EMBEDDING INTO OUR LIVES

Embedding into Our Lives

New Opportunities and Challenges
of the Internet

EDITORS

Louis Leung

Anthony Y. H. Fung

Paul S. N. Lee

The Chinese University Press

Embedding into Our Lives: New Opportunities and Challenges of the Internet
    Edited by Louis Leung, Anthony Y. H. Fung and
    Paul S. N. Lee

© **The Chinese University of Hong Kong**, 2009

ISBN: 978–962–996–368–2

THE CHINESE UNIVERSITY PRESS
The Chinese University of Hong Kong
SHA TIN, N.T., HONG KONG
Fax: +852 2603 6692
    +852 2603 7355
E-mail: cup@cuhk.edu.hk
Web-site: www.chineseupress.com

Printed in Hong Kong

Contents

Introduction vii
    Louis Leung, Anthony Y. H. Fung, and Paul S. N. Lee

Part I   The "Fitting" Capacity of the Internet into Our Lives

1. Internet Usage Patterns: An Examination of How
   Interactive Features and Processes Are Utilized in
   the United States 3
      Sally J. McMillan

2. The Roles and Importance of Internet Activities,
   New Media Use, and Leisure Participation on
   Leisure Satisfaction 27
      Louis Leung and Paul S. N. Lee

3. The Socio-Economic Impact of Intelligent Spaces:
   Who Is in Control? 53
      Michael Lyons

**Part II   The "Linking" Capacity of the Internet to the
Outside World**

4. Surfing the News: The Internet and Traditional News
   Consumption 83
      Lars Willnat

5. Examining the Use of and Preference for Online
   News in the Context of Intermedia Competition 101
      Hsiang Iris Chyi and Jay Hao-Chieh Chang

6. Online Journalism: The Psychology of Mass
    Communication on the Web 127
    S. Shyam Sundar

7. The Effects of Context Clutter and Advertising Repetition
    on Attitudinal and Behavioral Changes toward an
    Online Advertisement 145
    Vicky Wing Kei Ng and Hsiang Iris Chyi

8. Questioning Dis-intermediation: Rethinking the
    Internet's Political Economy 165
    Korinna Patelis

9. Online Games, Cyberculture and Community: The
    Deterritorization and Crystallization of Community
    Space 189
    Anthony Y. H. Fung

Part III   Capacity of the Internet to Enhance Our "Position"

10. Reconstructing E-government 209
    Sharon Strover and Karen Gustafson

11. Good Governance through E-governance? —
    Assessing China's E-government Strategy 235
    Junhua Zhang

12. The 2004 European Parliament Election, the Internet
    and Emergence of a European Public Sphere 269
    Nicholas W. Jankowski and Renée van Os

13. Shifting Approaches to Governing E-commerce: From
    Promoting New Technology to Controlling Uses 297
    Stephen D. McDowell

14. The Development of E-commerce in Online News
    Media: Toward a Core Partnership Strategy 323
    Alice Y. L. Lee and Clement Y. K. So

15. The Role of the Internet in Cultural Identity 347
    George A. Barnett

About the Editors 369
About the Contributors 371
Index 377

—m—

Introduction

Louis Leung
Anthony Y. H. Fung
Paul S. N. Lee

This edited volume conveys a strong message that the development of the Internet is at a crossroads and, on its 38th birthday, it is increasingly entrenched or embedded into our everyday lives. Adopting the "embedded media perspective" by Howard (2004), the aim of this book is to explore, from both the *individual* and *institutional* levels, how the Internet is embedded in our lives. The concept "embeddedness of the Internet" is used to describe how deeply our social and individual lives are involved in the Internet. In fact, "embedded media" is an analytical frame used to depict the way that "new" media have become — or are becoming — such an accepted part of everyday life. In the beginning, the new technology was an option for the wealthy, the specialist or the enthusiast. But today, it presents itself as a whole new way of liberating users and of offering them even greater control over their lives. Most household technologies like radio, television, and washing machines all started out like that. After a while, the technology becomes more widely accepted and easier to use. The once new and exciting technology then starts to become a necessary part of our lives rather than being an exclusive choice. We are now almost forced to use it and people even start to depend on it. Today, we can think about automobiles, automatic teller machines (ATM), mobile phones, and e-mails, to name a few, to realize and appreciate how dependent we have become on technologies. British writer Tom Standage (1991), in his book *The Victorian Internet,* described technological embeddedness using the term "invisible technology" — meaning that "technology has matured to become so embedded in, or integrated to, our everyday lives that we don't really notice it any more" (p. 54).

In discussing Internet embeddedness, Howard (2004) explains that the capacity and constraints of social life online can be conceived in terms of three measures: *fit, link,* and *position.* In terms of *fit,* embedded Internet goes well with daily routines of our social lives without demanding changes in our old habits. This means that Internet has entrenched and immersed in the background and surroundings of our everyday lives, we find difficult to give it up. In contrast, less ubiquitous and ill-fitting technologies are not easily embedded in our daily lives. With respect to *link,* this concept measures how effective and efficient Internet enables (or constraints) us to link to the outside world — to who and what we want to know — as compared to traditional media. Today, Internet is considered a highly embedded medium because we can telework at home without going to the office, read news online, express opinions on blogs, and in constant touch with friends and loved ones via the Internet more efficiently. There are many major benefits of the Internet which make it a more embedded medium because, as many would agree, the Internet is a fluid and multimodal medium which is sensitive to sensory appeals. Further, the Internet is very responsive with much interactivity, flexibility, less space and time constrained, and with the capacity to deliver non-linear content. Finally, in terms of status, its main idea is to ask a very important question, "What production or consumption capacity do technologies have for enriching our political, economic, and cultural lives?" This means that how we can use our ability to integrate Internet into our lives to improve our social *position* and life quality by increasing information and understanding. In other words, the more Internet can help us form (or hold us back from forming) our political views, become healthier and wealthier, or turn into smarter consumers, the more embedded the Internet has become.

The book is divided into three parts dealing with how the Internet functions in both individual and institutional dimensions, covering: (1) an overall introduction of the general uses, the current status, recent developments, the divergent usage patterns, and the social, psychological, and economic "fitting" capacity of the Internet in a converging media environment; (2) the "linking" capacity of the distinctive multimodal and interactive Web features influencing news consumption, online advertising, and social interaction in our growing Internet-embedded societies; and (3) the capacity of the

Internet which explicates, in both democratic and non-democratic states, how e-governance, political deliberation, and participation can enrich our economic, cultural, and political "position" online.

Part One, "The 'Fitting' Capacity of the Internet into Our Lives," focuses on the profiles of Internet users and socioeconomic and psychological impact of the Internet on users. In Chapter 1, McMillan presents two qualitative studies that add depth to the understanding of the *fitting* capacities of the Internet in the U.S. in 2004. This chapter sets a useful analytical tone by contrasting the usage and interactivity patterns of two very different groups of users — the young and the elderly. The first study explores young people's uses of, and opinions about, and the commercial aspects of the Internet. The overriding insight that emerged from this study was the pervasiveness of the commercial aspects of the Internet that affect every area of the lives of young people. The second qualitative study examines the opposite end of the spectrum of American Internet users — senior citizens. In particular, individuals aged 65+ revealed how they use the Internet for health communication and the overriding theme was dependency. This sample of senior citizens has come to depend on the Internet as a source of information about health-related issues.

Leung and Lee, in Chapter 2, test a conceptual model of leisure satisfaction among Internet users in Hong Kong in 2002 and to examine how it is related to technologically mediated leisure activities and non-media-related traditional leisure. They found that despite the strong contribution from non-media-related leisure activities, technological leisure activities were significant determinants of leisure satisfaction. They also found that entertainment-oriented Internet activities (such as playing online games, listening to music, and surfing the Internet for fun), as well as the use of new media (such as playing computer games, watching VCDs, DVDs, LDs, and chatting on ICQ), tend to displace or be substitutes for a large number of traditional leisure pursuits. These *fitting* capacities of the Internet seem go well with daily routines of our social lives. Their study successfully associated media-related activities (e.g., Internet use, new media use, and mass media use) to various components of leisure satisfaction. Specifically, socializing via the Internet, playing computer games, and reading newspapers were almost as powerful as non-media-related leisure participation (such

as talking to family or friends face-to-face, participating in
community or religious activities, doing physical exercise, shopping,
and taking evening classes) in predicting leisure satisfaction.

Turning to new opportunities of the Internet in Chapter 3, Lyons
studies the socioeconomic *fitting* capacity of intelligent spaces
based on work carried out under the Eurescom Project P1302 in
2004. He reviews the concept of "pervasive computing" or "ambient
intelligence" (AmI) in future online services. With the wide-spread
use of sensors, microprocessors in most goods, and a
communications infrastructure connecting different devices, Lyons
agues an intelligent environment or i-space can be created and
respond to people's needs without recourse to a complex and non-
intuitive interface. Lyons believes that the i-space vision could have
great potential for both individuals and businesses provided that
such intelligent systems are steered in the right directions. While
i-space applications allow people to have more control over their
lives, or reduce the time they spend on routine and mundane
activities, in the workplace these applications increase an
organization's ability to monitor the performance of its employees,
partner companies and competitors, as well as customer behaviors.
Regardless of whether the i-space technologies can be implemented
or not for both individuals and institutions, Lyons's discussion
addresses a primary but often forgotten vision of the Internet: above
all else, it must serve the people and must be relevant to them.

Part Two, "The 'Linking' Capacity of the Internet to the
Outside World," focuses on the opportunities and challenges of
the Internet with respect to online news, online advertising, and
social relationships. Willnat in Chapter 4 examines the potentially
growing impact of Internet news consumption on traditional sources
of news. Based on five national surveys conducted by Pew in 1998,
2000, 2002, 2004, and 2006 in the U.S., he found that the
consumption of Internet news was positively associated with the
use of traditional sources of news in all five surveys. Overall, this
study indicates that time spent on the Internet to *link* to the outside
world is used to supplement rather than to displace overall news
consumption.

In Chapter 5 Chyi and Chang explore the competition between
online and traditional news media from the standpoints of use and
preference in one of the most media-rich cities in the world — Hong

Kong — in 2002. Contrary to Willnat, they found that online news does not compare favorably with the traditional news media such as television, newspapers, and radio. Television was perceived as the preferred news medium and online news as the medium that was liked least. They also point out that online news is gaining in importance in terms of use, but that it lacks any competitive advantage in terms of media preference. They caution that, although use of one media form tends to be taken as an indicator of its popularity and diffusion, one should not underestimate the potential influence of the media preferences of news users on their media selection decisions.

In Chapter 6, Sundar discusses the psychology of mass communication on the Web and points out that certain values on the variables associated with the four Web features (agency/sourcing, navigability, interactivity, and multimodality) are better than others in creating user engagement with the content *linking* to the outside world. Based on a series of previous research studies prior to 2004, he argues that "audiovisual modality" does not always improve the user's opinion of the content but should be used with careful consideration of the overall experience needs of the audience. This study found that text is better than audio in modality, medium is better than low in interactivity, a strong information scent is preferred over a weak one in navigability, and self is over news-editors as a source or agent. He concluded that a key value of these Web features lies in their ability to alter the degree to which the content is the focus of user attention and evaluation. And these linking capacities in the forms of Web features are also important factors affecting our ability to connect to the outside world.

In Chapter 7, Ng and Chyi explore the impact of the Internet on advertising. They investigate whether an ad appearing on a cluttered Web page and repeated use of the same banner ad on the web page have an influence on the perception of the ad in 2004. Their findings reveal that both factors exert a significant influence on attitudes toward the ad — a highly cluttered Web page has a negative impact while repetitive advertising produces positive effects. However, neither of them have any effect on attitudes toward the brand nor on intentions to purchase, but advertising repetition does have a positive effect on the attitude toward the Web page. This study generates results that would be useful and usable, especially at the institutional level, for both advertising practitioners and web designers to extend the *linking* power of the Internet.

In Chapter 8, Patelis problematizes the current "dis-intermediation narrative" of the Internet from a radical political economy perspective. The dis-intermediation narrative apparently arises from concern over the digitally disempowered communities but the discourse has slowly degraded to deal only with the issue of exclusion and has been reduced to some key terms such as "the digital divide." Seemingly, with their urgent need for access and infrastructure, American policy makers have legitimately built this issue and the question of balance into their telecommunication policy documents. Globally, regulators have also started to accept the dis-intermediation narrative uncritically for the info-telecommunications sector. Patelis argues precisely that the narrative is built on an extremely illusory image: the creation of a huge highway, a technologically enabled labyrinth that is like a free market place, or a network society in which we are all *linked* digitally. Even without the potential risks, including loss of privacy or control, in such a digitalized society, the dominant narrative undermines the idea that the message of communication matters to regulators.

Fung, in Chapter 9, presents a specific angle on the *linking* capacity of the Internet from a cultural perspective: how the Internet plays a central role in maintaining and re-crystallizing community networks under conditions of urbanization. Specifically, this chapter focuses on the study of the uses of online games by the young in a small community in Hong Kong. Using ethnographic methodology, he argues that while community space was deterritorized by development, urbanization and the decline of village life, online communities help to re-crystallize some forms of community for the young and help to reterritorize a miniature community space in 2003. The optimism in his thinking is based on the fact that the *linking* capacity provided by the virtual community in an online game environment enables us not only to create a new virtual space for communication, but also to regain some physical space for interaction that had been lost. He argues that virtual spaces are not independent of physical space, but rather that the latter is in fact more dependent on the formation of the virtual space.

Following on from the *linking* domain, Part Three, "Capacity of the Internet to Enhance Our 'Position'," includes chapters focusing on e-government with deliberative work in the U.S., in China, and in Europe. Strover and Gustafson in Chapter 10 dissect the complex processes by most western e-governments work and remind us that e-government also has its dark face in our increasingly networked societies. While not excluding the fact that e-government and the technologies developed could increase the opportunities for the public to participate in online activities in 2003, they dispute the argument that participatory democracy is a primary factor in the implementation of e-government in the U.S. E-government may multiply such opportunities, but in fact this simply substitutes a sense of knowing *about* something for actually *doing* something about it. It could be that citizens would be primarily interested in the availability of government services online but would be less concerned with the possibility of using e-government as a means of political participation to enhance their position or status.

In Chapter 11, Zhang examines whether good governance can be achieved through e-governance by focusing on China's e-government strategy. He investigates the Chinese government's websites in 2003 and attempts to explicate the motivation behind China's plan to develop e-government and its current strategy. Zhang argues that because of the internal political changes in China, its e-government strategy reflects the situation in which an authoritarian system prioritizes the legitimacy of the status quo over the building of an e-government that would promote participation and democracy. On that precondition, e-government in China reflects primarily the government's concern with the technological aspects of public administration, and also the nation's efforts to enhance governmental functionality, professionalism and effectiveness by connecting central and local administrations. Zhang is quite pessimistic about the ability and quality of the future development of Chinese e-government to improve social and political position of its citizens. He perceives that it would be very different from that of developed countries.

Jankowski and van Os, in Chapter 12, consider a broader global picture of e-government, which they perceive as being a kind of information source that is actually not unique nor very different from the situation in many western countries. Their chapter is part of a pan-European collaborative empirical investigation examining the websites of 11 countries for features related to the provision of information about the elections to the European Parliament in 2004. Using the research results from two of the Web spheres dealing with the elections, they found that the actors in the two countries placed the primary emphasis on the provision of information, and offered only limited opportunities for enhancement of political position through civic engagement. A skeptical reading of this analysis suggests that the parties and candidates envisaged only a very limited purpose for the Web, and used it only to provide electronic versions of campaign materials prepared primarily for other modes of distribution.

In Chapter 13, McDowell examines shifts in policy research and debate about the governance of electronic commerce at the institutional level in the U.S. and in multilateral forums over the past decade. He argues that we have seen a shift toward an emphasis on the control of the use of economic transactions, as well as Internet technology, and away from the real need to facilitate electronic services and transactions in order to enhance our political, economic, and cultural lives (positions). In reality, in spite of the huge growth in e-commerce companies such as Amazon, online service providers (e.g., travel, hotels, consumer electronics), Internet access providers (e.g., AOL and MSN) and internet portals and search engines (e.g., Google and Yahoo), there are few signs that the vital discussion of e-commerce applications in manufacturing and wholesale trade is happening. McDowell urges that the specific nature of those purposes and uses of the Internet that could facilitate e-commerce practices and applications should be re-visited.

In examining the development of e-commerce in online news media, Lee and So in Chapter 14 evaluate the e-commerce performance of 26 online news media in five regions between 2001 and 2003. They found that the online news media were not able to fill the role of multi-dimensional electronic traders. Instead, they had redirected their e-commerce strategies, and were once more focusing on their in-house products and services. Lee and So point out that news sites around the world are clinging to the same development orbit — a return to the core fundamentals of the news industry. The establishment of partnerships is still regarded as a useful tool for survival, and the core partnership principle has become the guiding strategy for news sites involved in e-commerce to enhance their institutional position.

Finally, in the last chapter (Chapter 15), Barnett, based on network analysis of the international Internet in 2004, studies the role of the Internet in exerting the influence of the U.S. on cultural identity across the globe. He argues that, given the convergence of global culture, and since the U.S. is the core nation in the international flow of information and controls the world's channels of communication, the Internet will serve as an additional vehicle for the U.S. to impose its domination in the field of cultural identity. According to the theory of cultural convergence, the increased communication among the peoples of the world via the Internet will lead over time to a diminution in the differences between national cultures, leading eventually to the formation of a single global culture. Barnett foresees that one possible outcome of this process is that unique national cultures will disappear, and national differences will be gradually replaced by a single transnational identity, but also that that identity would be dominated by the U.S.

We are grateful to the contributors to this volume, especially those who were willing to share original work covering their research into a wide range of issues arising from the new challenges and opportunities brought about by the Internet which has been deeply embedded in multiple spheres of our lives.

References

Howard, P. H. (2004). "Embedded media: Who we know, what we know, and society online". In P. H. Howard and S. Jones (eds.), *Society Online: The Internet in Context*, pp. 1–27. Thousand Oaks, CA: Sage.

Standage, T. (1999). *The Victorian Internet: The Remarkable Story of the Telegraph and the Nineteenth Century's On-line Pioneers.* New York: Walker.

PART I

· · · · · · · · · ·

The "Fitting" Capacity of the Internet into Our Lives

Internet Usage Patterns: An Examination of How Interactive Features and Processes Are Utilized in the United States

Sally J. McMillan

Introduction

Americans tend to view the Internet, like many other aspects of their lives, from a self-centered perspective. Americans who know anything about the history of the Internet are more likely to focus on the role of the United States government in developing the protocol for Internet data transfer (TCP/IP) than on the role of a Swiss researcher in developing the graphical user interface that has come to be know as the World Wide Web (Leiner et al. 2000).

The United States is no longer the world leader in connectivity technology as other countries have played "leap frog" in expanding technologies such as broadband services. But the experience of Internet users in the United States can provide a framework for understanding Internet users and uses. The author of this research is an American. Nevertheless, the intent of the chapter is not to engage in American self-examination, but rather to provide insight into how one, large, industrialized nation that played a role in the development of the Internet is evolving as the technology grows worldwide.

A brief profile of demographic and psychographic trends in U.S. Internet use are provided followed by a brief overview of interactivity as it applies to Americans' Internet use. This study also provides an overview of two qualitative research projects that examine two unique populations in the United States: young people who have been raised on digital technology and senior citizens who are beginning their Internet use relatively late in life. A brief conclusion section suggests some possible future trends and research topics.

Demographics and Psychographics

Approximately two-thirds of all Americans are online (Madden 2006). According to a Harris Interactive poll (Greenspan 2002), 55 percent of American adults access the Internet from home, 30 percent at work, and about 20 percent access the Internet from a school, library, cyber café or other location. Fifty-three percent of internet users have broadband access from home (Fox 2005).[1] Fast access is important, because researchers have found that American Web users are impatient (Thilmany 2003). Web users typically visit only the first three results shown from an online search and one in five searchers spend 60 seconds or less at a Web document found by the search engine.

Women and men are now online in about equal numbers, but distribution by age is not uniform (Fox and Madden 2005). Table 1.1 summarizes difference in penetration by generation.

Table 1.1 Internet Penetration by Age

Age	Percent Online
12–17	87
18–24	82
25–29	85
30–34	83
35–39	80
40–44	76
45–49	73
50–54	68
55–59	68
60–64	55
65–69	57
70–75	26
76+	17

Source: Pew Internet and American Life Project.

Different demographic groups use the Internet in different ways. Madden (2003) reports that female Internet users frequently seek health or religious information while males seek news, financial information, sports information, and political news. Among minority populations, African-Americans most often focus on school-related research and religious and spiritual information while Hispanics report a high level of instant messaging and music downloading. Those with higher socio-economic status participate in a much broader range of activities than those with more modest income and education. These activities range from looking for government information, online banking, and participating in online auctions. The young like instant messaging and downloading music while older Internet users are more likely than younger users to get online information about health and government.

Demographics alone do not tell the full story of the Internet user. Dutta-Bergman (2002) found that psychographic variables accounted for more variance in Internet use than did demographic variables. In particular, innovativeness was a strong predictor of Internet use. Consumerism was also a fairly strong predictor as was concern about health issues.

Horrigan (2003) identified eight primary types of Internet users in the U.S. based on a combination of demographic and psychographic characterizations as summarized in Table 1.2. The first four types are high-end users: Young Tech Elites, Older Wired Baby Boomers, Wired Generation Xers, and Wired Senior Men. The other four groups have a more low-tech orientation: Young Marrieds, Low-Tech Older Baby Boomers, Unwired Young Baby Boomers, and Low-Tech Elderly. One of the key differences between the high-end and low-tech users is their use of the interactive capabilities of the Web.

Interactivity

The level of interactivity in which individuals participate was identified as a key differentiation in the user groups outlined in Table 2. The four groups categorized as Trendsetting Tech Elite are more likely to engage in interactivity than are the four Lower-Tech Groups. But what is interactivity in the context of computer-mediated communication?

Table 1.2 Eight Types of U.S. Information Technology Users

Type	% of Pop.	Average Age	Gender	Technologies Used	Online Activities
The Trendsetting Tech Elite					
Young Tech Elites	6	22	Predominantly male	100% Internet 100% Cell phone 80% DVD	Interactive aspects such as downloading music, creating online content, participating in online groups
Older Wired Baby Boomers	6	52	Predominantly male	100% Internet 82% Cell phone	Information gatherers especially for news and work related research. High on online transactions
Wired Generation Xers	18	36	About equal male/female	100% Internet 82% Cell phone	Wide range of online activities, just slightly less interactivity than Young Tech Elites
Wired Senior Men	1	70	Predominantly male	100% Internet for about 10 years	Information gathering and some online transactions
Lower-Tech Groups					
Young Marrieds	15	24	About equal male/female	66% Internet 56% Cell phone	Less education than Young Tech Elites and less Internet activity
Low-Tech Older Baby Boomers	21	54	Slightly more female	51% Internet 60% Cell phone	Lower-than-average income and education, relatively little Internet experience
Unwired Young Baby Boomers	16	39	Slightly more female	45% Internet 69% Cell phone	Broad but not deep usage of Internet. Positively inclined toward Internet, but lack much time for it.
Low-Tech Elderly	16	73	Slightly more female	12% Internet 39% Cell phone	Get most of their information needs from television and newspapers.

Source: Pew Internet and American Life Project.

One of the earliest and most frequently cited definitions is Rafaeli's (1988) idea of interactivity as an expression that embodies references to earlier expressions. Ten years later, Ha and James (1998, p.461) wrote: "Interactivity should be defined in terms of the extent to which the communicator and the audience respond to, or are willing to facilitate, each other's communication needs." A twenty-first century definition took a consumer-based focus (Schumann, Artis, and Rivera 2001): "Ultimately it is the consumer's choice to interact, thus interactivity is a characteristic of the consumer, and not a characteristic of the medium. The medium simply serves to facilitate the interaction." Another researcher defined the concept as (Kiousis 2002, p.355): "Both a media and psychological factor that varies across communication technologies, communication contexts, and people's perceptions."

McMillan and Hwang (2002) reviewed literature that defines interactivity based in features (the characteristics of the communication environment that make it interactive), processes (actually using an interactive feature), and perceptions (whether or not users perceive the communication environment to be interactive). McMillan (2002) also identified three different "types" of interactivity: human-to-human, human-to-computer, and human-to-content. Table 1.3 shows how these ways of viewing interactivity might be brought together.

Perceptions of interactivity are a valuable tool for researchers who want to understand how consumers respond to interactivity. But for the purpose of this study, the two most important aspects of interactivity are features and processes. What do we know about ways that Americans are actually using the interactive capabilities of the Internet?

The Pew Internet and American Life Project has been tracking Americans' uses of the Internet for several years. The organization provided an analysis of American's Internet Activities (*Internet Activities*, 2004). Table 1.4 summarizes those activities in terms of the primary ways in which they facilitate interactivity.

The most popular Internet application is e-mail, which is a clear example of human-to-human interaction. But Table 1.4 makes it clear that the most popular "type" of interactivity among Americans is human-to-computer interaction. In fact, only those interactions participated in by more than 50 percent of Americans are included

Table 1.3 Putting Together the Parts of Interactivity

	Human-to-Human	Human-to-Computer	Human-to-Content
Features	• Instant messaging • E-mail	• Navigational tools such as menus • Search tools	• Tools that facilitate personalized content • Unique content forms
Processes	• Participating in an IM chat • Sending/ receiving e-mail	• Navigating a Web site • Using a search engine	• Creating a personalized home page • Seeking out news stories in multiple media formats
Perceptions	• Believing that IM and e-mail facilitate communication • May be based in personal interest or involvement with topics of communication	• Finding a Web site easy to control and engaging • May be based in experience with the technology as well as interest/ involvement with topic	• Believing that customized and in-depth content is interactive. • May be based in time available for viewing content.

in the table because the list of computer interactions is so long (other activities range from 44 percent who check for sports scores or information to 8 percent who look for information about domestic violence).

Many of the tools that facilitate two-way communication between persons are used by relatively few Americans. Only about one quarter participate in chat or online auctions and less than 10 percent go to online sites to meet people or make telephone calls online. Although more than 50 percent go to sites that provide support for medical conditions, it should be noted that not all of these are using the two-way communication functions of these sites; some are simply searching for information.

Table 1.4 Most Popular Ways That Americans Interact on the Internet[2]

Human-to-Human	Human-to-Computer	Human-to-Content
91% Send e-mail	88% Use a search engine to find information	21% Use Internet to post photos
54% Go to a Website that provides information or support for a specific medical condition or personal situation	83% Research a product or service before buying it	20% Share files
47% Send an instant message	80% Do an Internet search to answer a specific question	19% Create content for the Internet
25% Chat in a chat room or in an online discussion	79% Search for a map or driving directions	7% Create a Web log or "blog"
22% Participate in an online auction	76% Look for information on a hobby or interest	
16% Take part in an online group	75% Check the weather	
8% Go to a site to meet people online	73% Look for information about movies, books, or other leisure activities	
7% Make a telephone call online	69% Get news	
	67% Surf the Web for fun	
	66% Get travel information	
	66% Look for health/medical information	
	66% Look for information from a government Website	
	61% Buy a product	
	57% Buy or make a reservation for travel	
	53% Look up phone number or address	
	53% Research for school or training	
	52% Watch a video clip or listen to an audio clip	
	52% Do job-related research	

Source: Pew Internet and American Life Project.

The least popular form of interactivity among Americans seems to be human-to-content interaction. Only about one-fifth of Americans share photos or computer files or create content. And less than 10 percent are active participants in the creation of Web logs (blogs). But human-to-content interaction may be increasing (Greenspan 2004). When a large range of content-creation activities was considered, about 44 percent of American users reported that they have participated in at least one content-creation activity such as uploading pictures, posting to newsgroups, and creation of personal Web pages. Further evidence of the expanding role of human-to-content creation is the heavy use of blogs by younger Americans. Among those in the 12-28 age range, about 20% have created their own blogs — as contrasted with less than 10% in any other age group.

Profiles of Extremes

Not all Americans use the Internet in the same in the way. As the research reported earlier makes clear, young Americans are more likely to be active users of the Internet. Those who are young, highly educated, and from high-income families are particularly likely to be classified among the technologically elite who use the Internet in highly interactive ways. On the other end of the spectrum are America's senior citizens who are age 65 and older. This group is least likely to be online, most likely to be classified as low-tech, and often likely to describe attempts to interact online as a struggle. To help provide a better understanding of these two ends of the demographic and interactivity spectrum, brief reports of qualitative research related to these two groups of Internet users is provided below.

College Students and Commercialization

McMillan and Morrison (2004) examined college students' uses of and opinions of the commercial aspects of the Internet. Commercialization has been an ongoing trend since the Internet grew beyond its government-based roots in the early 1990s. Approximately 61 percent of Americans report that they have purchased a product online (*Internet Activities*, 2004). But research suggests that it is the Young Tech Elites who take the most hands-on approach to Internet interactions and are the trendsetters for the future of Internet use (Horrigan 2003). Commercialization is important to track among these trendsetters, because Forrester Research predicted that online sales would account for 10 percent of all retail sales in the U.S. by 2008 (Rush 2003).

A study of America's college class of 2001 reported that these young people, most of whom started grammar school in 1985 when the Internet was rapidly expanding in government and research use, and high school in 1993 when the Internet was first becoming widely available to the public, were now almost 100 percent connected to the Internet (Miller 2001). These young people have been called the n-generation because networking is second nature to them (Tapscott 1997) and the e-generation because they are connected to all things electronic (Boiarsky 2002). The e-generation is one of the most active in online commerce activities. In the U.S., college students spent $1.4 billion online in 2001 (Tedeschi 2002).

Using grounded theory (Corbin and Strauss 1990; Strauss and Corbin 1990), McMillan and Morrison (2004) examined essays written by 72 college students about their experiences and expectations of commercial aspects of the Internet. Five axial codes, or key ideas, were identified: ration, emotion, social interaction, personalization, and privacy/security.

Ration

Many participants' responses focused on rational reasons for using commercial aspects of cyberspace and rational responses to that use. They often reported that shopping online was easy and inexpensive. For example, one young woman wrote: "I don't have to run to the store when I need a certain book or a birthday present. I can order it online and just have it sent where and whenever I need it to ultimately go and that cuts another hassle out of my day."

Online commercial activities other than shopping also had rational appeal. For example, banner ads were seen as "tips" about things they might find interesting and corporate Web sites provided a wealth of information that helped them get through class assignments.

The ability to do quick price comparisons was viewed as a major benefit of online commerce for many participants. Some used this information to then go to traditional retail outlets to purchase while others purchased online. But price was only one of the information-search factors reported by participants. They also reported comparing product features and seeking input from other users through bulletin boards and chat rooms in a way that had substantially altered their pre-Internet shopping behavior.

Many reported that their online behaviors were sometimes mirrored in offline commercial activities. But they often stressed that their online behavior was more rational because the medium gives them more depth and permanency of information.

Emotion

While ration-related responses tended to dominate many of the participants comments, they also evidenced strong emotional responses to the commercialization of cyberspace. Emotional responses included e-commerce as a relief from boredom, online communication with sellers as a way to overcome confusion, and online purchasing as a kind of "comforting" experience. For example, a young woman wrote: "I feel a sense of relief and comfort knowing that my need will be met without my having to go anywhere or do anything but simply click and safely enter my credit card number."

Use of the Internet for "relief from boredom" was expressed by several participants. Many expressed a cross-over between this online surfing and fulfilling other emotional needs such as supporting daydreams about vacations and enabling activities like designing an engagement ring. Positive emotional responses were not always dream-like. In fact, many reported finding great satisfaction in pursuing very directed behaviors. A young man reported: "It certainly gets me more involved in companies and their products and that's a lot of fun."

But not all emotional responses were positive. Participants also reported apprehension and fear. A young man wrote: "Technology of the future scares me and I am a bit pessimistic about the whole thing." However, many participants reported that these kinds of negative emotions were more associated with older generations than with peers of their own generation. Among college-age students, negative feelings about online shopping were far less likely to be driven by techno-phobia than by other factors. Many who reported that they don't shop online indicated that they simply loved the traditional shopping experience.

Participants also expressed some potential negative consequences in becoming overly involved in cyber-commerce. Many used words such as "obsession" and "addiction" to refer to their commercial uses of cyberspace. Other less-than-positive emotional responses included frustration with online advertising, and impatience with the computing environment.

Social Interaction

Many of the participants wrote about shopping and social interaction. For some, the ability to shop online reduced the need for unwanted interactions with clerks. Many compared online shopping to real-world interactions with sales clerks noting that sales clerks were just one of the annoyances that online shopping could eliminate.

Other participants, however, expressed negative responses to the lack of a social interaction in the online buying environment. In discussing why he still buys airline tickets offline, one young man noted: "I personally favor talking to an airline agent rather than interacting with the Internet because I feel more comfortable and can ask questions when needed." Others expressed the need to have clerks help them find the right fit in clothes and the right products to meet their needs.

Several participants also indicated that shopping was a social activity for them. To shop online would spoil that social pleasure.

Participants also talked about the ways in which their peers influenced their commercial uses of cyberspace. In many cases friends shared similar beliefs and behaviors and helped to reinforce individual attitudes and actions. In other cases, friends, family members and roommates provided the social "push" to get the participants to begin commercial activity in cyberspace. If the participants saw other people succeed in online shopping, they were more willing to try it for themselves.

Finally, many participants addressed the transformation that online commerce has brought to society. Some saw this transformation in a primarily positive light. But many participants speculated about the potential downside of a society in which the act of shopping was transformed from a social activity into an isolated experience.

Personalization

The fourth key theme that emerged from the data was that participants saw cyberspace as a place for personalized commercial interactions. Advertising could be targeted to them, Web sites could present them with products and services specifically tailored to their needs, and they could control their experiences at commercial Web sites.

Participants seemed to recognize that they would have to do some work and possibly give up some personal privacy (see the next section for more discussion of privacy issues) to obtain personalized information. But they felt that this was a price worth paying.

Participants also seemed to recognize that personalization would require more work on the part of the marketer. Several reported on internships and summer jobs at which they had been required to use the Web and related technologies to learn more about very specific consumer groups. But they recognized that with the work came rewards.

Privacy/Security

Many participants commented on issues related to the potential loss of privacy as cyberspace becomes more commercialized. They often linked the issue of privacy with the security of online transactions. The issues of privacy, identity theft, and credit card fraud were often intertwined.

Many participants reported a relationship between experience in online shopping and concerns about privacy and security. Their first experiences often affected future behaviors. Many times the first attempt to shop online was pleasurable, but others found it frustrating. However most of these Young Tech Elites reported that their concerns about security and privacy had been reduced as they had more experiences with online shopping.

After identifying the five axial coding categories, the researchers conducted selective coding. The process of selective coding takes the qualitative data that has been "broken apart" in the axial coding process and puts it back together. Taken together, how do these thematic categories help us understand what the e-generation can tell the rest of society about how coming of age concurrently with the commercialization of cyberspace has affected their lives? In the selective coding process, the researchers agreed that a single overarching concept is woven throughout all of the axial codes: pervasiveness. What the e-generation is telling us is that the commercialization of cyberspace is affecting every aspect of their lives.

It affects their private lives in both rational and emotional ways. It makes it easier to find information and make rational purchases. It makes them feel good and gives them something fun to do when they are bored. The pervasiveness of commercial cyberspace applies to their interactions with others as well. Friends help support them as they learn to conduct commerce online. Their buying behaviors become similar to those of others in their social group. They talk with their friends and classmates about Internet advertising campaigns and the marketing potential of the Internet. These respondents also saw the commercialization of cyberspace as central to their future careers. While they might have concerns about how to balance issues of personalization and privacy in their own lives, they were virtually unanimous in their belief that these technologies would benefit their careers and make their jobs more interesting.

Senior Citizens and Health Communication

As illustrated in Table 1.2, the Low-Tech Elderly are at the opposite extreme of the Young Tech Elites. The Americans who are age 65 and older are the least likely to be online (see Table 1.1). A project conducted by Generations on Line, a non-profit group devoted to increasing Internet usage among older adults, found that among those aged 65 and older health information was a favorite use of the Internet (Vastag 2001). As illustrated in Table 4, using the Internet for health-related topics is related to both human-to-human and human-to-computer interactivity. Among older adults, health-related Internet use is particularly strong (Fox and Rainie 2002).

McMillan (2004) gathered data from 20 senior citizens (8 women and 12 men) who use the Internet. The goal of this study was to provide insight into how these older Americans use this technology for health communication. E-mail interviews were conducted with participants, all of whom are online and all of whom identified themselves as being health-conscious individuals.

The same grounded theory approach (Corbin and Strauss 1990; Strauss and Corbin 1990) that was used in analyzing the essays of young people was used to examine the e-mail responses provided by these senior citizens. Five key axial themes emerged that help explain how older Americans are using the Internet for health information: alternatives, authority, information richness, social context, and skills.

Alternatives

One of the first themes to clearly emerge from the data is that the Internet is seen as an "alternative" in many different ways. First, many of the participants reported using the Internet to find information on "alternative" health-care options ranging from acupuncture to use of Valerian Root Extract for sleep and mood disorders. Not all of the Web uses were for alternative medicine. In fact, the majority of participants reported using the Web to search for more "routine" information such as information on bursitis, abnormal pap smears, and dyslexia. But even in these cases, the Internet often seemed to be a kind of alternative, or supplement, to other information sources. Several participants compared the Internet to a library and noted that it was both more up-to-date and more convenient than the library.

Many also saw the Internet as reducing the need for extended interpersonal interactions with physicians or other health-care professionals. The health-care provider was often at the nexus of discussions of alternatives. Participants often saw their search for alternative medicine to be in contradiction to what their physician recommended. Many participants expressed the need to seek out alternative information sources because their physicians were too busy to spend time talking to them about their health concerns. A retired nurse reported that: "With most MD visits, the physicians seem VERY rushed and not predisposed to having detailed conversations with patients." Many participants echoed this feeling.

Authority

The previous theme, which focuses on alternatives, is closely related to a second important theme: authority. Many participants reported that doctors resented patients who seemed to be using the Internet as a way of usurping the traditional position of authority held by the doctor. Even when seniors trusted the authority of the doctor, they did not always place unconditional faith in medical practitioners. In fact, they often reported that they by-passed their doctor to conduct Internet searches on topics ranging from gouty arthritis to care and development of grandchildren.

Another prevalent authority-related issue was the question of how to evaluate the credibility of online sources. Tactics used for evaluating source credibility ranged from relatively simple trust to more sophisticated techniques. For example, one gentleman reported that he evaluates trustworthiness of information by comparing several sites "to determine if the information is reasonable." Several reported relying primarily on "common sense."

Many participants reported checking sources of information. Among the most common indicators of authority were certification of the writer (i.e. is he/she a medical professional), organizational affiliation (e.g. university researchers generally had the highest level of credibility), and currency of the information.

Many participants also reported that they used personal sources to "triangulate" the information they got from the Internet. Information from family members who are medical professionals, friends who were experiencing similar health challenges, and personal physicians was used as a kind of "balancing force" to challenge or verify information found online.

Information Richness

Despite sometimes having reservations about the authority and reliability of Internet information sources, most participants found the Internet to be a very rich source of information. For example, a man wrote: "I enjoy using the computer, and I enjoy the instant gratification of finding the answers I need without all the extra effort to be found in ANY other method of research." Most reported that information they were able to find online was clear and well written.

For example, a woman wrote: "The doctors and their staff members that write for the Net are very clear with their explanations. I find their work easy to read and understand. I may think some of it is not my cup of tea, but at least I have the exposure for knowledge."

Many participants expanded on the first theme of alternative information by noting that the information that they received not only provided different insights but also more depth of information than they were able to get from other sources. Several other participants also reported that the Web sometimes gave them too much information. For example, a woman wrote: "I really try to avoid looking up health-related issues as much as possible, because the information is too lengthy, and too time-consuming for me to bother." But for many others this wealth of information provided a source of pleasurable exploration.

Several participants noted that the Internet as information source gave them more flexibility for information search and retrieval than do other media. They found that they could get the depth of information that was appropriate for their current search needs and time demands. For example, a man wrote: "I like the flexibility I have: do it on my schedule, as long as I want to, day or night."

Social Context

Throughout their discussions of Internet use, many participants revealed that the health information they gleaned was integrated into their social lives. While they might spend solitary time online searching and evaluating information, the information that they found was often shared with others. In fact, many of the participants reported that they were a kind of "information source" for friends and family members who did not regularly use the Internet. The participants' ability to use this tool made them both an innovator and leader among their friends and family members.

A woman wrote: "My two sisters are a bit lazy as far as looking up things, but read whatever I share. They are six and eight years older than me. Maybe tired and well worn is better than lazy. They appreciate having most of it searched out for them." A man echoed this idea by reporting that he often does Internet search for family members. But he also indicated that his role was expanding from simple information source to educator. He is teaching family members to use the Internet so that they can search for their own information.

The social context of Internet use often extended into other communication environments. For example, a man wrote: "I share Internet information with my family or friends regarding things in which I think they may be interested. If it is relevant for them, they enjoy it. Sometimes this sharing is in conversation and other times it is with printed copies."

Many participants reported that when they shared health information with others, those friends and family members expressed appreciation. In fact, as they become known as individuals who are capable of finding health information online, friends sometimes seek them out for help with difficult health information problems.

Skills

Even though these senior citizens often held positions as information resources for friends and family members, many reported that they felt frustrated because they were not more adept at using the technology. A woman wrote: "I do become frustrated in searching, and I think that is mostly my fault, because I'm not a computer expert!!"

Others, however, identified aspects of the technology that made their learning process easier and less frustrating. Specifically, the ability to search at their own speed was seen as an advantage. For example, a woman wrote: "It is very comfortable and educational. I don't have to study at another person or group's pace."

Most participants seemed to have fairly unsophisticated search skills. Most reported using the search engine that is provided with their Internet service. However, some of the participants did indicate search skills that were a bit more sophisticated. One man reported using "everything from Department of Health and Human Services, FDA and other governmental programs, services and benefits."

In review of the themes identified in axial coding, the key understanding that seems to emerge from this data is that the Internet is a valuable source of health information to these senior citizens. While some occasionally find it frustrating or believe that it provides too much information, most find it to be an important, maybe critical, form of health communication. In short, they need the Internet. It has become a critical health-communication tactic.

Several factors seem to be related to this growing dependence on the Web. Doctors are often too busy to take the time that these senior citizens want to discuss all aspects of their health. Other information sources are often viewed as too tedious. For participants, using the Web is much easier than going to the library. And the Web also lets them pursue their information search at a pace that is comfortable to them. Participants noted that the Web opened new possibilities for them as it let them pursue alternative medicines as well as alternative information sources. As participants have explored multiple uses of the Web, they have come to find it almost indispensable.

These participants are early adopters (Rogers 1995). A relatively small percentage of older Americans are online. For these early adopters the sense of need extends beyond themselves. Friends and family need these early adopters to provide them with the information that they (the non-adopters) have not yet learned to get for themselves. Use of information technology helps to define participants' position as central to their communities. They need to stay current with technology because others are depending on them. Authority is shifting. Participants are finding that doctors are losing some of the "god-like" authority that they once had. Additionally, these Internet users are finding themselves to be among the new sources of authority. Because they can find the information online, their friends and family depend on them as a new source for information.

The need for technology described by these participants is also associated with frustration. Several pointed out that they had never had any formal training in using the Internet. They had to teach themselves and they are not always confident in their ability to find health information online. They are not certain of the best search techniques. They are not always sure how to check the validity of their sources. They often take this frustration offline and talk to others both about the techniques of Internet use and about the possible validity of the information they have found. Thus, Internet-related health communication is not a strictly online phenomenon. Rather, the information that they get online becomes integrated into both their social lives and their interactions with health professionals.

Summary and Conclusion

Americans are active Internet users, but some are more active than others. In general those who are younger and who have higher socioeconomic status are the most active Internet users and partake in the greatest range of interactive activities. But for most Americans, interactivity focuses primarily on the ability to use navigation tools to control what the computer presents to them (human-to-computer interaction). While almost all American Internet users send e-mail, it is the only human-to-human communication activity participated in by more than 50 percent of the U.S. population. And human-to-content interaction is even less common.

Statistics often provide just a broad view of the big picture. To better understand two "extreme" populations (the Young Tech Elite and Low-Tech Elderly), this study reports on two qualitative studies. Dutta-Bergman (2002) noted that innovativeness, consumerism, and concern about health issues help to predict who will use the Internet. The qualitative studies reported in this chapter explore all three of those psychographic variables. College students are often on the leading edge of communication technologies. Senior citizens who participated in the research were also innovators. They are the early adopters within their age cohort. The study of students focused on the second key psychographic variable, consumerism, while the study of seniors focused on health. Thus these qualitative studies are ideally focused to help provide more depth of understanding of American Internet users.

As expected, most young people are comfortable with Internet technology and see commercialization of cyberspace as a positive trend for the future. But the Internet is more for them than just a tool to be used for rational information searching. It is also an entertainment vehicle and they find entertainment not only in interacting with friends but also in their commercial interactions. They recognize a variety of interactive functions and participate in interactive processes ranging from clicking on banner ads to buying goods and services online. The commercialization of the Internet is also affecting their social lives. It can reduce the social frustration of dealing with sales clerks, but it may also eliminate the social pleasures of the shopping experience. For these young people the Internet is a personal experience. It is not just an information source or entertainment venue, it is a "place" that they can make their own. They recognize that there may be some loss of privacy as they reveal personal information to commercial entities, but that seems a tradeoff they are willing to make. These young people have found that the Internet is a pervasive force in their lives. They have come to depend on it.

The experiences of the older Americans are both similar to and different from those of the young. The older Americans also seem to be fairly interactive in their Internet use — they communicate by e-mail (human-to-human interaction), search Web sites for health information (human-to-computer interaction), and sometimes even contribute to the content of the Internet by posting their own responses to health information they find online (human-to-content interaction). But for seniors each kind of interactivity is subtly different than it is for young people. Seniors see e-mail as a supplement to their "real world" communications, while for some young people e-mail is a primary communication tool. Seniors struggle to learn how to conduct efficient searches and to effectively evaluate the information they find while young people see the Internet as an easy way of gathering all types of information. For seniors, the Internet is an "alternative" while for young people it is their first choice for information seeking.

A particularly interesting contrast is the social context of Internet use for these two groups. Among young people, the Internet is a viable social context in its own right — a place where they can meet friends and conduct business. For seniors, the Internet is merely a supplement to their social lives. They take information that they get online and share it with friends and family.

While each of the qualitative studies reported in this chapter identified themes unique to a specific target group, the two studies can also be examined together for further insight into the American Internet user. Some of the themes found in the two studies are very similar (e.g. Social Interaction and Social Context). Table 1.5 suggests that the 10 different themes found in the two studies can be grouped into three primary categories: reasoned responses, affective responses, and personal responses. While specific experiences were different for the two groups of users, their overall responses seemed to fit these general categories.

The final selective coding process for both qualitative studies

Table 1.5 Summary of Themes from the Two Qualitative Studies

Overarching Factor	Related Themes from Study of College Students	Related Themes from Study of Senior Citizens
Reasoned Responses	Ration	Information Richness Alternatives Authority
Affective Responses	Social Interaction Emotion	Social Contexts
Personal Responses	Personalization Privacy/Security	Skills

resulted in identification of very similar themes: pervasiveness in the case of young people and dependency in the case of seniors. Both groups feel a need for the Internet. But that need is somewhat different. For young people, the Internet is an integral part of virtually every aspect of their lives. For seniors, the Internet is primarily a tool that helps them manage their lives.

The future of the Internet in the United States is still to be written. It will be important to continue to maintain statistics on how use is growing and changing among various demographic and psychographic groups. It will be important to continue to study interactive features, processes, and perceptions in the American context. Future qualitative research is also needed to gain more depth of understanding of what the Internet actually means in the lives of Americans.

Notes

1. Broadband means that the user has a high-speed dsl, cable, wireless, t-1, or fiber optic connection at home.
2. Percentages represent that percent of the Americans online who participate in the listed activity.

References

Boiarsky, C. (2002). "This is not our father's generation: Web pages, the Chicago lyric opera, and the Philadelphia orchestra". *Journal of Popular Culture*, 36 (1): 14–24.
Corbin, J. and Strauss, A. L. (1990). "Grounded theory research:

Procedures, canons, and evaluative criteria". *Qualitative Sociology*, 13 (19): 3–19.

Dutta-Bergman, M. J. (2002). "Beyond demographic variables: Using psychographic research to narrate the story of Internet users". *Studies in Media and Information Literacy Education*, 2 (3). Available online: http://www.utpress.utoronto.ca/journal/ejournals/simile.

Fox, S. (2005). *Digital divisions*. Pew Internet and American Life Project. Available online: http://www.pewinternet.org/pdfs/PIP_Digital_Divisions_Oct_5_2005.pdf.

——— and Madden, M. (2005). *Generations online*. Pew Internet and American Life Project. Available online: http://www.pewinternet.org/pdfs/PIP_Generations_Memo.pdf.

——— and Rainie, L. (2002). *Vital decision: How Internet users decide what information to trust when their loved ones are sick*. Pew Internet and American Life Project. Available online: http://wwqw.pewinternet.org/reports/toc.asp?Report=59.

Greenspan, R. (2002). "Two-thirds hit the net". *ClickZ Stats*. Available online: http://www.clickz.com/stats/big_picture/geographics/print.php/5911_1011491.

———. (2004). "Creating, contributing content catching on". *ClickZ Stats*. Available online: http://www.clickz.com/stats/big_picture/applications/article.php/3319651.

Ha, L., and James, L. (1998). "Interactivity reexamined: A baseline analysis of early business web sites". *Journal of Broadcasting & Electronic Media*, 42 (4): 457–474.

Horrigan, J. B. (2003). *Consumption of Information Goods and Services in the United States*. Washington, D.C.: Pew Internet and American Life Project.

Internet Activities (2004). Washington, DC: Pew Internet and American Life Project.

Kiousis, S. (2002). "Interactivity: A concept explication". *New Media & Society*, 4 (3): 355-383.

Leiner, B. M., Cerf, V. G., Clark, D. D., Kahn, R. E., Kleinrock, L., Lynch, D. C., Postel, J., Roberts, L. G., and Wolff, S. (2000). *A brief history of the Internet*. Available online: http://www.cs.ucsb.edu/~almeroth/classes/F03.176A/papers/history.html.

Madden, M. (2003). *America's Online Pursuits: The Changing Picture of Who's Online and What They Do*. Washington D.C.: Pew Internet and American Life Project.

———. (2006). *Internet penetration and impact*. Pew Internet and American Life Project. Available online: http://www.pewinternet.org/pdfs/PIP_Internet_Impact.pdf.

McMillan, S. J. (2002). "Exploring models of interactivity from multiple research traditions: Users, documents, and systems". In L. Liverow and S. Livingstone (eds.), *Handbook of New Media*, pp. 162–182. London: Sage.

———. (2004). *Ubiquity Extends to Senior Citizens: A Qualitative Exploration of How Seniors Use the Internet for Health-Related Information.* Paper presented at the Association of Internet Researchers Conference, Brighton, Great Britain.

——— and Hwang, J. S. (2002). "Measures of perceived interactivity: An exploration of communication, user control, and time in shaping perceptions of interactivity". *Journal of Advertising,* 31 (3): 41–54.

——— and Morrison, M. (2004). *Commercialization of cyberspace: Experiences and expectations of young consumers.* Paper presented at the Association for Education in Journalism and Mass Communication Conference, Toronto, Canada.

Miller, M. (2001). "A snapshot of the class of 2001". *Public Relations Tactics* 8 (9): 21–22.

Rafaeli, S. (1988). "Interactivity: From new media to communication". In R. P. Hawkins, J. M. Wiemann, and S. Pingree (eds.), *Advancing Communication Science: Merging Mass and Interpersonal Process,* pp. 110–134). Newbury Park, CA: Sage.

Rogers, E. M. (1995). *Diffusion of Innovations* (4th ed.). New York: Free Press.

Rush, L. (2003). *U.S. E-commerce to see significant growth by 2008* [Web]. CyberAtlas. Available online: http://cyberatlas.Internet.com/markets/retailing/article/0,,6061_2246041,00.html (accessed September 7, 2003).

Schumann, D. W., Artis, A., and Rivera, R. (2001). "The future of interactive advertising viewed through an IMC lens". *Journal of Interactive Advertising,* 1 (2). Available online: http://jiad.org.

Strauss, A. L. and Corbin, J. (1990). *Basics of Qualitative Research: Grounded Theory, Procedures and Techniques.* Newbury Park: Sage.

Tapscott, D. (1997). *Growing up Digital: The Rise of the Net Generation.* New York: McGraw-Hill.

Tedeschi, B. (2002, March 11). "Internet executives take a look at a moving target". *The New York Times,* p. 8.

Thilmany, J. (2003). "Web searchers measure site's appeal in seconds". *Mechanical Engineering,* 125 (10): 12.

Vastag, B. (2001). "Easing the elderly online in search of heath information". *Journal of the American Medical Association,* 285 (12): 1563–1564.

The Roles and Importance of Internet Activities, New Media Use, and Leisure Participation on Leisure Satisfaction[1]

Louis Leung

Paul S. N. Lee

Introduction

Technology and Leisure

As technology continues to evolve at a rapid pace, it exerts a substantial influence on everyone's lives. Over the years, various household technologies have made their way into homes and have greatly changed the way people work, live, learn, and, more importantly, spend their leisure time. Television and VCRs already have a considerable influence on leisure (Jeffres, Atkins, and Neuendorf 1995; Lin 1992; Massey and Baran 1990). Karaoke stereo players, DVD, MP3, large screen digital television, satellite television, digital home cameras, MSN, blogs, album, iPod, and iPhone are the latest leisure-related appliances on the market. Technology may transform patterns of social life, from finding new friends and sharing a new hobby, to chatting on ICQ and getting the latest news. Technological leisure is no longer tailored for the young. Early baby boomers and seniors are catching up with younger generations to whom surfing the Net is second nature. Mature computer users are finding that cyberspace is changing their lifestyle — the way they communicate and find information, and the way they engage in leisure activities.

It is possible to identify the public's main leisure activities: things that most people do, and which account for considerable proportions of their leisure time and/or spending. Martin and Mason (1998) suggested that the big three are the media, eating and drinking, and holidaymaking. Eating and drinking head the spending league, tourism is in second place, and home entertainment (mostly TV-related) is third. However, in terms of time use, home entertainment is in first place. In the 1990s, adults in the U.S. watched television for well over 20 hours per week on average. If time spent attending to all the mass media is aggregated, it amounts to approximately half of all leisure time (Martin and Mason 1998).

Today, although the information revolution promises to touch every aspect of our lives, far less clear is the impact of media technology on participation in traditional leisure pursuits (e.g., sports, arts, and outdoor recreation) and experience of leisure. Historically, there has always been a relationship between technology and leisure, but the increasing use of the Internet and computer gaming technology during leisure time is facilitating a transformation in contemporary leisure activity. This study examined the implications of this technological change for leisure satisfaction.

Functions of Leisure

People participate in leisure activities for experiences that are enjoyable and personally satisfying, to relax and escape from the stresses of everyday life, and to improve their health (Iso-Ahola 1997). Via leisure participation, adolescents acquire knowledge of the sociocultural environment, practice social and cooperative skills, experience intellectual or physical attainments, and explore a variety of peer, family, and community roles (Iso-Ahola 1980; Willits and Willits 1986). It has also been claimed that leisure is related to self-esteem, feelings of control, lifestyle, and self-identity (Iso-Ahola 1980). All uses of leisure seem capable of making people feel better provided the leisure is structured and involves activity and social contact (Hendry, Shucksmith, Love, and Glendinning 1993). Leisure contributes to life satisfaction by providing "basic" experiences which are beneficial wherever they are obtained — activity, social contact, achieving goals, and being appreciated by others. Leisure's psychological and social functions make it an important contribution to the quality of people's lives — the greater the leisure satisfaction, the greater the life satisfaction (Garton and Pratt 1991; Keller 1983; Ragheb and Griffith 1982; Stones and Kozma 1986).

In addition to establishing leisure functions and patterns of leisure behavior, family leisure provides opportunities for social bonding (Kelly and Kelly 1994). The parent-child relationship is not the only one in which leisure plays a part. Opportunities for bonding between husbands, wives, siblings, and other family members also occur during leisure (Orthner, Barnett-Morris, and Mancini 1994). It is often during periods of casual family leisure, either in home-centered technological leisure or non-media-related leisure activities, that important values, decision-making skills, and issues of self-image are addressed or shared. For example, in a study on functions of the VCR in the home leisure environment, Lin (1992) found that the VCR serves three functions. First, like the television set, it provides home entertainment. Second, it can displace other leisure activities owing to advantages in cost and convenience as an alternative leisure vehicle. Third, and most importantly, the VCR has a social utility function because video viewing can be considered as a social event to enhance social goals. Through interaction and socialization with family members, children learn family values and how to get along with others. All these functions of leisure are important determinants of how satisfied people are with their leisure experiences.

Against this backdrop, the purposes of this study were: (1) to examine the displacement or supplement relationships between the degree of participation in non-media-related traditional leisure activities and media–related activities (with particular attention being paid to the use of the Internet and other new media technologies), and (2) to assess the extent to which media-related and non-media-related leisure pursuits can influence leisure satisfaction.

Review of the Literature

Leisure Participation

Alongside existing leisure technologies, computer technology and the Internet are emerging as important locations of contemporary leisure activity, creating new spaces for leisure participation. The Internet, e-mail, instant messaging, blogs, and online games have led to the formation of thousands of groups discussing a range of topics, playing games, creating contents on YouTube, and entertaining each other (Smith and Kollock 1999). These virtual spaces represent changing leisure activities and experiences which have implications for the societal and individual experience of leisure and well-being.

Leisure is often divided into a number of separate categories, such as indoor and outdoor leisure, sport, countryside recreation, arts and entertainment, and tourism. The home has always played some role in leisure provision, if for no other reason than that most people have always spent a good part of their lives there and have needed some amusements to occupy themselves. One major development in home-centered leisure is also linked to substantial commercialization but involves those activities associated with *new technology*. The expansion of television ownership in the 1950s and 60s radically changed home-centered leisure and at the end of the twentieth century, 95% of all households owned at least one television set (Brown, 2004). Since then a succession of technological developments — color television, stereo systems, VCRs, electronic games systems, CD/DVD players, home computers, the Internet, satellite and cable television, and interactive television — have brought into the home a whole array of leisure-related, electronic gadgetry that has totally revolutionized home leisure.

At the end of the 1990s, 38% of households in the U.S. possessed a personal computer compared with 18% a decade earlier and the ratio of households possessing a VCR had increased from 1 in 5 in 1983 to 4 in 5 in 1999 (Brown, 2004). Using a personal computer and modem or broadband link it is possible to play interactive online games with friends, without those friends having to leave their respective homes. With all these choices for home-centered leisure, one important task is to examine closely how participation in traditional leisure such as sports, arts, and outdoor leisure is displaced, if at all, by technology-based, media-related, and home-centered leisure. Therefore, a research question is posed:

RQ$_1$:   What effect, if any, do media-related activities (such as Internet use, new media use, and mass media use) have on participation in traditional leisure?

Leisure is said to play an important role in psychological well-being. Kelly and Kelly (1994) found that people who report high leisure satisfaction are also likely to indicate high family satisfaction and positive family relationships. Leisure plays a dynamic role in individuals' lives, and it would be useful and important to know how the satisfaction gained from leisure choices related to personal and social adjustment, especially in the consumption of other technology-based leisure activities, and in turn to overall happiness (Beard and Ragheb 1980).

Leisure Satisfaction

Leisure satisfaction is defined as the positive feeling of contentment one perceives because of meeting personal needs through leisure participation (Seigenthaler 1997). Leisure satisfaction is comprised of distinct categories of effects on individuals participating in leisure activities. These effects are viewed as certain personal needs which are met through leisure. The literature has identified several needs which leisure activities may satisfy. These component categories represent the theoretical rationale upon which leisure satisfaction is based. Devised by Beard and Ragheb (1980), the Leisure Satisfaction Scale (LSS) proposed six leisure satisfaction components, which are: psychological benefits, educational benefits, social benefits, relaxation benefits, physiological benefits, and aesthetic rewards. The sensation experienced during or following a leisure activity is considered an indication of the degree of contentment an individual experiences as a result of the activity (Beard and Ragheb 1980). A higher score was indicative of greater benefits from leisure activities.

Past research has found that people feeling greater contentment resulting from the satisfaction of felt needs are more likely to participate in a large repertoire of different activities than those who are less contented (Mobily, Leslie, Lemke, Wallace, and Kohout 1986; Searle and Ise-Ahola 1988). Similarly, the more leisure activities people engage in, the more satisfied they would be with their leisure activities. Leisure satisfaction was thus hypothesized to moderate, or alleviate, the levels of experienced stress (Beard and Ragheb 1980). In past research, relationships between some leisure domains and perceived stress have been studied in a variety of settings (Ragheb and McKinney 1993; Tice and Baumeister 1997); however, relationships between leisure satisfaction and technological leisure activities (such as Internet use and new media use) have rarely been addressed directly.

Bandura (1989) argued that factors influencing the decision to adopt technological leisure activities are mutually reinforcing. This means that external environment (such as opportunities for leisure), personality traits (such as attitudes towards the Internet), cognitive factors (i.e., likes and dislikes due to satisfaction from certain leisure activities), and adoption behaviors (the degree of participation in various leisure activities) are likely to involve multi-way reciprocal effects. It seems appropriate to examine further, how different domains of leisure satisfaction could play a role in affecting the adoption of various clusters or repertoires of media-related and non-media-related leisure activities. Conversely, it is also fitting to investigate how the tendency to structure one's time on media-related and non-media-related leisure participation might be an important factor influencing leisure satisfaction in a mutually reinforcing relationship.   .

Furthermore, demographic characteristics should also be considered to constitute structural facilitators in explaining leisure satisfaction because they designate one's place in the structure of society and thus may dictate opportunity and leisure satisfaction. Literature related to socioeconomic status (SES) provided a good example of how demographic characteristics may be related to opportunities (Jeffres, Neuendorf, and Atkins 2003). The effects of SES on leisure preferences and satisfaction may operate differently at different levels of social class, demonstrating the significance of additional demographic characteristics as facilitators of leisure activities. As a result, this study also explored how demographics, together with other factors such as Internet activities, new media use, mass media use, and leisure participation, can predict leisure satisfaction. Based on these conceptual frameworks, we ask two final research questions:

RQ$_2$:   How can leisure satisfaction and demographics predict size of repertoire in (a) Internet, (b) new media, (c) traditional mass media, and (d) leisure activities?

RQ$_3$:   What are the roles of and how important are technological leisure activities (i.e., Internet use, new media use, mass media use), non-media-related leisure participation, and demographics in predicting different components of leisure satisfaction?

Method

Sample and Sampling Procedures

Data were gathered from a probability sample of 1,192 respondents, using a face-to-face structured questionnaire interview during the months of October to December 2002. Respondents were eligible members of randomly generated households from the Census and Statistics Department of Hong Kong. If there was more than one eligible respondent living in the household, the person who was between the ages of 15 and 64 and had had the most recent birthday was interviewed. Interviewers were trained university students. A total of 238 households were discarded when interviewers found them to be vacant, for non-residential use or ineligible, had no response after having visited more than three times, or encountered a respondent who declined to take part in the study. In addition, eligible respondents were all PC users and had access to the Internet at home. Of the 954 qualified households, 696 successfully completed the questionnaires, resulting in a 73% response rate. However, only Internet users (N = 388) were included in the analysis.

The sample consisted of 46.7% males and 53.3% females. The mean age was 36.8, with 30.3% in the 35–44 age group, 21.6% who were 25–34, 20% who were 15–24, 19.7% who were 45–54, and 8.5% who were 55–64. This age distribution closely resembled the 2001 population census in Hong Kong. Of the 696 respondents, 41.9% were high school graduates, 24% were college graduates, 19.5% had completed junior high, and 13.4% only had grade school education. In terms of income, the mean was at the income bracket of US$2,565 –$3,205 a month. Over 38% were managers, administrators, professionals, or associate professionals, 19.4% were clerks, 14.3% were service or sales workers, 10.8% were craft and related workers, 9.8% had elementary occupations, and approximately 5% were plant and machine operators and assemblers.

Measurement

Leisure satisfaction. Beard and Ragheb's (1980) Leisure Satisfaction Scale (LSS) was adopted to assess leisure satisfaction. Based on needs theory, the instrument contained 51 questions asking respondents to indicate the applicability of each statement to him/her on a five-point scale ranging from "almost never true for you" (1) to "almost always true for you" (5) and assessed six leisure satisfaction components: psychological benefits, educational benefits, social benefits, relaxation benefits, physiological benefits, and aesthetic rewards. A higher score was indicative of greater benefits from leisure activities (e.g., "My leisure activities give me a sense of accomplishment"; "My leisure activities contribute to my emotional well-being"). However, to make the questionnaire short (i.e., can be administered in less than 20 minutes) and focused on the roles media-related and non-media-related activities play in individuals' leisure satisfaction, only the psychological, social, and relaxation domains were included. This is because physiological, educational, and aesthetic rewards benefits were less relevant in the context of leisure satisfaction from technological leisure activities. As a result, a short form of only 12 items, four items on each subscale, was used. The component structure of the modified LSS has been empirically validated and reconfirmed using factor analysis with three factors emerging (eigenvalues greater than 1.0 and accounting for 57.66% of item variance), namely relaxation, psychological, and social dimensions (see Table 2.1). The present study obtained an alpha reliability of .87 (subscales ranged from .74 to .77) as compared to .93 reported by Beard and Ragheb (1980).

Internet activities. Respondents were asked how often they use a list of 11 Internet activities: learning from the Internet, searching for information, reading news online, listening to music, playing games, surfing for leisure and entertainment, purchasing, using services on the Internet (such as paying bills, account transfer, and booking tickets, etc.), communicating with somebody you didn't know before, communicating with somebody you knew before, and talking about aspects of your inner world to other people. A 5-point Likert scale was used with "0" meaning never, "1" = seldom, "2" = sometimes, "3" = often, and "4" = very often. Principal components factor analysis with Varimax rotation yielded four factors with eigenvalues greater than

Table 2.1 Factor Analysis of Leisure Satisfaction (Internet Users)

How often do you feel the following statements are true to you?	Mean	SD	Factors		
			1	2	3
Relaxation					
1. your leisure activities help relieve stress	3.60	.80	.773		
2. your leisure activities help you to relax	3.78	.76	.732		
3. your leisure activities contribute to your emotional well being	3.60	.74	.674		
4. you engage in leisure activities simply because you like doing them	3.78	.81	.640		
Psychological					
5. your leisure activities give you a sense of accomplishment	2.94	.88		.806	
6. your leisure activities help you to learn about myself	3.10	.91		.781	
7. you use many different skills and abilities in your leisure activities	2.71	.97		.656	
8. your leisure activities give you self-confidence	3.25	.87	.449	.641	
Social					
9. you have social interaction with others through leisure activities	3.42	.89			.779
10. your leisure activities help you to learn about other people	3.20	.82		.420	.674
11. your leisure activities have helped you to develop close relationships with others	3.12	.90			.664
12. you associate with people in your free time who enjoy doing leisure activities a great deal	3.27	.89			.564
13. the people you meet in your leisure activities are friendly	3.50	.79			.555
Eigenvalue			4.77	1.63	1.10
Variance explained			36.70	12.50	8.46
Cronbach's alpha			.74	.77	.76

Scale used: 1 = almost never, 2 = seldom true, 3 = sometimes, 4 = often true, 5 = almost always true; N = 386

1.0, explaining 64.37% of the variance. As shown in Table 2.2, these factors are entertaining, socializing, information seeking, and e-commerce, with alpha ratings equaling .71, .70, .58, and .62 respectively. In addition to clustering Internet activity items into four factors, a composite Internet activity repertoire measure was also constructed. The same 11 Internet activities were collapsed into a single variable indicating the overall size of the Internet activities, with scores ranging from zero to 44. The Cronbach's alpha for internal consistency of the Internet activities repertoire equals .75.

New media use. Respondents were asked how much time they spent on the six most popular new media technologies in their leisure time, namely, chatting on ICQ, e-mailing, and talking on the phone measured in minutes per day; and playing computer games, listening to CD, MD, MP3, and watching VCD and DVD assessed in minutes per week. As with the Internet activity repertoire, a new media repertoire variable was also created after the six variables were recoded and standardized into five categories, with "0" = never, "1" = seldom, "2" = sometimes, "3" = often, and "4" = very often. Possible scores ranged from zero to 24, with a high score indicating larger repertoire size in new media use.

Traditional media use. Four traditional mass media variables were included in the analyses: printed newspaper reading, TV watching, magazine reading, and radio listening. Respondents were asked to report the average time spent on these media in a normal day. Newspaper reading, TV watching, and radio listening were measured in minutes per day, while magazine reading was measured in minutes per week. Comparable to the Internet repertoire and new media repertoire, a mass media use repertoire was also introduced after the four variables were standardized into five categories, with "0" = never, "1" = seldom, "2" = sometimes, "3" = often, and "4" = very often, with possible scores ranging from zero to 16.

Leisure participation. The leisure participation scale consists of seven items broadly describing various leisure activities in Hong Kong families, including physical exercise, talking to family and friends face-to-face for more than 10 minutes, going window shopping, playing mahjong, participating in community or religious activities, going to evening school, and doing voluntary work. For each of the seven items, respondents rated how often they engaged

Table 2.2 Factor Analysis of Usage Pattern of the Internet

How often do you use the following Internet services?	Mean	SD	Factors			
			1	2	3	4
Entertaining						
1. playing games on the Internet	2.59	1.26	.79			
2. listening to music on the Internet	2.93	1.22	.77			
3. surfing for leisure & entertainment	3.36	.98	.69			
Socializing						
4. talk about things of your inner world to other people on the Internet	2.05	1.02		.78		
5. communicate with somebody you knew before on the Internet	3.42	1.08		.77		
6. communicate with somebody you didn't know before on the Internet	2.16	1.09	.51	.54		
Information seeking						
7. searching information on the Internet	3.70	.86			.79	
8. watching news on the Internet	3.07	.93			.69	
9. learning from the Internet	2.82	.90			.67	
e-commerce						
10. to get service on the Internet (e.g., paying bills)	2.81	.62				.86
11. purchasing on the Internet	2.74	.64				.83
Eigenvalue			3.32	1.56	1.17	1.04
Variance explained			30.16	14.13	10.66	9.42
Cronbach's alpha			.71	.70	.58	.62

Scale used: 1 = never, 2 = seldom, 3 = sometimes, 4 = often, and 5 = very often; N = 387 in the given activities on a 5-point Likert scale, with "0" = never, "1" = seldom, "2" = sometimes, "3" = quite often, and "4" = very often. The scale had an acceptable internal consistency level with alpha = .70. An index similar to the one established and validated by Mobily, Lesile, Wallace, Lemke, Koliout, and Morris (1984) was also created to assess the traditional leisure repertoire. Again, the seven leisure activities were standardized and added to create a scale with data ranging from zero to 28.

Social locators. Also included were sociodemographic variables such as age, gender, education, income, marital status, and occupation.

Results

Effect of Media-related Activities on Traditional Leisure Participation

To answer the first research question, we examined the tendency to structure one's time on activities to see whether a particular set of media-related activities would increase (supplement/complement) or decrease (displace/substitute) the levels of non-media-related leisure participation. To do this, we adopted a standardized *relative proportion* of time spent on each new media and mass media use variable instead of the actual time reported by the respondents for further analyses. First, we calculated the total new media and mass media activities time budget (i.e., the sum of the total time spent on all new media and mass media activities on an average day, including e-mail, chatting on ICQ, playing computer games, talking on the phone, listening to CD, MD, MP3, watching VCD, DVD, LD, newspaper reading, TV watching, radio listening, and magazine reading). Then the time spent on each item was divided by the total time budget to obtain the *relative proportion* of time spent on each new media or mass media activity. The same procedure was used to obtain the relative proportion of time for traditional leisure participation. This approach in assessing the time spent on each activity is more accurate when comparisons or correlations are made (Lee & Leung, 2004). As a 5-point Likert scale, instead of the actual time spent, was reported for Internet activities, no relative proportion of time was calculated for these variables.

Table 2.3 Correlation between Internet Activities, New Media Use, Mass Media Use, and Traditional Leisure Participation

Traditional Leisure Participation

Media-related Activities	Physical exercise	Talking w/ family & friends	Window shopping	Playing mahjong	Participating in community/ religious activities	Going to evening school	Doing voluntary work
Internet Activities							
Entertaining	-.28***	-.28***	-.16**	-.13**	-.27***	-.26***	-.24***
Socializing	-.11*	-.09#	-.05	-.10#	-.02	.01	.01
Information seeking	-.02	-.02	.02	-.08	.00	.07	.06
e-commerce	-.04	-.04	-.04	.02	-.04	.02	-.04
New Media Use							
e-mail	.17**	.17**	.15**	.09#	.18***	.18***	.21***
Chatting on ICQ	-.14**	-.14**	-.06	-.12*	-.09#	-.13*	-.06
Playing computer games	-.26***	-.29***	-.30***	-.18**	-.21***	-.22***	-.27***
Talking on the phone	.11*	.19***	.22***	.10*	.15**	.18***	.16**
Listening to CD, MD, MP3	-.10*	-.04	-.02	-.03	-.04	-.08	-.09
Watching VCD, DVD, LD	-.20***	-.22***	-.24***	-.22***	-.14**	-.15**	-.15**
Mass Media Use							
Newspaper reading	.38***	.42***	.35***	.33***	.28***	.24***	.27***
Television watching	.29***	.33***	.34***	.30***	.20***	.22***	.23***
Radio listening	.10*	.02	-.01	-.02	.03	.02	.03
Magazine reading	.06	.07	.09	.06	.03	.09	.04

#p <= .1; *p <= .05; **p <= .01; ***p <= .001; N = 327

As Table 2.3 shows, zero-order correlations indicated many significant but negative relationships between leisure participation variables and media-related activities. Specifically, entertainment-oriented Internet activities (such as playing online games, listening to music online, and surfing the Internet for entertainment), as well as the use of new media (such as chatting on ICQ, playing computer games, and watching VCD, DVD, LD), tended to displace or be substitutes for a large number of leisure pursuits (such as physical exercise, talking with family and friends face-to-face, window shopping, playing mahjong, participating in community/religious activities, going to evening school, and doing voluntary work). On the contrary, heavy use of e-mails, talking on the phone, newspaper reading, and television viewing in fact complemented a wide range of traditional leisure pursuits.

Predicting Size of Repertoire

Table 2.4 shows regression analyses results on the influences of leisure satisfaction and demographics on size of repertoire of Internet use, new media use, mass media use, and traditional leisure. As expected, the social dimension of leisure satisfaction was significantly linked to repertoire size of Internet activities (β = .16, p < .01). This indicates that the greater satisfaction respondents had with the social component of leisure satisfaction, the more they would engage in various activities using the Internet, such as chatting on ICQ, forum, and talking about aspects of their inner world to other people. These active Internet users were predominantly young and highly educated. The size of the new media repertoire was also significantly linked to psychological (β = .16, p < .01) and social (β = .12, p < .05) dimensions of leisure satisfaction. This suggests that people who use leisure to satisfy their social and psychological needs tended to use new media (such as playing computer games, talking on the phone, listening to music on CD/MD/MP3, and watching videos on VCD/DVD) for similar functions. People with a large new media repertoire were mostly young boys with a low household income.

Interestingly, the mass media repertoire was not associated with any leisure satisfaction components. However, heavy users of mass media were older and better educated. Lastly, relaxation (β = .09, p < .05), psychological (β = .23, p < .001), and social (β = .29, p < .001) dimensions of leisure satisfaction were predictive of a traditional non-media leisure repertoire. This shows that non-media leisure participation still plays an important role in fulfilling our social, psychological, and relaxational needs from activities such as sports, talking to family and friends, doing voluntary work, and going window-shopping. People who were involved in a large number of non-media-related leisure activities were predominantly highly educated females with a high household income. Among the four regression equations, 6% to 29% of the variance was accounted for.

Predicting Leisure Satisfaction

Finally, the last research question was concerned with the relative influence of media-related activities (such as use of the Internet, new media, and mass media) on the evaluation of overall and various

Table 2.4 Regression of Leisure Satisfaction and Demographics on Size of Repertoires in Internet Activities, New Media, and Leisure (Internet Users Only)

Predictor Variables	Size of Repertoire			
	Internet Activities β	New Media β	Mass Media β	Traditional Leisure β
Leisure Satisfaction				
Relaxation	n.s.	n.s.	n.s.	.09*
Psychological	n.s.	.16**	n.s.	.23***
Social	.16**	.12*	n.s.	.29***
Demographics				
Age	−.47***	−.28***	.11#	n.s.
Gender (Female=1)	n.s.	−.14**	n.s.	.13**
Educational level	.16**	n.s.	.23***	.17**
Monthly household income	n.s.	−.10*	n.s.	.13*
R^2	.30	.17	.08	.24
Final adjusted R^2	.29	.15	.06	.23

Notes: Figures are standardized beta coefficients from final regression equation with all blocks of variables included for the entire sample.
p <= .1; * p <= .05; ** p <= .01; *** p <= .001; N = 327

dimensions of leisure satisfaction when non-media-related traditional leisure participation and demographics were considered simultaneously. To isolate the contribution of media-related activities as well as non-media-related leisure pursuits, hierarchical regressions were conducted. That is, Internet use, new media use, use of mass media, traditional leisure participation, and demographics were entered into separate blocks of four independent equations. A total of four Internet activities variables were entered as the first block, out of which only socializing was a significant predictor of the overall (β = .14, p < .01), relaxation (β = .13, p < .01), and social (β = .17, p < .01) dimensions of leisure satisfaction. This indicates that active Internet users who use the Internet as a socializing tool tended to evaluate their overall, social, and relaxation leisure satisfaction higher. This finding may be due to the fact that people who were able to talk about aspects of their inner world to other people on the Net are more satisfied socially and emotionally. Furthermore, e-commerce also showed a positive linkage with the social component of leisure satisfaction (β = .10, p < .05). This may be due to the fact that Internet users enjoyed sharing information with friends on good bargains available online. The first block alone accounted for 2% to 5% of the variance (see Table 2.5).

Table 2.5 Stepwise Regression of Internet Activities, New Media Use, Mass Media Use, Traditional Leisure Participation, and Demographics on Leisure Satisfaction

Predictor Variables	Leisure Satisfaction			
	Overall β	Relaxation β	Psychological β	Social β
Block 1: Internet Activities				
Entertaining				
Socializing	.14**	.13**		.17**
Information seeking				
E-commerce				.10*
ΔR^2	.03	.02	.00	.05
Block 2: New Media Use				
e-mail				
Chatting on ICQ				

Predictor Variables	Leisure Satisfaction			
	Overall β	Relaxation β	Psychological β	Social β
Playing computer games	.19***	.17**	.20***	
Talking on the phone				.14**
Listening to CD, MD, MP3				
Watching VCD, DVD, LD				
ΔR^2	.05	.03	.05	.02
Block 3: Mass Media Use				
Newspaper reading	.11*		.10*	.13**
TV watching				
Radio listening				
Magazine reading				
ΔR^2	.01	.00	.01	.01
ΔR^2 *, Media-related variables only*	*.09*	*.05*	*.06*	*.08*
Block 4: Leisure Participation				
Physical exercise	.14**	.11*	.20***	
Talking with family or friends face to face	.15**	.16**		.13**
Window shopping	.13**		.14**	.14**
Playing mahjong				
Participating in community or religious activities	.14**			.22***
Going to evening school	.13**	.12*		.11*
Doing voluntary work			.17**	
ΔR^2 *, Non-media-related Leisure participation variables only*	*.11*	*.06*	*.08*	*.12*
Block 5: Demographics				
Age				
Gender (Female=1)				
Educational level				
Monthly household income				
ΔR^2	.00	.00	.00	.00
R^2	.23	.13	.16	.21
Final adjusted R^2	.20	.11	.14	.20

Notes: Figures are standardized beta coefficients from final regression equation with all blocks of variables included for the entire sample.

[#] $p <= .1$; * $p <= .05$; ** $p <= .01$; *** $p <= .001$; N = 328

Six variables of new media use were entered into the equations as the next block. They contributed significantly to the variance explained (change in R square ranged from 2% to 5%, p < .001). The contribution came mainly from playing computer games (β = .19, p < .001 for overall; β = .17, p < .01 for relaxation; and β = .20, p < .001 for psychological components of leisure satisfaction). Talking on the phone was also significantly linked to social leisure satisfaction (β = .14, p < .01). These results indicate that the more respondents played computer games and communicated with family and friends on the phone, the higher they evaluated their relaxation, psychological, and social leisure satisfaction.

Newspaper reading in the third block (i.e., mass media use) was found to be a positively significant but relatively weak predictor of the overall (β = .11, p < .05), the psychological (β = .10, p < .05), and the social (β = .13, p < .05) dimensions of leisure satisfaction. This particular finding suggests that newspaper reading satisfies Internet users' psychological and social needs for the information they need in keeping abreast of the situation in the world so that they can participate in conversations intelligently with friends and family. Newspaper reading only contributed 1% of the variance explained.

Non-media-related leisure participation was entered next in the fourth block. With the exception of playing mahjong, all non-media-related leisure participation contributed significantly to the evaluation of leisure satisfaction. Physical exercise predicted relaxation (β = .14, p < .01) and psychological (β = .20, p < .001) leisure satisfaction; talking with family and friends face-to-face and going to evening school helped with relaxation (β = .16, p < .01 and β = .12, p < .05 respectively) and social (β = .13, p < .01 and β = .11, p < .05 respectively) gratifications; window-shopping aided the feeling of psychological (β = .14, p < .01) and social (β = .11, p < .05) fulfillment; participating in community or religious activities benefited social rewards (β = .22, p < .001); and doing voluntary work brought psychological contentment in leisure satisfaction (β = .17, p < .01). This block yielded an increase in R square of 11% for overall, 6% for relaxation, 8% for psychological, and 12% for social dimensions of leisure satisfaction.

Finally, demographics were entered as the last block.

Surprisingly, no significant contribution was found. Overall, media-related activities, including use of the Internet, new media, and mass media, contributed a total of 9% of variance explained for overall, 5% for relaxation, 6% for psychological, and 8% for the social dimensions of leisure satisfaction. In comparison to the variance explained in the non-media leisure participation block, it appears that media-related activity variables were comparable predictors to the non-media-related leisure pursuits for the evaluation of leisure satisfaction. The total variance accounted for by the five blocks was 20% for overall, 11% for relaxation, 14% for psychological, and 20% for social leisure satisfaction.

Conclusions and Discussion

Our purpose was to test a conceptual model of leisure satisfaction among Internet users and to examine how it is linked to technologically mediated leisure activities and non-media-related traditional leisure. The present research investigated the interrelationships of the use of the Internet, new media technologies, and mass media in conjunction with traditional leisure participation to explain satisfaction in leisure. Important insights on these interrelationships emerged from the study. As anticipated, significant relationships were found between leisure satisfaction and home-based, media-related leisure activities. Despite the strong contribution from non-media-related leisure activities, technological leisure activities were significant determinants of leisure satisfaction. Using the Internet as a socializing tool, playing computer games, talking on the phone, shopping online, and reading newspapers enhanced self-determined relaxational, psychological, and social dimensions of leisure satisfaction. These relationships are in line with earlier findings that media use variables (such as VCR and newspaper use) complement non-media social activities in stimulating social leisure behaviors (Jeffres, Atkins, and Neuendorf 1995). The conclusion supports a basic premise that as individuals experience higher levels of satisfaction in their leisure, they will also experience increases in the respective leisure activities repertoire in a mutually reinforcing relationship — whether or not the activities are related to technology.

Displacement Effect of Media-related Leisure on Traditional Leisure Activities

Looking at the zero-order relationships between the technologically-mediated or media-related leisure variables and leisure participation, it may be seen that entertainment-oriented Internet activities (such as playing games and listening to music online and surfing the Internet for fun), as well as the use of new media (such as playing computer games, watching VCD, DVD, LD, and to some extent, chatting with someone on ICQ to relax), tend to displace or be substitutes for a large number of traditional leisure pursuits, as indicated by the negative relationships between these variables. These findings support previous research which suggested that media use, generally viewed as "entertainment" and "expressive activities," except TV watching, would be more functional substitutes of traditional leisure activities because they are more likely to provide similar uses and gratifications (Jeffres, Neuendorf, and Atkins 2003).

However, the reverse occurs for e-mailing, talking on the telephone, reading newspapers, and watching TV, which are positively correlated with almost all of the leisure participation variables. This suggests that, for many, the usage patterns of these technological leisure activities are often instrumental in nature, such as communicating with family and friends via the phone and e-mail, as well as obtaining information and entertainment from newspapers and TV. Participation in traditional leisure seems to be unaffected by these technological leisure activities, which actually complement or supplement traditional leisure. More importantly, this finding may also suggest that the Internet is assuming a larger role in the home; however, this is not at the direct expense of TV time. TV remains the pre-eminent and primary entertainment medium in the home. It seems that households are simply clearing more time for both types of leisure, the technological leisure and the traditional leisure, or in other words, they engage in them simultaneously.

Media-related vs. Non-media-related Leisure and Leisure Satisfaction

We see a predictive role for higher social leisure activities, both facilitated through technological leisure and non-media-related traditional leisure, on leisure satisfaction. Specifically, those satisfied with their leisure level reported a heavy use of the technologically-mediated socializing repertoire which included the descriptors of communicating via the Internet (such as e-mail, ICQ, forums, etc.), playing computer games with friends, and talking on the phone. In Hong Kong, chatting on ICQ, playing computer games, and talking and texting via mobile phones are popular activities which form part of the contemporary leisure lifestyles for a significant number of children, young people, and adults. They are increasingly part of existing social networks and involved in the creation of new social networks of gamers and virtual communities. In addition, the strongest leisure satisfaction predictors among non-media-related socializing descriptors were talking with family or friends face-to-face, going window shopping with friends, and participating in community and religious activities. This finding supports past research indicating that leisure participation, especially for socializing, is a social space providing opportunities for interpersonal activity (Kelly, Steinkamp, and Kelly 1986).

It is also worth noting that, in contemporary society, traditional leisure activities and spaces (e.g., cinema, socializing, clubs, and sports) exist alongside those that are technological (e.g., computer games and the Internet). In fact, traditional notions of leisure spaces and activities may also be reproduced technologically in virtual leisure spaces (e.g., computer games reproducing sporting activities, shopping, socializing, and exchanging information). Technological leisure activities fulfill the same functions as those considered traditional; they provide relaxation, stimulation, escape, social interaction, and the development of self-identity (Kelly 1983).

Finally, the lack of significance exerted by demographic variables on leisure satisfaction may suggest that the results reinforce the need to move beyond social locator variables, as variance attributable to demographics in leisure satisfaction is becoming less effective (Jeffres and Atkins 1996; Leung 2003; Leung and Wei 1998).

Limitation of the Study and Future Research

Although the conceptual model of leisure satisfaction is based on sound theoretical assumptions and was empirically supported, the present results should be interpreted in light of the methodological limitations of the study. We used a correlational design, which does not establish causal proof of the observed relations. The data were recorded at a single moment in time; consequently, one cannot predict what could happen over time with respect to the observed relations. Therefore, several explanations for our finding can be proposed. For example, there is a possibility that greater time spent in leisure participation may cause a decrease in media-related activities. Alternatively, an increase in media-related activities may cause a decrease in leisure participation. Use of quasi-experimental and longitudinal designs will improve the strength of the findings. Another limitation of this study is its reliance on self-reported measures. The results should be considered in context, and not be generalized to other populations without further investigation. A more precise and perhaps elaborate measure might have yielded different results. As the data of this study are based on a sample from a predominantly Asian society, there is also a need for replication on a more heterogeneous population and larger sample and other cultural setting, so as to increase generalizations and to determine the associations between the constructs. In addition, some of the scale reliabilities for Internet activities were lower than .70. Future research should explore the associations of these constructs with higher scale reliabilities.

Future research should explore the other mediator variables that could possibly explain the weakness or lack of correlations between leisure satisfaction and other measures. Furthermore, with the advent of the mobile Internet, wireless gadgets, such as iPod and iPhone, are set to invade new areas of personal life and leisure. Teenagers appear to be the most avid users of the mobile Internet, notably in markets where it is at an advanced stage of development, for example, downloading cartoon animations or "avatars" to represent the user when entering chat rooms or sending messages. These would be new additions to the expanding media menu of leisure opportunities. Therefore, as distinctions between mass media continue to blur over time — such as telephony, television, and the Internet beginning to compete in program delivery — it is important to repeat this research to assess changes in leisure opportunities and experiences. The Internet provides multiple leisure spaces that support a variety of leisure activities, suggesting changes in the interactional, spatial, and temporal experience of leisure. These changes demonstrate the need to research the multiplicity of uses of new technologies and the Internet in leisure, and the implications of this for individual psychological and physical well-being.

We recognize that the study was conducted in 2002 and due to availability of more applications (such as MSN, blog, album, MP3, iPod, and iPhone), the findings will be different today. However, the aim of the study was not to demonstrate how specific media-related leisure activity can contribute significant influence in explaining leisure satisfaction comparable to non-media-related activities. The purpose of the study was to test a broad conceptual model of leisure satisfaction among internet users and to examine how it is linked to technologically mediated leisure activities and non-media-related traditional leisure. We understand that there will be new electronic gadgets with new potentials to occupy our leisure time. This study provides an exploratory basis to conclude that technological leisure activities in broad terms, such as those we engaged in with the Internet, are significant determinants of leisure satisfaction which complement or supplement traditional leisure.

Note

1.   The work described in this paper was fully supported by a grant from the Research Grant Council of the Hong Kong Special Administrative Region. (Project no. CUHK 4315/01H).

References

Bandura, A. (1989). "Human agency in social cognitive theory". *American Psychologist* 44: 1175–1184.

Beard, J. G. and Ragheb, M. G.. (1980). "Leisure satisfaction: Concept, theory, and measurement". In S. Iso-Ahola (ed.), *Social Psychological Perspectives on Leisure and Recreation.* Springfield, IL: Charles C. Thomas.

———. (1980). "Measuring leisure satisfaction". *Journal of Leisure Research,* 12 (1): 20–33.

Brown, D. (2004). "Communication Technology Timeline". In A. E. Grant and J. H. Meadows (eds.), *Communication Technology Updates,* 9th edition, pp. 7–46. Boston: Focal Press.

Garton, A. F. and Pratt, C. (1991). "Leisure activities of adolescent school students: Predictors of participation and interest". *Journal of Adolescence* 52: 305–321.

Hendry, L. B., Shucksmith, J., Love, J. G., and Glendinning, A. (1993). *Young People's Leisure and Lifestyles*. London: Routledge.

Iso-Ahola, S. E. (1980). *The Social Psychology of Leisure and Recreation*. Springfield, IL: Charles C. Thomas.

———. (1997). "A psychological analysis of leisure and health". In J. T. Haworth (ed.), *Work, Leisure and Well-being*. London: Routledge.

Jeffres, L. W. and Atkin, D. (1996). "Predicting Use of Technologies for Communication and Consumer Needs". *Journal of Broadcasting & Electronic Media* 40: 318–330.

Jeffres, L. W., Atkins, D., and Neuendorf, K. (1995). "The impact of new and traditional media on college student leisure preferences". *World Communication* 24 (2): 67–73.

Jeffres, L. W., Neuendor, K., and Atkin, D. (2003). "Media use and participation as a spectator in public leisure activities: Competition or symbiosis?" *Leisure Studies* 22: 169–184.

Kelly, J. R. (1983). *Leisure Identities and Interactions*. London: George Allen & Unwin.

———. (1994). "Multiple dimensions of meaning in the domains of work, family, and leisure". *Journal of Leisure Research* 26 (3): 250–274.

———, Steinkamp, M. W., and Kelly, J. R. (1986). "Later life leisure: How they play in Peoria". *The Gerontoaist* 26: 531–537.

Lee, P. and Leung, L. (2004). *Assessing the displacement effects of the Internet*. Paper presented at the International Conference on Internet Communication in Intelligent Societies. School of Journalism & Communication, The Chinese University of Hong Kong, July 8–10.

Leung, L. (2003). "Impacts of Net-Generation Attributes, Seductive Properties of the Internet, and Gratifications-Obtained on Internet Use". *Telematics & Informatics* 20 (2): 107–129.

Leung, L. and Wei, R. (1998). "Factors Influencing the Adoption of Interactive TV in Hong Kong — Implication for Advertising". *Asian Journal of Communication Implication* 8 (2): 124–147.

Lin, C. A. (1992). "The functions of the VCR In the home leisure environment". *Journal of Broadcasting & Electronic Media* 36 (3): 345–352.

Massey, K. and Baran, S. (1990). "VCRs and people's control of their leisure time". In J. Dobrow (ed.), *Social and Cultural Aspects of VCR Use*, pp. 93–105. Hillsdale, NJ: Lawrence Erlbaum.

Martin, W. B. and Mason, S. (1998). *Transforming the Future: Rethinking Free Time and Work*. Leisure Consultants, Sudbury.

Mobily, K., Leslie, D., Lemke, J., Wallace, R., and Kohout, F. (1986). "Leisure patterns and attitudes of the rural elderly". *Journal of Applied Gerontology* 5: 201–214.

Mobily, K., Leslie, D., Wallace, R., Lemke, J., Kohout, F., and Morris, M. (1984). "Factors associated with the aging leisure repertoire. The Iowa 65+ rural health study". *Journal of Leisure Research* 16: 338–343.

Orthner, D. K., Barnett-Morris, L., and Mancini, J. A. (1994). "Leisure and family over the life cycle". In L' Abate (ed.), *Handbook of Developmental Family Psychology & Psychopathology*. New York: John Wiley & Sons.

Ragheb, M. G., and Griffith, C. A. (1982). "The contribution of leisure participation and leisure satisfaction of older persons". *Journal of Leisure Research* 14: 295–306.

Ragheb, M. G., and McKinney, J. (1993). "Campus recreation and perceived academic stress". *Journal of College Student Development* 34 (1): 5–10.

Searle, M. and Ise-Ahola, S. (1988). "Determinants of leisure behavior among retired adults". *Therapeutic Recreational Journal* 2: 38–46.

Seigenthaler, K. (1997). "Health benefits of leisure. Research Update". *Parks and Recreation*, 32 (1): 24–31.

Smith, M. A. and Kollock, P. (eds.). (1999). *Communities in Cyberspace*. London: Routledge.

Stones, M. J. and Kozma, A. (1986). "Happiness and activities as propensities". *Journal of Gerontology* 41:85–90.

Tice, D. and Baumeister, R. (1997). "Longitudinal study of procrastination, performance, stress, and health: The cost and benefits of dawdling". *Psychological Science* 8 (6): 455–458.

Willits, W. L. and Willits, F. K. (1986). "Adolescent participation in leisure activities: 'The less, the more' or 'the more, the more'?" *Leisure Sciences* 8: 189–206.

3

—⟋ᨏ⟍—

The Socio-Economic Impact
of Intelligent Spaces:
Who Is in Control?[1]

Michael Lyons

Introduction

Future on-line services will exploit "pervasive computing" or "ambient intelligence" (AmI). This assumes wide-spread use of sensors, microprocessors in most goods, a low-cost communications infrastructure connecting these devices together and advanced artificial intelligence to interpret the data generated. An intelligent environment or "intelligent spaces" (i-Spaces) is created that can respond to people's needs without complex and non-intuitive interfaces. If this vision is achieved, the impact will be revolutionary: changing totally the way people interact with each other and their environment. This chapter aims at exploring both the potential benefits of emerging services and the technical and institutional issues that need to be resolved if the benefits of i-Spaces are to be attained.

The i-Spaces vision has two drivers: The first is an aspirational dream of "invisible technology", in which unobtrusive, adaptive and sometimes unseen devices embedded in everyday objects will be available to support users in their home and working lives. This idea is captured in terms such as AmI, "calming technology" and i-spaces.

The second is a technologically driven vision, based on the following trends:

- Falling cost of computing (Moore's Law), resulting in widespread use of microprocessors in a wide range of consumer items and commercial equipment;
- Even more rapid reduction in the (marginal) cost of transmission, both fixed line and mobile;
- Development of new wireless technologies (Bluetooth, IEE802.11x etc., IR systems);
- Increasing availability and capability of cheap tags and sensors;
- Increasing capability of AI — a crucial element in ensuring the technology becomes "invisible."

The development of i-Spaces will create a system of trillions of interconnected entities, ranging from the most humble object to the most complex. Each entity will have both communications and computing capabilities. They will be able to communicate information, interpret it and process it. This vision leads us to envisage new ways of living and working and, for companies, new ways of creating value and organising businesses (Lyons et al. 2004).

New business (value creation) opportunities may arise through the development of new infrastructures (such as sensor nets), new operating systems (already a key battleground — Santo, 2001) and a wide range of applications including intelligent management systems to support both businesses and individuals. This range of potential applications reflects the pervasive nature of the underlying technologies, but will also present problems for companies seeking to exploit the opportunities. As Odlyzko (1999) points out, the spread of pervasive computing or i-Space technologies will "ignite an explosion of innovation that will destroy any stability that might exist." In this dynamic environment, "new players and new business ideas will be emerging constantly … no company will be certain of its commercial environment, even in the short-term. If companies are to succeed in the long-term they will need to be constantly innovating." (Pearson, Lyons, and Greenop 2000). But eventually, user expectations will start to stabilise and more permanent business forms will emerge.

It is often difficult to grasp the implications of i-Space technology; the twin characteristics of pervasiveness and invisibility mean its impact can only be seen indirectly through the way people live and work. The technology is largely an enabler — it can impact on many industries in many different ways. Similarly, the concept of "invisible technology" is intuitively attractive, but again can be applied to many different applications and products. Clearly, there are great uncertainties about what will be a successful i-Space application. In this paper, we look at how people respond both to current ICT and to proposed i-Space applications with a view to identifying characteristics of successful applications.

This paper draws on work carried out under a recent Eurescom project P1302 — PROFIT (Potential pRofit Opportunities in the Future ambient InTelligence world). This studied the socio-economic impact of Ambient Intelligence and sought to understand some of the factors which will determine the success or otherwise of new AmI or i-Space services.

Characteristics of Intelligent Spaces

The vision driving i-Spaces is described in many different ways: ubiquitous computing (Weiser 1991), pervasive computing (IBM 1999) and ambient intelligence (ISTAG 2001). Although there are some differences in the scope and emphasis of these visions, the overlaps are so large that the terms are frequently used interchangeably. The characteristics of the vision are based largely on expected developments in information and communications technology and have three main aspects:

- Pervasive communications
- Ubiquitous sensors and actuators
- Embedded intelligence

Pervasive Communications

Much of the current interest in i-spaces arises from the introduction of new wireless protocols (such as blue-tooth) which offer a means of enabling local devices to communicate with each other. Consumer electronics companies such as Philips are introducing such systems into a number of consumer goods. Bluetooth provides a means for developing wireless home networks. Other wireless protocols such as IEEE802.11, IEE802.16 and 3G offer broadband communications over larger distances, thus enabling a household's devices (which can, of course, include PCs, PDAs and phones) to connect to the global networks.

Ubiquitous Sensors/Actuators

A second feature of the i-Space vision is the widespread presence of sensors and actuators (Nagel 2000). Initially, these are simply carrying out tasks internal to the individual items of equipment (for example, temperature sensors in a washing machine to monitor the washing programme, and relays to operate motors, pumps etc.). However, when combined with pervasive communication and embedded intelligence (see below) this technology opens the possibility of linking together individual consumer goods and standalone sensors to form a seamless "intelligently aware" environment.

Embedded Intelligence

Increasingly, microprocessors are being incorporated in a large number of household goods — TVs, washing machines, fridges, cars etc. There is thus a huge amount of raw processing power being introduced into the home — most of which is hidden and invisible to the user. The capabilities of artificial intelligence are also developing rapidly, so that it is possible for devices and applications to monitor the wider environment (including the words and actions of humans) and to respond to, or even anticipate, individual needs.

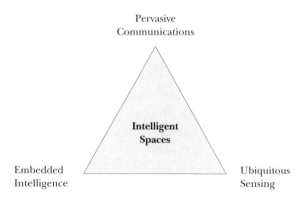

i-Spaces

How these capabilities can be exploited for the benefit of both individuals and businesses is the key challenge of the i-Space vision. The different descriptions referred to above emphasise the three characteristic capabilities to varying extents. Ubiquitous computing, as its name implies, concentrates very much on the embedded intelligence of technology. Its emphasis on "calming" human-centred technology (Weiser 1991) is highly dependent on intelligent systems providing intuitive interfaces and appropriate information to the user in such a way that the underlying technology becomes invisible. Ambient intelligence and i-Spaces build on this vision, to include the sensor and actuator networks that enable a continuous interaction between individuals and their environment. And all these visions assume some degree of communication between individual devices, between devices and humans, and between humans.

Thus, an i-Space is an environment that responds and adapts intelligently to the presence of the individuals within it, and anticipates needs including the need to communicate and interact with other i-Spaces. The pervasive communications strand is similar to ideas of seamless, mobile and broadband communications networks that are seen as key enablers of the Information Society.

The concept of an i-space emphasises an aspect often neglected in discussions of ubiquitous computing or pervasive ICT — the notion of boundaries. Spaces are bounded both physically and logically; access to these spaces may be restricted to particular people, or at particular times. Yet, the full benefit of i-Space technology comes from its ability to extend information horizons — potentially to a global level, for like today's internet, the future network will enable interactions between anyone (or anything) connected to the network, regardless of physical location. One challenge for the technology will be to protect those spaces from intrusive and unauthorised access by others. Where access to the wider network is via some form of gateway, then the individual has control over what passes through this, and can switch it off completely if desired. However, not only is an "off-switch" a clumsy and unsatisfactory method of control, but it could also become an impossibility. In the future, i-Spaces may be created by individual consumer goods in a house exploiting short-range radio communications to form an "ad hoc" network. It is easy to see how such networks could combine with neighbouring networks: under these circumstances, the individual has little control over what is communicated with the outside world.

The EC's Institute for Prospective Technological Studies discusses the concept of a virtual residence (IPTS 2003, p. 80) as a means of clarifying the difference between private and public "by providing a visual and mental model for representing the online private space of people, families or households in Ambient Intelligence". A similar concept could be applied to other restricted spaces such as the virtual office or virtual club. Such a picture also allows one to visualise the breakdown of barriers. When working from home, there is an overlap between the "virtual office" space associated with work, and the "virtual residence" associated with the physical home. Where separate equipment is used for work and home, the boundaries in cyberspace are relatively clear. However, if people use the same device to access or control both home and work data and equipment, then the boundaries become ill-defined, as do rights and their associated responsibilities.

Benefits of i-Spaces: Automating the Mundane

There are two routes by which i-Space technology may enter the home. One is through the embedding of microprocessors and wireless communications into domestic (brown and white) goods. An important part of the i-Space vision is the ability of devices in the home to monitor both themselves and usage. This means that any faults can be notified directly to the manufacturer or maintenance organisation and repairs put in hand immediately. More ambitious visions envisage refrigerators, for example, monitoring usage and food (using tags on the food items themselves) and offering warnings of food approaching use-by date, or even re-ordering food automatically, based on observed usage or offering dietary advice. All such activities imply a shift from selling a good (product) towards providing a service (instead of a washing machine, a clothes cleaning service is provided; instead of a refrigerator, a food storage service). This not only implies a shift in the thinking of manufacturers/ suppliers but also the need for new infrastructures and services related to service fulfilment.

A second route is through the introduction of i-Space technologies to support home or remote working. Firms may provide equipment for their employees to use at home, or self-employed people may purchase the equipment to support their own business activities. Here the emphasis is on intelligent support to deliver appropriate information in a timely manner, and the facilitation of group working. This approach has underpinned a number of published scenarios demonstrating the potential impact of i-Spaces and AmI (e.g. ISTAG 2001, WWRI 2002; MIT 2000). Many of these scenarios are technology driven and in many (though not all) cases there is an emphasis on efficiency in terms of using time, interactions with others etc. as effectively as possible. The interface of personal activities and work activities is a key element of many scenarios. However, some of the visions (e.g. the "road warriors" travelling the globe, but simultaneously in contact with both work and home) describe a lifestyle which is both alien to many, and one not sought after or attractive to many people. The frenetic juggling of multiple interactions described in some scenarios is a marked contrast to the vision of "calming technology" described by Weiser (1991) and a reminder that the way the technology is used depends on a wide range of social, political and economic factors.

A survey of i-Space and ambient intelligence scenarios identified a number of key application areas (Eurescom 2004a):

- Communications/Messaging
- Leisure/Entertainment
- Collaboration/Teleworking
- E-Government
- Safety/Location based
- Live independently/Health
- Financial security/Financial services
- Data across the web/Information services
- Quality of life /Monitoring;
- Education

Some specific applications described in the scenarios included:

- "Digital me": A device for controlling access by voice at a particular time, and could decide which calls to ignore.

- Identity verification: a device verifying identity and unifying identity-related information.
- Taste and preference adaptor: a device altering things to your own tastes and preferences e.g. room lighting, news, TV programmes etc.
- Guardian angel: a device to "look after them" — e.g. telling people when they are ill or stressed, remembering where things have been left, stop them when running a bath that is too hot.
- Device as "agent": a device which acts as an individual's agent — e.g. ordering groceries, looking for and ordering cheaper insurance etc.

All these applications depend on embedded intelligence and at least local (within a room or house) communication, but the use made of sensors/actuators or global communications varies widely.

As part of the Eurescom project, fieldwork was undertaken in the UK, Norway, Finland and Hungary. The survey was carried out by means of over 30 interviews with a range of people working both in small businesses and in corporations. The small businesses included a number of "lifestyle businesses" where the main driver was quality of life rather than profit maximisation.

Interviewees were asked about their use of ICTs to support both the maintenance of work-home boundaries and the integration of these domains, with a view to understanding the likely impact of i-Space technologies (Eurescom 2004b). In addition, interviewees were asked about their feelings towards proposed i-Space applications (see above) in order to gain some insight into customer acceptance of these services.

For the Eurescom interviewees, the main advantages of the i-Space technologies were found to be in automating the mundane (reducing the time spent on routine and trivial activities) and helping people to be more in control of their lives (Eurescom 2004b). Thus, devices such as "digital-me" were seen as potentially useful if they helped individuals to manage the many different interactions made possible in an i-Space. Similarly, systems that notified individuals of the need for maintenance of domestic goods, or that made suggestions for ordering food etc, on the basis of monitored usage, offered ways to simplify people's lives. Whilst such findings do not identify which specific services will be successful, they do indicate characteristics that people will value and suggest ways of marketing them.

However, it should be noted that overall, the responses from the Eurescom interviewees to the proposed applications were largely negative. This may in part reflect a suspicion of new technology and bad experiences with existing technology, but the concerns expressed were common to most interviewees and indicate the issues that need to be solved if the technology is to be widely accepted. Whilst people generally welcomed the idea of systems that offered support for their chosen life-styles, they were much less happy with systems that acted autonomously on their behalf. There was a strong feeling that the technology should help the individual to control their life, but that it should not take control itself. In fact, the concept of control is central to much of the debate, as most of the perceived problems and disadvantages of the i-Space technologies are also related to issues of control.

Negative responses to the technology included:

- Privacy concerns — how to control access to and the use made of the (very personal) data gathered by i-Space applications.
- A concern that some of the devices would take over (the device controlling the human rather than vice versa). For example, the guardian angel might prevent people from undertaking activities it (the device) considered dangerous or the taste and preference adaptor would not recognise changes in taste, thus inhibiting spontaneity.
- A concern that choices made by an agent, or advice provided by the taste and preference adaptor, might not be independent but influenced by the provider of such services. Again this is an issue of who is ultimately in control of the technology.
- There was a concern about the risk of identity theft in an environment when transactions are being made remotely, and possibly without direct intervention by the individual.
- There was considerable scepticism about the ability of the applications to cope with the variability and unpredictability of human behaviour.
- Finally there was a concern about our becoming overly

dependent on technology. Although a valid concern, it is the one that is most affected by unfamiliarity — as applications become more widespread and are found to be reliable, this concern should fade.

Home-Work Interface

Issues of control also arise in considering the impact of i-Spaces on the home-work interface — this was a specific concern of the Eurescom survey and these issues are discussed next.

One of the main impacts of ICT has been a marked increase in the number of people working from home for at least part of the time. For example, data from the e-Living project show that in the UK — 8% of people use the Internet to work from home, while a further 12% work at home using a PC (e-living 2004). Understanding how people use the current generation of ICTs to mediate between the home and work roles provides clues as to how i-Spaces may be used in the future. An important focus of the Eurescom field-work was the study of how ICTs support both the maintenance of work-home boundaries and the integration of these domains, with a view to understanding the likely impact of i-Space technologies (Eurescom 2004b).

The home-work interface also means looking at several different i-Spaces. The dominant space is the home. A second major space is the i-Office, but work may also take place on the move, so vehicles and public spaces also need to be considered. One of the key findings of the Eurescom survey was that people had very different views about the extent to which they wanted to merge the work and home roles. Some, particularly small businesses, saw it as part of their service to be available at any time. Other people, more often lifestyle (hobby) businesses and corporate employees, sought to maintain a clear separation between work and home. Both groups, however, used ICT to control the degree to which work and home activities were integrated. i-Space devices will therefore need to stop incoming messages or data from work at home or home at work. A form of "off switch" is necessary, which is more sophisticated than powering down. In practice, few people maintained a strict work and home separation; work activities would be done in the home, and home activities could be done at work. Thus, context-aware applications that needed to identify whether a particular person was acting in a home or work role would not be able to use simple cues such as location.

Institutional Issues and Control

As noted above, the Eurescom interviewees' perceptions of i-Space technologies were sceptical of the benefits. Two areas of concern were highlighted. One is that of control — who controls the technology, who controls the data or information generated by the technology and to what extent is the user being controlled by someone or something else. The second, related, concern is a scepticism about whether the technology is capable of the level of intelligence needed to, for example, filter incoming communications (digital me), adapt to changing tastes and preferences, or act as an autonomous agent.

The issue of system intelligence is largely a question of technological development and is discussed below. However, we first consider the wider issues of "control." It is important to note that the determining factor in this case is not primarily the technology but rather, the interplay of a variety of institutional factors. These include social and corporate norms, the legal framework and economic drivers.

In the context of the work-home interface, there are several issues of control that need to be considered:

1. The extent to which the employee is in control of when and how they work;
2. The extent to which the user has control over the data generated within an i-Space, particularly his or her own home.
3. The extent to which the user wants to be in direct control of the system, or is willing to trust the system. This is related to the degree of intelligence within the system and is considered in more detail below.

Controlling Boundaries

Prior to the industrial revolution, most craft workers worked at home, and life and work was an integrated whole. The introduction of factories and later office work led to a very clear separation between work and home life, with firm boundaries being set in both time (working hours) and space (work location separated from home). The introduction of ICT has enabled more workers to re-integrate their work and home lives, leading to a blurring of the work-home boundary. There is no doubt that many people find it advantageous to be able to spend more time at home. The greater flexibility in both time and place of work gives individuals the freedom to juggle home and work responsibilities — all the more important in a world where most men and women work, and care of children or elderly relatives has to be shared. Growing use of the Internet for a variety of commercial transactions also enables people to sort out home issues (e.g. purchasing or paying bills) in the work environment.

There is little doubt that flexible working practices can be of benefit to both employees and employers. Thus, a survey within BT found that the ability to work flexibly was perceived as a perk and helped to retain staff. However, although the technology enables people to blur the work-home boundaries, the Eurescom survey showed that most people, especially those working for a corporate employer, still wished to maintain a distinction between work and home. This was typically achieved by simple, low technology methods such as switching off equipment, disconnecting from the corporate network and (for small businesses) having separate phones for private and business calls. An application such as "digital-me" which could automatically screen and prioritise calls (a task often achieved currently by the use of CLI or an answer phone) was seen as offering a useful service, although there was considerable scepticism over whether such a system could work in practice (see intelligence below).

The concern to maintain some distinction between work and home raises issues about who controls the boundaries. For the most part, interviewees were either self-employed or creative knowledge workers — groups that could reasonably exercise some control over these boundaries. Significantly, it was profit-making small businesses that were least inclined to impose a strict separation between home and work. While this was usually expressed as a matter of personal choice, it is also the case that such businesses may be the least able to restrict their work time for fear of damaging reputation and customer relationships.

Within the corporate sphere, the ability to maintain a separation between work and home depends very much on the norms of both the corporation and wider society. In the USA, where a high priority is placed on the demands of the economy, separating home and work life has become problematic for many workers: "The long arm of the job has reached into employees' homes, their nights, their weekends, and their vacations, as technology designed to make work less onerous has made it more pervasive." (Beatty 2001). Quoting a book by Jill Andresky Fraser (Fraser 2001), Beatty describes how work is encroaching into the time people spend at home and talks about "job spill": What Fraser calls "job spill" is "the dirty little secret behind many a corporation's thriving bottom line." Half of all households own pagers and half of those who own pagers have been beeped during a vacation." (Fraser 2001). It is important to recognise that the driver for these trends is not the technology — much of which, as Beatty notes, was developed to make life easier — but the extreme competitiveness of the US commercial environment, which forces firms to find new ways to increase productivity and reduce costs.

It does not have to be like this, but it is important for both companies and employees to have a clear understanding of expectations. For example, Microsoft UK recently introduced advanced technology (smart phones, tablet PCs and broadband at home). However, in a survey conducted with the Work Foundation "the most prominent response from the 443 staff involved was their demand for an 'agreed etiquette' and 'clarity of expectations' from Microsoft's management as to when work ended and their home life began. Staff felt stressed by the 'ambiguous expectations' about how available they should be, … given that the technology enabled them to work 24 hours a day."

In response, Microsoft "… issued guidance to all its UK staff on when they should turn off their mobile phones and disconnect from the internet at home, following a six-month trial of the latest mobile technology." (*Daily Telegraph* 2003). The guidelines stressed the fact that "the smart phone is a business enabler to empower employees to work more flexibly. The provision of a smart phone in no way requires users to either view or respond to business-related mails or calls out of office hours." Similar guidance was issued for tablet PCs and Internet access, "making it clear to staff that they remain in charge when it comes to how 'available' they are at home."

A final conclusion of the study was that after an initial drop, due to a learning curve, the company saw an increase in the productivity of its workers — evidence that where the technology is introduced in a way that leaves employees in control of the boundaries, there are gains by both employees (increased flexibility in managing home and work activities) and employer (increased productivity).

Microsoft UK is not the only example of good practice. BT has for many years promoted teleworking, both for its own staff and its customers. The author of this paper works from home at least part of the time, and has benefited from the greater flexibility and productivity offered by teleworking.

Controlling the Work or Controlling the Worker?

A consequence of working from home is that the i-Office is extended into the home. As Wright and Steventon (2004) note, employees are more acquiescent to corporate "Big Brother" in the i-Office. But will this acquiescence extend to extensive monitoring in the home environment? And where are the boundaries drawn when personal and work lives merge? Workplace monitoring is already widespread and likely to increase in scope (see e.g. Pearson and Lyons 2003, p. 93; Schulman 2001; Hazards 2004). An employer may have a right to monitor the work of the employee but if, for the employee, the prime benefit of home working is greater flexibility in when or how they work, then systems that impose rigid working practices on individuals will undermine both the benefits of, and enthusiasm for, home working.

A number of new systems are emerging including Enterprise Resource Management, Supply Chain Management, Customer Relations Management and Employee Relationship Management. Benefits claimed for these systems include faster and greater responsiveness to market changes, and greater efficiency in the use of resources. The capabilities of these systems will be greatly enhanced by i-Space technologies: much greater information on process performance and status will be gathered in real time, leading to greater control of both processes and service. By taking over much of the routine information transfer and recording, and ensuring process information is delivered to individuals in a timely and controlled way, these systems could both improve efficiency and reduce information overload. However, these same systems will involve the monitoring and storage of far larger amounts of information about individuals than is currently possible. Used inappropriately they could result in unacceptable levels of monitoring of both consumers and employees resulting in suspicion on the part of consumers and causing stress in employees (Smith et al. 1990); if system design emphasises efficiency then the result may be counter-productive with high levels of monitoring and control inhibiting the innovation essential for survival in an increasingly competitive environment.

De Tienne (1993), in a largely optimistic article, listed nine predictions about the way ICT would develop:

- Monitoring systems will become "evasion proof";
- Monitoring systems will provide suggestions to employees for performance improvement;
- Monitoring systems will give employees access to information about their own performance;
- Monitoring will be used as part of a results-oriented focus;
- Monitoring will primarily be used as a coaching device;
- Monitoring systems will facilitate group work and team-oriented approaches to work;
- Pay will be more closely connected with employee performance;
- The number of electronically monitored employees who work at home will increase;
- There will be increased attempts to pass legislation that regulates monitoring.

De Tienne clearly saw the use of ICT systems as a means to provide support and coaching for the users. Unfortunately, her article contained a number of examples (often in call centre environments) where existing systems were used primarily as means of control, to impose compliance and uniformity on the workforce. Common criticisms of the then current monitoring systems were that they were only used to speed up work, and that there was too much emphasis on quantity of work rather than quality (DeTienne 1993). Ten years later, little seems to have changed: indeed, more recent work by Head (2003) suggests that if anything, the situation has worsened for many workers. The introduction of advanced ICT-based management systems (such as Enterprise Resource Planning [ERP] and Customer Relationship Management [CRM] Systems) has led to a deskilling of the work, strictly enforced work practices and constant, real-time monitoring of performance. Furthermore, Head notes attempts to impose the same systems and disciplines on professional activities hitherto thought outside the scope of process re-engineering. He discusses efforts by Managed Care Organisations (MCOs) in the US to monitor, control and impose a single "best practice" on medical physicians (Head, 2003). Not surprisingly, this approach has met serious resistance both from patients and the medical profession. But the drivers: a concern for efficiency, the need to minimise costs, and the belief that a single, standardised approach is the best way to achieve this, are common to many businesses.

However, the technology does have the potential to support individual workers. By providing feedback on performance, monitoring systems can help both individuals and teams to improve. Monitoring programmes can ensure that successful strategies discovered by one team member can be shared with others. For example, Fast Data Technology's "Fast Tracker" (an on-line employee management system) enables co-workers to monitor each other's web surfing, helping them to discover the best practices of successful co-workers (Fast Data Technology 2004). Context-sensitive support can ensure appropriate information is delivered to an individual, thus relieving them of the need to remember vast amounts of detail that may only be used occasionally. Work flow systems can "talk" employees through complex procedures, thus helping workers to concentrate on key issues. The move to web-based quality management systems means ready access to the latest version of the system and avoids problems due to individuals keeping out-of-date paper versions. Because these systems should only deliver information when needed, they will reduce the problems of information overload. Furthermore, by enabling closer monitoring of workers' output by employers, it will be possible to develop remuneration systems that are far more closely related to performance, either of individuals or teams.

As software becomes more intelligent and context-aware, so the ability to interpret employee behaviour and activity will increase. Any "inappropriate" behaviour can be flagged, either as feedback to the employee, or as an alert to a human supervisor. Unlike human surveillance systems, the machines will never lose concentration or get bored. If used to coach employees, by presenting information or hints at appropriate times, such systems could be accepted and, indeed, found helpful. The fact that such help comes from a computer rather than a person may even be an advantage for some people: in the UK it has been found that young males, in particular, are happier to seek help and confide their problems in a neutral, computer-mediated environment (Samaritans).

Given that the emerging ICT and i-Space technologies can be used both to control and to coach employees, it is worth considering why the trend seems to be so firmly towards control at present. There are four drivers:

- The technology needed to monitor and control is, in general, simpler and largely in place. In contrast, coaching systems require a higher level of intelligence that has yet to be developed.
- The emergence of a "risk society" (Regan 2002, p. 386) in which institutions use surveillance as a means of managing risk: information collected about an individual and their activities is compared with standard profiles ("good/bad"; "trustworthy/untrustworthy") to decide how to deal with that individual.
- The justification for these systems is usually on ground of cost reduction. ERP and CRM systems etc. offer the potential to replace (costly) experts with expert systems and (cheaper) unskilled people (Head 2003).
- Finally, there is the attitude of managers: "Most business people, without knowing it, see the service world through the lenses of manufacturing goggles ... They are influenced by historical traditions in business training, strategy techniques and organisational theory, all rooted in manufacturing." (Reichfield and Markey 1990). Foremost amongst these traditions are the manufacturing production line and scientific management, with their emphasis on standardised procedures, measurement and control.

A more holistic view of a company's operations may be necessary: rules and procedures tend to grow over time, in response to specific failures, or to meet growing regulatory and legal requirements. The more these are automated, the less freedom individuals have to ignore them. A different view of the workplace (Bell et al. 2002) described it as a bundle of services, noting that "employee self-service is an emerging and rapidly evolving set of applications." If the i-Office and other work related systems are to live up to the promise of helping and supporting individuals, rather than being seen as a tool of control, then use and control of the tools must move towards the workers, rather than remain with the employer.

Ownership and Control of Information

There is a widespread concern about the implications of ICT for the privacy of consumers (Pearson and Lyons (year??), pp. 89–92) which is already thought to be slowing the development of e-commerce. This concern is likely to increase in the future: an announcement that Benetton intended to sew RFID tags into its clothing range caused a deluge of complaints by customers, and resulted in the project being postponed (Shabi 2003). The development of i-Spaces greatly increases the extent of monitoring and surveillance: "This will be possible not only because this intelligent environment will be able to detect what people are doing in their everyday lives ... but also because it will connect and search isolated databases containing personal information." (IPTS 2003, p. 75). Thus it will be increasingly difficult for people to find a space where they have "the right to be left alone" — one of the earliest definitions of privacy. As with employee monitoring, the issue is not monitoring per se, but rather the use made of the monitoring taking place, by whom and the extent to which an individual can control this monitoring. But such monitoring is an integral part of i-Spaces, without which the vision of an intelligent, responsive and adaptive environment is not feasible. Thus, a balance between the private and the public must be found.

A key driver for the gathering of personal information by corporations is that personal information is increasingly being seen as a valuable asset, especially in the areas of direct marketing, financial services and health care. Customer information allows firms to develop specific offers (products/services) for individual customers and to target advertisements more effectively. The information may also be sold to other interested parties.

At present, customer information consists of that generated during a transaction, information freely given by customers (e.g. through surveys) and information on Internet usage gained by, for example, cookies. Future information may be far more extensive: RFID tag technology could in the future enable remote identification of everything a person owns or is carrying. Such information may be used to establish ownership, but could also be used to identify individual tastes and preferences for many different types of goods; digital satellite systems already enable the operators to record individual viewing habits; future systems which, for example, monitor and maintain stock levels in one's refrigerator are also recording individual diet. Coupled with monitoring of health and exercise levels, a detailed picture of an individual's lifestyle (healthy or otherwise) is built up - of obvious value to life and health insurers.

There are several approaches to overcoming these issues:

- Government Regulation. Regulation typically places broad limits on what information can be stored, gives individuals the right to inspect and correct information and places a duty on the organisation to store the information securely. However, individuals cannot themselves place restrictions on what information is stored, or how it is used.
- Self-regulation. The pressure for self-regulation comes from two sources: pressure from consumers themselves, which is restricting the growth of e-commerce, and the threat of government regulation. A number of schemes are emerging that offer consumers some degree of control over the use of personal information. These include e-TRUST (an audited labelling and certification programme, whereby web-sites declare certain levels of privacy) and the Platform for Privacy Protection (P3P) of the Internet Privacy working Group (Dyson). Using P3P, an individual's computer agents can seek web-sites with which to do business, having specified what types of privacy policy are acceptable, or should be avoided. Similarly, web-sites can describe their privacy policies and negotiate with individual agents. This is a step towards the

long-term dream of pervasive computing in which individuals have electronic agents which represent them in transactions within the all-pervasive web (ISTAG 2001; Greenop and Cupidi 2002).

• Anonymization services: in which an intermediary hides the identity of the person undertaking a transaction. Some simply anonymize users, so it is no longer possible to identify who is searching a Web site. Others may settle bills anonymously on behalf of clients. However, consumers must be able to trust the integrity of the sites. Some sort of external audit may be necessary, much as an audit process is a key feature of e-TRUST. In the future, anonymization services may merge with or be superseded by the agent-based approach.

In the long term, i-Space technologies will enable individuals to control both access to, and the use of, personal information by third parties. The same technology which is reducing the cost of data gathering and collection also offers the possibility of greater control of information by the individual. Scholz (2001) argues that by reducing the transaction costs of controlling personal information, individuals can gain and enforce property rights over their personal information. They will also be able to monitor and track the usage of personal information by those gathering it. This transparency in usage will itself act as a check on abuses of privacy (Brin 1998).

By allowing individuals to enforce property rights over their personal information, a market in this information is likely to develop (Scholz 2001). Where consumers control what information is passed to companies, and for what purpose, the value of such information is likely to increase. For example, consumers who give personal information to a supplier in return for receiving offers of goods and services tailored to their own interests and preferences are more likely to respond to such offers, thus increasing the effectiveness of direct marketing campaigns.

All these approaches treat privacy as a private good. Regan (2002) suggests this approach is unlikely to achieve the levels of privacy desired by individuals unless it is extremely easy to make the necessary choices. Firms and other institutions have strong incentives to gather large amounts of personal information, both to develop improved marketing and to avoid risk by monitoring and profiling individuals. However, to choose to protect that information can cost the individual both time and money. This is, of course, the opportunity for intelligent agent technology.

Regan suggests that looking at privacy as a "common good" may offer alternative policy approaches because it draws attention to the costs of overusing personal information. In this view, personal information is seen as a "common pool" resource and, like all such resources is subject to a "tragedy of the commons." Regan identifies three ways in which overuse of personal information can have a negative impact:

- Overload: as more personal information is collected, costs (e.g. of storage, search, validation, processing etc.) increase for both subjects and users.
- Pollution: over time, information can become irrelevant, inaccurate and out-of-date, contaminating the pool.
- Over-harvesting: as more and more users take out the same information, the value of that information becomes of less value to any one user.

Such degradation of the common resource will reduce the effectiveness of both public service and commercial activities.

Control of Services

Interviewees were very concerned that the advice and actions taken by intelligent systems should be independent of any third party. This was particularly the case for services offering medical or health support and advice. There is clearly an issue of trust here — many of the i-Space systems are designed to learn individual preferences and will, after an initial period, act in the interests of their user. However, those users must feel confident that the device is not being manipulated by any other organisation. It is important for providers of intelligent devices and services to be sensitive to the expectations of their customers. Failure to do so can have serious consequences, as TiVo discovered. TiVo is a personal video recorder (PVR) that will automatically scan programme listings and record onto a hard disc everything it is programmed to. This is a classic example of technology "automating the mundane" and it has been very much sold on the basis that the customer has control over what they watch and when they watch it. But this control is not unrestricted – the machines can also be used to monitor viewing habits. This latter facility could be useful in letting the machine learn user's tastes and suggest other programmes they may be interested in.

However, the machines can also be remotely set to record specific programmes. In 2002, this facility was used to record a BBC sitcom "Dossa and Joe". The idea was to experiment with the use of the machines to market new TV programmes. No-one was forced to watch the programme, but some people might be tempted to try it. But the response from TiVo subscribers was fury, much of it related to the fact that they were not given any option over whether or not to record the programme (Wells 2002). More recently, users found their TiVo had recorded trailers from the Discovery Channel (BBC 2003). In this case, the problem seems to have been a technical fault rather than deliberate action; but as with "Dossa and Joe," it was perceived by viewers as an invasion of privacy. PVRs such as TiVo and Sky Plus have not been as successful as expected. The reasons for this are not clear, but the fact that viewers are not as in control of the machines as they were led to believe will not have helped sales.

Intelligence and Control

A key element of the i-Space vision is that of intelligent systems and agents which can understand and adjust to an individual's situation and anticipate needs. It is this intelligence that enables the context-awareness of applications, which is assumed to be both attainable and desirable. Yet, this is the aspect of the vision that aroused most scepticism amongst our interviewees.

Some authors have questioned whether this is as straightforward as the vision suggests. Erickson (2000) points out that the term "context aware" obscures two key aspects: 1) the object of context-aware systems is that they should take action autonomously, and 2) *the ability to recognise the context and determine the appropriate action requires considerable intelligence.* It will be recalled that interviewees were very concerned about autonomous systems that removed control from individuals. Here, though we focus on the second issue — that of intelligence.

It is worth considering what is meant by "intelligence." It is well known that intelligence as measured by IQ tests reflects only a limited set of verbal and logical skills. Increasingly, it is recognised that people demonstrate multiple intelligences. Thus, Gardner (1993) identifies seven types of intelligence:

1. Verbal
2. Mathematical-logical
3. Spatial (e.g. artists, architects)
4. Kinaesthetic (e.g. dancers, sports players)
5. Musical (e.g. composers, musicians)
6. Interpersonal (e.g. leadership, nurturing relationships, conflict resolution, social analysis)
7. Intrapsychic (e.g. psychological insights, inner contentment).

It is clear from this list, that developments in artificial intelligence have not explored the full range of intelligences listed here, but have largely focussed on the academic intelligences: mathematical-logical intelligence and, to a lesser extent, verbal. Yet, systems that could recognise context, that is identify the specific role a person is playing at a given time, and their mood, would require very high levels of the interpersonal and intrapsychic intelligences. These are related to what Goleman (1996) calls emotional intelligence. As Goleman points out, emotions play a key part in making decisions in a world where information is incomplete and uncertain. But emotions do not seem to be based on logic or rule sets.

In contrast, computer systems make decisions on the basis of a rule set. Erickson (2000) gives a number of examples of how autonomous action by rule-based systems can lead to problems. One could, of course, add further rules (this is what learning agents do), but building a rule set that can cover any situation (including unforeseen situations) becomes unmanageable. Erickson suggests that in many situations, rather than taking autonomous action, the systems should pass on information and let humans make the decisions: "humans are good at recognising contexts and determining what is appropriate." Similar concerns are expressed by Walker et al. (2002) in the context of embedded computing in cars. Like Erickson, they suggest that ultimately individuals should retain control of the system. Both papers reflect a view that systems should not be autonomous but support human beings who retain ultimate control and responsibility.

Conclusion

The development of i-Space technologies will have a radical impact on the way individuals interact with other individuals and with companies, both as consumers and employees. i-Space technologies will have a profound effect, not only on the products and services offered, but also on the way companies are organised and managed.

The hidden but pervasive nature of i-Space technology opens up many possible services and applications. Some possible applications have been described in a range of i-Space and ambient intelligence scenarios. A survey of individuals' attitudes to both current ICT and to proposed i-Space applications has been completed as part of a Eurescom study. Although such a survey cannot predict successful applications, the results did give clues to the characteristics of a successful service and also evidence of potential barriers to success.

i-Space applications that allowed people to have more control over their lives, or reduced the time spent on routine and mundane activities were seen to be the most beneficial. However, there is considerable concern about privacy issues and the question of who really is in control of the technology. ISTAG (2001, p.15) also noted a "consistent demand for some kind of volume control or on/off switch that would allow people to decide what level of access they have on an issue and when." Service providers will need to be sensitive to these concerns and ensure their actions do not breach customer expectations.

i-Space technologies will also be adopted in the workplace; they offer greater flexibility both in where people work and in how they work. However, they also increase an organisation's ability to monitor the performance of employees, partner companies, competitors and customer behaviour. Companies may have to make judgements about how far to exploit these capabilities.

The field survey showed ICT is already used to mediate the boundary between work and home. In a corporate environment, where individuals have retained overall control of the technology (as at Microsoft), such flexibility has been shown to improve productivity and can improve employee retention.

However, providing such control is not easy with a technology where a key function is the constant monitoring of individuals and their environment. Intelligent systems can help with both the privacy and control issues, but this depends very much on the trust people place in their suppliers. The question of control will be crucial in determining the extent and rate at which i-Spaces will develop. Although most i-Space visions assume future applications will be autonomous and able to act without user involvement, users are sceptical of such visions. This scepticism arises both from doubts about the capabilities of the technology, and from concerns about privacy and the independence (from third parties) of such applications. In practice, some degree of end-user control over the way the systems use information and interact with individuals will be essential, if i-Spaces are to be accepted both in the home and at work.

Note

1.   The author would like to thank the many colleagues in Telenor, Elissa, Hungarian Telecom, BT, and Eurescom who have worked on the Eurescom project P1302 - PROFIT. In particular, Rebecca Ellis, Morgan Potter, Di Holm, Rosita Venousiou and Peter Stollenmayer.

References

BBC. (2003). *TiVo slated for "invading privacy"*. Available online: http://news bbc.co.uk/1/hi/entertainment/tv_and_radio/2756497.stm.

Beatty, J. (2001). *White Collar Sweatshop.* Politics and Prose Column. Atlantic Unbound, June 7. Available online: http://www.theatlantic.com/ unbound/polipro/pp2001-06-07.htm.

Bell, M., Hayward, S., Tunick, M. D., Murphy, K., and Young, C. (2001). *The Agile Workplace: Supporting people and their work.* Available online: http:// www4.gartner.com/1_researchanalysis/focus_areas/special/ agile_workforce/agile.jsp.

Brin, D. (1998). *The Transparent Society: Will Technology Force Us to Choose Between Privacy and Freedom?* New York: Perseus Publishing.

Daily Telegraph. (2003). *When it's OK to switch off Microsoft rewrites its rulebook for the "always on" generation.* 13th November.

DeTienne, K. B. (1993). "Big Brother or Friendly Coach". *The Futurist*, September/October, pp. 33–37.

Dyson, E. *Labeling Practices for Privacy Protection.* National Telecommunications and Information Administration (NTIA). Available online: http://www.ntia.doc.gov/reports/privacy/selfreg5. htm.

e-living. (2004). *Work, Home And Work At Home: Final Report - Implications For The New Economy And New Forms Of Work.* Deliverable D11.5. Available online: http://www.eurescom.de/e-living/.

Erikson, T. (2002). "Some problems with the notion of Context-Aware Computing". *Communication of the ACM* 45 (2): 102–104.

Eurescom. (2004a). *Strategic business models for the new economy.* Deliverable D3, Project P1302. Edited by J. M. M. Potter. Available online: http://www.eurescom.de/public/projects/P1300-series/P1302.

Eurescom. (2004b). *Work/home boundaries and user perceptions of AmI: key issues and implications for business.* Deliverable D4, Project P1302. Edited by R Ellis.

Fast Data Technology. (2004). http://www.fastdatatech.com/fasttracker/features.shtml

Fraser, J. A. (2001). *White-Collar Sweatshop: The deterioration of work and its rewards in corporate America.* Quoted in Beatty (2001). Available online: http://www.eurescom.de/public/projects/P1300-series/P1302.

Gardner, H. (1993). *Frames of Mind: Theory of Multiple Intelligences.* New York: Perseus Books Group.

Goleman, D. (1996). *Emotional Intelligence.* London: Bloomsbury.

Greenop, D. and Cupidi, R. (2002). "Getting personal — Finding a place in cyberspace". *J. Communication Network* 1 (1): 31–37.

Hazards. (2004). *Hazards Magazine.* February. Available online: http://www/hazards.org/privacy.

Head, S. (2003). *The New Ruthless Economy: Work and Power in the Digital Age.* Oxford: OUP.

IBM. (1999). "Special Issue on Pervasive Computing". *IBM Systems Journal* 38 (4). Available online: http://www.research.ibm.com/journal/sj38-4.html.

IPTS. (2003). *Security and privacy for the citizen in the post-September 11 digital age: A prospective overview.* European Commission Inst. Prospective Technological Studies, July. Available online: http://www.jrc.es/home/publications/publication.cfm?pub=1118.

ISTAG. (2001). *ISTAG Scenarios for Ambient Intelligence in 2010.* EU February, 2001, Available online: http://www.cordis.lu/ist/istag-reports.htm.

Lyons, M. H., Potter, M., Holm. D., Venousiou, R., and Ellis, R. (2004). "The Socio-Economic Impact of Pervasive Computing: Intelligent Spaces and the Organisation of Business". *BTTJ* Special Issue on i-Spaces.

MIT. (2000). *Pervasive, Human-Centered Computing: MIT PROJECT OXYGEN.* Brochure, http://oxygen.lcs.mit.edu/publications/Oxygen.pdf, p. 10.

Nagel, D. J. (2000). "Pervasive Sensing". In P. Hamburger (ed.), *Proc. SPIE 4126, Integrated Command Environments.* pp. 71–82.

Odlyzko, A. (1999). *The Visible Problems of the Invisible Computer: A Skeptical*

Look at Information Appliances. Available online: http://firstmonday. org/issues/issue4_9/odlyzko/index.html.

Pearson, I. D., Lyons, M. H., and Greenop, D. (2000). "Cyberspace — From Order to Chaos and Back". *Journal of IBTE* 1 (1): 87–95.

Pearson, I. D., and Lyons, M. H. (2003). *Business 2010: Mapping the New Commercial Landscape.* London: Spiro.

Regan, P. M. (2002). "Privacy as a Common Good in the Digital World". *Information, Communication & Society* 5 (3): 382–405.

Reichfield, F. and Markey, Jr. R. G. (1990). *Loyalty and Learning; Overcoming Corporate Learning Disabilities.* Bain and Company Essays: The relations between loyalty and profits, p. 1. Quoted in Head (2003) p. 112.

Samaritans: Observation by the Samaritans, made at a meeting of the Telephone Helplines Association

Santo, B. (2001). "Embedded Battle Royal". *IEEE Spectrum* 38 (12): 36–41.

Scholz, P. (2001). "Transaction Costs and the Social Costs of Privacy". *First Monday* 6 (5). Available online: http://firstmonday.org/issues/ issue6_5/sholtz/index.html.

Schulman, A. (2001). *The Extent of Systematic Monitoring of Employee E-mail and Internet Usage.* Available online: http://www.sonic.net/~undoc/extent. htm.

Shabi, R. (2003). "The card up their sleeve". *The Guardian*, 19th July, 2003. Available online: http://www.guardian.co.uk/weekend/story/0,3605, 999866,00.html.

Smith, M. J. et al. (1990). *Electronic Performance Monitoring and Job Stress in Telecommunications Jobs.* Univ. Wisconsin-Madison Dept. Industrial Engineering and Communications Workers of America.

Walker, G. H., Stanton, N. A., and Young, M. S. (2001). "Where is Computing Driving Cars?" *Int. J Human-Computer Interaction* 13 (2): 203–229.

Weiser, M. (1991). "The Computer for the 21ˢᵗ Century". *Scientific American*, September, pp. 94–104. Available online: http://www.ubiq.com/ hypertext/weiser/SciAmDraft3.

Wells, M. (2003). "Big Brother: watchers and the watched". *The Guardian*, 7 September. Available online: http://www.guardian.co.uk/bigbrother/ privacy/yourlife/story/0,12384,785843,00.html.

WWRI. (2002). *Towards Technologies, Systems and Networks beyond 3G: Work package 1 — Sector Analysis: Scenarios for the wireless telecoms market 2002–2010*, October. custom@analysys.com

Wright, S. and Steventon, A. G. (2004). "Intelligent Spaces: The Vision, the Opportunities and the Barriers". *BTTJ Special Issue on i-Spaces.*

PART II

The "Linking" Capacity of the Internet to the Outside World

4

—⋘—

Surfing the News: The Internet and Traditional News Consumption

Lars Willnat

Introduction

One of the oldest and most frequently repeated media-related predictions is that television will soon be replaced by computer-based activities, such as surfing the Internet (Negroponte 1995). While it is unlikely that people will give up television completely for Internet-based activities, the nation's online population has grown steadily over the past years. According to the Pew Internet & American Life Project (2006), about 73 percent of all Americans in 2006 said they use their computers to access the Internet or to send and receive email. The increase in the overall number of Internet users has been accompanied by exponential growth in online news consumption. While audiences for traditional news sources such as television and newspapers have dwindled during the past decade, more and more Americans turn to online sources for news. Overall, the number of people who go online for news at least three days a week has grown from just two percent in 1995 to an astonishing 46.6 percent in 2006 (Pew 2006).

The steady increase in online news consumption has led to worries about the demise of traditional mass media news in the near future. While traditional news media have been quick to move their content online in order to capture Internet audiences, media scholars are especially concerned about the self-selective nature of online news consumption, which could accelerate audience fragmentation.

Studies of online use, however, have shown that, though Internet usage has increased dramatically in the past years, this increase has not greatly affected consumption of traditional mass media by Internet users. Norris (1998), for example, found that Internet users tend to be heavier-than-average users of newspaper and radio news, especially those who engaged in political discussion and contacting. Sixty-six percent of those who went online for news said they follow national news most of the time, compared to just 47 percent of those who do not use the Internet. Similarly, Robinson et al. (2000) found no significant evidence that Internet usage reduces time spent with media or social activities. In fact, Internet users reported significantly higher use of print news media and movie attendance.

The Internet's lack of influence on traditional news consumption can be partly explained by the fact that people spend far less time getting the news online than they do getting news from traditional media sources. According to a recent Pew study (2006), while about half of all Americans (48%) say they spend at least 30 minutes watching television news during a typical day, and about a quarter spend that much time reading the newspaper (24%) or listening to radio news (22%), only about nine percent say that they spend at least a half-hour each day getting the news online.

Thus, instead of diminishing news audiences, online news might be emerging as a supplement to — not a substitute for — other traditional news sources. However, given the exponential growth of online news consumption and the attraction of the Internet to the younger generation, the questions remains whether this pattern will continue or whether online news sources will gradually come to replace traditional news sources.

The goal of this study is to explore the potentially growing impact of online news consumption on traditional news usage. Unlike previous analyses, however, this study will track the impact of online news on the use of traditional mass media news sources such as television, newspapers, radio, and magazines between 1998 and 2006. Data for this study come from five representative telephone surveys conducted by Pew between 1998 and 2006. Because each of the biannual surveys contains the same questions regarding respondents' news exposure, this study is able to map the influence of online news on traditional mass media use over time. Obviously, tracing such an effect is important due to the exponential growth in the number of Americans going online for news during the past years.

Literature Review

Previous studies of the impact of the Internet on traditional mass media usage have focused on the so-called "displacement" hypothesis (Nie and Hillygus 2002). The displacement hypothesis is rooted in the notion that time spent with daily activities is largely a zero-sum phenomenon: Because there are only 24 hours in a day, time spent on one activity must be traded off against time spent on other activities. Accordingly, various studies have demonstrated that increased time on the Internet often comes at the expense of other activities, specifically television viewing (Kayany and Yelsma, 2000) and face-to-face social interactions (Nie and Hillygus 2002).

Other studies, however, have shown that Internet usage does not impact other daily activities (Kestnbaum et al. 2002; Franzen 2000) or that it might even have a positive impact on newspaper reading and radio news listening (Stemple III et al. 2000). The explanations offered in these studies are typically based on either the "efficiency" hypothesis or the "multi-tasking" hypothesis. Studies based on the first hypothesis usually argue that the Internet increases efficiency, so Internet users actually have <u>more</u> time for other activities (Franzen 2000). Studies based on the multi-tasking hypothesis, on the other hand, propose that technologically advanced individuals tend to be the type of people who are able to fit more activities into the same time (Robinson et al. 2000). Thus, as individuals use the Internet more and more, they become increasingly able to squeeze other activities into the remainder of their day. Thus, while it is likely that the average American only spends a finite amount of time each day consuming news (thus making Internet news competition a zero-sum game), online news might serve as a supplement to the traditional mass media news most people consume during a typical day.

To investigate how the use of online news interacts with traditional news consumption, this study focuses on the actual time people spend using the news online and offline. Previous studies testing the impact of Internet usage on the consumption of traditional news have resulted in mixed findings depending on methodology and type of data used. Nie and Erbring's (2002) analysis of a 1999 *Knowledge Networks* online survey of 4,113 respondents, for example, found that the more time people spend using the Internet, the more likely they are to report reduced time watching television and reading newspapers. However, the authors failed to control for respondents' demographic characteristics that, in other studies, have proven to be important factors in determining online news usage.

A more sophisticated analysis of another *Knowledge Networks* online survey conducted among 5,500 respondents in 2002, conversely, found that time spent on the Internet indeed comes at the expense of time spent on social activities, hobbies, reading, and television viewing (Nie and Hillygus 2002). The analysis, which controls for demographics, living arrangements, marital status, sleep time, and other daily activities, indicates that there is a negative relationship between television viewing and home Internet use. Overall, the study found that, compared to non-users, heavy Internet users spend about 17 percent (or 24 minutes) less time per day watching television and 24 percent (or 5 minutes) less time reading newspapers. Music consumption, on the other hand, was higher among heavy Internet users — possibly a result of the fact that music can be easily consumed while surfing the Internet.

Support for the time-displacement theory was also found in a panel survey conducted among 963 adult respondents between June 2001 and March 2002 (Shklovski et al. 2002). The authors show that, over time, television viewing decreased among heavy Internet users but increased among non-users.

Other studies generally do not support the time-displacement hypothesis. Based on a national telephone survey conducted in 1995, for example, Robinson, Barth, and Kohut (1997) detected little evidence of the expected displacement of traditional media by Internet or home computer usage. Indeed, users of these "new" technologies reported significantly higher use of print news media and attendance at movies. These differences were reduced (but still significant) after adjustment for new technology users' higher levels of education and income.

A similar analysis of a telephone survey conducted in 1998 among 3,993 adults combined a sample of 2,000 randomly selected respondents with a screened sample of 1,993 online users. It also found no significant or consistent evidence that Internet usage reduces the amount of time spent with traditional mass media (Robinson et al. 2000). In fact, the findings indicate that Internet users have a more active social life than non-users. The authors state, "These results reinforce the conclusion that personal computer/ Internet use may have more in common with time-enhancing home appliances such as the telephone than they do with the time displacing technology of television" (p. 1).

Similarly, Neustadl, and Robinson's (2002) analysis of the 2000 GSS survey of 2,817 adult respondents provides little support for the conclusion that greater Internet usage is related to lower television or newspaper usage. While Internet users were found to watch less television than non-users, this difference is largely explained by demographic differences between the two groups. On the other hand, online users were more likely to read newspapers, even after controlling for demographic predictors. The authors conclude that "as of year 2000, it appeared that the Internet was slightly more of a stimulant to Americans' use of more traditional media, rather than a suppressor of it" (p. 114).

Cole and Robinson's (2002) secondary analysis of a national telephone survey conducted in 2000 among 2,096 adult respondents also indicates little consistent evidence of decreased media consumption among heavier Internet users. Internet users did report five hours less television viewing per week, but only 1.5 hours less after adjustments for demographics were taken into account. On the contrary, the study found significant evidence of more book reading, video-game playing, and music listening among Internet users, even after adjustment for demographic factors.

Overall, it is clear that neither the time-displacement nor the multi-tasking hypothesis can be dismissed yet. While general Internet usage might have peaked in the past years, it is obvious that more and more people are going online to obtain their news. Thus, while people still get most of their daily new from the mass media, the trend towards online news might slowly decrease the time people spend with traditional mass media news every day. On the other hand, online news might be used primarily as a supplement rather than a displacement, as indicated by various previous studies. Should that be true, users of online news actually might spend more time with traditional mass media new than non-users.

Based on the above discussion, the following three research questions are presented:

RQ1: Does online news usage decrease or increase the time people spend with traditional news sources such as television news or newspapers?

RQ2: Who are the people most affected by a potential displacement or supplement effect of online news usage?

RQ3: If a displacement or supplement effect can be identified, how has this effect changed between 1998 and 2006?

Methods

This analysis of traditional media and online news consumption is based on five representative, national surveys conducted by Pew in 1998, 2000, 2002, 2004, and 2006 (Pew Biennial Media Consumption Surveys). All five surveys contain the same questions about mass media and online news usage (with very few exceptions), asking respondents how long they used each medium during the previous day. While the surveys also contain a series of specific questions about program choices, this study will focus on respondents' use of television and radio news, newspapers, news magazines, and online news.

The focus on a single day's news activities in all five surveys allows us to examine if heavy users of online news also report lower levels of traditional media use on an average day. Moreover, since all questions were asked exactly the same way in each of the five surveys, we will be able to compare the results across time. To ensure that comparisons across time are not affected by demographics differences between the samples, the five survey samples were compared on various key demographics. As expected, no significant differences in terms of sex, education, income, and race were found.

In all five surveys, mass media consumption was assessed by asking respondents if they had used a specific news medium "yesterday." If respondents answered yes, a follow-up question asked them to estimate how much time they spent either reading a daily newspaper, watching news programs on television, listening to news on the radio, or reading news magazines. The time spent with television, newspapers, and radio was measured on a four-point scale ranging from 1 = "less than 15 minutes" to 4 = "one hour or more." News magazine usage, on the other hand, was measured on a seven-point scale ranging from 1 = "less than 5 minutes" to 7 = "one hour or more." Respondents who answered that they did not use a specific medium the previous day were considered non-users and coded as 0.[1] Similarly, online news consumption was measured by first asking respondents if they went online yesterday, then asking them to rate how many days per week they "go online to get news" on a five-point scale (5 = "every day"). Respondents who did not use the Internet the previous day or who stated that they never use the Internet for news were considered non-users and were coded as 0.

In addition to the news media consumption measures, all analyses control for the effects of key demographic variables such as sex, education, income, race, and party identification.[2] Previous studies of Internet usage have shown that younger, well-educated, male respondents are more likely to use the Internet as a news source (Pew, 2002; 2004).

Findings

To investigate the trends in mass media and online news consumption between 1998 and 2006, we first compared the percentage of respondents in each survey who said that they used newspapers, television news, radio news, or online news "yesterday." As Table 4.1a and 4.11b show, the number of people who use newspapers has declined somewhat between 1998 and 2006, while more people are consuming television- and online news. The use of radio news, on the other hand, has remained stable between 1998 and 2006. For example, the percentage of respondents who said that they used newspaper "yesterday" dropped from 48.8 percent in 1998 to 44.8 percent in 2006. The biggest declines in newspaper consumption are found among respondents who are between 30 and 49 years old (–8.6%), have no high school degree (–9.2%), or belong to a minority (African-American –7.6%; Hispanics –5.1%).

The percentage of respondents who used television "yesterday," on the other hand, increased slightly from 58.5 percent to 59.8 percent between 1998 and 2006. The only decline in television news consumption is found among those 65 years or older (–3.6%). The slight increase in television news usage, however, is overshadowed by

Table 4.1a Use of Newspaper and Television News as a Function of Key Demographic Variables 1998–2006

	Newspaper Use					Television News Use				
	1998 %	2000 %	2002 %	2004 %	2006 %	1998 %	2000 %	2002 %	2004 %	2006 %
All	48.8	47.8	42.7	44.2%	44.8	58.5	54.7	55.9	61.1%	59.8
Sex										
Male	51.8	51.0	46.3	50.8	48.6	57.7	53.3	56.0	60.5	59.4
Female	48.1	45.2	40.0	38.8	41.8	59.2	56.0	55.8	61.6	60.0
Age										
18–29	32.0	31.1	26.2	22.8	24.5	46.1	47.5	40.0	40.4	49.3
30–49	46.1	45.6	36.2	39.5	37.5	53.6	48.7	51.8	59.1	53.0
50–64	59.5	56.5	52.9	52.4	50.2	62.7	56.5	60.8	66.3	64.0
65+	66.4	65.4	58.4	60.3	61.7	74.4	73.5	72.7	75.6	70.8
Education										
Less HS	37.8	31.5	18.3	31.3	28.6	52.7	51.8	42.7	65.6	54.4
HS Grad	42.4	45.2	42.2	37.4	40.2	58.5	56.5	53.9	59.3	59.4
Some College	48.6	47.1	44.4	40.5	42.9	60.9	58.9	61.3	58.7	62.1
College Grad	60.5	56.7	50.0	56.3	54.1	58.5	50.2	58.6	63.4	59.0
Race										
White	n/a	48.8	45.4	46.5	47.3	n/a	54.1	56.3	61.8	59.3
Black	n/a	42.4	34.0	32.6	34.8	n/a	63.6	60.5	61.6	68.5
Hispanic	n/a	40.0	33.0	32.6	34.9	n/a	46.7	46.2	54.7	55.3
Other	n/a	43.3	32.5	41.4	36.9	n/a	49.3	51.2	54.3	57.9

Note: All percentages refer to those respondents who used the specific media yesterday.

Table 4.1b Use of Radio and Internet News as a Function of Key Demographic Variables 1998–2006

	Radio Use					Internet News Use				
	1998 %	2000 %	2002 %	2004 %	2006 %	1998 %	2000 %	2002 %	2004 %	2006 %
All	48.9	42.7	38.8	40.7%	48.4	13.7	25.1	27.3	30.3%	44.8
Sex										
Male	51.9	47.0	45.7	45.2	44.7	18.5	33.0	34.6	34.7	53.4
Female	46.2	39.1	35.6	37.1	33.5	9.5	18.3	22.0	26.8	41.1
Age										
18–29	46.1	36.4	31.8	26.4	28.9	21.0	33.4	34.5	37.2	44.8
30–49	53.6	50.4	47.7	47.1	43.2	15.5	30.0	32.5	36.9	49.8
50–64	46.1	44.4	42.6	47.1	40.3	8.5	18.8	28.0	31.5	47.0
65+	44.5	30.0	29.2	32.6	32.7	5.0	9.3	10.4	10.7	37.1
Education										
Less HS	43.2	23.2	25.0	27.5	22.8	8.1	7.2	6.1	9.2	32.5
HS Grad	41.9	36.2	32.1	33.5	31.2	5.9	13.9	16.1	17.1	36.0
Some College	50.5	44.1	42.7	41.1	41.8	13.7	29.7	29.9	32.1	45.2
College Grad	57.2	54.9	51.0	50.6	46.8	24.0	39.8	44.2	47.6	55.1
Race										
White	n/a	43.8	40.0	42.6	39.9˙	n/a	25.4	28.6	30.2	47.3
Black	n/a	38.4	32.7	32.6	35.1	n/a	17.2	16.3	24.6	38.8
Hispanic	n/a	33.3	38.1	29.5	35.1	n/a	33.3	22.7	30.5	36.9
Other	n/a	37.3	51.2	34.3	36.8	n/a	31.4	33.8	45.7	57.7

Note: All percentages refer to those respondents who used the specific media yesterday (Internet use every day & 3–5 days per week).

the much more substantial gains in online news usage. Overall, the percentage of respondents who said that they went online for news "yesterday" increased more than threefold from 13.7 percent in 1998 to 44.8 percent in 2006. Since younger and more educated people were more likely to use online news in 1998, the most significant jumps in online news consumption are found among the older and less educated respondents. Among those who are between 50 and 64 years old, for example, online news consumption increased from 8.5 percent in 1998 to 47 percent in 2006. Similarly, among respondents without an advanced degree, online news consumption jumped from 5.9 percent in 1998 to 36 percent in 2006. On average, however, online news consumption was highest among the middle-aged and the more educated respondents.

These findings suggest that especially the more educated and older Americans have become less regular users of traditional news sources, instead relying on online news more frequently. Nevertheless, the trend toward more regular online news consumption does not necessarily imply less time spent with traditional news sources.

Table 4.2 analyzes the relationship between online news consumption and usage of traditional news sources in more detail. Overall, while online news usage has increased from about one day per week to more than two days per week (see Internet total), the decline in the consumption of traditional news has been minimal, ranging from one to four minutes a day depending on the type of media.

Moreover, the comparison of heavy Internet users (those who go online every day) with non-Internet users does not support the notion that the time spent with online news is negatively correlated with the time spent with traditional news sources. Compared to 1998, heavy Internet users in 2006 spent about 2.8 minutes less per day with newspapers (non-Internet users: −.03 minutes) and 6.5 minutes less with news magazines (non-Internet users: −2.3 minutes). Television and radio news consumption, on the other hand, increased slightly among heavy Internet users (+.03 minutes for television news and +1 minute for radio news) but decreased among non-users (−.03 minutes for television news and −2.8 minutes for radio news) between 1998 and 2006.[3]

To fully understand how the fast growing use of online news

Table 4.2 Use of News Media as a Function of Internet Exposure 1998–2006 (in minutes per day)

	1998 (N = 1,499)	2000 (N = 1,593)	2002 (N = 1,551)	2004 (N = 1,493)	2006 (N = 2,013)	Change 1998–2006
Internet x Newspaper						
Never	18.4	17.9	17.8	18.1	18.1	–0.3
1–2 days	16.9	16.6	15.4	15.6	15.5	–1.4
3–5 days	25.7	20.0	16.8	18.6	17.9	–7.8
Every day	23.2	18.9	20.7	20.4	20.4	–2.8
Average	**18.8**	**17.8**	**16.9**	**17.8**	**17.5**	**–1.3**
Internet x TV News						
Never	28.8	28.1	29.3	33.5	28.5	–.03
1-2 days	29.1	25.8	27.4	26.7	26.8	–2.3
3-5 days	30.2	23.1	27.3	33.0	27.2	–3.2
Every day	29.6	24.4	29.4	28.7	29.9	+0.3
Average	**28.7**	**25.8**	**27.6**	**30.5**	**27.9**	**–.08**
Internet x Radio News						
Never	15.6	12.3	13.0	14.1	12.8	–2.8
1–2 days	18.5	16.8	18.8	15.5	15.9	–2.6
3–5 days	23.4	18.4	17.3	19.6	19.4	–4.0
Every day	18.6	17.5	21.0	22.3	19.6	+1.0
Average	**16.9**	**14.7**	**15.8**	**16.7**	**17.3**	**+0.4**
Internet x Magazines						
Never	3.7	2.6	1.3	1.4	—	–2.3
1–2 days	8.3	5.0	3.6	1.2	—	–7.1
3–5 days	7.7	4.5	3.8	1.3	—	–6.4
Every day	8.4	5.8	4.1	1.9	—	–6.5
Average	5.0	3.9	2.6	1.4	—	–3.6
Internet Total (days per week)	.89	1.67	1.74	2.80	2.12	**+1.23**

Note: The values in this table represent approximations because of recoding of the original scores (see endnote 3).

might be related to a possible decline in traditional news consumption, it is necessary to control for demographic variables such as sex, age, education, income, and race. As previous studies have shown, all of these variables strongly affect Internet usage and, as we might assume, online news usage as well. Table 4.3 shows the results of a series of multivariate OLS-regressions that test the impact of online news consumption on each medium (television news, newspapers, radio, and magazines) between 1998 and 2006, controlling for the effects of key demographic variables and traditional mass media usage (excluding the main dependent variable).

Overall, the findings confirm that online news usage is <u>not</u> negatively associated with the time spent using traditional news sources as implied by the time-displacement hypothesis. In cases where significant relationships are found, it appears that respondents who spend more time with Internet news also consume more traditional news sources, therefore supporting the multi-tasking hypothesis. For example, in 1998, 2004, and 2006, respondents who spent more time with Internet news also read more newspapers. Similarly, heavier users of Internet news were more likely to spend more time reading news magazines in 2000, and they listened to more radio news in 2002, 2004, and 2006.

While the positive correlations between the use of online news and traditional news consumption are relatively weak, they are significant, surviving controls for important demographic variables such as sex, age, education, and income. Moreover, the fact that no negative correlations were found in any of the five surveys conducted between 1998 and 2006 suggests that the use of online news does not compete with traditional news consumption in a zero-sum time scenario as has been suggested by some earlier studies (Nie and Erbring 2002; Nie and Hillygus 2002; Shklovski et al. 2002).

In order to investigate more specifically the impact of online news consumption among certain demographic subgroups, four separate multivariate OLS-regressions were run for respondents who are (1) less than 40 years old, (2) have a college degree, (3) have incomes above $40,000, and (4) are male. As in the previous analyses, the impact of online news usage is tested for each news media separately, controlling for the effects of key demographic variables and traditional news consumption.

Table 4.3 Impact of Internet News on Traditional News Media Use 1998–2006 (standardized betas)

		TV News	Newspaper	Radio News	Magazines
1998	Television	—	.14***	.06*	.09**
	Newspaper	.15***	—	.03	.04
	Radio	.06*	.02	—	−.07*
	Magazines	.08***	.04	−.07*	—
	Internet News	.05	.08**	.05	.03
2000	Television	—	.09***	−.03	.12***
	Newspaper	.09***	—	.02	.06*
	Radio	−.03	.02	—	.00
	Magazines	.12***	.05*	.00	—
	Internet News	.01	.01	.04	.10***
2002	Television	—	.12***	.00	.09*
	Newspaper	.13***	—	.03	.06*
	Radio	.00	.03	—	.03
	Magazines	.08**	.06*	.03	—
	Internet News	.03	.06	.07*	.05
2004	Television	—	.10***	.07**	.06*
	Newspaper	.10***	—	.01	.06*
	Radio	.07**	.00	—	−.05
	Magazines	.06*	.05*	−.05	—
	Internet News	.01	.06*	.08**	.03
2006	Television	—	.19***	.07**	—
	Newspaper	.20***	—	.02	—
	Radio	.07**	.02	—	—
	Magazines	—	—	—	—
	Internet News	.01	.05*	.07**	—

Note: All regressions models control for sex, age, race, education, income, and party identification.

p <= .1; * p <= .05; ** p <= .01; *** p <= .001

Overall, the findings shown in Table 4.4 indicate that the associations between online news usage and traditional news consumption are <u>positive</u> but inconsistent. Higher levels of online news consumption, for example, correlate positively with higher exposure to television news among younger men in 1998, but only among college graduates in 2002. Similarly, the use of online news is

Table 4.4 Impact of Internet News on Traditional News Media Use Among Specific Audiences 1998–2006 (standardized betas)

		TV News	Newspaper	Radio News	Magazines
1998	Less than 40 years old	.10*	.10**	.02	.08
	College Graduates	−.03	.11*	.02	.05
	Income above $40,000	−.03	.10*	.02	.04
	Men	.09*	.05	.02	.05
2000	Less than 40 years old	.03	.07	.10*	.09*
	College Graduates	.02	−.04	−.05	.09
	Income above $40,000	.03	.04	.05	.19***
	Men	.00	.08*	.05	.10*
2002	Less than 40 years old	.08	.03	−.02	.08
	College Graduates	.11*	.09	.11*	.03
	Income above $40,000	.07	.07	.11**	.04
	Men	.01	.05	.02	.05
2004	Less than 40 years old	−.03	.01	.06	.12***
	College Graduates	.01	.01	.13***	−.03
	Income above $40,000	.02	.01	.13***	−.01
	Men	−.01	.03	.08*	.01
2006	Less than 40 years old	.02	.05	.06	—
	College Graduates	.01	.08*	.09*	—
	Income above $40,000	.04	.05	.08**	—
	Men	.01	.08*	.09*	—

Note: All regressions models control for media use, sex, age, race, education, income, and party identification.
p <= .1; * p <= .05; ** p <= .01; *** p <= .001

positively associated with newspapers consumption among younger, more educated, and wealthier respondents in 1998, but only among male respondents in 2000 and male college graduates in 2006. Online news consumption also correlates with higher levels of radio news usage among younger respondents in 2000, and wealthier, male college graduates in 2002, 2004, and 2006. Finally, exposure to online news is positively associated with the use of news magazine among younger, wealthier men in 2000, but only among the younger respondents in 2004.

Overall, these findings suggest that the supplementary impact of

Internet news usage might be dynamic and is likely to affect the four demographics groups in different ways across time. It is likely, however, that some of these demographic differences will slowly disappear with the growing acceptance and use of online news among the majority of Americans.

Conclusions

The findings of this study show that online news consumption is not likely to decrease, but rather, boost the time spend with traditional news sources. While heavy users of online news spent slightly less time with traditional news sources in 2006 as compared to 1998, this observed decrease at the aggregate level does not translate to the individual user level. When factors such as demographics and the use of other traditional mass media are controlled, the findings indicate that online news consumption is in fact <u>positively</u> associated with news exposure in traditional mass media such as newspapers, radio, and news magazines. While inconsistent, these positive associations survive controls for important demographic factors such as sex, age, education, and income. Overall, these findings indicate that users of online news are supplementing rather than displacing their overall news consumption with time spend on the Internet. This is a rather remarkable finding considering the fact that the time people spend with online news has more than doubled between 1998 and 2006.

Notes

1. **Traditional Media News Consumption:** "About how much time did you spend reading a daily newspaper yesterday?"; "About how much time did you spend watching the news or any news programs on TV yesterday?"; "About how much time, if any, did you spend listening to any news on the radio yesterday, or didn't you happen to listen to the news on the radio yesterday?" (Answer categories: less than 15 minutes, 15–29 minutes, 30–59 minutes, 1 hour or more, don't know/refused). "About how much time did you spend reading magazines yesterday?" (Answer categories: less than 5 minutes, 5 to less than 10 minutes, 10 to less than 15 minutes, 15 to less than 20 minutes, 20 to less than 30 minutes, 30 minutes to less than one hour, one hour or more, don't know). **Online News Consumption:** "How frequently do you go online to get news?" (Answer categories: every day, 3 to 5 days per week, 1 or

2 days per week, once every few weeks, less often, never, don't know/ refused).

2. **Sex:** (Male, Female), **Age:** "What is your age?" **Education:** "What is the last grade or class that you completed in school?" (Answer categories: none, or grade 1–8, high school incomplete, high school graduate, business, technical, or vocational school after high school, some college, no 4-year degree, college graduate, post-graduate training or professional schooling after college, don't know/refused). **Race:** "What is your race?" (Answer categories: White, Black, Asian, other) **Income:** "Last year, that is in ___, what was your total family income from all sources, before taxes? Just stop me when I get to the right category" (Answer categories: less than $10,000, $10,000 to under $20,000, $20,000 to under $30,000, $30,000 to under $40,000, $40,000 to under $50,000, $50,000 to under $75,000, $75,000 to under $100,000, $100,000 or more, don't know/refused). **Party Identification:** "In politics today, do you consider yourself a Republican, Democrat or Independent?"

3. In order to compute the consumption of traditional and online news in minutes per day for each medium, the original scores for **newspaper, radio, television news use** were recoded as follows: "no use" = 0, "less than 15 minutes" = 15, "15 to 29 minutes" = 30, "30 to 59 minutes" = 45, "one hour or more" = 60. **News magazine use** was recoded as follows: "no use" = 0, "less than 15 minutes" = 15, "5 to less than 10 minutes" = 15, "10 to less than 15 minutes" = 15, "15 to less than 20 minutes" = 30, "20 to less than 30 minutes" = 30, "30 to less than 60 minutes" = 45, "60 minutes or more" = 60. **Internet news use** was recoded as follows: "every day" = 7, "3 to 5 days" = 4, "1 to 2 days" = 1.5, "once every few weeks" = .05, "less often" = .01, "never" = 0.

References

Cole, J. and Robinson, J. (2002). "Internet use, mass media and other activity in the UCLA data". *IT & Society* 1 (2): 121–133.

Franzen, A. (2000). "Does the Internet make us lonely?" *European Sociological Review* 16 (4): 427–438.

Kaynay, J. and Yelsma, P. (2000). "Displacement effects of online media in the socio-economical context of households". *Journal of Broadcasting & Electronic Media* 44: 215–230.

Kestnbaum, M., Robinson, J. P., Neustadtl, A., and Alvarez, A. (2002). „Information technology and social time displacement". *IT & Society* 1 (1): 21–37.

Negroponte, N. (1995). *Being Digital.* New York: Alfred A. Knopf.

Neustadtl, A. and Robinson, J. P. (2002). "Use differences between Internet users and nonusers in the General Social Survey". *IT & Society* 1 (2): 100–120.

Nie, N. H. and Erbring, L. (2002). "Internet and mass media: A preliminary report". *IT & Society* 1 (2)" 134–141.

Nie, N. H. and Hillygus, D. S. (2002). "Where Does Internet Time Come From? A Reconnaissance". *IT & Society* 1 (2): 1–20.

Norris, P. (1998). *Who surfs? New technology, old voters and virtual democracy in America.* Paper presented at the third annual meeting of the John F. Kennedy Visions of Governance for the Twenty-First Century, Bretton Woods, July 1998.

Pew Research Center Biennial News Consumption Survey (1998). *Internet news takes off.* Accessed on 5 July, 2007, from http://people-press.org/reports/display.php3?ReportID=88.

—— (2000). *Internet sapping broadcast news audience.* Accessed on 5 July, 2007, from http://people-press.org/reports/display.php3?ReportID= 36.

—— (2002). *Public's news habits little changed by September 11.* Accessed on 5 July, 2007, from http://www.people-press.org. http://people-press.org/reports/display.php3?ReportID=156.

—— (2004). *News audiences increasingly politicized.* Accessed on 5 July, 2007, from http://people-press.org/reports/display.php3?ReportID=215.

—— (2006). *Online Papers Modestly Boost Newspaper Readership.* Accessed on 5 July, 2007, from http://people-press.org/reports/display.php3?PageID=1064.

Pew Internet & American Life Project (2006). *Home Broadband Adoption 2006.* Accessed on 5 July, 2007, from http://www.pewinternet.org/pdfs/PIP_Broadband_trends2006.pdf.

Robinson, J., Barth, K., and Kohut, A. (1997). "Personal computers, mass media, and use of time". *Social Science Computer Review* 15: 65–82.

Robinson, J. P., Kestnbaum, M., Neustadtl, A., and Alvarez, A. (2000). „Mass Media and social life among Internet users". *Social Science Computer Review* 18 (4)" 490–501.

Robinson, J. P., Kestnbaum, M., Neustadtl, A., and Alvarez, A. (2002). "Information technology and functional time displacement". *IT & Society* 1 (2): 21–36.

Stempel III, F., Hargrove, T., and Bernt, J. (2000). "Relation of growth of use of the Internet to changes in media use from 1995 to 1999". *Journalism & Mass Communication Quarterly* 77: 71–79.

Shklovski, I., Kraut, R., Kiesler, S., and Boneva, B. (2002). *Impact of Internet use on TV watching: How research details shape conclusions.* Accessed on 5 July, 2007, from http://www-2.cs.cmu.edu/afs/cs.cmu.edu/user/kraut/www/RKraut.site.files/articles/Shklovski-CACM_draftv1.5.doc.

Examining the Use of and Preference for Online News in the Context of Intermedia Competition

Hsiang Iris Chyi

Jay Hao-Chieh Chang

Introduction

Over the last decade, the rapid development of Internet technologies and the diffusion of the World Wide Web have created a new media landscape where offline and online news media co-exist and compete for audience attention. After years of experimentation, many online news sites have established a substantial user base, which presents a challenge to traditional news media of television, newspapers, and radio. As news users face more media options and the market relation between online and traditional news media becomes increasingly complex, the factors underlying user attention, consumption, and satisfaction deserve more scholarly attention.

From the perspective of media economics, this study examines 1) current use patterns to illumine how traditional news media co-exist with online media in such a highly competitive, rapidly evolving media environment; and 2) the user perceptions and preferences driving these trends. Past research has successfully employed behavioral measures to track media use patterns. Theoretically, this study goes beyond the scope of previous studies by using both behavioral and attitudinal measures at the same time, thereby presenting a more comprehensive picture of the competitive advantage — or lack of it — of online news compared with traditional news media.

From the standpoints of use and perception, this study examines the relationship between online and traditional news media in one of the most media-rich cities in the world — Hong Kong — where more than 20 online news services compete with newspapers, television, and radio stations, targeting a single media market of 6.8 million residents. A media-rich city as such provides an ideal research setting for studying intermedia competition and consumer preferences over different media products.

Media Markets in Hong Kong

Television is the dominant medium in Hong Kong. There are two domestic free television broadcasters (TVB and ATV) in Hong Kong, and each operates two channels — one in Cantonese and the other in English. There are more than 50 cable television channels. Fifteen local dailies (two in English and the rest in Chinese) actively serve this newspaper market — for a detailed account of Hong Kong's the television and newspaper markets, see So, Chan, and Lee (2000). Hong Kong has 13 radio channels, operated by two commercial companies (Commercial Radio and Metro Broadcast) and one government-funded station (RTHK). There are 788 publications in the magazine market, of which 557 are Chinese, 106 English, 108 bilingual, and 17 are in other languages. These magazines cover a wide variety of subjects (Information Services Department, HKSAR Government, 2004), but entertainment-oriented periodicals rather than elite news magazines (such as Time and Newsweek) dominate the market.

Online news sites, at the end of 2002, included 18 local media websites, twelve of which were operated by local newspapers and six by TV or radio stations. In addition, an online-only news aggregator (www.now.com.hk) and several portals also provided online news services.

Literature Review

Intermedia Competition

Intermedia competition, i.e., between-industry competition, has been a fundamental concern in media economics (Picard 1989). The broadcast TV networks face challenges from cable and VCRs (Litman 1998). The cable industry competes with telephone companies, DBS, and wireless services (Carroll and Howard 1998). In some cases, competition from outside the industry poses a greater threat to firms operating in markets without substantial intramedia competition. For example, most U.S. newspapers are local monopolies, and the decline in readership — especially among young people — is at least indirectly related to the use of other media (Picard 1998). In 2004, only 23% of those under age 30 reported having read a newspaper yesterday — down from 26% in 2002 (Pew Research Center 2004).

The Pew Research Center (2004) also documented other trends in media consumption, such as the decade-long slide in network news viewership — 34 percent regularly watched network TV news in 2004, down from 60 percent in 1993. Radio audience has remained stable — 40 percent of Americans reported listening to radio news yesterday. As people seem to move away from traditional news media, online news readership has increased from just 2 percent in 1995 to 29 percent in 2004. These evolutions call for scholarly research on how online and traditional news media compete and co-exist in such a complex media environment.

Several influential media economic theories attempt to describe intermedia competition between the new and old media industries. The theory of the niche (Dimmick 2003; Dimmick, Chen, and Li 2004; Dimmick, Kline, and Stafford 2000) states that the rise of a new medium will compete with the established media for consumer time, satisfaction, and advertising dollars. The possible consequences of competition include exclusion (i.e., replacement, when the new medium replaces the old) and displacement (when the new medium takes over some of the roles that were played by the old medium). In the literature of intermedia competition, competitive exclusion is rarely observed, and the displacement effect is more likely to occur (Dimmick, Chen, and Li 2004).

Past research has found that displacement often occurs when a viable new media technology is introduced (Althaus and Tewksbury 2000; Dimmick, Chen, and Li 2004). Displacement as a theoretical concept may reflect various dimensions of media use, such as time, functions, contexts, motivations, and gratifications. In mass communication research, many studies (Althaus and Tewksbury 2000; Dimmick, Chen, and Li 2004) have measured the displacement effect in terms of time — time spent on one medium in relation to others. Because media compete for audiences, and audience numbers affect advertising dollars, user time spent on different media has important economic consequences for media organizations.

Time Displacement Effect of Internet Use on Traditional Media Use

The growing popularity of the Internet as a new medium and its potential to take audiences away from the traditional news media have been studied by both academics and media analysts (Brown 2000; Noack 1998; Outing 1999). Surveys conducted by the Pew Research Center in 2000 and 2003 showed that there was a remarkable increase in online news use and a significant decrease in the viewing of television news (Pew Internet & American Life Project 2003a). Stemple, Hargrove and Bernt (2000) also found a substantial increase in the use of online news, together with a decline in the viewing of television news. Dimmick et al. (2004) documented the displacement effect of online news on the traditional news media among individuals who used Internet news and at least one other daily news medium regularly. Respondents were asked to report the change in frequencies of using traditional news media after beginning to use Internet news. Results showed that the displacement effect was largest for television, with 33.7% of respondents reporting that they watched television news less often after having started to use online news, followed by newspapers (28%), cable (22.6 %), and radio (22.2%). It seems clear that Internet use tends to lead to a decrease in time spent on television.

Based on previous time displacement studies (Dimmick, Chen, and Li 2004; Pew Internet & American Life Project 2003a; Stemple, Hargrove, and Bernt 2000), this study attempts to gauge the displacement effect of Internet use on time spent on traditional media in a different market — Hong Kong. Therefore, this study proposes this research question:

RQ1:   Does Internet use lead to a decline in time spent on traditional media (TV, newspapers, radio, and magazines)?

Overlap: Beyond Time Displacement

While previous research has documented the competition-based time displacement effect of the Internet on traditional news media (especially television), many researchers have identified a fairly common phenomenon characterizing Internet and newspaper consumption — Internet users are more likely to be newspaper readers. Two national surveys conducted in 1995 and 1999 found that Internet news users were more likely to be newspaper readers (Stemple and Hargrove 1996; Stemple, Hargrove, and Bernt 2000). A 1998 survey of Austin residents found that print readership was strongest among readers of that same newspaper's online edition and identified the substantial overlap of online and print readerships (Chyi and Lasorsa 2002). Tewksbury (2003) analyzed the 2000 survey data collected by the Pew Research Center and found online newsreaders more likely to read newspapers, watch CNN, and listen to radio news but less likely to watch local and network TV news than non-Internet users. Dutta-Bergman (2004) also analyzed the 2000 Pew Research Center survey data and found online news users interested in seven specific content areas more likely to follow news in the same categories on traditional media than non-users. In other words, although Internet users may report a decline in time spent on traditional media (including newspapers), they are more likely to be newspaper readers than non-Internet users.

The simultaneous use of online and print news points to the need to scrutinize people's media selection behavior as a dynamic process. To assess the competitive advantage of online news in relation to traditional news media, measuring gains and losses in time spent on particular media must be complemented by understanding the rationale behind the audience's media selection behavior. According to Fidler (1997), the relationship between any new and existing media is characterized by "coevolution and coexistence rather than sequential evolution and replacement" (p. 24).

Media Preference

Previous research on the relationship between online and traditional media focusing on behavioral measures (e.g., time spent on different media or simultaneous use of multiple media channels) must be supplemented by research on fundamental attitudinal factors such as liking or preference that drive the media selection process. As the new and old media co-evolve, cross-media differences as perceived by users carry important implications regarding the competitive advantage of online news in the context of intermedia competition.

A review of literature identified several studies exploring media perception or preference using different approaches. Most focused on user preference over different delivery technologies. Mueller and Kamerer (1995) asked 62 readers to rate their preference between a web site and a traditional newspaper. The participants indicated a preference for the web site only for its topic search function, but found the new medium to be "unappealing to browse leisurely, inappropriate for all news material, uncomfortable to travel through, not preferable over traditional newspaper, and more difficult to read than a traditional newspaper" (p. 11). An experimental study of news delivery formats (Schierhorn, Wearden, Schierhorn, Tabar, and Andrews 1999) explored the attitudes of potential readers toward portable document viewers (PDV), the Web, and print newspapers, and found an overwhelming preference for the PDV format. The traditional newspaper was rated as being more preferable than the Web format. Chyi and Lasorsa (1999, 2002) in their surveys asked respondents whether they would prefer online or print newspapers with the same content and at the same price. They found that the print format was preferred even among Web users — 72% said they would prefer the print edition (2002).

Some studies focused on perceived quality of news content and the effect of news format on recall. In an exploratory focus group study, Chyi (2002) examined the perceived value of online and offline news. Participants, who were all online news users, were asked to create an analogy to illustrate their consumption of print and online newspapers. Most of the analogies conveyed notions of quality — for example, print newspapers were compared to a "home-cooked, balanced meal," and online newspapers were compared to "junk food." Print editions of newspapers were perceived to be of better quality and to have more in-depth information. Tewksbury and Althaus (2000) found readers of the online version of the *New York Times* were less likely to recognize and recall events that occurred during the exposure period than readers of the print version.

Sundar (1999) identified four criteria — credibility, liking, quality, and representativeness — that are important to news users in their assessment of print and online news content. Although the criteria that are employed by news users in the assessment of news content carried by online and offline media seem to be rather similar (Sundar, 1999), users' perceptions of the different news media may result in a certain degree of preference.

To present a more comprehensive picture of the intermedia competition between online and traditional news media, this study measures both general liking or preference as well as media preference under specific conditions, in order to assess the competitive advantage of online news compared with other more established news media. To examine general liking toward online and traditional news media, this study proposes the following research question:

RQ2: Regarding general liking, how would online users rate online news as opposed to newspapers, TV news, and radio news? What factors have an influence on liking for online news?

In addition to the measure of general liking, this study also employs several hypothetical measuring items to gauge online news users' preferences for different media. Based on previous studies (Chyi and Lasorsa 1999, 2002) on users' format preference between online and print newspapers from the other-things-being-equal standpoint, this study further examine format preference among Hong Kong Internet users by asking:

RQ3: Given the same content and the same price, would online news users prefer a print newspaper or the online edition?

One way to measure media preference is to ask respondents how difficult they would find it to give up different media items. A national survey conducted by the Pew Research Center in 2002 found that about half of all Americans (48%) said it would be very difficult to give up their television, and 39 percent would find it hard to give up the Internet. Only 19 percent said that they would find it hard to give up newspapers, and 13 percent said the same about magazines

(Pew Internet & American Life Project 2003b). To further examine this rivalry between television and computers, this study proposes the following research question:

RQ4: If asked to make a trade-off decision, would online news users choose to keep their television or their computer?

Given the limited media spending, intermedia competition is salient whenever consumption decisions are made. The principle of relative constancy proposed by McCombs and Eyal (1980) contends that the percentage of personal income spent on mass media is relatively constant. When one medium gains popularity and prominence, it chips away the money originally invested in other media. In other words, the media usage patterns may change, but overall spending on the media remains relatively constant. A number of studies empirically testing the principle of constancy produced mixed results (McCombs and Son 1986; Fullerton 1988; Noh and Grant 1997). Whether the principle of relative constancy holds or not, media spending decisions are almost always made within one's budget constraint. As several Hong Kong online news sites started charging for news access after the economic downturn starting in 2000, fee-based online news services may compete with traditional news media for the limited money that is available to be spent on news media consumption. Chyi (2002) discussed users' negative perception of online news and the lack of paying intent and suggested that online news might be inferior goods. A U.S.-based consumer survey found that 70 percent of online adults could not understand why anyone would pay for content online (Jupiter Media Metrix 2002). This study investigates how people respond to different fee-based news sources such as cable television news, paid online news services, newspapers, and magazines differently by asking this research question:

RQ5: Given additional income, which fee-based news medium would online news users consume?

Internet news is characterized by real-time transmission and its unprecedented boundary-transcending capacity. However, a 2003 Pew Center survey shows that most Americans (57%) would turn to television first in the event of a terrorist attack. Another 15 percent said that they would turn to radio, and only eight percent said that would turn to news websites first. Even Internet users said that they would turn to the television first and radio second (Pew Internet & American Life Project 2003c). This study examines such media selection preference in Hong Kong by asking:

RQ6: Which news medium would online news users turn to first for information about breaking news events?

Method

A random-sample telephone survey of Hong Kong residents aged 15 or over was conducted over five days in November 2002 to investigate the general public's consumption of and attitudes toward online and traditional news media.

Sampling

A systematic random sample was drawn from the Hong Kong phone directory, which covered Hong Kong Island, Kowloon, and the New Territories, together yielding a combined population of 6,815,000 (Hong Kong Census & Statistics Department 2003). The "plus one" sampling method was used, which adds one to the last digit of each number sampled, to ensure that every residential telephone (including unlisted and new numbers) had an approximately equal chance of being included (Landon and Banks 1977).

Data Collection

Data were collected between 13 and 17 November 2002. Graduate and undergraduate students completed 853 interviews after undergoing a training session. The sample size of 853 yielded a standard sampling error of ± 3.4 percentage points at the 95 percent confidence level. The response rate was 44 percent.

Survey Instrument

The survey, which took an average of 15 minutes to complete, focused on the use of, and attitudes toward, traditional and online media. The questionnaire was developed according to the results of a focus group of ten college students in Hong Kong. Revisions were made based on the results of a pretest.

Respondents were presented with questions regarding television use, newspaper use, computer knowledge, Internet use, and news website use.

The displacement effect of Internet use on traditional media use was measured by asking this question:

> Since you started using the Internet, how much time do you spend on newspapers/TV/radio/magazines? 1) Much more 2) More 3) The same 4) Less 5) Much less.

General liking toward different news media was measured by the question:

> Please indicate how much you like the following news media by assigning a grade between 0 to 10 for each (0 means "do not like it at all," and 10 means "like it very much"): TV news _____/ Online news _____/ Newspapers _____/ Radio news _____.

Based on previous research (Chyi and Lasorsa 1999, 2002), the following hypothetical question measured the format preferences for online or print newspapers, without specifying the name of a particular newspaper:

> Imagine that you are provided with both print newspapers and online newspapers with the same news content and at the same price. Which would you prefer?

Several more hypothetical questions measured media preference under specific conditions, namely, the trade-off between television and computers, willingness to pay for fee-based news products given extra income, and information source for breaking news, respectively:

> If you could only keep either a TV or a computer, which would you choose? 1) TV 2) Computer.
>
> If you had some extra money to spend every month, which of the following news media would you be most likely to consume? 1) Newspapers 2) News magazines 3) Paid TV news channels 4) Paid online news websites.
>
> Which of the following news media would you turn to first for

information about breaking news events? 1) TV 2) Radio 3) Online news 4) Other.

Finally, demographic information such as gender, age, education, and income were collected.

Results

A comparison with the 2001 census data published by the Hong Kong Census & Statistics Department (2003) showed that the sample deviated from the population in the following aspects: 1) The sample over-represented people aged 15–24 (16.4% in the population vs. 28.1% in the sample) and under-represented those 65 or older (13.3% in the population vs. 8.6% in the sample). 2) The sample over-represented those with tertiary education (16.4% in the population vs. 24.9% in the sample) and under-represented those with elementary or less education (28.9% vs. 16.1%). Overall, the sample was slightly younger and better-educated but still was reasonably representative of the population.

Traditional Media Consumption in Hong Kong

The survey documented the public's use of traditional media in Hong Kong. Television was the dominant medium in Hong Kong in terms of penetration. Of all the respondents, 97 percent watched television on a daily basis. On average, television viewers spent more than 2.5 hours watching television per day. Cable penetration was 28 percent.

With 15 local daily newspapers, newspaper penetration was high — 89 percent of all respondents read newspapers regularly, spending an average of 57 minutes per day reading newspapers.

The survey did not measure time spent on radio, but ACNielsen reported that 52 percent of the general public listened to radio in the one-week period before their survey. On average, people spent 1.18 hours a day listening to radio (ACNielsen 2002).

Internet Usage and Online News Consumption in Hong Kong

Results showed that 63 percent of all respondents aged 15 or above used a personal computer at home or work on a weekly basis. Computer users rated their computer knowledge on an 11-point scale (with 0 being not at all knowledgeable and 10 being extremely knowledgeable). The mean was 5.6.

Of all respondents (N = 853), 58 percent used the Internet, and 46 percent used online news. Table 5.1 compares the difference between online news users, other Internet users, and non-Internet users in demographics and media usage. Unsurprisingly, online news users were much younger, better educated, and with higher income. ANOVA tests also found significant differences in time spent on watching television ($F[2, 827] = 4.879$, $p<.01$) and reading newspapers ($F[2, 752] = 9.948$, $p <.001$) among the 3 types of users. *Post hoc* tests found that online news users spent significantly less time watching television ($p<.01$) and reading newspapers ($p<.001$) than non-Internet users.

The following analysis focused on the online news users (n = 396) because their experience of using online news made cross-media comparisons reasonable. On average, online news users (n = 396) had 38 months of Internet experience at the time of the study, and were online for 2 hours and 13 minutes per day. Forty-seven percent spent up to one hour online, 23 percent spent between 1 and 2 hours, 19 percent spent between 2 and 4 hours, and 12 percent spent more than 4 hours online on a typical day.

Among the 18 media news sites available at the time of the study, the most visited ones were the online editions operated by the leading newspapers. About 76 percent of online news users visited one or more local news sites during the one-week period before the study. Forty-one percent visited one local news site, another 22 percent visited two sites, and 14 percent visited three or more sites. About 21 percent of online news users also visited non-local news sites during the previous week, of which more than half said that they visited U.S.-based news sites such as *CNN.com*.

Displacement Effects

To address the first research question regarding the time displacement effect of Internet use on traditional media use, online users were asked to report any change in time spent on TV, newspapers, radio, and magazines after starting to use the Internet.

Table 5.1 Comparing Online News Users, Other Internet Users, and Non-Internet Users

	Online news users (46.4%)	Other Internet users (11.5%)	Non Internet users (42.1%)
Gender (%)			
Male	50.1	46.9	41.0
Female	49.9	53.1	59.0
Age (%)			
15–24	44.0	42.3	6.5
25–34	26.3	19.6	8.2
35–44	20.7	26.8	20.2
45–54	6.4	8.2	30.2
55–64	1.6	3.1	15.4
65+	1.0	0.0	19.4
Education (%)[a]			
Elementary or below	1.3	0.0	37.4
Form 1–3	8.9	16.7	26.4
Form 4–5	35.2	45.8	24.1
Form 6–7	12.5	16.7	5.5
Tertiary	42.1	20.8	6.6
Monthly Income (%)			
No income	35.7	38.9	55.7
1–10,000 (Hong Kong dollar)[b]	20.7	20.0	26.0
10,001–20,000	20.2	25.6	15.3
20,001–30,000	11.9	10.0	2.1
30,001–40,000	5.9	1.1	0.9
40,001–50,000	2.8	0.0	0.0
50,001+	2.8	4.4	0.0
Media use (min)			
Average time watching TV per day	143.8	162.3	169.5
Average time reading newspapers per day	50.9	53.3	64.8
Average time online per day	132.8	126.2	–

Note. N = 853. Base = people aged 15 or above.

[a] Forms 1–7 is the equivalent of grades 7–13; tertiary is the equivalent of college or higher.

[b] HK$7.8=US$1

Table 5.2 Percentage of Online News Readers Who Used Traditional Media More, Less, or About the Same after Starting to Use the Internet

	TV	Newspaper	Radio	Magazine
More[a]	2%	14%	4%	3%
The same	63	68	71	68
Less[b]	35	17	26	28
N	(396)	(395)	(385)	(386)

[a] More = more or much more.
[b] Less = less or much less.

Table 5.2 shows that 35 percent of online news users reported they spent less or much less time watching television and only 2 percent reported an increase since they started using the Internet ($p<.001$). Also significantly more respondents reported a decrease in the time spent on radio and magazines than reporting an increase — 26% vs. 4% for radio ($p<.001$), 28% vs. 3% for magazines ($p<.001$), which, however, is not the case for newspapers (17% vs. 14%, not sig.). Cross-media comparison found significantly more respondents reporting a decrease in time spent on TV than on newspapers ($p<.001$), radio ($p<.01$), and magazines ($p<.05$). In other words, the displacement effect of Internet use on television was the strongest.

Media Preference

The second research question asked how online users would rate online news as opposed to newspapers, TV news, and radio news in terms of general liking. Results show that online news users clearly differentiated their liking for online and traditional news media (Table 5.3). Repeated measures ANOVA analysis indicated a significant difference among the general liking ratings for different news media ($F[3,1074] = 60.95$, $p<.001$). *Post hoc* analysis using paired-sample t-tests with Bonferroni correction to safeguard against Type I error (with significance criterion being set at $\alpha=.05/6=.008$) demonstrated that differences in general liking ratings between any pair of the four media except for newspaper and radio are statistically significant ($p<.001$). In other words, television was perceived by online news users as the most likable news medium and online news the least likable.

Table 5.3 General Liking toward Traditional and Online News Media among Online News Users

	Mean Liking (SD)
TV news	7.1 (1.6)
Newspaper	6.5 (1.8)
Radio news	6.1 (2.1)
Online news	5.5 (2.1)

Notes: N=396; using repeated measures ANOVA, $F(3,1074)=60.95$, $p<.001$.

Bivariate correlation analysis showed that liking for online news is positively correlated to education ($rho = .095$, $p<.05$), time spent online per day ($r = .160$, $p<.01$), and computer knowledge ($r = .212$, $p<.001$). Regression analysis further investigated what factors have an influence on liking for online news. Table 4 shows that the only significant predictor in the overall equation ($p<.01$) is computer knowledge ($\beta = .166$, $p<.01$).

The third research question dealt with the preference between

Table 5.4 Hierarchical Regression Analysis of Predictors of Liking for Online News

Predictor Variables	Regression 1	Regression 2	Regression 3
Gender (female)	−.081	−.066	−.059
Age	−.049	−.010	.028
Education	.132*	.115	.070
Income	−.055	−.054	−.075
Web use	.141	.096	
TV use	.020	.020	
Newspaper use	−.057	−.061	
Computer knowledge	.166**		
Broadband access	.093		
R^2	.03	.05	.08
Adjusted R^2	.01	.03	.05
Sig. F Change	.082	.067	.005

Note. Cells contain β weights. $*p < .05$; $** p <.01$; n = 330.

online and print news formats on the basis of other things being equal. When asked whether a print or online news format would be preferred given the same content and the same price, 83 percent of online news users said that they would prefer the print edition; only 17 percent would prefer the online edition ($p < .001$).

Open-ended, follow-up questions probed the reasons behind this format preference. Most (77%) of those who preferred the online format (n = 65) mentioned the convenience factor. In comparison, those who preferred the print edition (n=312) cited convenience (28%), dislike of the online reading experience (20%), habit (15%), and the fact that paper is more tangible (10%) as reasons for their preference for the print format.

The fourth research question asked whether televisions or computers were considered to be indispensable when online news users were forced to make a trade-off decision. Among all respondents (N = 853), 70 percent said that they would keep the television, and only 30 percent said that they would choose the computer ($p<.001$). Among online news users (n=396), 53 percent said that they would choose the television and 47 percent said that they would choose the computer. The difference is not statistically significant at the .05 level.

The fifth research question dealt with responses to fee-based news media. When asked which paid news medium they would consume if they had extra income to spend, 38 percent of online news users said that they would use that money for access to cable television news, 27 percent said that they would spend it on news magazines, 17 percent said that they would buy newspapers, and only 12 percent said that they would spend the extra money to pay for online news. Follow-up questions were asked to probe the reasons behind such decisions (Table 4.5). Whichever medium respondents decided to pay for, the most common reasons seemed to be the existence of more information or content, and convenience.

Discussion

Overall, this study has demonstrated how different news media co-exist in the highly competitive market of Hong Kong. In terms of use, the Internet has a displacing effect on television. However, regardless of how media preference is measured (i.e., in general terms or under

Table 5.5 Medium That Would Be Consumed Given Extra Income and the Reasons for the Choice

Extra income spent on ___ (% of respondents)	Top 3 Reasons
Paid TV news channel (38%)	1. Other (33%) 2. For more information/content (24%) 3. Convenience (16%)
News magazine (27%)	1. Other (41%) 2. For more information/content (27%) 3. Convenience (10%)
Newspaper (17%)	1. Habit (29%) 2. Other (28%) 3. For more information/content (16%)
Paid online news (12%)	1. For more information/content (37%) 2. Other (27%) 3. Convenience (13%)

Note: N=396.

specific conditions), the Web as a news medium appears to be less favorable than television and/or newspapers.

The last research question assessed media preference in a specific situation in which people would be in need of timely information. When asked which news medium (television, radio, or the Internet) they would turn to first to obtain breaking news, about two-thirds (66%) said that they would turn to the television first. Eighteen percent said that they would turn to online news, and 12 percent said that they would rely on the radio.

Displacement Effect

Consistent with the findings of previous displacement research, this study also found a substantial decline in the time spent on television viewing among Hong Kong online news users. One possible reason is that television viewing is more likely to be rooted in the home, whereas other news media consumption is less confined to the home. One can, for example, read newspapers on public transport, listen to the radio while jogging, and surf the Internet while at work, but it is less likely that one would watch television anywhere but in the home. Such a confinement poses limitations to television use if people, with access to a variety of news media, have fulfilled their information needs elsewhere during the day.

Although the displacement effect of the Internet on television is significant, one should be cautious when interpreting the results. The characteristics of different news media allow news receivers to access various news media at different times and places to fulfill different needs. Simply taking the displacement effect of Internet use as evidence of its competitive advantage may give a misleading picture of the market relation between online and offline news media.

In other words, the decrease in time spent watching television news in this sense should not be taken as a sign of a decline in the market competitiveness of the medium. In fact, the Internet as a news medium did not receive a high ranking in any of the preference measures employed in this study as television did.

Media Preference

To explore users' attitudes toward online news from different perspectives, this study measured general liking as well as several more specific preference variables. It is acknowledged that not all the preference measures shared the same conceptual definitions — some were framed more broadly than others. For example, the TV-vs.-computer trade-off question measured preference toward "the computer" as opposed to preference toward "online news" as in the question on breaking news channel selection. By doing so, this study managed to investigate preference for online news from different but related angles. Most importantly, this study has demonstrated that, no matter how preference was measured, online news seemed to be considered a compromise or even the last resort for news consumption in various contexts. It may serve the purpose of information seeking, but consumption gratifications may not be as satisfactory.

Regarding the competition between online and print newspapers, Hong Kong users, like their U.S. counterparts (Chyi and Lasorsa 2002), preferred the print format on the other things being equal basis. Respondents who preferred the print format seemed able to cite diverse reasons for their preference, but those who preferred the online format failed to mention anything other than convenience. It seems that Internet-specific features such as timeliness, interactivity, and searchable databases were not perceived to be as important, even to online news users.

In terms of fee-based media preference, given hypothetical income, online news was ranked as the least attractive news medium after paid television news, magazines and newspapers. The lack of paying intent on a comparative basis suggests that fee-based online news lacks competitive advantage when competing with fee-based traditional news media. The results seem to suggest a potential failure of the subscription model that many online publishers have been advocating since the economic downturn starting in 2000.

In terms of which medium would be used for obtaining breaking news information, most respondents said they would turn to television first, a result that is consistent with the findings of the Pew Center study (Pew Internet & American Life Project, 2003c). According to Althaus and Tewksbury (2000), consumers are intentional, selective, and strategic in their use of different media for different purposes. One of the most common and, perhaps most important, purpose for news consumption is information seeking or surveillance. Despite the fact that online sites are capable of providing up-to-the-minute news updates, television still is perceived as the best choice for information-seeking purposes in this particular scenario. One plausible reason is that television news is characterized by a stronger visual appeal. Convenience may also be a factor — turning on one's TV still is easier than going online and locating a particular news website.

Overall, respondents unmistakably expressed their disliking of online news in the highly competitive media market of Hong Kong. Most of the results reconfirmed what previous studies have found in the U.S. market, despite all the differences distinguishing one geographic market from the other. While the Internet has a displacement effect on time spent on television, online news lacks competitive advantage when users make media selection decisions in different contexts.

Implications

The findings of this study have practical as well as theoretical implications. The Internet as a news medium still is evolving. Online news organizations should think beyond usage to create a more satisfactory user experience. As for advertisers, overlooking the media preference factor may lead to unwise allocations of advertising money, especially because it is an industry rule to assign the greatest economic value to the time spent by media consumers on a certain medium. However, these findings show that it is advisable to take the factor of media preference into consideration in addition to the time factor when making media planning and buying decisions.

Theoretically, as indicated in the findings of this study, use and media preference are two distinct factors. Although use tends to be taken as an indicator of popularity and diffusion, one should not underestimate the potential influence of media preference on the media selection decisions of news users. Even if people spend less time on a particular medium, they may still perceive it to be favorable. In other words, time is not everything. More time spent on a medium does not guarantee favorable attitudes.

Future studies should look into online news users' persistent disliking for the online medium using different methodological approaches (such as controlled experiments or in-depth qualitative analysis). Intermedia competition also can be examined from different perspectives (such as enjoyment, vividness, modality, etc.). Online news users' buying intent for both the news media products and the products that are advertised through these news media also carries important economic implications. Such studies should provide more insight into the economic nature of online news and its competitive advantages and disadvantages in its competition with traditional media.

References

ACNielsen. (2002). "Broadcasting services survey 2002 executive summary". Accessed on 24 June, 2003, from http://www.hkba.org.hk/hkba/en/doc/Exe%20summary-E(Final).doc.

Althaus, S. L. and Tewksbury, D. (2000). "Patterns of Internet and traditional news media use in a networked community". *Political Communication* 17: 21–45.

Brown, M. (2000). "Bringing people closer to news". *Adweek* 41 (40): IQ26.

Carroll, S. L. and Howard, H. H. (1998). "The economics of the cable industry. The economics of the television networks: New dimensions and new alliances". In A. Alexander, J. Owers, and R. Carveth, (eds.), *Media Economics: Theory and Practice*, pp.151–174. Hillsdale, NJ: Erlbaum.

Chyi, H. I. (2002). *No one would pay for it? Web content as inferior goods*. Paper presented at the Fifth World Media Economics Conference, Turku, Finland, May 2002.

Chyi, H. I. & Lasorsa, D. (1999). Access, use and preference for online newspapers. *Newspaper Research Journal, 20*: 2–13.

Chyi, H. I. and Lasorsa, D. L. (2002). "An explorative study on the market relation between online and print newspapers". *Journal of Media Economics* 15: 91–106.

Dimmick, J. W. (2003). *Media Competition and Coexistence: The Theory of the Niche*. Mahwah, NJ: Erlbaum.

Dimmick, J., Chen, Y., and Li, Z. (2004). "Competition between the Internet and traditional news media: The gratification-opportunities niche dimension". *Journal of Media Economics* 17: 19–33.

Dimmick, J., Kline, S., and Stafford, L. (2000). "The gratification niches of personal e-mail and the telephone: Competition, displacement and complementarity". *Communication Research* 27: 227–248.

Dutta-Bergman, M. J. (2004). "Complementarity in consumption of online news types across traditional and new media". *Journal of Broadcasting & Electronic Media* 48: 41–60.

Fidler, R. (1997). *Mediamorphosis: Understanding New Media*. Thousand Oaks, CA: Pine Forge Press.

Fullerton, H. S. (1988). "Technology collides with relative constancy: The pattern of adoption for a new medium". *Journal of Media Economics* 1 (2): 75–84.

Hong Kong Census & Statistics Department. (2003). Accessed on 3 March, 2003, from http://www.info.gov.hk/censtatd/eng/hkstat/index.html.

Information Services Department, HK SAR Government (2004). "The media". Accessed on 3 May, 2004, from http://www.info.gov.hk/hkfacts/media.pdf.

Jupiter Media Metrix (2002). "Bumpy road from free to fee: Paid online content revenues to reach only $5.8 billion by 2006, reports jupiter media metrix". Accessed on 6 January, 2003, from http://banners.noticiasdot.com/termometro/boletines/docs/consultoras/jupiter/2002/jupiter_Paid_Online_Content_Revenues.pdf.

Landon, Jr., E. L. and Banks, S. K. (1977). "Relative efficiency and bias in plus-one telephone sampling". *Journal of Market Research* 14: 294–299.

Litman, B. R. (1998). "The economics of the television networks: New dimensions and new alliances". In A. Alexander, J. Owers and

R. Carveth, (eds.), *Media Economics: Theory and Practice*, pp. 131–149. Hillsdale, NJ: Erlbaum.

McCombs, M. E. and Eyal, C. H. (1980). "Spending on mass media". *Journal of Communication* 31: 153–158.

McCombs, M. E. and Son, J. (1986). *Patterns of economic support for mass media during a decade of electronic innovation.* Paper presented at the meeting of the AEJMC, Norman, OK.

Mueller, J. and Kamerer, D. (1995). "Reader preference for electronic newspapers". *Newspaper Research Journal* 16: 2–13.

Noack, D. (1998). "America's newsrooms bend to the Internet". *Editor & Publisher* 131 (8): 14.

Noh, G.. and Grant, A. E. (1997). "Media functionality and the principle of relative constancy: An explanation of the VCR aberration". *Journal of Media Economics* 10 (3): 17–31.

Outing, S. (1999). "News sites audience closing in". *Editor & Publisher* 132 (14): 29.

Pew Internet & American Life Project. (2003a). "America online pursuits". Accessed on 3 May, 2004, from http://www.pewinternet.org/pdfs/ PIP_Online_Pursuits_Final.PDF.

———. (2003b). "Consumption of information goods and services in the United States". Accessed on 3 May, 2004, from http://207.21.232.103/ pdfs/PIP_Info_Consumption.pdf.

———. (2003c). "The Internet and emergency preparedness: A joint survey with *Federal Computer Week* magazine". Accessed on 3 May, 2004, from http://www.pewinternet.org/pdfs/PIP_Preparedness_Net_Memo.pdf.

Pew Research Center for the People & the Press. (2004). "Online news audience larger, more diverse". Accessed on 12 December, 2004, from http://people-press.org/reports/pdf/215.pdf.

Picard, R. G. (1989). *Media Economics.* Beverly Hills: Sage.

———. (1998). "Economics of the daily newspaper industry". In A. Alexander, J. Owers, and R. Carveth, (eds.), *Media Economics: Theory and Practice*, pp. 111–129. Hillsdale, NJ: Erlbaum.

Schierhorn, C., Wearden, S. T., Schierhorn, A. B., Tabar, P. S., and Andrews, S. C. (1999). "What digital formats do consumers prefer?" *Newspaper Research Journal* 20: 2–19.

So, C., Chan, J. M., and Lee, C.-C. (2000). "Hong Kong SAR (China)". In Shelton A. Gunaratne (ed.), *Handbook of the Media in Asia*, pp. 527–551. New Delhi: Sage.

Stemple, III, G. H. and Hargrove, T. (1996). "Mass media audience in a changing media environment". *Journalism and Mass Communication Quarterly* 73: 549–558.

Stempel, III, G. H., Hargrove, T., and Bernt, J. P. (2000). "Relation of growth of use of the Internet to changes in media use from 1995 to 1999". *Journalism and Mass Communication Quarterly* 77: 71–79.

Sundar, S. S. (1999). "Exploring receivers' criteria for perception of print and online news". *Journalism and Mass Communication Quarterly* 76: 373–386.

Tewksbury, D. (2003). "What do Americans really want to know? Tracking the behavior of news readers on the Internet". *Journal of Communication* 53: 694–710.

Tewksbury, D. and Althaus, S. L. (2000). "Differences in knowledge acquisition among readers of the paper and online versions of a national newspaper". *Journalism and Mass Communication Quarterly* 77: 457–479.

6

—Λ\\—

Online Journalism: The Psychology of Mass Communication on the Web

S. Shyam Sundar

Introduction

Although much is made about how the World Wide Web has changed the practice of journalism and related functions such as advertising and public relations, the fundamental content of mass communication has remained the same. Mainstream online news carries roughly the same content as traditional media such as newspapers and television. The values that characterize news and the nature of advertising and marketing appeals remain largely unchanged. What is different however is the process by which news and advertising are (1) produced by journalistic professionals and (2) disseminated to Web users. Several researchers have examined the former with a focus on production contingencies introduced by the technology of the medium (e.g., Boczkowski 2004; Singer 2004). However, these changes in organizational practices and packaging by media professionals would be of little value if the products of their efforts were of no enduring psychological importance. In order to assess this, it is useful to look at the effects upon users caused by the new style of dissemination enabled by the Web. In particular, it would be necessary to assess the cognitive, attitudinal, and behavioral consequences of those features of form (rather than content) that are most distinctive in the new medium and serve to alter production styles. Across dozens of studies conducted at our lab and related programs of research in the last decade or so, four features of the Web have stood out as being psychologically critical — agency/sourcing, navigability, interactivity, and multimodality. This chapter will describe one significant study pertaining to each feature and highlight its role in shaping a unique psychology for mass communication on the Web.

Agency/Sourcing

For quite some time now, the field of human-computer interaction (HCI) has been emphasizing the use and importance of agents. Lately, these agents have taken on human attributes, including embodiment and conversations (e.g., Cassell 2000). This trend probably arose out of an innate need for a human or human-like sender of information that is distinct from the medium (Laurel 1993). Traditional communication media, most notably radio and television, clearly have a human presence. While listening to the radio, it is obvious that a human being is transmitting the information (be it news or entertainment) to us. The same is true for television and newspapers. However, the computer as a medium does not have such an obvious human presence, making some researchers wonder about the locus of users' psychological attributions while working on a computer (e.g., Sundar and Nass 2000). To whom or what are the users orienting when interacting with the computer? Are they mentally constructing a programmer as Sundar (1994) suggests, or are they simply treating the computer itself as a human being in accordance with the argument forwarded by "media equation" researchers (Reeves and Nass 1996; Nass and Moon 2000)? Regardless, this is indicative of a psychological need for agency while receiving mediated communications. Social psychologists and communication researchers have long studied the importance of agency under the concept label of "source". Indeed, the source or sender is the starting point in all major models of communication.

On the Web, the concept of source becomes quite complicated because the technology of the internet allows for a variety of sourcing options. Online news sites of traditional newspapers (e.g., *nyt.com*) follow a sourcing pattern that is identical to their newspaper counterparts. The masthead itself identifies the entire newspaper staff as the collective source or gatekeeper of the day's news. The agency here is quite obvious. But, on news aggregator sites, assigning agency becomes somewhat tricky. On a site like *drudgereport.com*, it is clear that the gatekeeper is Matt Drudge when you are on the main screen with the menu of news headlines. Once you click on a headline, you are transported to another Website, often another online news site, and the story you read is the result of gatekeeping performed by that site and not drudgereport.com. However, to the extent it is salient to you that you landed on the story as a result of going to drudgreport.com, you are likely to assign agency to Matt Drudge. But, how will you assign agency while browsing online news via *Google News*, the beta site (http://news.google.com/) that uses an algorithm to aggregate news from thousands of news sources on the Web? Here, a non-human entity performs the gatekeeping function, so will you assign agency to the technology itself?

To make matters more complicated, the Web offers still other types of sources. Collaborative filtering systems such as the one used by amazon.com let users have a say in what is hot and what is not. Most major news sites feature a section listing the most e-mailed stories of the day, thus according readers a role in gatekeeping. Here, the audience as a collective serves as the source. Web technology also allows single users to act as sources, as in the case of portal sites whereby a given user acts as his or her own gatekeeper of content by specifying a priori the types of content he/she would like to receive. In essence, the receivers themselves can serve as sources, thus turning the traditional engineering flow models of communication on their heads.

In these instances, the receiver is not the only source that is psychologically relevant. The computer technology probably remains a salient source in the minds of news readers. Not to mention the original news producer, especially if it is a well-known news organization. In sum, online news not only offers a variety of different sources but also a variety of layers in sourcing. In the common occurrence of a forwarded news story by a friend via e-mail, the friend is the proximate source of that information, but there most likely are other sources that are psychologically relevant — a newsgroup perhaps, where a posting might have alerted the friend to the story, or a portal or aggregator site where the friend came upon the story. One layer removed from this is the online news site that officially "published" the article. Not to mention the news organization that produced the story itself. All these are "sources" of news, but none may be psychologically relevant to the reader. We have often heard acquaintances say that they read this or that on the computer or got something off the Web. In these instances, the only relevant sources are the computer technology and Web medium respectively.

Sundar and Nass (2001) attempted to make sense out of the confusing array of sourcing possibilities in online media by proposing a typology of communication sources that distinguished between such technological sources and professional gatekeepers as sources. These two types of sources were in turn distinguished from so-called receiver sources. In all, the typology identifies four distinct sources: (1) "Visible" source, referring to the sender in traditional communication models (e.g., anchorperson of evening broadcast news or editorial staff of a news organization as signified by its masthead/logo); (2) "Technological" source, referring to the computer itself or some interface element or software product that sifts through information and selects a subset of it for user consumption; (3) "Audience as Source," referring to any situation that highlights the usage patterns of the collective audience as a heuristic offered to users for determining the relative worth of different pieces of information (e.g., collaborative filtering systems online or call-in shows on TV); and (4) "Self as Source," referring to interfaces that allow the individual user to act as gatekeeper of content, as in customized portals (e.g., *myYahoo.com*).

These four types of sources were operationalized in an experiment involving exposure to six online news stories via a menu screen containing a larger number of stories. All study participants were exposed to the same six stories, but differed in who/what they thought was the gatekeeper/selector of the stories. One-fourth of the subjects was told that these stories were selected by news editors (i.e., visible sources), another fourth was told that they were selected by the computer terminal they were using, and another fourth was told that they were selected by other users of the online news service. The final fourth was led to believe, by way of a pseudo-selection task, that they themselves (i.e., individual respondents) chose the news stories from the larger set. Following exposure to each news story, participants filled out a paper-and-pencil questionnaire assessing their perceptions of the story's credibility, liking, quality, and representativeness (which refers to the degree to which an individual story represents the stereoptypical attributes of a news story, and can be seen as a proxy for newsworthiness — see Sundar 1999).

Despite the fact that all participants read identical stories, statistically significant differences were found across the four conditions. On average, when a given story was attributed to other users, it was rated higher on liking and quality than when the same story was ostensibly selected by news editors. Even computer as a source led to higher evaluations of story quality than news editors. Moreover, participants rated computer-selected stories as being higher in quality than those selected by themselves. When other users chose the stories, they were rated higher in liking, quality, and representativeness than when the same stories were ostensibly selected by oneself.

While perceived objectivity (unlike self and news editors, the computer is objective in gatekeeping decisions) may be cited as a reason for differences between computer as source and other conditions, Sundar and Nass (2001) discuss several possible reasons for participants privileging other users over self as sources of news stories. Among them is the bandwagon effect (if everyone thinks the story is good, then I should, too), the democracy effect (all online users have a say in the news decision-making process) and the role played by prior expectations about sources — we usually expect ourselves to do much better than other users in choosing something for our consumption, but given that the stories chosen for the experimental stimuli were of average quality that was unlikely to evoke strong emotions, self may have been penalized for not meeting expectations while others may have been rated high for surpassing initially low expectations.

If the self as source is rated so poorly, then one wonders what the psychological value is of the much-hyped phenomenon of customization. Does this mean that the recent industry trend toward customization in online content is simply marketing hype without much consequence to users? Not quite. A recent experiment on customized Web portals showed that users' attitudes were positively affected by personalization (Kalyanaraman and Sundar 2006). The more tailored the site is to the user, the more positive the attitudes. Searching behavior appears to be inhibited by greater customization (users presumably see information that they want without having to extensively seek it), although users tend to navigate their way to the main page more often. This is indicative of a need to orient toward one's own signature page.

In sum, it appears that while customization of a news-and-information site is quite desired by online users, the own-ness heuristic is a negative cue in the particular context of news selection that adversely affects content evaluation. The reasons for this may lie in the theoretical mechanisms governing the psychological connection between personalization and user attitudes toward the site. For instance, Kalyanaraman and Sundar (2006) identified perceived interactivity as a significant mediator of this relationship. It may be argued that the greater interactivity of heightened customization may bring users in closer contact with the content (Sundar and Kim 2005), thus forcing deeper scrutiny of the merits of the content, and given that Sundar and Nass (2001) chose mediocre stories for their experiment, participants were more likely in the self condition to rigorously — and hence critically — evaluate the average nature of those stories. Likewise, other mediators such as perceived relevance and perceived involvement may play a role in users' evaluations of content resulting from customization. As Sundar (in press) observes, the me-ness fostered by customization serves to psychologically entrench the sense of personal agency of the user in the communication, resulting in a greater sense of ownership and responsibility for the content.

The variable nature of agency/sourcing in computer and internet technologies has many important implications for mass communication via this new medium. To begin with, there is a greater tendency to assign agency to the physical manifestation of the medium itself (e.g., the front-end computer supplying news and entertainment). This has psychological consequence given that we commonly factor in the source while psychologically responding to mass communication of any kind. For example, Sundar (2004a) showed that we tend to be loyal to particular computer terminals by repeatedly visiting them even though functionally equivalent alternative terminals are just as easily accessible. We may associate particular computers in our midst with particular types of mass communication — personal laptop for visiting portal sites, home desktop computer for music and entertainment sites, office desktop computer for news sites, and so on. Such source-content association is likely to influence our perceptions of the nature of mass-communicated content as well as our experience of it.

The multiplicity of sources in computer-mediated mass communications has implications as well. Future research would do well to understand the psychological processes underlying our assignment of agency to particular sources in the chain of sources embedded in most online communications. How do particular sources become salient in the minds of users and not others? And how do users handle multiple sources and source combinations? Answers to such questions can significantly aid the design of interfaces (i.e., agents) as well as that of Websites (in the way they portray various sources and cue users about them) and allow for various options for agency. Practice and theory will also benefit from a richer understanding of the cognitive heuristics triggered by particular sources (or instantiations of agency), including self as source, during reception of content so that we can better appreciate user reactions to content.

Navigability

Unlike traditional media, the Web medium allows the user to move from one place to another. The term "cyberspace" accurately emphasizes the spatial aspect of this medium, perhaps the most distinctive feature of mass communication via the Web. A wide array of menus, buttons and hyperlinks invites online news readers to navigate a given Website (or even a single online news story for that matter) in highly idiosyncratic ways, presenting numerous navigational opportunities, each with its own psychological effect. May, Sundar and Williams (1997) were among the first in our field to document the differential psychological effects of different hyperlinking strategies, due clearly to the differential navigation of the site prompted by those strategies. Kalyanaraman, Mahood, Sundar, and Oliver (2000) documented the powerful effect of search-engine output on users' perception of the nature of underlying content in particular and internet content in general, with clear implications for their exploration of the Web. And the aforementioned study on customized portals by Kalyanaraman and Sundar (2006) showed how personalization can actually inhibit exploratory navigation while enhancing visits to the main page, perhaps as a landmark during navigation. All of this suggests a variety of ways in which navigability of Web interfaces and sites can be controlled by site designers.

More importantly, all these signify different ways in which navigational cues can be transmitted to online users. Unlike task-based interactions on the Web that tend to be planned, if not strategic, and closed-ended, news reading is relatively open-ended and non-strategic. The user is typically willing to go where the news takes him or her, foraging for relevant and/or interesting information. Using information foraging theory (Pirolli, Card, and Van Der Wege 2001), Sundar, Knobloch-Westerwick, and Hastall (in press) posit that users are heavily influenced by the "information scent" (Pirolli 2003) provided by so-called "proximal cues" (cues in the immediate environment) about "distal information." For example, the particular words that are underlined to indicate a hyperlink constitute a proximal cue. If those words serve to peak a reader's interest, then that particular hyperlink is said to possess a strong scent. If it's of lesser interest, then it is said to carry a weak scent. If the reader finds it completely inconsequential, that means this proximal cue does not carry any information scent and therefore is unlikely to be clicked upon by the user.

The display and layout of online news are insufficiently suggestive of prominence of particular stories over others; indeed newspapers do a much better job of leading readers toward the more newsworthy stories. Instead, most online news sites simply have a headline (with a hyperlink), often arranged according to their recency rather than importance (Sundar and Nass 2001). This puts the onus on the content of the headline to provide a reasonable proximal cue about the underlying distal information. Most online news sites have headlines for more stories than is typically possible for one person to consume on a daily basis. It is fairly customary for newspaper readers to browse through the entire issue every morning. With online news however, careful selection of some stories over others is inevitable. And this selection is governed by the information scent transmitted by proximal cues embedded in and around the headline. The strength of scent emanated by the text of the headline is in large part the personal domain of the reader because it depends on the degree of overlap between the topic of news and the reader's own background and interests. Outside of the text, there exist other cues in the headline or lead that can potentially aid decision-making about navigation toward the underlying story or some other headline and story.

Taking the lead from news aggregator sites such as Google News, Sundar et al (in press) identified three major non-content cues that newsbots provide without the need for human editorial involvement — the source of the underlying story (usually a news organization) that appears under the headline on the main page of Google News; the recency of upload of the story that appears right next to the headline; and the number of related articles on the same topic floating about on the Web at any given time (basically the number of other online sources carrying the same story, apart from the source that supplied the headline and lead featured on the site). They called these "news cues" and proposed that each cue triggers a particular heuristic or shortcut in the minds of readers — that the credibility of the attributed source would trigger the "professional expertise" heuristic based on reputation while the number of related articles (NRA henceforth) cue would trigger the same heuristic but based on professional consensus across a variety of journalistic outlets, and that NRA itself would cue the bandwagon heuristic while the recency information cues the timeliness heuristic. They hypothesized that perceived message credibility would be significantly influenced by the credibility of the attributed source of the underlying story as well as by the NRA cue, that perceived newsworthiness of a given news item would be affected by the NRA cue as well as the recency cue, and that self-reported click-likelihood would be influenced positively by the NRA cue.

A large online experiment involving 523 participants from 19 countries was conducted to test these propositions. Two levels of attributed source credibility (high, low) were factorially varied with three levels of upload-recency (7 or 29 minutes; 11 or 12 hours; and 45 or 48 hours) and six levels of NRA (7/8, 171/174, 338/342, 502/ 512, 716/721, and 938/944) in a within-subjects experiment that involved participants browsing a main page of 12 headlines and leads for five minutes, followed by exposure to each headline and lead on a separate page with the attendant questionnaire eliciting perceptions about underlying story and click-likelihood. (Given the within-subjects nature of the study, participants were exposed to all levels of all variables across the 12 leads, and more than once. For example, every participant was exposed twice each to the six NRA levels across the 12 leads and four times to the three recency levels. Therefore, the numbers within each level of these two variables were varied slightly in order to avoid sensitization to the purpose of the investigation). The three news cues were placed around the headline and lead in exactly the same fashion as Google News.

Results overwhelmingly showed a main effect for NRA, but not in the predicted monotonic positive direction. Instead, there was a bipolar effect pattern such that leads with most and least NRA were rated the most credible, most newsworthy, and most likely to be clicked upon, followed by the two middle conditions (300+ and 500+), with the remaining two conditions (100+ and 700+) scoring the lowest. This effect pattern was quite similar to behavioral patterns recorded when participants browsed the main screen and the links thereof for five minutes (Knobloch, Sundar, and Hastall 2005) thus ratifying the connection between user perceptions of news leads and their actual news-reading behavior measured in terms of exposure duration. NRA is a unique cue it seems, evoking the freshness heuristic at the low end and the bandwagon heuristic at the high end (Sundar et al., in press).

Source credibility emerged as a significant cue, indirectly affecting user perceptions of message credibility. In general, if the story is attributed to a high-credibility news source, then it appears that recency and NRA cues do not matter in user evaluations of the underlying story's credibility. But when the source is of low credibility, the other cues become psychologically important and indeed cumulate in their influence upon news perception. Therefore, although Sundar et al (in press) found support for their source-primacy proposition, they also found evidence for a cue-cumulation effect under conditions of low source credibility.

The implications of this research for navigability of an interface are obvious. Clearly, even in the context of non-strategic browsing, users are responding systematically to cues on the interface. They appear to process these cues heuristically and make quick inferences about distal information, based on which they structure their next move within the interface. System architects may use a variety of navigational structures to ease users' wayfinding through the system, but the best aids for navigation in the context of online news are cues related to newsworthiness of the underlying story or stories. To the extent features of the Website emphasize cues that lend insight into traditional news values and trigger heuristics related to decision-making, they are likely to aid navigability of the news site regardless of the overall design quality and architecturally soundness of the layout and interior layers. Navigation is not simply a random activity for users to be drawn blindly into some elaborately structured network of paths within the site. Instead, it is a highly deliberate activity dictated by the degree to which proximal cues in the interface promote the value of distal information by way of revealing the pedigree, relevance or quality of that information. Navigational cues that accurately trigger useful heuristics will ultimately impact the usability and effectiveness of all interactive systems, particularly those delivering news.

Interactivity

The central goal of building navigability in online sites is to enable idiosyncratic interaction between the user and the system. Some sites allow for a great deal of interaction whereas others follow the shovelware approach, i.e., simply slap on content from the print edition to the online site. The latter does not utilize the interactive potential of the medium and therefore encourages reception of content in a manner that is similar to one's experience with traditional, passive mass media such as newspapers and television. But, does this make a difference to how we process and perceive information?

Investigations into the psychological effects of interactivity have been marred by controversy about the definition of the concept, with most scholars preoccupied with typologizing, rather than theorizing about, interactivity (Bucy 2004). Some scholars view interactivity as any interface feature that promotes dialogue between user and system (Sundar, Hesser, Kalyanaraman, and Brown 1998) while others view it as speed of system response (Steuer 1992). At the message level, interactivity is seen as the degree of contingency built into a series of message exchanges. Original conceptualized by Rafaeli (1988) for computer-mediated communication contexts such as bulletin boards, this conceptualization has recently been adapted for analyzing the effects of interactivity in Web-based mass communication as well.

Consistent with Sundar's (2004b) suggestion to theorize about interactivity effects along the lines of classic triumvirate of psychological dependent variables (knowledge, attitudes, and behavior), studies employing contingency-based interactivity have shown differences on different outcome variables depending on the nature of the mass-communicated content. For example, a study with interactive news showed that interactive devices such as rollovers and tabs promote clicking activity and are associated with increased recognition memory for news embedded in deeper layers. Some interactive features such as drags were psychophysiologically significant, with their use triggering a deceleration of heart rate, indicating heightened attention. In general however, greater the variety of interactive devices used in a story, lesser the exact recall (albeit higher the recognition) and poorer the user rating of the structure (Sundar and Constantin 2004). Clearly, the use of certain interactive devices that are behaviorally as well as cognitively demanding can have negative consequences for site perceptions. Alternatively, a smooth interactive flow of messages can induce positive affect especially with persuasive messages. In a study with interactive advertisements, Sundar and Kim (2005) showed that contingency in message delivery has profoundly positive effects. Marketing units with three or more layers of messages contributed to significantly more positive Aad (attitudes toward the ad) compared to their counterparts with lesser number of layers. They were also associated with significantly higher levels of perceived product knowledge, perceived product involvement, and behavioral intention. Peripheral cues such as animation ceased to have an effect in high-interactive ads probably due to the fact that contingency demands central processing of message stimuli.

This finding echoes the result obtained in an experiment with a political Website wherein a candidate's platform positions were interactively delivered to users (Sundar, Kalyanaraman, and Brown 2003). In the low interactivity condition, the Website was one scrollable page with candidate's positions organized under topics and sub-topics. In the medium interactivity condition, the same content was broken up into two layers, with the front page providing introductory information and topic headings that are hyperlinked to a second page that contained the topic-specific information including all the sub-topics. In the high interactivity condition, the site content was further fragmented such that the second layers featured the topic, but did not go into subtopics. Instead, the subtopic headings appeared in the second layer with hyperlinks to a third layer. If a user landed on a particular subtopic, then it is because of idiosyncratic selection on his or her part in the previous two layers. The layer headings emphasized the path taken to get there, thus entrenching the contingency manipulation. Clearly, this operationalization is consonant with users' lay definition of interactivity. On a 10-point scale that asked study participants to rate the level of interactivity of the Website, significant mean differentiations were found across the three between-subjects conditions in the expected direction. On impression-formation items however, an inverted V-pattern emerged with participants being most positive about the candidate in the medium condition, there being virtually no difference between the low and high conditions. As suggested by the study with interactive news, high interactivity appears to be associated with cognitive burden that results in lowered ratings for site characteristics (the candidate in this case).

Among the implications for mass communication are that contingent interactivity is most likely processed centrally and therefore likely to bring site content under stricter scrutiny. Message-based interactivity is not simply a bells-and-whistles feature that can peripherally influence user perceptions of a Website. This means interactivity is a double-edged sword — while it can enhance user involvement with site content, it can also result in an amplified response to content characteristics such that good content is rated even more positively than it would be in a less interactive site, but perhaps more worrisome, the effects of bad content would be more apparent in such a site.

Alternatively, the functional view of interactivity views the concept in terms of the number of dialogue-enhancing features present on the interface — features such as a button to send an e-mail to the site, a feature that allows one to view a picture from a different angle, a link to a chatroom related to site content, and so on. There is some evidence to suggest that the sheer presence of such features can add up to an overall positive impression of the site, implying a peripheral processing of interactivity in this case (Sundar et al. 1998).

Designers of sites for online mass communication are often enamored by the interactive potential of the medium and build in many dialogue-enhancing features and contingency-enhancing layers. What these serve to do is reduce the massness of mass communication by either promoting interpersonal communication through the dialogue-enhancing interactive features or breeding customization in one's experiencing of site content. Therefore, interactivity serves to turn on its head the traditional distinction between mass and interpersonal communication, forcing scholars and designers alike to reconceptualize the notion of "mass communication" on the Web. It may be less useful to view Websites as vehicles for disseminating packaged content to a vast audience base than to view them as venues that allow vast number of users to idiosyncratically experience continually evolving content.

Multimodality

The multimedia nature of computers and the internet has received considerable popular attention. Traditional print media are predominantly textual, with picture as a common additional modality. Broadcast media are either audio only (as in radio) or both audio and video (as in television). To be sure, traditional media do feature more than one modality of presentation, appealing to more than one of the five senses. What makes computers special is their ability to allow simultaneous presentation via multiple modalities and the affordance to switch modalities within the same system, often in a given Website or even a particular presentation. Mass communicators on the Web have gone to great lengths to produce and digitally publish content in a number of modalities, with many Websites featuring lavish productions. Advertisers have employed newer modalities such as animation and pop-ups to garner user attention. However, it's not entirely clear whether multimedia presentations raise the effectiveness of mass communication.

In an early attempt at assessing the psychological significance of multiple modalities of presentation, Sundar (2000) examined the processing and perception of online news as a function of five different modality conditions: text only, text plus pictures, text plus audio, text plus picture plus audio, and text plus picture plus video. Theories from cognitive psychology such as dual coding (Paivio

1986), which argue for the existence of multiple encoding systems specializing in verbal and visual stimuli, were used to hypothesize a double-dose advantage of multiple modalities over a single modality. On the other hand, theories that focus on limited processing capacity (Lang 2000) were invoked to suggest that multiple modalities may overload the cognitive system to the point of degrading memory. The experiment measured memory for both news stories and advertising content on the page. Recognition for story details was highest for text and text + picture conditions and lowest for the text + picture + video condition, implying that the presentation of news via a multitude of modalities serves to hinder encoding of story details. An assessment of story recall measures ratified this trend by showing that text + picture led to the best retrieval of content, significantly higher than text + picture + audio. Clearly the addition of audio hindered encoding as well as storage of story information. Somewhat the reverse pattern was found with memory for advertisements. While multimedia conditions did not make a difference to ad recall, ad recognition for the audio and video conditions was significantly higher than for text + picture condition. One possibility is that the ads received greater attention in the multimedia conditions as a consequence of study participants waiting for their downloads to appear on the screen. Another possibility is that reception of audio and video modalities may have triggered the passivity endemic to traditional broadcast media, resulting in lowered attention to story and greater susceptibility to contextual interference (the ads in this case).

The immersive quality of multimedia enhancements and their vividness in general may be thought of as qualities that would result in a positive appraisal of the news site. On the other hand, studies have shown that text only (or, at the most, text with picture or graphic) is associated with the most positive attitudes (e.g., Steuer 1994; Gopal 1996). Sundar's (2000) study found that the addition of the audio download to a text + picture story led to lower ratings of coherence and quality of site design. Video did not seem to have the same negative effects. Something about the combination of pictures and audio appears to trigger negative evaluations of the site. Perhaps it's the idea of listening to audio when staring blankly at a picture. In this sense, audio is not as seamless as audiovisual in promoting engaged reception of news content. Analysis of story perception measures revealed that both video and audio downloads appeared to detract from perceived news quality of a text + picture story. Clearly, involvement of broadcast media triggers heuristics about the journalistic quality of online news stories. Sundar (2000) suggested that perhaps the audio and video quality did not compare in fidelity to that found on FM radio and cable television respectively, and therefore were evaluated relatively poorly. These considerations highlight the enormous amount of theoretical work that lies ahead in determining the psychological effects of multimedia presentations of online news. Clearly, the addition of audiovisual modalities does not appear to be a runaway success, with text still being the safest bet in promoting processing as well as positive perceptions of news stories. Perhaps adding newer modalities that are unique to the medium (such as animation) may enhance the psychological value of online news, especially with stories that have the kind of detail that can best be visualized with the aid of novel modalities. Alternatively, the cognitive superiority of text may lie in the fact that it is consciously, rather than automatically, processed, with multimedia constituting a natural experience of mediated stimuli requiring little or no mental conversion.

Online news providers have to be careful in the way they deploy the multimodal output capable in Web-based media. From the data, it appears as though multimedia sites are somewhat more successful in conveying the message of advertisers. Moreover, industry trends and Web site awards favor the use of multimedia, generally speaking. Given this, it might be tempting to actively employ multiple modalities of output, but it could come at the cost of fully conveying information to the news reading public — an essential social-responsibility function of the news media. As the Web gets more sophisticated, users will increasingly get a choice of textual vs. multimedia presentations, which might serve to alleviate some of the negative effects of multimedia. The next frontier beyond customization of multimodal output is the system's invitation of multimodal input from the user. Considerable HCI research has already focused on interfaces that process two or more inputs (speech, gaze, head movements, etc.) in a coordinated manner (Oviatt 2003). When news Websites begin to accept multimodal input, we will see a completely new dynamic in the way users process and perceive online news.

Conclusion

Certain values on the variables associated with the four aforementioned Web features are better than others in creating user engagement with content (e.g., text better than audio in modality, medium better than low in interactivity, strong over weak information scent in navigability, and self over news-editors as source or agent). More than their value as peripheral cues in the message context, these features affect users by the degree to which they facilitate user involvement with content. They can stimulate an effortful consideration of mass-communicated content or detract users from meaningfully engaging with it. This is where content effects take over. Once the structural features deliver the content to the user, the quality of that content will dictate the resulting effects. Therefore, a key value of these Web features lies in their ability to alter the degree to which content is the focus of user attention and evaluation.

These technological features are also powerful because they suggest cognitive heuristics during their operation or even simply by their presence on the interface. Different agents or sources signify different cues about their functionality (in the case of online news, their gatekeeping style). Likewise, navigational gateways in online sites are rich with cues suggesting the nature and potential value of underlying or distal information. The type of interactivity present in an interface (dialogue vs. contingency) can dictate the degree to which content is peripherally processed or centrally processed in part because each particular interactive device triggers heuristics relating to its functionality (e.g., whether it exists just to add bells and whistles or to address a specific communication need). Likewise, each modality appears to be associated with a heuristic and, as a consequence, processed quite differently than other modalities. Over time, with novelty effects fading away, the particulars of these heuristics may change, but it appears that users tend to depend on heuristics for aiding their cognitive processing, evaluations, and action decisions while interacting with online content.

The fundamental stance taken by the consumer of online mass communication is one of interacting with the content rather than merely receiving it. All the new technological features exist in part to facilitate this approach to media consumption by offering varying levels of customization (i.e., content tailored to meet the individual user). While self-as-source signifies the most extreme form of customization by allowing the user to be the gatekeeper of information, navigable interfaces aid the user in the process of customization by allowing for idiosyncratic browsing of the site. Interactivity is clearly geared toward meeting the needs of individual receivers — interactive devices allow the user to initiate and view particular parts of the content whereas contingency-based devices afford the user to dictate the nature and content of message transmission. Finally, modality options on an interface allow the user to customize his or her experience of online content by offering different forms of perceptual representation of content, from simply text to video to virtual reality. Therefore, at some fundamental level, the psychological value of these technological features lies in their ability to offer customized experiences of mass communication. This clearly changes the very core of the concept of mass communication by suggesting that the content of online mass communication is far from being monolithic and indeed highly demassified with the arrival of technological features unique to this new medium.

References

Boczkowski, P. J. (2004). "The processes of adopting multimedia and interactivity in three online newsrooms". *Journal of Communication* 54 (2): 197–213.

Bucy, E. P. (2004). "Interactivity in society: Locating an elusive concept". *The Information Society* 20: 373–383.

Cassell, J. (2000). "Embodied conversational interface agents". *Communications of the ACM* 43 (4): 70–78.

Gopal, Y. (1996). "Selling in cyberspace: An investigation of modality effects on cognitive processing of persuasive communication on the Internet". Unpublished doctoral dissertation, University of Georgia, Athens.

Kalyanaraman, S. and Sundar, S. S. (2006). "The psychological appeal of personalized content in Web portals: Does customization affect attitudes and behavior?" *Journal of Communication* 56 (1): 1–23.

Kalyanaraman, S., Mahood, C., Sundar, S. S., and Oliver, M. B. (2000). *Priming effects of accidental exposure to internet pornography: An experimental study of construct accessibility in search engine output.* Paper presented at the 83rd annual convention of the Association for Education in Journalism and Mass Communication, Phoenix, AZ.

Knobloch, S., Sundar, S. S., and Hastall, M. R. (2005). *Clicking news: Impacts of newsworthiness, source credibility, and timeliness as online news features on news consumption.* Paper presented at the 55th annual conference of the International Communication Association, New York, NY.

Lang, A. (2000). "The limited capacity model of mediated message processing". *Journal of Communication* 50 (1): 46–70.

Laurel, B. (1993). *Computers as Theatre.* Reading, MA: Addison-Wesley.

May, M., Sundar, S. S., and Williams, R. B. (1997). *The effects of hyperlinks and site maps on the memorability and enjoyability of web content.* Paper presented at the 47th annual conference of the International Communication Association, Montreal, Canada.

Nass, C. and Moon, Y. (2000). "Machines and mindlessness: Social responses to computers". *Journal of Social Issues* 56 (1): 81–103.

Oviatt, S. (2003). "Multimodal interfaces". In J. A. Jacko and A. Sears (eds.), *The Human-computer Interaction Handbook*, pp. 286–304. Mahwah, NJ: Lawrence Erlbaum.

Paivio, A. (1986). *Mental Representations: A Dual-coding Approach.* New York: Oxford University Press.

Pirolli, P. (2003). "Exploring and finding information". In J. Carroll (ed.), *HCI Models, Theories and Frameworks: Toward a Multidisciplinary Science*, pp. 157–191. San Francisco, CA: Morgan Kauffmann Publishers.

Pirolli, P., Card, S. K., and Van Der Wege, M. M. (2001). "Visual information foraging in a focus + content visualization". In J. Jacko and A. Sears (eds.), *Proceedings of the SIGCHI Conference on Human Factors in Computing Systems, Seattle, WA*, pp. 506-513. New York: ACM Press.

Rafaeli, S. (1988). "Interactivity: From new media to communication". In R. Hawkins, J. Weimann, and S. Pingree (eds.), *Advancing Communication Science: Merging Mass and Interpersonal Processes*, pp 124–181. Newbury Park, CA: Sage.

Reeves, B. and Nass, C. (1996). *The Media Equation: How People Treat Computers, Television, and New Media Like Real People and Places.* New York: Cambridge University Press/CSLI.

Singer, J. B. (2004). "Strange bedfellows? The diffusion of convergence in four news organizations". *Journalism Studies* 5 (1): 3–18.

Steuer, J. (1992). "Defining virtual reality: Dimensions determining telepresence". *Journal of Communication* 42: 73–93.

———. (1994). "Vividness and source of evaluation as determinants of social responses toward mediated representations of agency". Unpublished doctoral dissertation, Stanford University, CA.

Sundar, S. S. (1994). *Is human-computer interaction social or parasocial?* Paper presented at the annual conference of the Association for Education in Journalism and Mass Communication, Atlanta, GA.

———. (1999). "Exploring receivers' criteria for perception of print and online news". *Journalism & Mass Communication Quarterly* 76 (2): 373–386.

———. (2000). "Multimedia effects on processing and perception of online news: A study of picture, audio, and video downloads". *Journalism & Mass Communication Quarterly* 77 (3): 480–499.

———. (2004a). "Loyalty to computer terminals: is it anthropomorphism or consistency?" *Behaviour & Information Technology* 23 (2): 107–118.

———. (2004b). "Theorizing interactivity's effects". *The Information* Society 20 (5): 387–391.

———. (in press). "Self as source: Agency in interactive media". In E. Konijn, M. Tanis, S. Utz, and A. Linden (eds.), *Mediated Interpersonal Communication*. Mahwah, NJ: Lawrence Erlbaum Associates.

———, Hesser, K., Kalyanaraman, S., and Brown, J. (1998). *The effect of Website interactivity on political persuasion*. Paper presented at the 21st General Assembly & Scientific Conference of the International Association for Media and Communication Research, Glasgow, UK.

——— and Nass, C. (2000). "Source orientation in human-computer interaction: Programmer, networker, or independent social actor?" *Communication Research* 27 (6): 683–703.

——— and Nass, C. (2001). "Conceptualizing sources in online news". *Journal of Communication* 51 (1): 52–72.

———, Kalyanaraman, S., and Brown, J. (2003). "Explicating Web site interactivity: Impression formation effects in political campaign sites". *Communication Research* 30 (1): 30–59.

——— and Constantin, C. (2004). *Does interacting with media enhance news memory? Automatic vs. controlled processing of interactive news features*. Paper presented at the 54th annual conference of the International Communication Association, New Orleans, LA.

——— and Kim, J. (2005). "Interactivity and persuasion: Influencing attitudes with information and involvement". *Journal of Interactive Advertising* 5 (2). Available online: http://www.jiad.org/vol5/no2/sundar.

———, Knobloch-Westerwick, S., and Hastall, M. R. (in press). "News cues: Information scent and cognitive heuristics". *Journal of the American Society of Information Science and Technology*.

7

—ⁿⁿ—

The Effects of Context Clutter and Advertising Repetition on Attitudinal and Behavioral Changes toward an Online Advertisement

Vicky Wing Kei Ng
Hsiang Iris Chyi

Introduction

According to the Interactive Advertising Bureau (2004), online advertising revenue reached $2.3 billion in the first quarter of 2004, a 39% increase over Q1 2003, suggesting the reviving confidence in this particular advertising medium since the market downturn during 2001–2002. Despite this quantitative growth, the click-through rate keeps dropping, and questions regarding online advertising effectiveness remain.

Since the first banner ad appeared in 1994 (Bayan 2001), the online advertising industry has been developing various strategies to compete for Internet users' attention. While the banner still is the dominant form of online advertising and accounts for 29% of total online ad spending (Interactive Advertising Bureau 2003), ads of larger sizes and in more intrusive forms of presentation contribute to a more cluttered online landscape. The diffusion of broadband technology also provides Web publishers with more flexibility for presenting multimedia content online. As a result, a banner ad is often placed in a cluttered context. While research on the effect of context clutter on print advertising effectiveness exists, such an effect in the online environment has not been fully understood.

In addition, to increase ad impressions, some advertisers place banner ads in different parts of a Web site or even replicate the same ad on the same Web page. Such media buying strategies, aiming at maximizing the effect of a single ad by increasing the chance of exposure, are similar to the advertising repetition practice seen in television and print media buying. This study empirically examines whether repeated use of the same ad increases advertising effectiveness in the online environment.

A controlled experiment investigates the effects of advertising clutter and advertising repetition on people's attitudinal and behavioral responses to an online advertisement. The hierarchy of effects model serves as the theoretical framework, so advertising effectiveness is measured in terms of attitude toward the Web page, attitude toward the ad, attitude toward the brand, and purchase intent.

Literature Review

Hierarchy of Effects

For decades, the hierarchy of effects paradigm has served as the basis for measuring advertising effectiveness (Weilbacher 2001). Models along this line have assumed a particular sequence of stages that consumers pass through until they reach their decision at the end. The defining-advertising-goals-for-measured-advertising-results (DAGMAR) model introduced by Colly (1961) assumes a sequence of awareness, comprehension, conviction and action for advertising effects to take place. McGuire (1978) introduced the information-processing model (IPM) assuming a sequence of presentation, attention, comprehension, yielding, retention and behavior. The most common set of relationships is that attitude toward the ad tends to have a direct impact on attitude toward the brand, which in turn tends to have a positive effect on purchase intention (Brown and Stayman 1992).

Elements in these hierarchy-of-effects models have been widely used as the attitudinal and behavioral measures in the history of advertising research. With the advent of Internet advertising, hierarchy-of-effects models remains a useful framework to understand how people react to Internet advertising messages

(Bruner and Kumar 2000; Cho 1999; Dahlen 2001; Shamdasani, Stanaland, and Tan 2001).

Effectiveness of Internet Advertising

The unique characteristics of the Internet as an advertising medium have expanded the scope of advertising research to include some unique variables relevant to advertising effects. One such variable is click-through, which leads to voluntary exposure (Cho 1999, 2003). Click-through is the basis of a performance-based online advertising model in which non-click, involuntary ad exposures are not perceived as valid outcomes in the real-world practice. Some researchers thus took click-through as the dependent variable in effectiveness research (Cho 2003; Li and Bukovac 1999; Sundar and Kalyanaraman 2004). However, click-through is not the only measure of advertising effectiveness. Briggs and Hollis (1997) found exposure to banner ads alone creates advertising effects. In addition, as click-through rates keep dropping, ad impressions (involuntary exposures) remain an important and realistic measure in the advertising industry. Therefore, this study focuses on people's attitudinal and behavioral responses to a banner ad after an involuntary exposure.

Based on previous research (Bruner and Kumar 2000), this study measures advertising effectiveness in terms of attitude toward the ad, attitude toward the brand, and purchase intent. In addition, a new construct "attitude toward the Web site," an antecedent in the hierarchy of effects, with a positive impact on attitude toward the ad, attitude toward the brand, and purchase intent (Bruner and Kumar 2000; Stevenson, Bruner, and Kumar 2000) is also a focus of this study.

A review of previous research identified a number of factors found to exert influences on advertising effectiveness. Some are advertisement characteristics such as ad size (Li and Bukovac 1999), animation (Heo and Sunder 2000; Lang, Borse, Wise, and David 2002; Li and Bukovac 1999), animation speed (Sundar and Kalyanaraman,2004), and ad frequency (Lee and Sundar 2002). Some are user characteristics such as Internet experience (Bruner and Kumar 2000; Dahlen 2001; Lee and Sundar 2002) and product involvement (Cho and Leckenby 2000). Some are context characteristics such as Web site reputation (Shamdasani, et al. 2001) and relevance between the advertised product category and Web site content (Cho 1999). This study examines the effects of a context-related factor (context clutter) and an ad-related factor (ad repetition) on Internet advertising effectiveness.

The Effect of Context Clutter

Previous research suggests that media context exerts influence on attention, comprehension, and attitude toward the advertising message embedded in the context. For example, television advertising researchers found program-induced viewer mood (Aylesworth and MacKenzie 1998; Coulter 1998) and program-advertising congruity (Kamins, et al. 1991; Sharma 2000) affect advertising effectiveness. Context also affects print advertising effectiveness. Norris and Colman (1992) found that the more involved readers are when reading an article in the magazine, the less they recall the ad accompanied. Along these lines, it is essential to also examine whether context influences advertising effectiveness in the online environment where multiple ads, text, graphics, and multimedia elements compete for attention.

A related concept is advertising clutter — the density of advertisements in a media vehicle. According to Ha (1996), one of the possible dimensions of clutter that constitute the density perception and account for clutter's negative effects on information processing is the number of ads as well as the proportion of ad space in a media vehicle. Previous research on traditional advertising showed that a highly cluttered environment distracts people's attention from the target ad and thus creates a negative impact on attitudes toward the advertising vehicle, the ad, and the advertised brand (Elliott and Speck 1998; Ha 1996; Kent 1993; Webb 1979). A recent study found background complexity had negative effects on attitudes toward the Web page, the ad (a commercial), the brand and purchase intent (Stevenson et al., 2000). This study attempts to examine whether such effects also apply to banner ads. Moreover, in today's Internet environment, animated banners have emerged as one of the major ad formats. According to Li and Bukovac (1999), animation gets more attention and triggers quicker response than static banners. While animation may bring attention to the target ad, it also serves as a major cause of distraction for competing advertising messages. Because animated ads substantially contribute to a Web page's density perception, this study defines context clutter as the proportion of animated graphics to the total viewable area of a Web page. To examine the effect of context clutter on advertising effectiveness, this study tests the following hypotheses:

H_{1a}: Context clutter will have a negative effect on attitude toward the Web page.

H_{1b}: Context clutter will have a negative effect on attitude toward the ad.

H_{1c}: Context clutter will have a negative effect on attitude toward the brand.

H_{1d}: Context clutter will have a negative effect on purchase intent.

The Effect of Advertising Repetition

Advertising repetition refers to ads of the same brand based on the same creative ideas appear more than once in the same advertising vehicle. Previous research indicates the relationship between ad repetition and advertising effectiveness is characterized by an inverted-U curve (Batra and Ray 1986; Pechmann and Steward 1989), suggesting that low to moderate level of repeated exposure generates better message effects and more favorable attitudes because advertising repetition provides more opportunities for viewers to process the advertising message, which in turn, enhances people's attitude toward the ad, the brand as well as their purchase intent (Batra and Ray 1986; Berger and Mitchell 1989; Campbell and Keller 2003; Hawkins and Hoch 1992). In the online scenario, as any Web page may carry multiple ad messages simultaneously, this study attempts to examine whether repeated use of online ads (within a reasonable range — e.g., twice) on the same page enhances attitudes toward the ad, the brand, and purchase intent. In addition, as previous studies suggest that attitude toward the Web page is positively associated with attitudes toward the ad, the brand and purchase intent (Bruner and Kumar 2000; Stevenson et al. 2000), the effect of ad repetition on attitude toward the advertising vehicle is also hypothesized. To examine the effect of ad repetition on advertising effectiveness, this study tests the following four hypotheses:

H_{2a}: Advertising repetition will have a positive effect on attitude toward the Web page.

H_{2b}: Advertising repetition will have a positive effect on attitude toward the ad.

H_{2c}: Advertising repetition will have a positive effect on attitude toward the brand.

H_{2d}: Advertising repetition will have a positive effect on purchase intent.

Method

A total of 131 college students participated in a between-subject 2 (content clutter) X 2 (advertising repetition) factorial experiment. Subjects were randomly assigned into one of the four treatment groups: 1) highly cluttered context with ad repetition, 2) highly cluttered context without ad repetition, 3) lowly cluttered context with ad repetition, and 4) lowly cluttered context without ad repetition (Table 7.1). Their attitudinal and behavioral responses to an online advertisement — i.e., attitudes toward the Web page, the ad, the brand, and paying intent — were measured in the post-test.

Table 7.1 2 x 2 Factorial Design (4 Treatment Groups)

		Advertising Repetition	
		Yes	No
Context Clutter	High	Group 1	Group 2
		2 animated target ads	1 animated target ad
			1 animated non-target ad
		8 animated ads	8 animated ads
	Low	Group 3	Group 4
		2 animated target ads	1 animated target ad
			1 animated non-target ad
		8 static ads	8 static ads

Experimental Treatment Conditions

Context clutter is defined as the proportion of animated graphics to the total viewable area of a Web page. To enhance ecological validity, the level of clutter was determined with reference to the leading web sites in town[1]: high clutter contains 10 animated graphics, and low clutter contains 2 animated graphics.

Advertising repetition also was operationalized into two levels: no repetition (an ad occupying only one advertising spot) and repetition (the ad appearing on two spots on the same Web page).

Dependent Measures

Four dependent variables are: attitude toward the Web page, attitude toward the ad, attitude toward the brand, and purchase intent.

Attitude toward the Web page was measured by asking participants to indicate how much they agree with each of the following eight statements on a seven-point scale (7 = strongly agree; 1 = strongly disagree): "This is an interesting Web page"; "This is a friendly Web page"; "This is a boring Web page"; "The Web page contains multi-dimensional contents"; "This is an informative Web page"; "I am satisfied with the content on this Web page"; "I enjoy reading this Web page"; and "I like this Web page." This scale, modified based on previous research (Bruner and Kumar 2000; Shamdasani et al. 2001), measures respondents' attitude toward the Web page.

Attitude toward the ad was measured by asking participants to indicate how much they agree with the following eight statements on a seven-point scale (7 = strongly agree; 1 = strongly disagree): "This is an interesting ad"; "This ad attracts my attention"; "This ad has good visual effects"; "This ad makes me dizzy"; "This is an entertaining ad"; "This ad is annoying"; "I like this ad"; and "This is a good ad." This scale, modified based on the previous research (Cho 1999; Ha 1996), measures respondents' attitudes toward the target ad.

Similarly, attitude toward the brand was measured by the following five statements: "This is an interesting brand"; "This is a friendly brand"; "This brand is attractive"; "This is a good brand"; and "I like this brand." This scale was also developed based on previous research (Shamdasani et al. 2001).

Purchase intent was measured by this question: "If there is a chance, how likely will you buy the advertised product?" Participants indicated their buying intent on a seven-point scale (7 = very likely; 1 = very unlikely).

Pre-Test

A pre-test was conducted to determine the type of Web page and the advertised product for the study. Altogether 87 college students participated in the pre-test by filling out a questionnaire. Results showed that portals would be the most familiar context for online ads and therefore the portal was chosen as the context for this study.

To determine the advertised product or service, the goal is to identify a product of low to moderate interests among potential participants to prevent any personal bias from being introduced into the results. Respondents were asked to rate on a seven-point scale (7 = very important; 1 = not at all important) the degree of importance of different product categories including credit cards, mobile phones, soft drinks, computer products, travel, cars, personal care products, insurance, music products, chewing gum, camera and films, and movie-related products. Five product categories receiving below-the-average scores were: cars (2.52), insurance (2.46), gum (3.20), soft drinks (3.48), and credit cards (3.49).[2] Cars, insurance, and credit cards were then excluded because high-involvement products as such generally require more information seeking and a one-shot ad exposure is less likely to trigger purchase intent. Finally, soft drinks instead of chewing gum was selected as the product category because soft drinks tend to cover a larger consumer base.

Stimuli

A prototype Web page for a hypothetical portal was developed as the advertising context. A fictitious lemon tea brand "LemTea" was assigned to the target ads so that the subjects' experience with or perception of existing brands would not interfere with the results. The target ad was placed in the upper part of the Web page to increase the chance of being noticed by the subjects.

Procedure

The experiment was administered to each participant individually in a computer laboratory. Upon arrival, subjects were randomly assigned into a treatment group and were asked to read through the instructions before accessing the Web page. To disguise the purpose of the experiment, participants were told that they would help evaluate a front page prototype of a Web site targeting young viewers to be launched next month (without active links). They were asked to pay attention to everything on the Web page for as long as they wished and were then asked to fill out a questionnaire. Once the respondent started working on the questionnaire, they were not allowed to visit the Web page again.

The post-test questionnaire consists of four sections: 1) evaluation of the Web page, 2) recognition of target ad, 3) evaluation of the ad and the brand, and 4) demographic and psychographic information.

The overall process took about 10–15 minutes. Upon completion, subjects received some snacks and were dismissed after a debriefing session.

Findings

Reliability of Measures

Attitude toward the Web page was measured by eight attribute statements on a seven-point scale. Cronbach's alpha was .89, suggesting a highly reliable scale. A composite score "attitude toward the Web page" (Attweb) was constructed by using the average scores of the eight attributes. The overall mean was 4.63 (N = 131).

Attitude toward the ad was measured by eight attribute statements on a seven-point scale. Cronbach's alpha was .88. After excluding two attributes ("this ad makes me dizzy" and "this ad is annoying"), Cronbach's alpha was improved to .93. Therefore, a composite score of attitude toward the ad (Attad) was constructed by using the average scores of the six remaining attribute statements. The mean was 4.54 (N = 131).

Attitude toward the brand was measured by five attribute statements. Cronbach's alpha score was .91. A composite score

(Attbd) was constructed to represent each respondent's overall attitude toward the brand by using the average scores of the five attribute statements. The mean was 3.98 (N = 131).

Purchase intent was measured by a single questions "if there is a chance, how likely will you buy the advertised product?" The mean was 4.46 (N = 131).

Manipulation Check

Manipulation check was conducted to make sure the manipulation of context clutter was effective. A three-item scale measured the perceived amount, proportion, and density of animated graphics on the Web page. Cronbach alpha was .91. A composite score was calculated for each treatment group. A t-test revealed that the amount of animated graphics perceived by the subjects in the highly cluttered group was significantly higher than that by those in the lowly cluttered group (mean = 3.276 vs. mean = 2.284, t = 8.726, $p <$ .001). Therefore, the manipulation was successful.

Data Analysis

Multivariate analysis of variance (MANOVA) was conducted to examine the effects of the two independent variables (ad repetition and context clutter) on people's overall reactions toward the ad, which include attitude toward the Web page, attitude toward the ad, attitude toward the brand as well as purchase intent. Several univariate F-tests examined the effects of independent variables on each dependent variable.

Hypotheses Testing

Effects of Context Clutter and Advertising Repetition on Overall Attitudinal and Behavioral Measures. Table 7.2 presents the results of the MANOVA test. The multivariate main effects of context clutter and advertising repetition on the variate of people's overall reactions toward the ad (which was formed by the four dependent variables) were significant, repectively (for context clutter, Wilk's Lambda = .888, F[4,124] = 3.929, $p <$ .01; for advertising repetition, Wilk's Lambda = .925, F[4,124] = 2.504, $p <$ .05). However, the interaction

Table 7.2 The Effects of Context Clutter and Ad Repetition on Overall Reactions toward the Ad (MANOVA)

	Wilk's Lambda	F	Significance
Context Clutter	.888	3.929	$p < .01$
Ad Repetition	.925	2.504	$p < .05$
Context Clutter x Ad Repetition	.981	.608	$p = .658$

between the two independent variables was not significant (Wilk's Lambda = .981, $F[4,124]$ = .608, p = .658).

The Effect of Context Clutter. Several F-tests examined the effect of context clutter on each of the four dependent variables.

The hypothesis (H_{1a}) predicting the negative effect of context clutter on attitude toward the Web page was not supported (F [1, 127] = 1.948, p = .165) (see Table 7.3).

The hypothesis (H_{1b}) predicting the negative effect of context clutter on attitude toward the ad was supported (F [1,127] = 6.939, $p < .01$) (see Table 7.4).

The hypothesis (H_{1c}) predicting the negative effect of context clutter on attitude toward the brand was not supported (F [1,127] = .000, p = .999) (see Table 7.5).

The hypothesis (H_{1d}) regarding the negative effect of context clutter on purchase intent was not supported (F [1,127] = .787, p = .377) (see Table 7.6).

The Effect of Advertising Repetition. Several F-tests examined the effect of ad repetition on each of the four dependent variables.

The hypothesis predicting the positive effect of ad repetition on attitude toward the Web page (H_{2a}) was supported (F [1,127] = 4.295, $p < .05$) (see Table 7.3).

The hypothesis predicting the positive effect of ad repetition on attitude toward the ad (H_{2b}) was supported (F [1,127] = 5.270, $p < .05$) (see Table 7.4).

The hypothesis predicting the positive effect of ad repetition on attitude toward the brand (H_{2c}) was not supported (F [1,127] = .389, p = .534) (see Table 7.5).

The hypothesis predicting the positive effect of ad repetition on purchase intent (H_{2d}) was not supported (F [1,127] = 1.641, p = .203) (see Table 7.6).

Table 7.3 Univariate F-Test on Attitude toward the Web Page

Variables		n	Mean	SD	F	df	significance
Context clutter	(HC)	64	4.725	.651	1.948	1	n.s.
	(LC)	67	4.530	.951			
Ad repetition	(ADR)	66	4.771	.785	4.295	1	$p < .05$
	(NAD)	65	4.477	.837			
Two-way	(HCA)	32	4.828	.677	.372	1	n.s.
interactions	(HCNA)	32	4.621	.617			
(Clutter x ad	(LCA)	34	4.717	.881			
repetition)	(LCNA)	33	4.337	.995			

HC: highly cluttered context
LC: lowly cluttered context
ADR: with ad repetition
NAD: without ad repetition
HCA: highly cluttered context with ad repetition
HCNA: highly cluttered context without ad repetition
LCA: lowly cluttered context with ad repetition
LCNA: lowly cluttered context without ad repetition

Table 7.4 Univariate F-Test on Attitude toward the Ad

Variables		n	Mean	SD	F	df	significance
Context clutter	(HC)	64	4.313	1.016	6.939	1	$p < .01$
	(LC)	67	4.764	.969			
Ad repetition	(ADR)	66	4.737	.998	5.270	1	$p < .05$
	(NAD)	65	4.346	.999			
Two-way	(HCA)	32	4.594	.976	1.001	1	n.s.
interactions	(HCNA)	32	4.031	.990			
(Clutter x ad	(LCA)	34	4.873	1.013			
repetition)	(LCNA)	33	4.652	.923			

HC: highly cluttered context
LC: lowly cluttered context
ADR: with ad repetition
NAD: without ad repetition
HCA: highly cluttered context with ad repetition
HCNA: highly cluttered context without ad repetition
LCA: lowly cluttered context with ad repetition
LCNA: lowly cluttered context without ad repetition

Table 7.5 Univariate F-Test on Attitude toward the Brand

Variables		n	Mean	SD	F	df	significance
Context clutter	(HC)	64	3.978	.938	.000	1	n.s.
	(LC)	67	3.979	.956			
Ad repetition	(ADR)	66	4.030	.982	.389	1	n.s.
	(NAD)	65	3.926	.908			
Two-way	(HCA)	32	4.025	.9126	.004	1	n.s.
interactions	(HCNA)	32	3.931	.975			
(Clutter x ad	(LCA)	34	4.035	1.057			
repetition)	(LCNA)	33	3.921	.853			

HC: highly cluttered context
LC: lowly cluttered context
ADR: with ad repetition
NAD: without ad repetition
HCA: highly cluttered context with ad repetition
HCNA: highly cluttered context without ad repetition
LCA: lowly cluttered context with ad repetition
LCNA: lowly cluttered context without ad repetition

Table 7.6 Univariate F-Test on Purchase Intent

Variables		n	Mean	SD	F	df	significance
Context clutter	(HC)	64	4.56	1.332	.787	1	n.s.
	(LC)	67	4.36	1.334			
Ad repetition	(ADR)	66	4.61	1.311	1.641	1	n.s.
	(NAD)	65	4.31	1.345			
Two-way	(HCA)	32	4.69	1.230	.044	1	n.s.
interactions	(HCNA)	32	4.44	1.435			
(Clutter x ad	(LCA)	34	4.53	1.398			
repetition)	(LCNA)	33	4.18	1.261			

HC: highly cluttered context
LC: lowly cluttered context
ADR: with ad repetition
NAD: without ad repetition
HCA: highly cluttered context with ad repetition
HCNA: highly cluttered context without ad repetition
LCA: lowly cluttered context with ad repetition
LCNA: lowly cluttered context without ad repetition

Discussion

This study has examined the effects of context clutter and advertising repetition on people's attitudinal and behavioral responses to a banner ad in an experimental setting. Findings revealed that both factors influenced people's attitude toward the ad but no effect was found at the brand evaluation level or beyond. In addition, advertising repetition had a positive impact on people's attitude toward the Web page.

The Effect of Context Clutter

One of the most important findings of this study is that cluttered context has a negative effect on attitude toward the online ad — a result consistent with previous research (Stevenson et al. 2000). An ad stands out more easily in a relatively simple context, while context clutter would distract attention from the ad and thus prevent viewers from fully comprehending the message and formulating more favorable attitude toward the ad. In other words, advertising practitioners should place banner ads on a simpler context to generate better advertising results.

It was also hypothesized that context clutter would result in a less favorable attitude toward the advertising vehicle — the Web page. Surprisingly, this is not the case. There are two plausible explanations. First, according to Bruner and Kumar (2000), people tend to perceive complex Web pages as more interesting, which may create a positive impact on attitude toward the page. In the present study, cluttered Web page was indeed rated as more interesting ($t = 3.153$, df $= 129$, $p < .01$). Therefore, the increased interestingness may cancel out the negative effect of the clutter.

Another possibility is that the student subjects used in this study — all were active Internet users, with an average of four years of online experience, spending three hours online per day — are in general more robust against the use of animated graphics because animation is such a common practice in the online environment, especially in Hong Kong. As a result, subjects did not perceive the Web page cluttered with animation as less favorable. Replicating the study using different subjects may reveal whether participant characteristics make a difference.

This study failed to identify the effect of context clutter at the level of brand evaluation. According to the hierarchy-of-effects theories, effects on or beyond the brand evaluation level are naturally more difficult to achieve. Besides, the use of a fictitious brand and the one-shot exposure design also may account for the lack of significant differences in brand attitude and purchase intent. Using a fictitious brand may avoid introducing any individual bias about the brand to the study (Shamdasani et al. 2001). However, as the target brand is unknown to the subjects, it is difficult to establish a relationship with a brand by a one-shot exposure. Multiple exposure (across time) of the target ad, or using an existing brand together with a pre- and post-test experimental design may alleviate the problem.

In addition, the absence of context effect on brand evaluation could be related to the way the hypotheses were constructed. The present study hypothesized that context clutter would directly affect attitude toward the brand. However, effects on the brand evaluation level might have been mediated by other factors (e.g., attitude toward the ad) and thus no direct effect of context clutter on brand evaluation could be observed. As attitude toward the ad has been postulated to be a mediating variable in the process through which advertising affects attitude toward the brand as well as purchase intent (Belch, Lutz, and MacKenzie 1986), future studies should look into the mediating effect of attitude toward the ad to better understand whether context clutter affects brand attitude and purchase intent.

The Effect of Advertising Repetition

Subjects in this study demonstrated more favorable attitudes toward a repeated ad, occupying two ad spots, than a stand-alone ad. It seems repetition does allow viewers to process an advertising message (online and offline) more thoroughly and results in more favorable attitude toward the ad. In other words, this relatively new media buying strategy effectively enhances advertising effectiveness.

This study found no effect of advertising repetition on the brand evaluation level. As Giles and Rao (1995) found a positive effect of advertising repetition on relative brand preference and purchase intent for a familiar brand in a pre- and post- experimental design, future research may follow suit.

An interesting finding is that ad repetition creates a more favorable attitude toward the Web page. Most research investigated how context affects ad evaluation. Our finding seemed to suggest that the relationship could also be the other way around — the ad may affect context evaluation as well. One of the possible explanations is that the repeated target ad could serve as the focal point for attention. People exposed to the abundant information on a Web page would naturally focus on the most dominant element on the page and the existence of a focal point may make viewers feel comfortable and thus have better evaluation of the page. Further research should investigate this relationship to better understand how advertisements in return affect how people perceive an advertising vehicle.

Practical Implications

The results also carry practical and actionable implications for advertising practitioners and Web publishers. While many Web designers utilize animation to create visual effects, a highly cluttered context may actually induce undesirable effects on attitude toward the ad. On the other hand, the benefit of buying two advertising units for the same ad on a single Web page — a relatively new online media buying strategy — has gained empirical support, because ad repetition creates a positive impact on ad and Web page evaluations. Internet advertisers may maximize advertising effectiveness by replicating their ads on a relatively simple Web page. Web publishers may consider refraining from overusing animated graphics and may sell ad space on a less cluttered Web page at higher rates.

Overall, this study contributes to advertising research by investigating how context clutter and ad repetition affect advertising effectiveness on a new advertising medium, the Internet. This study also takes into consideration the unique characteristics of the online medium. Although not all the hypotheses were supported, the effects of context clutter and ad repetition on advertising effectiveness have been documented. The findings would serve as the groundwork for future research on Internet advertising effectiveness.

Limitation of Current Research

This study was conducted in a laboratory setting and thus suffers from the external validity problem inherent in experimental design. In the laboratory, subjects were asked to scrutinize every item on the Web page — something they normally would not do in the real world. In addition, they were not given the chance to interact with the Web page by clicking on the hyperlinks. Therefore, one should keep in mind the plausible impact of the artificial setting on the subjects' responses to the online ad when interpreting the results.

In addition, content clutter was operationalized as the number of animated graphics with the assumption that animation is the major cause of distraction. But other factors such as color, typeface, font size, and ad formats may also constitute context clutter. Future research should investigate whether different dimensions of context clutter also affect advertising effectiveness.

Notes

1. They are: www.esdlife.com, www.mingpaonews.com, www.appledaily. com.hk, www.yahoo.com.hk, www.hongkong.com, www.msn.com.hk, www.netvigator.com, www.sina.com.hk, etc.
2. The average was 3.91.

References

Aylesworth, A. B. and MacKenzie, S. B. (1998). "Context is key: The effect of program-induced mood on thoughts about the ad". *Journal of Advertising* 27 (2): 17–31.

Batra, R. and Ray, M. L. (1986). "Situational effects of advertising repetition: The moderating influence of motivation, ability, and opportunity to respond". *Journal of Consumer Research* 12 (4): 432–445.

Bayan, R. (2001). "Banner ads — still working after all these years?" *Link-Up* 18 (6): 2–8.

Belch, G. E., Lutz, R. J., and MacKenzie, S. B. (1986). "The role of attitude toward the ad as a mediator of advertising effectiveness: A test of competing explanations". *Journal of Marketing Research* 23 (May): 130–143.

Berger, I. E. and Mitchell, A. A. (1989). "The effect of advertising on attitude accessibility, confidence, and the attitude-behavior relationship". *Journal of Consumer Research* 16 (Dec): 269–279.

Briggs, R. and Hollis, N. (1997). "Advertising on the Web: Is there response before click-through?" *Journal of Advertising Research* March/April: 33–45.

Brown, S. P. and Stayman, D. M. (1992). "Antecedents and consequences of attitude toward the ad: A meta-analysis". *Journal of Consumer Research* 19 (1): 34–51.

Bruner II, G. C. and Kumar, A. (2000). "Web commercials and advertising hierarchy-of-effects". *Journal of Advertising Research* January/April: 35–42.

Campbell, M. C. and Keller, K. L. (2003). "Brand familiarity and advertising repetition effects". *Journal of Consumer Research* 30 (September): 292–304.

Cho, C. H. (1999). "How advertising works on the WWW: Modified elaboration likelihood model". *Journal of Current Issues and Research in Advertising* 21 (1): 33–50.

———. (2003). "The effectiveness of banner advertisement: Involvement and click-through". *Journalism and Mass Communication Quarterly* 80 (3): 623–645.

——— and Leckenby, J. D. (2000). *The Effectiveness of banner advertisements: Involvement and click-through.* Paper presented to the Advertising Division at the annual convention of the Association for Education in Journalism and Mass Communication, Phoenix, AZ, August 9–12, 2000.

Colly, R. H. (1961). *Defining Advertising Goals for Measured Advertising Results.* New York: Association of National Advertisers.

Coulter, K. S. (1998). "The effects of affective responses to media context on advertising evaluations". *Journal of Advertising* 27 (4): 41–51.

Dahlen, M. (2001). "Banner advertisements through a new lens". *Journal of Advertising Research* 41 (4): 23–30.

Elliott, M. T. and Speck P. S. (1998). "Consumer perceptions of advertising clutter and its impact across various media". *Journal of Advertising Research* 38 (1): 29–41.

Giles, D. S. and Rao, R. C. (1995). "Can repeating an advertisement more frequently than the competition affect brand preference in a mature market?" *Journal of Marketing* 59 (2). Accessed on 15 July, 2004, from *ProQuest* Database.

Ha, L. (1996). "Observations: Advertising clutter in consumer magazines: Dimension and effects". *Journal of Advertising Research* 36 (4): 76–85.

Hawkins, S. A. and Hoch, S. J. (1992). "Low involvement learning: Memory without evaluation". *Journal of Consumer Research* 19 (September): 212–225.

Heo, N. and Sundar, S. S. (2000). *Emotional responses to Web advertising*. Paper presented at the Advertising Division of the annual convention of the Association for Education in Journalism and Mass Communication, Phoenix.

Interactive Advertising Bureau (2003). "IAB/ PWC release final full year 2002 Internet ad revenue figures". Accessed on 15 July, 2004, from http://www.iab.net/news/pr_2003_6_12.asp.

———. (2004). Internet ad revenue report, Quarter 1 2004. Accessed on 15 July, 2004, from http://www.iab.net/news/pr_2004_5_24.asp.

Kamins, M., Marks, L. J., and Skinner D. (1991). "Television commercial evaluation in the context of program induced mood: Congruency versus consistency effects". *Journal of Advertising* 20 (2): 1–14.

Kent, R. J. (1993). "Competitive versus noncompetitive clutter in television advertising". *Journal of Advertising Research* 33 (2). Accessed on 15 July, 2004, from *ProQuest* Database.

Lang, A., Borse, J., Wise, K., and David, P. (2002). "Captured by the World Wide Web: Orienting to structural and content features of computer-presented information". *Communication Research* 29 (3): 215–245.

Lee, S. Y. and Sundar, S. S. (2002). *Psychological effects of frequency and clutter in Web advertising*. Paper presented at the 52nd annual conference of the International Communication Association (ICA), Seoul, Korea.

Li, H. and Bukovac, J. L. (1999). "Cognitive impact of banner ad characteristics: An experimental study". *Journalism and Mass Communication Quarterly* 76 (2): 314–353.

McGuire, W. J. (1978). "An information-processing model of advertising effectiveness". In H. L. Davis and A. H. Silk (eds.), *Behavioral and Management Sciences in Marketing*, pp. 156–180. New York: Ronald.

Norris, C. E. and Colman, A. M. (1992). "Context effects on recall and recognition of magazine advertisements". *Journal of Advertising* 21 (3): 37–47.

Pechmann, C. and Stewart, D. W. (1989). "Advertising repetition: A critic review of wearin and wearout". *Current Issues & Research in Advertising* 11: 1–2, 285–330.

Shamdasani, P. N., Stanaland, A. J., and Tan, J. (2001). "Location, location, location: Insights for advertising placement on the Web". *Journal of Advertising Research* 41 (4): 7–21.

Sharma, A. (2000). "Recall of television commercials as a function of viewing context: The impact of program-commercial congruity on commercial messages". *Journal of General Psychology* 127 (4): 383–397.

Stevenson, J. S, Bruner II, G. C., and Kumar, A. (2000). "Webpage background and viewer attitudes". *Journal of Advertising Research* 40 (1/ 2): 29–35.

Sundar, S. S. and Kalyanaraman, S. (2004). "Arousal, memory, and impression-formation effects of animation speed in web advertising". *Journal of Advertising* 33 (1): 7–17.

Webb, P. H. and Ray, M. L. (1979). "Effects of TV clutter". *Journal of Advertising Research* 19 (June): 7–12.

Weilbacher, W. M. (2001). "Point of view: Does advertising cause a 'hierarchy of effects'?" *Journal of Advertising Research* 41 (6): 19–26.

8

—ᴍ—

Questioning Dis-intermediation: Rethinking the Internet's Political Economy

Korinna Patelis

The Dis-intermediation Narrative

The dis-intermediation narrative of the communication technologies in our society was developed throughout the first decade of the Internet's development as a result of the dominant trend and policy of re-regulation. It refers to a social discourse that claims an urgent need of access and infrastructure with the latter heavily regulated without paying serious heed to the content that mediated the public. The narrative was enthusiastically brought out during the 1990s through the dot.com bubble years and paved the way to the re-regulation of info-telecommunications industries worldwide. By the late 1990s with less than 4 percent of the world's population on-line, just about everybody accepted that existing barriers to entry to the Internet market threatened the web's equilibrium.[1] The Achilles heel of the dis-intermediation narrative was identified by policy makers worldwide: exclusion. Exclusion was carefully absorbed into the narrative. Later, the term digital divide, coined by American policy makers, was gradually incorporated in debate to address the issue and ensure that balance in the Web, and it quickly became an incremental part of the dominant policy approach allegedly countering political economy skepticism. Like sustainable development, interest in the environment, world peace and many other clichéd policy goals, the digital divide has now become a world problem. It is being addressed on an UN level and receives attention on a national level as well as supra national funding. Exclusion is therefore enshrined in the dis-intermediation narrative, establishing, that universal access to the Internet is the cure for the ills besetting the Internet's development, an imperative policy goal. The underlying assertion is that once the digital gap narrows, the Internet market will actually work perfectly.[2] The idea is that despite concerns with equality, the Internet is essentially a democratic, chaotic library under construction, a paradise of knowledge were every body can encounter anything once the gates are wide open to all of us; the technological grid which will grow through our contribution and participation. The narrative only allows for disagreement with regard to how this grid will expand, not on whether the end alleged end ideal — the digital free market of ideas — is actually desirable or plausible. Policy makers might disagree on how exactly the Internet might reach the point were it embodies the market, were the information society will be realized, but most agree that this is the teleology. The idea is that if we could actually make it work, the Internet, will provide us with the technological solution to social issues. This in turn verifies the underlying policy assertion that one needn't take a look at on-line communications per se to actually understand the Internet. The conceptual leap required to subscribe to this line of argument is the conflation of anarchy with pluralism, the idea that since the Web appears to be vast and its content randomly distributed, there is no point in taking a further look at it.

The dis-intermediation narrative has been widely criticized over and over again; in the mid-90s by authors adopting a radical political economy perspective (McChesney 1996, 1999; Elmer 2000; Rogers 2000; Patelis 2000; Schiller 1996, 1999; Schiller and McChesney 2001), later on by the various critical media scholars. The plethora and heterogeneity of criticisms voiced formed the counter approach to new media, an approach which argues that new media do in fact mediate communications — hence the term new media (Buttler 1999; Manovitch 2001). These critical approaches set out to examine the specific ways in which each medium does actually refashion communications: how hybrid forms the communication flows are being constituted, and how narrative structures are being produced. The re-mediation approach forms the basis of the majority of research in media studies. This paper is situated within this effort to approach new media critically.

Despite its predominance in research, the idea that new media and in our case the Internet, re-mediate communications is still largely marginal outside the realm of media studies. Policy and industry are oblivious to any criticism voiced in the Ivory Tower. Policy documents worldwide accept the dis-intermediation narrative uncritically adopting its key assumptions and reproducing them. This in turn reshapes Internet related markets. Indicative of this blindness is the term used to refer to new media policy. In the name of technological convergence nobody refers to "media policy" anymore; or to "new media policy" for that matter. The term "information society policy" is usually used hand in hand with the term "communications" as if mass media suddenly got abolished, and our world has already become unmediated. The paragraphs below critically analyze the ways in which mediation has been excluded from the regulatory agenda prior to 9/11 events. Such exclusion is proving to be incredibly problematic in with regard to understanding, controversial issues, such as "terrorism."

The Information Society Regulatory Paradigm

The dis-intermediation narrative lies at the heart of the current regulatory paradigm for the info-telecommunications sector.[3] The paradigm consolidated in the late nineties after a series of heated policy debates particularly in the E.U.,[4] under a substantially different political reality worldwide. In this paper this paradigm is referred to as the information society paradigm, a name policy makers routinely give to it, but is used here without really accepting that there is such a thing as the information society. The majority of info-telecommunication polices worldwide, particularly in the U.S. and in the E.U. are formulated within the information society paradigm,[5] despite anti-terrorist legislation. The declaration of principles in the UN organised world summit on the information society is a typical example, as is the E.U. Regulatory Framework for Communications, or the Millennium Digital copyright Act (WSIS 2003; E.U. 2002). The paradigm consolidates pivotal shifts in media policy, particularly for Western European media and the legacy of public service media; these are discussed throughout this paper.

The paradigm asserts and builds on an extremely illusive image: the creation of a huge highway, a technologically enabled labyrinth like free market place, a grid that carries just about everything. The information society is a place were individuals are all connected with each other through enabling technologies, they can freely exchange words, photos, images, all these things that are now digitised matter. The network forming the backbone of this information-saturated society is the Internet which forms a huge highway network where goods and services are carried across quickly fairly and easily. What is being carried is irrelevant, what is relevant is how it is being carried. Like real highways it is one that matters not what rides it. This image of the great info highway comes to replace the image of saturated commercial broadcasting. Fluidity and randomness come to replace structures and media driven agendas.

With this image as the end goal, broadly speaking within the information society paradigm info-telecommunication markets are being re-engineered vis-à-vis a set of policies which allegedly "protect" the workings of the free market. Three key type of policies are involved in this re-engineering: firstly, policies aiming at the safeguarding of private (mostly intellectual) property, secondly policies establishing at least some universal access mechanisms for consumers, thirdly policies that dismantle existing content regulation of any type, across media platforms. So the paradigm demands strict regulations on patenting and copyright and relatively inclusive pricing schemes for accessing the info-telecommunication infrastructure, and no regulation when it comes to content. Key issues in media policy are neatly excluded from the regulatory agenda and are substituted by concerns previously voiced with regard to non-media markets. So for example concern with universal access and pricing mechanisms (inclusion) replaces concern with pluralism. The implicit assumption behind this substitution is that the universal access automatically leads to pluralism since giving more people access to the Internet will automatically increase the number of people transmitting their opinions on-line and thus pluralize the Web. Pluralism is therefore defined in quantitative terms, to mean plural. By the same token ownership rules are relaxed [6] and intellectual property regulation replaces previous funding mechanisms offered to new markets entrants as it is assumed that intellectual property provides with the financial incentive for production. Finally concern with state censorship is replaced by privacy concerns.

A Critique from a Political Economy Perspective

What I would like to pinpoint in this paper is that the information society policy paradigm essentially extends some assumptions embedded in the regulation of U.S. communications and establishes an association between the free market communications regulation and new media.[7] A number quasi-neoliberal assumptions lie at the heart of the paradigm. These have been criticised over and over from political economists (e.g. Ramsey 1987) way before the Internet became commercialised, and after its commercialisation. In radical political economy of the mass media authors have repeatedly argued that Internet communications are not formulated in the some virtual democratic realm but reflect existing socio economic inequalities across the globe. Finally some argue that electronic commerce and electronic communication should not co-exist because they serve different needs for our societies, and therefore should be regulated by different frameworks as they are with other media.

At the heart of the paradigm, it ignores existing offline communication power and structures[8]. There is growing concern that the Internet will magnify existing communications inequalities instead of the opposite. The framework pays no attention to the fact that most content is actually produced by a few companies around the world, that there is media concentration affecting the content available online. In doing so of course it is unable to explain why specific websites are more popular than others. It also ignores that fact that most content produced in the world is actually copyrighted and already owned by media conglomerates. In the following analysis, I am going to discuss the problem of the paradigm in terms of content, access and those few intermediate companies that dictate the use of the Internet nowadays.

What Is Content?

First, within the information society paradigm there is very little concern with content. In refusing to acknowledge that communications are public, the paradigm holds content to be unimportant. Content becomes the inconsequential inner bit of a well rapped data packet. The Internet is simply a network that treats content as the object of exchange within the information society paradigm. Its exchange value is all that regulation acknowledges. Its sign and use value are irrelevant for society they are only relevant to the parties involved in the specific exchange of this specific content object. Policy abstracts substance from the term content. Policy is primarily interested in the property function of content. The paradigm is content blind. It equates new media with technology refusing to actually acknowledge that what is being regulated is not some pure form of technology. This is achieved in three key ways: first content is not mentioned or defined; secondly infrastructure is placed at the center of policy, and finally the term "information" replaces the term "content."

Nowadays, information society documents are also almost exclusively concerned with the so called infrastructure[9]. As mentioned earlier, infrastructure and access to infrastructure services is their primary focus to such an extent that content is often not mentioned. Policies focus more on cables, telecommunications, and networks and goes hand in hand with constant references to e-commerce and security. The issue is always whether the network is accessible and secure. On the most basic quantitative level there is very little reference to the term "content" in information society policy documents worldwide.

There is also the problem of definition of content. As a matter of fact, the term content is never defined. To take an example: is a press release reproduced in plain text on a web page content? Are the pages displaying results for the word "terrorism" on Goggle content? Are menus content? And if yes, who is the author of this content? In not defining content the paradigm fails to make regulatory and conceptual distinctions between the different types of content and as well as their functions. Such distinctions could actually be extremely useful in understanding on-line communication. Even the most obvious distinctions do not exist. For instance, isn't e-commerce content different from e-communications content like in the off-line world? Should they co-exist? This key argument is better understood through an analogy. The off-line equivalent of the perverse extension of advertorials on the web (actually buying a product whilst reading an advertorial — a key feature in numerous sites) would be the opportunity to buy a product during newscasts; or to buy a book on a telemarketing channel and at the same time contributing to a political campaign (this was actually possible on Amazon.com during the U.S. primaries 2004) or of being in a library reading about a type of sailing boat and be informed you can actually buy it on the spot. Shouldn't all these different types of content and service be distinct? Why are they distinct in the offline world? Replacing the example of the boat with the example of any weapon places the problem in perspective for those that would treat political economy anxiety with scepticism.

That references to the term "content" are sporadic is also due to the fact that the term "content" is often substituted with the term "information." There is an underlying assertion that "content" refers to something subjective whereas "information" refers to something objective, some tangible thing exchanged through enabling technologies, in short an object, unmediated and pure. The visual metaphor with which the windows operating system operates strengthens this assertion. Information is more real, more usable, and less constructed. So this distinction is useful to regulation in that it attempts to naturalise the idea the content is an object.

Access, Infrastructure and the Dis-intermediation Narrative

Second, the neat distinction between infrastructure and content defines the way in which access is perceived of with the information society paradigm. Access is defined in very narrow terms within the dis-intermediation narrative; by access to the Internet the narrative literally refers to material, to electricity, cables and PC. Access basically is synonymous to access to the Internet infrastructure. So a so called terrorist has access to the Internet if he/she can formally access the network. Similarly we have access to a terrorist web site if this is actually posted on-line irrespective on whether it actually visible through navigational tools.

This formal definition does not allow for a distinction between access to post information and access to receive information. This is reflected in the way access is actually measured. Predictably enough the global reports inquiring upon the term access almost never ask users whether this access actually includes the web's most celebrated features interactivity producing and posting content. Even major surveys published by E.U. and U.S. include information with regard to what type of content people do actually contribute to the web but only includes information on what they consume. The opposite is actually true of survey on business use. In fact we know very little about the people that produce content. Those reports that measure how much people contribute content have found that the portion of Internet users contributing content is a small minority of those using the web[10].

A political economy of the Internet which accepts this narrative would now proceed to give you an account of those who has access to the Internet and who has not what type of access is this access and so on. Indeed, unlike 5–7 years ago there are now plenty of studies from official sources providing data on ICT penetration and the divide. To an extent these provide us with an idea of the material boundaries within which on-line communication can occur.

In 2002 in the U.S. 53.6 percent[11] of the population was using the Internet. The EU average was lower with 40.4% of households with Internet penetration.[12]

Internet penetration rates really vary according to economic development and geopolitical position. We can take the E.U. as an example. The table above shows the percentage of households with

Internet Penetration in Households 2000–02

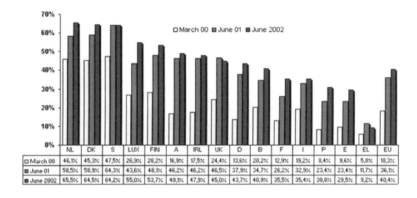

Source: European Commission (Eurobarometer)

Internet access in E.U. (prior to the enlargement). Note that there are countries in which Internet access is actually decreased. Britain and Greece (by 4 percent and 1 percent respectively). In general there is a north and south divide Southern EU countries have poor record of access, 30 for Spain, and Portugal and a really low 9.2 percent for Greece.

Info rich and poor are also divided because of income and literacy levels. For example access to the Internet in the U.S. depends on income. In 2002 according to the U.S government[13] 75.0 percent of people who live in households where income is less than $15,000 and 66.6 percent of those in households with incomes between $15,000 and $35,000 did not have access to the Internet. Education is also a huge issue. In the U.S. for example adults with low levels of overall education — 60.2 percent of adults (age 25 +) with only a high school degree and 87.2 percent of adults with less than a high school education. In countries where penetration rates are high ethnic origin in combination with knowledge of the English language is also a factor. For example 68.4 percent of all Hispanics and 85.9 percent of Hispanic households in the U.S. do not have access to the Internet.

What type of connection we have to the Internet also makes a difference. In the U.S. 80 percent of people access the Internet through dial up service but 11 percent have broadband access. According to one EU 16 percent of standard telephone lies are the access point for 72 percent of respondents and 16 with ISDN lines. Finally where do people can get access of the Internet is of major importance. To a large extent it influences the use we make as we are contracted to not make certain uses of the network by those providing the access. There is public use, private use and corporate use depending on the access point available. So for example personal use is not permitted in major business around the world. The consumption of pornographic material is prohibited in some access points. In Europe for example 71 percent of users use the Internet from home, 11 percent from public access places (and this has decreased in most countries) and 42 percent from offices. Access to the Internet grows as infrastructure develops through telecommunications investment and also as income level grows. In the late 90s there was evidence that showed that Internet use would grow at an amazing rate. The U.S. provides the best example with Internet usage rate growth of 20 percent annually since 1998 (Nation 2002). Statistics from Europe defy this evidence as Internet penetration is reaching a plateau of growth. Internet penetration rates doubled between 2001 and 2001 from 18 percent to 36 percent but grew by a mere 2 percent in the same year (BARO 2002).

E-mediaries and the World We Live in

Third, the distinction of content and carriage is an illusive assumption since it is actually impossible to distinguish between the two. This is mainly because software is both infrastructure and content and software is what on-line content is made off. Software constructs and distributes content on-line. Software is part of a wider system of taxonomy that operates on-line. This taxonomy weaves the web's infrastructure tight with its content, to such an extent, unlike other media, that it is actually impossible to distinguish between the two. In other words the web re-mediates through a complex system of taxonomy. This system of taxonomy has extraordinary mediating power both in quantitative and in qualitative terms. It potentially mediates the navigation of 1 billion users. This taxonomy firstly, assigns hierarchy to different content elements, and secondly defines the boundaries within which navigation must occur. It sets the limits of the narrative, and when the narrative is about terrorism we can understand how important this agenda setting affect actually is. This taxonomy is constituted by the interplay of various entities, what we could call e-mediators. On-line communications is compromised by a complex system of e-mediators. By an "e-mediator" one refers to an entity or process, which mediates the on-line experience imposing any kind of structure; that is a force that intervenes between the user and on-line content. By doing so it compromises the medium's promise of transparency and freedom; it interrupts the potential for direct exchange embedded in on-line communication. E-mediators are also the distributors of the Internet industry.

E-mediators include:

- Software
- Navigational tools: software that allow us to retrieve files over the Internet

- Filtering devices: software does not allow the retrieval of certain files
- Internet Service Providers
- Information brokers: companies that provide users with information chunked into smaller segments
- Portal sites: sites that are gateways to other sites
- Search engines: robots that crawl web sites
- Catalogues and indexes

The Web's taxonomy system assigns hierarchy to the different nodes of information one could encounter on-line and by doing so structures the on-line communication. It provides the narrative backbone of content. There are two dimensions to e-mediation, firstly there is structuration through the production of intertextuality, secondly there is structuration through classification. So in other words e-mediaries limit the supply of content by firstly adding a structured textual component and secondly by classifying information and adding layers of representation. This means that software and DNS constitute the Web's main navigation interface. Aside from these there are other e-mediaries which structure our on-line experience. These are mainly information brokers, that is companies that add structure to information by mining, indexing, cataloguing and classifying it; providing information on information is their key business. The workings of all these different type of e-mediaries intertwine and mix, re-mediating the web. The remediation process in which e-mediaries are involved is composed of the workings of each e-mediaries separately but actually constitutes one unified process and thus should be analyzed as such. So for example if we were examine how terrorist content is affected by this process we would have to look at the users client software, the software the content is written on, the software (usually a navigation tool) through which it becomes available and how the term terrorism is distributed through the current domain naming system.

E-mediaries are companies that develop services and products building on the simple fact that information and content available in a space is not accessible unless it is organized in some way. It is only through such organizational structure that the actual content differs from an amorphous bubble and can thus be of value. This is how a warehouse differs from a library. In a library information is classified, segmented, indexed and archived rationally so that users can find it more easily. Records summing up the content of information objects are produced so that users do not have to read through the entire range of material available to find that which is relevant. Information retrieval existed long before the Web was invented. Practically speaking it is actually impossible to organize material without applying some form of hierarchy, that is without assuming that some information is more important than others. In librarianship hierarchy is provided by well thought out methods that have been applied for decades for example the Dewey Decimal System of Classification. Information retrieval is based on cataloguing and indexing objects. These processes have traditionally been carried out by skilled professionals at a very high cost. Creating one single record for an item in a library or museum for example can cost $50 (Arms 2001:154). The indexes on the back of a book take up time to produce, for every index we find so useful there has been a librarian that has agonized over its creation. Non-automated indexing is of better quality than any other: the processing power, sophistication and detail that a human being can use to classify goes well beyond a computers ability to match a word with another. Humans understand meaning not form. Despite this due to the high cost of paying humans to index as well as the increasing quantity of information that needs to be catalogued computers are being increasingly used to automate the indexing and the information retrieval process.

The Web is no exception. The same logic applies to on-line content. Without some form of organization Internet content would be nothing more than an anarchic maze. We would not have the time to surf all Web pages and we would be lost in an infinite labyrinth. Time limitations add to the need for some structure as we cannot be surfing endlessly. So some entity has to set the boundaries of the user's on-line experience in order for the Internet to be used at all within existing time and other limits. As Fuller mentions: "Users need the interface to narrow their attention and choices so they can find the information and actions they need at any particular time. Real life is highly moded" (Fuller 1998). So even if it were possible to built software and other e-mediators that were technically transparent, and would thus to allow us to experience an infinite amount of content, this would not be possible because our time is limited, and thus we could not possibly experience an infinite amount of content. So theoretically the need for some organization of Internet content exists. In cyberspace the need for such organization has been appropriated by companies brokering information in various ways. Classification as a line of business has proven to be profitable. It is attracting audiences.

Software, DNS and Search Engines

The most basic structure that influences on-line communication by providing the basic text within which we read any computer mediated communication is the interface. It would be impossible to cover this issue within the constraints of this paper, though one has to mention that: every time a user logs on-line he has already made certain assumptions about information and how this is stored and manipulated in his/her pc. These assumptions do not often receive attention but nevertheless remain instrumental in structuring the on-line experience. Any interface and thus a piece of software is not transparent: it represents information and, in doing so, it essentially constructs information. Software and thus operating systems are culture, they are cultural texts, they mirror set assumptions about the world. Software is representation. Software constitutes a visual language and this, like any language, is structured. Software provides the cultural environment, the net material constraints and framework within which on-line communication can occur. This is a framework that reflects certain assumptions about users and the nature of information and, by doing so, reproduces such assumptions. For example it might strip an experience down to one or two components, namely the purely textual component of language like chat room software, or do the opposite.

Companies offering information retrieval services on the Web cash in on the fact that under the current DNS it is difficult to know the exact URL of an on-line resource and thus search engines are literally the only way millions of users world-wide can find what they are after.

Increasing reliance on search engines also partly stems from the construction of the Internet as a vast and chaotic landscape which search engines to an extent promise to make more usable. Many sites offering search services have evolved into portals and many portals offer search engines. Search engines have thus become gateways to the on-line world, offering services that go beyond merely indexing web pages. Search engines are more than on-line yellow pages. Attention to available on-line resources is distributed by search engines and consequently search engines are of paramount importance in structuring the on-line experience. Search engines are then one of the most important pieces of software that mediates and changes our web experience. Search engines perform automated searches for the retrieval of particular on-line material; essentially functioning like catalogues of available resources. Take the example of Yahoo that officially claims to be an "aggregator of content." Yahoo claims that its services are used by something like 219 million unique consumers, with 86 million of these registered 13 languages generating revenues of 717 million dollars.

Search engines have received little academic attention and their function is often considered to be technical, an operational matter of allocating attention to different Web-sites. Such a perception is in striking contradiction to popular wisdom in business circles according to which the exposure and inclusion of a Web site in search engine database is the primary task of on-line promotion and distribution. In fact placing a web site in search engine databases is itself a line of business; part of on-line advertising packages. Consider the following advert, for example: "SalesSecrets.com is in the business of providing the Industry's leading Search Engine Submission services. Our packages are geared towards businesses that are serious about not only putting their sites on Search Engines but also being at the Top of SE rankings, and seeing dramatic increases in Web traffic." (SalesSecrets.com). This line of business is based on knowledge on part of companies that search engines do not distribute all web pages of all parties on a equal basis. This is simply because search engines do not index all web pages and furthermore they do not rank results alphabetically or randomly.

The "Terrorism" Taxonomy

Because life is highly moderated by time, information brokers have gained amazing power on the Web. Categories have become ways of classifying content and the narrative backbone of web communications. The system of taxonomy however has been produced in an arbitrary first come first serve basis. It is not really systemic though it is obviously amazingly powerful. It sets the agenda for millions of Internet users but the problem is that the power to set this agenda is purely dependant on the power to remediate. This power is actually financially defined.[14]

This system of taxonomy becomes extremely important at times of geopolitical crisis. Contemplate, all of the above in relation to term "terrorism." The term terrorism compromises two qualities that seem perfect to test the taxonomy system described above: on the one hand there is no consensus in defining it. On the other it is the most controversial category for searching as it is very closely linked to a type of content that is considered criminal. It provides us with a pure example of the problems of disintermediation: a type of content that is not necessarily well defined and is considered dangerous is being randomly distributed through the webs commercial taxonomy.

For example, "terrorist" content is in fact unlikely to be visible within the Internet's current taxonomy system. When it is visible this is purely accidental. It is usually the automatic translation of off-line power to on-line power. Let's look at some examples. I would like to find out more about terrorism, without knowing a specific site that could provide me with terrorist content (whatever that might be), I would be likely to go to a search engine and run a search for terrorism. According to Google there are 8,740,000 websites that include some reference or information or content about terrorism on the web. Out of these the majority 8,270,000 have the word terrorism in their title. Out of these only 3,370 are in Arabic, 43,800 have terrorism in their title in the org domain, and out of these only 19 are in Arabic. There are 139,000 pages in the .com domain that have the term terrorism in their title. Out of these, only 16 are in Arabic where all others are in English. Nobody knows anything about these sites and nobody regulates access to them. Most importantly if I actually wanted some independent information about what terrorism is, I would not know which of these available sites share the best information!

The Critique of Information Society Problem and the Worry about Terrorism

The above described shifts are conceptually based on the idea of dis-intermediation. They fundamentally rely on the assumption that the

Internet is not a media but technology, meaning it does not re-mediate social meaning, it dis-intermediates meaning all together. The Internet is defined as technology that allows for direct access and fair exchange of pure meaning- of information, an exchange mechanism for independent signs, and a distribution platform of signs with no fixed signification. These pivotal policy shifts have re-regulated the info-telecommunications sector in radical ways. What has essentially been undermined is the idea that the message of communication matters to regulators and by extension to our society. What the paradigm essentially does is assert that communication is a private individual right, as opposed to a public good. This conceptual shift is phenomenal. The paradigm essentially deprives content of its flesh as it refuses to even acknowledge that content is not like any other product and it should not and cannot be regulated as if it is an object. In doing so it builds on the idea that there is in fact some new media void out there, a neat place were commercial global media have no power. This information society essentially gets rid of all issues with regard to the power to mediate; any idea of an agenda setting affect threatening pluralism becomes irrelevant. It essentially presents us an image of a loosely fragmented network of individuals that just exchange objects amongst each other. Once this is done any regulation occurs with regard to one specific exchange. Communication is therefore defined in negative terms: communications freedom from external restrictions, not freedom to communicate.

Because of 9/11 events, suddenly regulation has assumed its interest in one type of content. This despite the fact there is no regulatory paradigm that would make it feasible to recognise the difference between different types of content, let alone regulate them. Suddenly all of this illusion of freedom has to be contained within an anti-terrorist legislative framework, and thus exclude certain exchanges between sovereign parties, exclude that is so called "terrorist" related content and services.

I would like to suggest that this interest is actually contained within the information society paradigm. It merely cements the pivotal shift that has occurred. It is a different type of interest in content. It is an interest in a specific content object. Thus because it merely restricts what can be exchanged, it remains indifferent to the public need for independently produced, non-commercial content on terrorism. The anti-terrorist legislation passed in the U.S. as well as the one in the E.U. does not change the substance of the monumental conceptual shift in the regulation of communications. It does not suddenly assert that there is a need for a public sphere to discuss terrorism, accepting that they were wrong and maybe we did need some public service funded media for the web. On the contrary, legislation targets terrorist criminals but still remains unwilling to actually take a look at the function on-line communication has for society. Criminal content is considered to be the equivalent to exchanging an object that should not be exchanged like drugs or a real bomb. Legislators want to regulate communications as private not as public. This is why it is so hard to actually produce arguments against this censorship. Once you accept that freedom of speech is a negative right, the freedom from as opposed to freedom to, then speech looses its publicness. The result is a commercially saturated mess[15]: no official sources to find out more about terrorism, plenty of unofficial ones, commercially sponsored sites, and just a general randomness. An illusive dis-intermediated space were terrorist content is produced by official sources, so called terrorist sources and commercial companies. Is that the end goal?

Conclusion

The web is characterized by dis-intermedation. On the contrary there is a system of taxonomy distributing content remediating for users. The current regulatory paradigm is blind to this process. As a result despite its interest in content related to "terrorism" it cannot really regulate this. A regulatory regime that acknowledges the workings of e-mediation on-line and potentially funds independently run autonomous e-mediators is needed for the web to exit its current state of random commercial distribution.

Notes

1. The way in which access to the Internet is actually measured is problematic as is the notion of an Internet user. Variables and definitions vary. This article discusses the ways in which Internet use has actually been measured, in the paragraphs discussing the term access.

The figure quoted here is that one appearing at the NUA website at NUA.com back in 1999 under the category demographics.

2. The term digital divide was coined by the US Department of Commerce in the late nineties and appeared in the title of reports measuring the penetration of Internet use in the U.S. such as for example the one issue in 1998 tiled Falling through the Net: new data on the Digital Divide (US 1998).

3. The regulatory documents setting out the key parameters of this paradigm are infotelecommunication specific and don't just include any policy such as the US. Patriot Act. They would include: the Telecommunications Act of 1996, the EU Communications Framework, the Digital Millennium Act, eEurope Action Plan 2002: accessibility of public websites and their content.

4. The debate on the future of European Union media unfolded between 1996–1999 reaching its peak with the controversy on the green paper for the convergence of telecommunication and media. Opposition to the so called Bangeman approach to the information-society and the re-regulation of the media industries was voiced by media theories, policy makers and practitioners alike. The viewpoints debate are still archived on the europa server, Notable responses to the green paper are the one by the BECTU (CEC 1997).

5. The paradigm was defined in the nineties in the U.S.

6. In 2003 for example the FCC recently relaxed ownership rules in the U.S. despite opposition.

7. The regulation of communication in the U.S. does not reflect one monolith tradition and it would be unfair to only pay tribute to its pro-deregulatory.

8. This was a key argument voiced by the civil society declaration on the WSIS.

9. To use the European Union as an indicative example; The new framework s for regulating communications which consolidates the policy principles set out by the so called Bangeman approach to the Information society is composed of 6 directives:

    The Framework Directive, The Access and Interconnection Directive, The Authorisation Directive, The Universal service Directive, The Data protection Directive The Consolidated Directive on Competition in the market for communications services. Content not mentioned in the titles neither is it specifically mentioned inside the documents. It is consider the peripheral thing that rides the network.

10. The PEW Center for the Internet and society recently issued a report with such finding according to which only 13% of US Internet users

have their own web page and about 17% have posted material on the a web site.

11. In order to have data that is comparable this account, I use data from 2002 that is the latest complied data for many digital excluded countries.

12. It should be noted that household figures do not represent the entire population of a country depending on the homeless rate.

13. A nation on-line — survey.

14. One could still argue that this is not true of DNS as governments have at least some say on how their top country level domains are regulated.

15. A search on any popular search engine would provide access website the first 100 of which are not any way independent sites casting independent content. A notable example would be the terror portal or even terorrism.com which is a sponsored site.

References

Boczkowski, P. (1999). "Understanding the development of online newspapers: Using computer-mediated communication theorizing to study Internet publishing". *New Media & Society* 1 (1): 101–126.

Brook, J. and Boal, I. A. (eds.) (1995). *Resisting the Virtual Life: The Culture and Politics of Information.* San Francisco: City Lights Books.

Byfield, T. (1999). "DNS: A short history and a short future". In J. Bosma, et al. (eds.), *Readme: Filtered by Nettime-ASCII Culture and the Revenge of Knowledge.* Brooklyn: Autonomedia.

Cohen, E. and Mitra, A. (1999). "Analyzing the Web; Directions and Challenges". In S. Jones (ed.), *Doing Internet Research.* London: Sage.

Coleman, S. (1999). "The New Media and Democratic Politics". *New Media & Society* 1 (1): 67–74.

Communication Rights in the Information Society (CRIS): http://www.crisinfo.org/live/index.php

Dewey, M. (1876). "Classification and Subject Index for Cataloguing and Arranging the Books and Pamplets of a Library", facsimile reprint of the 1876 edition published in Amhurst, M. A. Forest Press Division, Lake Placid Education Foundation, Lake Placid, NY.

Elmer, G. (2002). *Critical Perspectives on the Internet.* New York: Rowan and Littlefield.

Gates, B. (1996). *The Road Ahead.* London: Penguin.

Golding, P. (1998a). "Global Village or Cultural Pillage". In B. McChesney, E. M. Wood, and J. B. Foster (eds.), *Capitalism and the Information Age.* New York: Monthly Review Press.

————. (1998b). "World Wide Wedge: Division and Contradiction in the Global Information Infrastructure". In D. K. Thussu (ed.). *Electronic Empires Global Media and Local Resistance*. London: Arnold.

Goldman Sachs. (1999). *Free for All: The Evolution of Internet Access Models*. New York: Goldman Sachs Investment Research.

Hall, S. (1996). "The Problem of Ideology: Marxism without Guarantees". In D. Morley and K. H. Chen (eds.), *Stuart Hall: Critical Dialogues in Cultural Studies*. London: Routledge.

Horwitz, R. (1989). *The Irony of Regulatory Reform: The Deregulation of American Telecommunications*. New York: Oxford University Press.

————. (1997). "The First Amendment Meets Some New Technologies: Broadcasting, Common Carriers, and Free Speech in the 1990's". *Theory and Society* 20: 21–72

Jenkins, H. and Thorburn, D. (eds.). (2003). *Democracy and New Media*. MIT Press.

Larsen, S. (2003). "The WSIS: whose freedom, whose information?" Available online: opendemocracy.net.

Mattelart, A. (2003). *The Information Society: An Introduction*. London: Sage Publications.

McChesney, R. (1993). *Telecommunications, Mass Media and Democracy — The Battle for the Control of U.S. Broadcasting 1928–1935*. New York: Oxford University Press.

————. (1996). "The Internet and U.S Communication Policy-Making in the Historical and Critical Perspective". *Journal of Communications* 46 (1): 98–124.

————. (1997). *Corporate Media and the Threat to Democracy*. New York: Seven Stories Press.

————. (1998). "Political Economy of Communication". In R. W. McChesney, E. M. Wood, and J. B. Foster (eds.), *Capitalism and the Information Age*. New York: Monthly Review Press.

Noris, P. (2001). *Digital Divide: Civil Engagement, Information Poverty, and the Internet Worldwide*. Cambridge: Cambridge University Press.

Noveck, B. (2003). "Unchat: Democratic solution for a wired world". *Boston University Journal of Science and Technology Law* 9 (1) at the Yale information society server.

Pew Internet & American Life Project. (2004). "Content Creation On-line report". Available online: www.pweinternet.org (accessed on 1 May, 2004).

Winseck, D. (2002). "Illusion of the perfect information and fantasies of control in the Information Society". *New Media and Society* 4 (1): 93–122.

Official Documents (Reports and Policy)
EC. (2003). *Statistical Pocketbook on the Information Society: Key Data.* Luxembourg: Office for the Official Publications of the European Communities.

E.U. documents
CEC. (2002). "Manuscript for the information brochure for the general public: Towards a knowledge-based Europe". The European Union and the Information Society.

Commission Decision No 163/2001/EC of the European Parliament and of the Council of 19 January, 2001 on the implementation of a training programme for professionals in the European audiovisual programme industry (MEDIA-Training) (2001-2005), *OJ L 026 27.01.2001 p.1.*

Commission Decision No. 2001/148/EC of 21 February, 2001 on the application of Article 3(3) (e) of Directive 1999/5/EC to avalanche beacons (Text with EEA relevance) (notified under document number C(2001) 194), *OJ L 055 24.02.2001 p.65.*

Commission Decision No. 2002/627/EC of 29 July, 2002 establishing the European Regulators Group for Electronic Communications Networks and Services (Text with EEA relevance), *OJ L 200 30.07.2002 p.38.*

Commission Decision No. 2003/375/EC of 21 May, 2003 on the designation of the .eu Top Level Domain Registry (Text with EEA relevance) (notified under document number C(2003) 1624), *OJ L 128 24.05.2003 p.29.*

Commission Decision No. 1151/2003/EC of the European Parliament and of the Council of 16 June, 2003 amending Decision No. 276/1999/EC adopting a multiannual Community action plan on promoting safer use of the Internet by combating illegal and harmful content on global networks, *OJ L 162 01.07.2003 p.1.*

Commission Directive 2002/77/EC of 16 September, 2002 on competition in the markets for electronic communications networks and services (Text with EEA relevance), *OJ L 249 17.09.2002 p.21.*

Commission Recommendation of 20 March, 2003 on the harmonization of the provision of public R-LAN access to public electronic communications networks and services in the Community (Text with EEA relevance), *OJ L 078 25.03.2003 p.12.*

Commission Recommendation of 23 July, 2003 on notifications, time limits and consultations provided for in Article 7 of Directive 2002/21/EC of the European Parliament and of the Council on a common regulatory framework for electronic communications networks and services (Text with EEA relevance) (notified under document number C (2003) 2647), *OJ L 190 30.07.2003 p.13.*

Council Resolution of 21 January, 2002 on the development of the audiovisual sector, *OJ C 032 05.02.2002 p.4.*

Council Resolution of 1 March, 2002 on the protection of consumers, in particular young people, through the labeling of certain video games and computer games according to age group, *OJ C 065 14.03.2002 p.2.*

Council Resolution of 25 March, 2002 on the eEurope Action Plan 2002: accessibility of public websites and their content, *OJ C 086 10.04.2002 p.2.*

Council Resolution of 25 June, 2002 on preserving tomorrow's memory — preserving digital content for future generations, *OJ C 162 06.07.2002 p.4.*

Council Resolution of 19 December, 2002 on interactive media content in Europe, *OJ C 013 18.01.2003 p.8.*

Council Resolution of 18 February, 2003 on a European approach towards a culture of network and information security, *OJ C 048 28.02.2003 p.1.*

Directive 2002/22/EC of the European Parliament and of the Council of 7 March, 2002 on universal service and users' rights relating to electronic communications networks and services (Universal Service Directive), *OJ L 108 24.04.2002 p.51.*

Directive 2002/21/EC of the European Parliament and of the Council of 7 March, 2002 on a common regulatory framework for electronic communications networks and services (Framework Directive), *OJ L 108 24.04.2002 p.33.*

Directive 2002/20/EC of the European Parliament and of the Council of 7 March 2002 on the authorization of electronic communications networks and services (Authorisation Directive), *OJ L 108 24.04.2002 p.21*

Directive 2002/19/EC of the European Parliament and of the Council of 7 March, 2002 on access to, and interconnection of, electronic communications networks and associated facilities (Access Directive), *OJ L 108 24.04.2002 p.7.*

Directive 2002/58/EC of the European Parliament and of the Council of 12 July, 2002 concerning the processing of personal data and the protection of privacy in the electronic communications sector (Directive on privacy and electronic communications), *OJ L 201 31.07. 2002 p.37.*

Directive 2003/98/EC of the European Parliament and of the Council of 17 November, 2003 on the re-use of public sector information, *OJ L 345 31.12.2003 p.90.*

G-7. (1995). G-7 Ministerial Conference on the Information Society. Theme Paper, Brussels, 27 January. Available online: http://www.ispo.cec.be.

OECD. (1995). Special Session on information Infrastructures — Towards

Realization of the Information Society. Working papers, Vol. IV, No.9 Paris.

———. (1997). Global Information Infrastructure-Global Information Society. (GII-GIS): Policy Recommendations for Action, OECD/GD (97) 138 Paris.

———. (2001). Communications Outlook.

———. (2003). Communications Outlook.

Regulation (EC) No 45/2001 of the European Parliament and of the Council of 18 December, 2000 on the protection of individuals with regard to the processing of personal data by the Community institutions and bodies and on the free movement of such data Council Resolution of 3 October, 2000 on the organisation and management of the Internet *OJ C 293 14.10.2000 p.3.*

Regulation (EC) No. 733/2002 of the European Parliament and of the Council of 22 April, 2002 on the implementation of the .eu Top Level Domain (Text with EEA relevance), *OJ L 113 30.04.2002 p.1.*

U.N. (2003). "Declaration of Principles: Building the Information Society: a global challenge in the New Millenium". WSIS-03/GENEVA/DOC/ 4-E.

United States Institute for Peace. (2004). Special Report 116.

US Congress. (1934). *The Communications Act of 1934*, 47 U.S.C. Available online: www.firstgov.gov.

———. (1996). *The Telecommunications Act of 1996*, Pub. LA. No. 104-104, 110 Stat. 5. Available on: http://www.fcc.gov/Reports/tcom1996.txt.

US Government, Dept. of Commerce. (1998). "Falling Through the Net II: New Data on the Digital Divide". Report released 28 July, National Telecommunications and Information Administration IA. Available online: http://www.ntia.doc.gov/ntiahome/net2/.

Online Games, Cyberculture and Community: The Deterritorization and Crystallization of Community Space

Anthony Y. H. Fung

Introduction

Each medium, independent of the content it mediates, has its own intrinsic effects which are its unique message. The message of any medium or technology is the change of scale or pace or pattern that it introduces into human affairs. The railway did not introduce movement, transportation or the wheel or even the road into human society, but it accelerated and enlarged the scale of previous human functions, creating totally new kinds of cities and new kinds of work and leisure. This happened whether the railway functioned in a tropical or northern environment, and was quite independent of the of the railway medium content itself. (*Understanding Media*, NY, 1964, p. 8).

What McLuhan writes about the railroad applies with equal validity to the media of print, television, computers and now the Internet. "The medium is the message" because it is the "medium that shapes and controls the scale and form of human association and action." (Eric McLuhan 2004, p. 9)

This is a quote from the official website of Marshall McLuhan in which his son Eric McLuhan explains "The Medium is the Message" in the FAQ session of the site. This explanation is pertinent to this study because my study tests this fundamental maxim on the medium of the Internet. But what is more important is that the quote illustrates one core theme of this study: communication technology has the power to change the "pace" and "scale" of a community, and in this sense, it can also be chaotic, disruptive and accelerate the disintegration of it. By the same logic, although communication technology itself cannot completely assuage our desire for community, it multiplies people interaction and this has the liberating effect that is reminiscent of community.

Ethnographic Study of Community and Use of the Internet

My study is an ethnographic study of the pattern of use on the Internet, and more specifically the youth community's use of online games in a relatively isolated and remote community. In this research, I do not intend to focus largely on the kinds of online games played in different settings. Instead, the study aims at understanding how the critical features of online games can influence communication patterns and spaces. Online games allow for many players to interact through the online network provided by PC communication devices. A common game that Chinese youth played in this study is called Legend of Jinyong in which players role-play characters from ancient China and play moves forward either individually or in groups and tribes. Despite being an adventure game with a warrior theme, communication in the form of virtual chatting is the most common activity on the site.

The study of community change and the uses of the Internet in this community represents a 6 month period from September 2002 to March 2003. During this period, together with a local historian, I visited Mui Wo at Lantau Island[1] and conducted many interviews with the community members. Among those, included were school principal, head of the village, person in charge of the community center, representatives of rural communities, rural land owners, ex-fishermen, ex-farmers and more importantly, youth and adults who have grown up in this community. I also participated in their community activities, informal youth gatherings, and helped organize activities in one of the community centers, during which I did participant observations. Although the persons studied represent a wide spectrum of ages and the use of the Internet is more or less a youth phenomenon, the conclusion that I would like to draw relates to community communication and its future direction and development.

The results of the study are based on a collection of narratives from the Mui Wo community as applied to the cultural history of communication technology. I admit that my observation and interviews represent a somewhat biased explanation of the community development and its connection to communication technology. However, this does not amount to technological determinism which argues that technology is the only bona fide reason for social and cultural change. As for empirical studies, we never know exactly — and are also not able to distinguish — if technological factors are the only social change agent. But what is valid and real is, among various social, economic and political factors, the perception of the neighborhood and the community about their cultural life and about the impact of the Internet upon themselves. The significance of this study lies in outlining a framework about how the emergence of online space affects community communication. The study also has implications for technology and social and community life.

The Study of Internet Space

The answers to whether the Internet has positive or negative consequences to our social life falls along two opposite points of view: the liberalist view and the critical view. The former argues that the Internet is structurally a non-hierarchical and distributed technology with immense potential for communication, organization and leadership, formation of identity and multiple discourses (Gierco 2002), and for its uses and adoption, it can be participatory and interactive in online communities which are deliberating, responsive and democratic in nature (e.g. Sproull and Kiesler 1991). The latter, the critical perspective, however, argues that the Internet creates more conflict — rather than plurality and diversity (e.g. Carnevale and Probst 1997) — and replicated structured society in a virtual world (Fung 2003).

Grounding the discussion of the Internet on the concept of space, this paper however approaches this question from a different dimension. Space here refers, not to exact geographical locations, but instead refers to the spatial dimension of communication in which community members can interact. While I put aside the question of whether this form of communication is oppressive, liberating, or both, this study aims at exploring the nature of this space, and how it influences communication.

In general, empirical studies which conceptualize the Internet using this spatial concept follow similar arguments to those of many general Internet adoption studies. Research conceived from the notion that the Internet as a disruptive technology is based on the argument that it creates a class-divided virtual space. Even when a new space is carved out and open for public uses, there are always the powerful elite in society controlling the content providers' access to people and people's access to content (Winseck 2002). As a consequence, space on the Internet still serves as the tool of the powerful.

On the other hand, liberalists tend to develop more complicated arguments about the potential of new communication technology, which politically is said to be serving as a site of resistance (Robins 1995) and individually as a psychological space in which human expectations can be met and fulfilled (Weibel 1990). Along the same line of thinking, the Internet in different forms can be argued to be transforming existing spaces for individuals as well as for organizations. For example, in the realm of education, Weis et al. (2002) argued that the Internet has transformed classrooms from spaces of delivery to spaces of active inquiry and authorship, whereas Kaufmann (2003) found that the Internet has created new spatial extensions for companies which may be conducive for them to develop distant business partners.

My study takes a third route which espouses that the Internet is a contested space (Conway, Combe, and Crowther 2003), which inevitably contains the dual and simultaneous functions either to empower the grassroots or to strengthen the existing organizations, the latter of which can reduce human autonomy and creativity. There are comparative studies which show that communication technology strongly anchors offline social and cultural groups to cyberspace which in turn strengthens social ties (Matel and Ball-Rokeach 2001). Using this proposition as a departure point, this study examines whether and how the Internet creates spaces for changing the actual communication space and the development of a community.

The Communication Development of Mui Wo and Its Main Villages

Before I present data showing changes in the community, I have to explain why the community of Mui Wo, situated at the eastern corner and the coastal region of Lantau Island, was chosen for this study. Lantau is the largest island in Hong Kong, and the Hong Kong Airport is located at the northern side of Lantau. It is connected to the urban area by the Tsing-Ma Bridge but the rest of the island, including Mui Wo is isolated and surrounded by mountains, and the island still relies on a ferry service which takes almost an hour to arrive at other urban areas.[2]

The name of the community "Wo" means that it is geographically a basin dissected from other communities on this Island. This unique geographical location means that the five major villages in Mui Wo, Chung Hau (涌口), Tai Tei Tong (大地塘), Luk Tei Tong (鹿地塘), Pak Ngan Heung (白銀鄉) and Mang Tong (白芒), were in essence situated close to each other and historically dependent on each others for trade, food and defense for over 200 years.[3] Most villagers now are descendents of migrants who came from China in exile during the 1940s and 1950s (Shiratori 1985: 156)[4] and the population was built up to 7000 in Mui Wo in the 1960s (Tsui et al. 1986: 187). Since the heyday of the villages, the population had been declining with less than two thousand people living there in the early 1990s.[5] The youth population also suffered a rapid decrease as they increasingly sought urban life in urban Hong Kong. However, external factors also disrupted natural population growth and furthered the decline of the community (Interview with Mr Yuen, a local representative). For example, the government's establishment of a public estate, namely Ngan Wan Estate to re-locate fishermen in the 1980s caused a short increase in population (Lui 2003: 106). Now the major public centers in Mui Wo include a sports complex, public library, a village association, a health clinic, a market place, banks and churches. Apart from these basic facilities, there are also hotels, vacation houses, souvenir shops for tourists, and a famous beach for tourists. On the whole, in terms of infrastructure, the communication facilities in the community are well developed. However, what has disappeared is the kind of space used for community interaction.

Public Spaces for Communication

The problematic regarding communication space did not exist when the entire community was perceived as a homogeneous ground for communication. For both formal and informal communication, adults participating in community customs and rituals gathered in front of major monument buildings such as the temple and in open areas and houses for the rural heads. For the younger generation, children would go to different villages (Interview with Mr Wong, organizer of youth center in Mui Wo). As one of the parents in the community said, "On the Hong Kong Island [the urban areas], there may be more gangs because they have to go downstairs and leave home." The very definition of going outside the home space in city area is seen as a potentially deviant behavior. However, the understanding of space in the rural area is different.

Here children outside the home are in space which is an extension of home. They are ordinary children because home in nearby. Here given that we have so many children in a family, we don't have the tradition of having our mother watching us. (Interview with Ms Wong, a local villager now working in an NGO in Mui Wo).

Historically, the only way for children and youth to communicate was to visit public spaces. There was no alternative. It was a period of low technology, no mobile phones, no televisions and no Internet. Because there was no communication technology linking home space with public space, physical presence was of the utmost importance; and, importantly, one could not remotely dictate the actions and behaviors of these public spaces. It was as described by Giddens (1984) a pre-modern society where space was not fixed, controlled and dictated for any institutional purpose and where the physical individual presence was closely connected to labor, work and production.

Second, as the public space was allocated for daily communication, the community members simply did not have a strong concept of private and public. The boundary between private and public communication appeared more blurred than it is in the urban residential areas nowadays. Communicating in public areas with other members was as common as communicating in one's home space. Describing the activities from his childhood 20 years ago, a villager said,

We played on the beaches and on the stream up on the mountain ... we caught fish in the stream and sometimes took people's vegetables.... And these [the act of eating people's crops] seemed not major problems. All these belonged to our community and we felt at home. We didn't lock our door [when we left home]. There is no strong distinction between the street in front of our house and our home. The public places are ours too (interview with Ms Wong).

This conceptualization of public space included privately owned farms and households, temples, streets, hills and open village squares[6]. In other words, the villagers territorized a large common area and regarded it as public space.

The Death of Mui Wo Community with Modern Communication

The change of community was due to external forces. Mui Wo was a typical community with a fishing and agricultural population (Shiratori 1985: 154). The change was first brought by the development and improvement of the infrastructure. In the mid-1960s, villagers in Mui Wo started to receive electricity (Kwok 2001: 183–184),[7] and almost a decade later, the government also extended its fresh water supply to the area (Ho, 2001: 158).[8] The postal service was established in 1963 and earlier in 1941, the telephone infrastructure was laid (Tsui et al. 1986: 31–32).[9] When the basic facilities were equipped, the community metamorphosed from being a traditional fishery port and farm community to being a tourist spot. This was followed by the improvement of ferry services. To accommodate the tourist industry, the coastal area of the community also had a complete new facelift with farmlands along the coastal area converted into a cultural and commercial center (Shiratori 1986: 155–156). Consequently, banks, hotels, restaurants, soft drink and souvenir shops were established around the pier.

Concurrent with the influx of "outsiders" due to tourism, households relocated from wooden houses and squatter areas in the 1980s to temporary government housing and later to public housing estates. When families were allocated to unfamiliar, newly built flats with large numbers of strangers, they started to lock the doors and barred entry to strangers, creating a more defined boundary for this private space. They could not feel safe in the community nor were they allowed to engage any public activities in those public areas defined by the authorities. The emergence of hippies during the 1960s brought in the culture of drugs and street fights after 1988 also further reinforced the notion of closing up space and drawing boundaries for what was considered to be legitimate communication space (interview). Parents could not allow their children to play, interact and communicate in public areas as they had in the past. Community members started to conceive of a stronger concept of private space reserved for dialogue and communication — with public space minimized for basic necessities for work, trade and school. A villager described the change with a sense of sorrow:

> I remembered at that time we didn't allow our children to go out. You couldn't see them in public places. [The community] was like a dead city. There was no sound of joy any more.... Afterwards, children seemed not know each other any more; they were like strangers (interview with a staff member working in an NGO in Mui Wo).

The modernization brought with it a short-lived economic prosperity but it came at the price of alienating the youth population who were virtually imprisoned by private home space. It was a deterriorization of public space in that it was no longer included and mapped for communication purposes.

The deterriorization was however not curbed by the "ushering in" of better communication infrastructures. At first the community had high hopes that communication technologies such as telephony and television could revitalize the community. However, practically, telephony served instrumental purposes, rather than informal ones, while television became a form of family entertainment, rather than a community activity. An old community leader said,

> I forgot when we exactly got a telephone.... But this was still different when we met and talked as a group. We didn't spend much time together since then. A lot of trivial things could be easily solved via telephony. The tradition of talking in the public area was lost (Interview with a local villager).

> ... we no longer gathered in public to "smell" the television set. All of us went back home and watched our television set. ... The public viewing in the past in a small shop faded out as we had our own space.

It seemed that the ensuing communication technologies did not have the power of extending the public space for communication, and failed to re-develop a public ritual of community interaction.

The Rise of Net Generation in the Community

The Internet has become popular in the community since 1996, appealing conterminously with online computer games. Like other media, when Internet use became widespread among the population, it became a device to crystallize people's relationships. As one of the parents in the community said,

> In the 80s, [when TV arrived at Lantau] kids brought along their chair, paid a little money, and sat together in a single shop watching television. I remembered, there was a shop for TV repairs in the 70s. We, usually in a group of tens, [as children] watched and heard about Superman there. The TV was the focal point of children ... Now, children have the focal point of the Internet. This is quite normal (Interview with Ms Wong).

In other words, mass media have lost its appeal for socialization and the Internet has replaced the former to crystallize community. The question is why online gaming is so attractive that it is able to crystallize online communities. One of the probable reasons, as other research has suggested is that the Internet provides an alternative space for students and youth to discuss affairs which are not allowed in any other medium. Informal interviews with the secondary school students in Mui Wo found that they rarely talk about schooling online; rather they talked about gossip, gaming and other consumption matters, arenas that they are not given a specific space to talk about at school. The online space can be regarded as an uncontrolled area where youth can talk about those "illegitimate" issues. The gaming environment also provides imaginative space for youth. For example, in combat role-play games, taking different pseudonyms in the virtual space, students serve as tribe leaders leading a group of Mui Wo friends. They fantasize themselves as being leaders, supporters, and triumphant warriors.

The existing literature on online communities would call them imagined communities in which subjects are imagined like people sharing and experiencing the same concerns, identity and interests and hence reorganizing space and dissolving boundaries (e.g. Mitra,

1997). However, the characteristics of the online communities formed seem to take a very different shape in Mui Wo. There is a strong sense of forming internal groups, and this fits in structurally with the design of the online games which requires the formation of virtual communities for collective action. The community is not so imaginative in the sense that the members are known to each other, and simply put, the youth replace the real communicative space with the virtual space. The groupings are similar to the real groupings as they are in the secondary schools in the community. In other words, the lost communicative space in real life is gradually reinstated by the virtual community.

Intact, communicative and cohesive as it is, this virtual community once worried principals and other senior community members. Given this public pressure, so far there has been no Internet café or game shops established in Mui Wo. As in most urban areas — closely matching media reporting on the subject — the local people worried about the adverse effect of the Internet: youth isolation, worsening relationship between parents and children, Internet addiction, and computer crimes, to name a few. In the late 1990s there was still a strong opposition from parents when broadband Internet was connected to households. Community members then started to realize that the Internet carries with it the side effect of anchoring children in their homes. This enables the parents to have better child control and monitoring. A parent mentioned,

> I'd rather see [my children] play online games at home than go out to some unknown places. I can at least keep track of them. Occasionally I ask them to bring some classmates home to play together. Home in any case is safer (interview with a staff NGO in Mui Wo).

The principal of the secondary school in Mui Wo also said that they also deliberately provided computer and internet access to their students after school hours. It also serves the same purpose of bounding the youth in a safer communicative space online and in some real safe locations offline such as computer labs in schools. Now all of the community members with children interviewed would approve of installing broadband Internet connections at home for their children.

Redeeming the Wasteland

The Internet, which was initially perceived to be a negative force for the youth in Mui Wo, turned out to be a strong vehicle for redeeming the communication spaces lost during the development of the community. The lost space here refers to space at two levels. The first level is the virtual space that the users created in the gaming environment. A secondary school student I talked to on a playground of Mui Mo said,

> Now we no long see many people playing here. This place used to be full of life and vigor. The place (of communication) now switches to households [where] we gather physically and virtually to play online games (interview with a student in a youth center).

It seems that online games have helped youth to extend space for communication online. Without it they would have remained anonymous. However, what is theoretically intriguing is that there seems to be a connection between virtual space and real space, which is the second level I referred to. This includes public physical grounds such as the space in front of the temples, seashores or mid-level hillsides. The same student explained how the online space could broaden the communication space offline,

> We meet on the Internet and wait at certain place [on a certain site of the computer warrior game] at a certain time to discuss [matters].... We will go out. Here, we do ask people to go out, for example, playing football, swimming or going to the [youth] center.... For some friends, we just meet, chat, quit the game and then meet [physically] offline (Interview with a student in a youth center).

This gamer implied that many real communicative activities taken up in space are in fact secondary to or an extension of the virtual space online. This is diametrically different from the commonplace conception that virtual space is developed for periphery communicative purpose after face to face communication. The empirical evidence suggests that virtual space has emerged to be the nexus for communication, around which new communication sites, including offline and online space, develop, flourish and get connected. Despite the subsidiary function of real space, online game helps the community to re-terrioritize some physical communicative spaces — including sports complex, playgrounds, youth centers — which they have long forgotten.

Gaming's Hyperplace and Spatial Extension

To explain the process of virtual communication formation with a version of geography and space (e.g. Mark 1998), we may borrow the concept of hyperplace. Hyperplace is a concept which describes the "electronic coupling of remote activities as well as environments that transcends the limit of functioning and settings of a physical space to support and accommodate a complex human activity of a higher order" (Takeyama 2001: 422). The notion of hyperplace can be traced back to Giddens' sociological notion (1984) of time-space distanciation which refers to the modern conditions under which time and space are systematically organized so that we can connect the presence and absence, and more important, extend our social relations over distant places by embedding other social systems. With the technological advancement of the Internet, such extensions of placeness are accelerated, united and connected by virtual space networks. Thus, hyperplace can be regarded as a form of telepresence, an experience of presence in a different location by means of a communication medium — the ability to control what happens at a distant location (Steuer 1993).

With regard to the community studied in this paper, the notion of hyperplace can be used to describe the aspects of interaction as well as the integration of people, objects and environments of geographically distributed real and physical locations. The interaction within the virtual community in the online game can be regarded as a hyperplace that (re)connect the different realms of the community, and it is this hyperplace which becomes the real center of communication, not the physical space in the community. Without such hyperplaces, the community members can not be bridged, and all the physical sites such as playgrounds, youth centers, and restaurants will become obsolete for communicative purposes.

Online Game: Linking the Virtual and the Real

This emerging Internet function is probably related to the development of online games. In a follow up even with a student,

I was directed to read the following statement about online games.

[Humans] all aspire for searching for the existences of reality in virtual world [and] crave for ideal fantasy out of the real world. This passion impresses the heaven and earth, and also impresses us (Xuanyuan Jian Online).[10]

To my surprise, I found out that the above saying is a promotional slogan of an online game. Complex, ambivalent and even mystical as if it were in the Chinese Confucian classics, the philosophy expressed reflects, first, the connectedness of reality and online space, and second, human reliance on the virtual world to sustain and perpetuate the reality. In other words, we cannot have a contented life without the sojourn of fantasy and temporarily escaping from reality. Here the virtual world functions to stabilize our chaotic and fast-changing world. If our society moves too rapidly and inadvertently towards self-breakdown, the virtual world can bring the collective whole back to the right track.

Based on the fieldwork evidence, this paper in fact espouses a similar argument: our real physical space for communication in our modern life has been eclipsed by a more hectic, complicated and uncontrolled urban life. What provides us with optimism is that the virtual community in an online game environment not only enables us to create new virtual space for communication, but also re-territorizes some physical space of interaction lost earlier. Online games in this sense reassembles subculture which itself is full of contradictions (Hebdige 1979). Parents hesitate to accept this subculture because it has distracted children from school and adult communication but they know that online games serve to bind youth communities together, and thus have slowed down the fragmentation of the community.

This paper suggests that the Internet in the form of computer games functions as space for youth to communicate. But the new virtual spaces are not independent of the physical space; rather the latter is more subject to the formation of the virtual space. The consequences are that youth now accustomed to not communicating in the real space in school, church, and communities and have instead turned to virtual space to cultivate deeper relationships. Virtual space becomes the primary community and the real space becomes secondary.

This may not be without reason for youth. As our space is more institutionalized and disembeded with humanistic presence, and continually fused with capitalist society (Giddens 1991), youth may want to recreate a community which is more ideal and which recaptures basic human interactions. In addition, they may no longer wish their presence and absence in real geographical terms to be in the hands of the others. With the autonomy of online space, their crystallization in the community can also be autonomous.

Epilogue

While there is a fear that online social ties will substitute for offline social bonds, and our social relationships could be reduced to online relationships (Kraut et al. 1988), this study disproves this proposition and suggests that the Internet can be used to both re-build and to cultivate social ties and activities.

Finally, I would like to suggest that McLuhan's conception of technology is not entirely wrong. The answer to the question about the value of technology and the Internet is not definite, and it always depends on how and when we apply it and for what and to what people. Communication infrastructure destroyed the community in Lantau but now online gaming is actually revitalizing our community and bringing communication back. In the past, everyone in the community could tell that technology had broken down the community relations because this technology was a mass medium. The Internet can now create an interactive platform for the community and by doing so can save it. This returns us to one Marshall McLuan's sayings, "Why is it so easy to acquire the solutions of past problems and so difficult to solve current ones?" (Official Marshall McLuan site 1986)

Notes

1. I would like to express my gratitude to Mr Shum Sze, a local historian who wrote about the cultural history of the community, and who accompanied me for visits in this study. And I am also indebted to Mr Ng, the Manager of the outdoor camp of the Hong Kong Playground Association at Lantau, who allowed me to serve as an organizer in their event.

2. Before the establishment of Lantau Link, Mui Wo played an important role in connection with Lantau and Hong Kong for sea and other parts of Lantau for land transportation. In the 1970s, an overall systematic transportation network of bus routes was established with Lantau as the terminus. However, since the Lantau Link was open in 1997, which is the vital connection to the airport, the value of Mui Wo being the midway to other part of Lantau has diminished.

3. With the five just mentioned, there are more than thirty villages in Mui Wo and they are scattered in the basin or on the hill-sides. Each of the villages belongs to one of nine districts in Mui Wo, which are Chung Hau District (涌口區), Tai Tei Tong District (大地塘區), Pak Ngan Heung District (白銀鄉區), Luk Tei Tong District (鹿地塘區), Wo Tin District (窩田區), Man Kok Tsui District (萬角咀區), Pak Mong District (白芒區), Tai Ho District (大蠔區) and Ngau Ku Ling District (牛牯塱區).

4. During this period and before the World War II, for security reasons, the villagers here built their houses adjacent to each other on the northwestern edge and far away from the coast, a place called Mui Wo Kau Tsuen. See Tsui et al (1986: 187–187). However, as the threat of pirate attacks lessened the villagers began to disperse and the new settlers built their houses wherever a site was available. See Shiratori (1985).

5. According to the 1981 and 1991 census, the population of Mui Wo was about 3711 and 1910 people (Hong Kong Government, 1991: 3).

6. For example, in Tai Tei Tong, there is a 100 year old Pak Tei Temple, where indigenous villagers gathered during important festivals. Pak Ngan Heung is a place for religious activities and celebrations for all villagers in the surrounding areas.

7. In 1957, the Hong Kong Government through the China Light Power Company decided to develop Lantau Island. In 1961, according to the Rural Electrification Scheme, CLP planned to supply electricity to the villages in the New Territories and the outlying islands. The construction would help supply electricity to 250 major villages in three years. This resulted in raising the living standards of the people in the New Territories and the outlying islands.

8. The Hong Kong Government built the Shek Pik Reservoir on Lantau in 1963, however, mainly to ease the rapid growth of population on Hong Kong Island. Despite the reservoir, most of the remote areas on Lantau and other outlying areas were still not provided with fresh water connections. Residents were forced to use well water and river water to meet daily basic needs and irrigation. The water improvement work was not completed until the 1970s.

9. Before 1941, it is said that there was only one wired phone installation located at Tai O Police Station. It is believed that two wireless phone installations were also located in Mui Wo and South Lantau in the early 1960s. A 3-minute call cost one dollar.
10. See report, marriage on "Xuanyuan Jian Network version," GM becomes the witness, *Sina.com* June 20, 2003. http://games.sina.com. cn/newgames/2003/06/06202677.shtml.

References

Carnevale, P. and Probst, T. (1997). "Conflict on the Internet". In S. Kiesler (ed.), *Culture on the Internet*, page no.? Mahwah, NJ: LEA.

Conway, S., Combe, I., and Crowther, D. (2003). "Strategizing networks of power and influence: The Internet and the struggle over contested space". *Managerial Auditing Journal* 18 (3): 254–263

Fung, A. (2003). *Bridging cyberlife and real life: A study of the online communities in Hong Kong*. Paper presented to Critical Cyberculture Studies: Current Terrains, Future Directions , sponsored by Ford Foundation, Resource Center for Cyberculture Studies, University of Washington, Washington , Seattle, USA, 9–11 May.

Giddens, A. (1984). *The Construction of Society: Outline of the Theory of Structuration*. Berkeley, CA: University of California Press.

———. (1991). *The Consequences of Modernity*. Stanford, CA: Stanford University Press.

Grieco, M. (2002). "Distributed Technology, Distributed leadership, Distributed Identity, Distributed Discourse: Organizing in the Information Age". In L. Holmes, M. Grieco, and D. Hosking (eds.), *Distributed Technology, Distributed leadership, Distributed Identity, Distributed Discourse: Organizing in the Information Age*, page no.? Aldershot: Ashgate Publishing.

Hebdige, D. (1979). *Subculture: The Meaning of Style*. London: Routledge.

Ho, P. Y. (2001). *Water For a Barren Rock: 150 Years of Water Supply in Hong Kong*. Hong Kong: Commercial Press.

Hong Kong Government. (1991). *Mui Wo Fringe Development Permission Area Plan*. Hong Kong: Planning Department.

Kaufmann, A., Lehner, P., and Todtling, F. (2003). "Effects of the Internet on the Spatial Structure of Innovation Networks". *Information Economics and Policy* 15 (3): 402.

Kraut, R., Lundmark, V., Patterson, M., Kielser, S., Mukopadhyay, T., and Scherlis, W. (1998). "Internet paradox: A social technology that produces social involvement and psychological well-being?" *American Psychologist*, 53 (9): 1017–1031.

Kwok, S. T. (2001). *A Century of Light*. Hong Kong: CLP Power Hong Kong Limited.

Lui, L. (2002). *Lantau*. Hong Kong: Joint Publication (in Chinese).

Mark, G. (1998). "Constructing a Virtual Geography: Narratives of space in a text-based environment". *Journal of Communication Inquiry* 22 (2): 152–176.

Matel, S. and Ball-Rokeach, S. (2001). "Real and virtual social ties: Connections in the everyday lives of seven ethnic neighborhoods". *The American Behavioral Scientist* 45 (3): 550–566.

Mitra, A. (1997). "Virtual Commonality: Looking for India on the Internet". In S. Jones (ed.), *Virtual Culture: Identity & Communication in Cybersociety*, pp. 55–79. Thousand Oaks, CA: Sage.

Robins, K. (1995). "Cyberspace and the world we live in". In M. Featherstone and R. Burrows (eds.), page no.? *Cyberspace/Cyberbodies/Cyberpunk*. London: Sage.

Shiratori, Y. (1985). *The Dragon Boat Festival in Hong Kong*. Tokyo: Ethno Historical Research Project, Sophia University.

Steuer, J. (1992). "Defining virtual reality: Dimensions determining telepresence". *Journal of Communication* 42 (4): 73–93.

Tsui, W. Y., Chueng, C. W., and Liu, D. S. (1986). *Mui Wo Economic and Social Changes, Chinese Anthropology Research Special Edition*. Hong Kong: Chinese University New Asia Academic Publication Editorial Board (in Chinese).

Weibel, P. (1990). "Virtual worlds: the emperor's new body." In G. Hattinger (ed.), page no.? *Electronics* 2, Linz: Veritas-Verlag.

Weis, T., Benmayor, R., O'Leary, C., and Eynon, B. (2002). "Digital Technologies and Pedagogies". *Social Justice* 29 (4): 153–167.

Winseck, D. (2002). "Netscapes of power: Convergence, consolidation and power in the Canadian mediascape". *Media, Culture and Society* 24 (6): 795–819.

.

. . . .

PART III

Capacity of the Internet to Enhance Our "Position"

Reconstructing E-government

Sharon Strover

Karen Gustafson

Introduction

Electronic government (e-government) is a relatively new phenomenon that has received a great deal of federal and state bureaucratic interest in the past ten years. Initially conceived more as a venue for demonstrating the utility of new technological innovations such as videotext, the earliest history of e-government almost appears to be one of a technology searching for an application. However, once home- and work-based computer and networked communication systems became more widely available, the idea of systems that could use different electronic communication means (email, web sites, listservs, and more currently even weblogs) to bring government closer to the people captivated scholars, critics and activists. However, the institutional development of e-government services has been disappointing: it generally appears to offer not visions of improved democratic processes but rather improved efficiencies for undertaking business-as-usual among government agencies.

Surveys of e-government users, both businesses and individuals, have focused primarily on qualities of the transactions between government sites and the individuals, as well as on assessing the types of uses that would bring more users to e-government portals. Very little work exists that explores e-government from a more open-ended, democracy-oriented framework, one that might echo the interests of the empowering citizens. In fact, in the US, operational, agency-based notions of e-government is disconnected from the actual user needs or understanding of systems' democratic implications. Rather, a consumer paradigm dominates most implementations as well as most analyses of actual e-government operations. As a potential architecture for accountability as well as control, for democracy as well as privacy intrusion, for efficiency as well as bureaucratization, e-government systems and ideas function as sites for examining how modern state institutions configure and conceptualize the power of new technologies.

Conceptualizing E-government

The idea of blending communication technologies with the goals and functions of government yields several alternative conceptions of e-government. At its most prosaic, it is "the civil and political conduct of government using information and communication technologies" (MvIver and Elmagarmid 2002, p. 31). At its most ambitious, it is e-democracy, a powerful tool to make government more accountable, accessible, and responsive to citizens, or even a political tool of citizenship.

According to Aldrich, Bertot, and McClure, e-government has existed in the U.S. since the late 1960s with the development of ARPAnet, the information network created through a partnership of military, academia, and private business interests (2002). Most early efforts at e-government were confined to individual agencies, with little interoperability (Aldrich, Bertot, and McClure, p. 350). Internationally, videotext services were deployed in European countries during the 1970s and 1980s to relay both government and private information, but only the French system, Minitel, is considered to be a success, and a limited one at that. The interactive and organizing potentials of such systems were only dimly appreciated in the 1980s.

McIver and Elmagarmid suggest that in the U.S., e-government services did not become a viable option for the broader public until the diffusion of the personal computer and dial-up network connections during the 1980s (2002, p. 3). The spread of non-proprietary, platform independent standards such as TCP-IP and

HTTP set the stage for the endorsing a National Information Infrastructure (NII) initiative by the U.S. government.[1] During the Clinton Administration in the early 1990s, government agencies were encouraged to bring their services and internal communication online, to join up with the *information superhighway*, a popular but ambiguous concept during this period. In the US, the National Performance Review (NPR) and NII initiatives supported this goal, and the NPR generated *Access America* as a government portal for citizens in September, 2000. The first NPR report distinguished the roles of citizen from consumer, but Chadwick and May point out that it later abandoned this distinction, instead addressing the needs of "customers" and coordination within and between government agencies, thereby neglecting the citizen (2003). *Access America* later became FirstGov (http://www.firstgov.gov/index.shtml), an umbrella site for users seeking federal information and services.[2] In the same time frame, numerous states also began to explore the possibilities of e-government.

In the past two decades, the concept of e-government has been surrounded by hopes for reinvigorated democracy and more accountability of government to its citizens. Many recent analyses point out the theoretical and practical difficulties of e-government implementations against a fabric of optimistic anticipation often captured in notions of e-democracy. E-democracy refers to "the thesis that accelerated communication of citizens and politicians through the means of ICT will lead to increased participation of citizens in the making of policy in democratic nations" (Kampen and Snijkers 2003, p. 492). Dahl (1985) for example suggests computer technology could help citizens get adequate information for informed deliberation so they could knowledgeably participate in the policy process. Likewise popular writers Dyson, Gilder, Keyworth, and Toffler (1994) argue that the Internet lends agency to citizens, and suggest that participation via the World Wide Web could actually supersede traditional government structures. One of the best known and perhaps most extreme examples of this view is John Perry Barlow's "Declaration of the Independence of Cyberspace," which excoriates established government for attempting to extend into online interactions. Barlow argues that the unique nature of the Internet will allow wholly new forms of governance to emerge, surpassing traditional governments' jurisdiction and authority.

We believe that from ethics, enlightened self-interest, and the commonweal, our governance will emerge. Our identities may be distributed across many of your jurisdictions. The only law that all our constituent cultures would generally recognize is the Golden Rule. We hope we will be able to build our particular solutions on that basis. But we cannot accept the solutions you are attempting to impose. (Barlow 1996).

In the middle of the 1990s, Barlow and other cyberspace utopians perceived the Internet as a revolutionary environment that would transcend traditional government and allow the creation of a new, egalitarian global society. As public use of the Internet grew unevenly and gaps in access became evident, these utopian proclamations generally faded.

The Internet is still seen by many theorists as a space for improved democracy, whether through more accountable representation or direct voter input, but e-government is now more commonly viewed by government itself as a means for modifying traditional government and citizen interactions, not as a space for a wholly new governing system. A central issue in current evaluations of e-government is whether or not online government truly improves the nature of government and citizen interactions. Although there are numerous ways government can be modified through adaptation to the online environment, it is likely that many attempts at putting government online do not fully take advantage of e-government potentials.

For example, many e-government sites consist mainly of text, with little opportunities for interactivity. One reason for this may be that in many cases, attempts at e-government deployment primarily consist of putting traditional documents and forms online, rather than using the new technologies to reconfigure the relationship between citizens and government. So much of the World Wide Web functions as a bulletin board, and it is not surprisingly that the heavy information role of government adapted easily to using the Internet in that mode. Established structures and modes of interaction are simply extended to the online environment, bypassing opportunities for critical reflection and potential change (West 2003; Ferber, Foltz, and Pugliese 2003). Abramson, Arterton, and Orren noted this tendency over a decade ago, observing that contemporary uses of communications technologies tended to reinforce pre-existing power relations, rather than actually alter the structure of relationships between stakeholders (1988). Hence it is not too surprising that e-government is frequently considered to be not necessarily an avenue to more participatory governance but rather a means to streamline communications within government agencies and to increase economy of government operations, what McIver and Elmagarmid refer to as *internalizing* and *externalizing* forms of e-government. Whereas internal e-government systems are meant to increase the efficiency of operations between and within government agencies, external e-government is based on "enabling citizens or government officials to interact with governmental processes" (2002, p. 7). In both cases, democracy is sidelined while efficiency is foregrounded. Unfortunately, increased fragmentation, loss of privacy, unequal access, and a loss of accountability among state agencies may be the price of enhanced government efficiencies.

Some critics are sanguine in extolling the benefits of e-government, avoiding discussion of the role of a governance system in their assessments of e-government. Moulder for example suggests that local e-government can enhance the information seeking abilities of citizens and businesses, streamlining permit applications, allowing improved internal communication between local agencies, and reducing the costs of material and labor (2002). Ferber, Foltz, and Pugliese (2003) are more cautious in their analysis, which examines how assumptions about the nature of democracy can affect e-government implementation — "views on how e-government can increase participation will vary depending on one's conception of democracy" (p. 158). E-government applications may increase citizen involvement, but this will depend upon the underlying assumptions of those implementing the system. The authors acknowledge that political participation varies depending upon the nature of the democratic political structure, which can promote different forms of democracy including direct citizen involvement, representative government, or interest group liberalism. Their analysis suggests that democratic participation can refer to the interactions of citizens deliberating over the common good, and the means to achieve the common good (2003). Borrowing from Benjamin Barber, the authors argue for "strong democracy" as a worthy goal of e-government, where electronic applications would promote greater direct participation in the political decision-making process. This means that dissemination of information is very necessary to citizens' deliberation in a democracy, but does not fulfill the potential of e-government, which must promote meaningful interactivity between citizens and the state. These assumptions are embedded in the actual design of e-government applications and public portals, which may inform citizens but not offer facilities for public discussion and interaction with government officials. Some assessments of e-government efforts do look closely at potentials for meaningful interactivity.

Differences in national attitudes also can affect the deployment and use of e-government. For instance, whereas several of the studies discussed below reveal Americans' distrust of government power, citizens of other countries are often more comfortable with moderate levels of state surveillance. The Hart-Teeter survey of 2003 examined e-government perceptions in Australia, Canada, Singapore, Spain, and the U.K., and found significant differences in user attitudes between the U.S. and these other countries. Among these countries, only the U.S. had a majority oppose a voluntary identification card (2003, p. 19). The UK had highest levels of support for national identification cards, which has many communities already deploying surveillance systems to discourage crime, indicating that British citizens may be much more accustomed than Americans to overt state surveillance.[3] This international survey of attitudes may also suggest that these other countries' citizens are more trusting of their state governments, and more willing to surrender personal information. Openness to sharing information is significant for e-government deployment, because many opportunities to participate in online governance require that the user give up personal information.

Although advocates herald the potential of e-government to strengthen citizen participation, more direct forms of democratic involvement are not always seen as desirable. In fact, some argue that hopes for direct online political participation are unrealistic, and that direct democracy can lead to the neglect of minority interests (Kampen and Snijkers 2003). Ferber, Foltz, and Pugliese agree with some of these cautions, reasoning that forms of e-government promoting direct democracy may be vulnerable to certain interest groups overwhelming government officials with input, such as email or straw votes. Bimber too suggests that greater individual participation could lead to more pluralism, and potentially greater fragmentation among citizens' interest groups (1998).

Getting to the nature of the governing process, Kampen and Snijkers argue that because everyday citizens cannot adequately research every issue that arises, they cannot make fully informed choices and are unable to see the interrelated nature of policy issues or the negotiation and compromise that underlie policy resolutions. Instead of direct democracy through e-government, Kampen and Snijkers call for increased representation: "Democracy by its nature converges to a tyranny so long as its population grows and the number of representatives is kept constant, simply because the ratio of the representatives to the represented tends to zero. Either way, the e-era requires more representatives to handle more information and represent more citizens." (p. 495). E-government applications can enhance the ability of citizens to monitor representatives and can increase trust in government activities, while not requiring citizens to take on the duties of direct participation on a daily or weekly level.

Accessibility is an important factor in e-government implementation: even if direct citizen participation is technologically feasible, not everyone will have equal access to the means of participation, and this can make those with access disproportionately powerful in the political process. Netchaeva (2002) agrees with this warning, and is skeptical of technology alone solving problems of participation and government. She writes, "the development of IT [information technology] systems and establishing government portals do not ensure the achievement of real democracy. Indeed, how can we talk about real democracy when even in the UK and US (where more than a third of the population is now online and nine out of ten people are working in information businesses), low-income and older people seldom use the Internet and still feel uncomfortable using IT?" (p. 470) Lan and Falcone (1997) similarly recognize that online government will not erase historical inequalities, and could potentially even reproduce them. They argue against technologically driven optimism, and claim that although e-government may offer citizens greater access to information, this information will always be filtered through established power structures. "Power does not reside with those who seek access to information but with those (primarily institutions) who will determine what information will be available and who will have access to it" (Lan and Falcone 1997, p. 255).

Jaegar (2002) goes so far as to state that current e-government strategies violate constitutional principles of federalism and the separation of legislative, judicial, and executive powers. Criticizing the Office of Management and Budget's 2002 E-Government Strategy, Jaegar finds that if "efforts to increase participation in Federal government services for citizens are taken to any more than a nominal level, the rights of states as independent governments may be violated" (p. 363). He argues that states should be allowed to choose their individual level of participation within the national e-government framework, and that the current agenda for e-government does not properly request the consent of the states. In addition, he finds that unifying portals, such as the federal government's FirstGov site, dangerously blur boundaries between separate branches of government, so that a single government group might achieve "hegemonic control over information, leading to many potential imbalances of power, both within in the government and to the citizens" (p. 360). This blending of different agencies' services and information provision could also lead to decreased accountability for individual government entities.

The following section will examine some of the e-government implementations in the US, as well as users' reactions, so that we can assess the extent to which some of these concerns are apt.

Studies of State and Local Sites

Currently, every state in the US has an e-government initiative, but with varied levels of quality. The notion of quality is subjective, and different critics conceptualize it in unique ways; there is no standard "rating" for e-government sites and services, and no single idea of government purpose or mission motivates them. Two recent surveys' ratings of e-government web sites or portals are discussed below, with an eye to illuminating the different criteria that are meaningful to scholars with different goals in mind.

In a 2003 analysis of state legislature websites Ferber, Foltz, and Pugliese found significant connections between the quality of particular states' sites and the demographic and political characteristics of the states' citizenry using five rating categories:

content, usability, interactivity, transparency, and audience awareness. The investigators evaluated fifty state sites drawn from the National Conference of State Legislators web site (www.ncsl.org), using a ten-point scale for determining quality in each of the five rating categories. They argue that better quality sites usually exist in states with higher rates of Internet access, education, per capita income, and voting participation, and they hypothesize that these statistics suggest higher levels of political participation — thus leading in turn to the idea that user demand may be driving "quality."[4] In states with lower averages in education and per capita income, state legislature sites received inferior ratings.

> Citizens who are already inclined to use the Internet, and have better access, are being provided with higher quality legislative web sites. Citizens on the wrong end of the digital divide appear to also be on the low end of the quality divide, as their states provide relatively inferior sites. These citizens, already less inclined to use the Internet in general, are less likely to interact with their state legislatures' relatively poor sites (Ferber, Foltz, and Pugliese, p. 161)

The authors criticized many of the sites for having almost exclusively one-way communication, with little opportunity for citizens to participate in government via the websites. The top ranked five states in the study are New Jersey, Minnesota, Alaska, Hawaii, and Connecticut; the five lowest states are Rhode Island, Illinois, California, Pennsylvania, and Mississippi. (They note that California and New York (ranked 43 out of 50) ranked lower than would be expected, because neither state possesses specific legislature sites, a situation that negatively affected each state's usability, transparency, and content scores.) Surprisingly, states with a significant presence of technologically-oriented industry and educational institutions (e.g., NY, CA, and PA) scored low in this analysis. Although the methods of rating the state sites are described in detail, the demographic and voting data used for the correlations are unclear, making these conclusions more weakly supported than those of the other studies reviewed here.

To illustrate how such rankings depend on alternative ideas of "quality," another major survey of e-government state sites reaches very different conclusions. In their fourth annual survey of state and federal websites, Brown University's Center for Public Policy examined 1,603 sites across all states, evaluating them for a wide variety of factors including responsiveness to user emails, literacy requirements, language translation availability, required user fees and premium areas, presence and number of online services, level of disability access, and indicators of privacy policies. In this survey Massachusetts, Texas, and Indiana are the top three rated states, and Alaska, New Mexico, and Nebraska comprise the bottom three. Texas is noted for offering fifty online services, a clear privacy policy, and numerous easily accessible links to useful information resources (West 2003). Overall, the report noted several significant trends in government websites: Eighty-nine percent of the sites conform to World Wide Web Consortium accessibility guidelines. As well, 44 percent of surveyed sites offered fully-executable online services, up from 33 percent in a 2002 study, and more sites had translation services (13 percent, up from 7 percent) and security policies (54 percent, up from 43 percent).

The disjuncture of rankings between these two studies suggests widely different standards. Ferber, Foltz, and Pugliese acknowledge the Brown study, suggesting that it did not consider the differing levels of quality among state web site features and only looked for the presence or absence of content and services. Although both surveys consider issues of interactivity, this is a primary focus for the Ferber, Foltz, and Pugliese study, but only one of many factors examined in the Brown University study. The Brown survey specifically addresses accessibility and privacy protection, and this may partially account for the divergence in the two studies' results. Also, whereas Ferber, Foltz, and Pugliese limited their study to state legislature sites, the Brown survey evaluated a wider variety of state sites and worked with a much larger sample.

Another study of e-government web sites focused on e-government at a local level. Musso, Weare, and Hale observe the entrepreneurial and participatory elements of municipal e-government interfaces, looking at local government websites in California during 1996 and 1997 (2000). The authors discuss several models of e-government and note the potential for new technologies to facilitate the reform of local governance through entrepreneurial and participatory paradigms. The entrepreneurial ideal emphasizes the delivery of services to citizens and private business development, while the participatory or civic ideal refers to cultivating interest groups and their involvement in decision-making processes. Their structured content analysis of 270 Californian municipal websites used 125 variables to establish the general emphases, information provision, and communication capabilities of each site as it assessed available links to businesses, tourism offices, and chambers of commerce, as well as links to city council contact information, local interest groups, and neighborhood organizations. Generally, the authors found that the sites' technology "is designed primarily to facilitate routine interactions between service providers and recipients (the entrepreneurial function) rather than direct citizen participation in policy making processes" (12). Only 14 percent of sites provided updated information about elections, and few sites provided links to local community organizations.

Table 10.1 Typology of Municipal Web Pages

Communication channels provided	Percentage of sites
Links to businesses, tourism or Chamber of Commerce	67.4
City Council member pages	14.1
Neighborhood organizations	13
Chat rooms/Bulletin boards	10

Adapted from Musso, Weare, and Hale, 2000

They conclude that the "vast majority" of sites in the study do not demonstrate either entrepreneurial or participatory reform models, instead focusing primarily on "superficial information and communication capabilities" (16). Those municipal sites that do incorporate characteristics of either reform model are most commonly oriented towards service delivery and management, rather than civic participation. Site users are offered few opportunities to network with community interest groups and engage in grassroots political organization.

These assessments, though varied, are not especially encouraging with respect to the interests of e-democracy. If anything, they conform to observations that e-government efforts are normative, and do little more than extend already existing government information and processes to a web environment. The following section reviews some of the empirical literature on users' responses to such efforts.

E-government Users

A handful of studies have looked at e-government users, both individuals and businesses. In general, such studies have been utilitarian, seeking formulas for achieving efficient e-government applications within the context of concerns about costs and efficiencies. Private research groups (e.g., Momentum Research Group, Hart Teeter), academics (Strover 2002; Strover and Straubhaar 2004; Strover et al. 2004) and non-profits such as the Pew Internet and American Life Project have sought to understand what users want from e-government and how it should be structured. Most such research is designed to answer questions related to optimizing already existing e-government portals, but they have little "good news" to report in terms of overall use and in terms of e-government's relationship to democratic practices.

The Momentum Research Group examined use patterns as well as demands for future use of e-government interfaces (2000), asking online individuals and businesses their preferences for e-government portals, funding models, and public-private cooperation in e-government development. In 303 interviews conducted with individual Internet users[5] and 106 interviews with businesses[6] they found that a majority of online adults had conducted an e-government transaction at least once, and a fifth of Internet users reported conducting a transaction within the past thirty days. Significant percentages of individual users reported interest in online services such as driver's license renewal. Individual citizens were primarily interested in accessing e-government services and information through local government sites, whereas business users reacted favorably to the concept of an overarching federal portal. In terms of funding models, the majority of individual and business respondents preferred the use of user or "convenience fees" to support e-government initiatives, in contrast to the use of taxpayer funding. Supporting e-government is a topic of some currency since these efforts are costly and have yet to be "self supporting" financially. Hence, pressure is on such programs to demonstrate their utility.

Surveying a broader base of users, the Hart-Teeter firm researched current US e-government users, users living in "best practice" cities, government employees, and Internet users in Spain,

Singapore, the U.K., Canada, and Australia to investigate how and where people use the Internet and how they use government sites (2003). The same group had conducted a similar study in 2001. In 2003 they found that seven out of ten surveyed Americans reported Internet access at home, work, or school, and one half of all Americans surveyed reported using a government website for information retrieval or other services. For self-identified Internet users, three quarters reported recent use of government sites. Those utilizing e-government information and services tended to be young, white, educated, and enjoying middle class income levels. Of these self-reported users of e-government, 80 percent identified as Caucasian, 68 percent were under age 50, and 44 percent earned household yearly incomes over $50,000.

The Hart-Teeter findings illustrate that trust and familiarity are two primary factors influencing use of e-government. Over a fifth of Americans surveyed reported concern over security and privacy issues to be limiting their use of government sites; although many believed that surrendering personal information to e-government websites could enhance service, they also considered submitting personal information to be risky. Americans' awareness of e-government has not changed much between the Hart-Teeter surveys of 2001 and 2003. In 2003 only 8 percent of those surveyed reported great familiarity with e-government, and 29 percent reported being somewhat familiar with online government. The study suggests, "this indicates that although e-government users may be aware of specific, individual online services, they do not relate those services to the broader concept of online government" (Hart-Teeter, p. 7). Although a majority of those surveyed reported high interest in using new services, such as automated address updates, 63 percent of those accessing e-government sites did so only to retrieve information such as office addresses, and only 23 percent accessed sites to actually conduct transactions such as tax filing or license renewal. Like the results of the earlier Momentum study, the Hart-Teeter survey found significant interest in a variety of proposed e-government services, including online voting. They conclude, "The American public is not ready for online voting. In some areas, Americans simply do not believe that more Internet technology means better government" (Hart-Teeter, p. 11). To illustrate, thirty percent of Americans favored online voting, but 54 percent strongly opposed the idea. In addition, only 19 percent of Americans felt it was a high priority for government to invest tax dollars into the development of online information and services; however, about 54 percent of those surveyed thought the government should proceed slowly with e-government deployment, and 44 percent of actual e-government users agreed with this statement. When asked about the most important potential benefit offered by e-government, users appeared most interested in increased accountability and efficiency. Overall, although the Hart Teeter survey demonstrates some acceptance and optimism in surveyed Americans' attitudes towards e-government, it also reflects caution and unfamiliarity.

The Pew Foundation's report, "How Americans get in Touch with Government" is based on a national random sample survey of 2,925 adults, and focused on how people evaluate using the Internet for contacting the government as opposed to other means of getting services and information (Horrigan 2004). In a technology-centric framework, the Pew survey assesses the strengths and weaknesses of the Internet as a conveyance for conducting business with the government. It finds that the Internet expanded information flows between government and citizens, and that Internet access helps people to contact government: Internet users do so far more often than do non-Internet users. However, insofar as people may have technological limitations (slow connect speeds), and needs that go beyond the typical panoply of e-government services, the Internet is not particularly helpful. In fact, this survey found that among people who contact government, most are likely to say they prefer to use the telephone rather than the Internet.

In Texas, opinion surveys were administered in 2000 and 2004 to gauge statewide public interest in e-government services and perceived potential or actual benefits (Strover 2002; Strover et al. 2004).[7] A third survey in 2004 also assessed business users of e-government services (Strover and Straubhaar 2004).[8] Echoing some of the concerns of the Hart-Teeter survey but expanding them to consider issues pertaining to the digital divide and access, this research sought answers to questions such as whether and under what circumstances people would use Internet-based government services, and how much people would be willing to pay for such online services, who had access to the Internet and where, and why people did not use the Internet. The study examined computer and

Internet use, finding some striking relationships in 2004 between minority ethnic group membership and using computers and the Internet in so-called "third places," public sites such as libraries and schools. This was significant in that a well-funded state program had invested millions in creating Internet access in exactly such places.

The study also examined privacy and security concerns of potential e-government users, and opinions regarding the economic support of proposed online government sites. Privacy concerns regarding the Internet grew from 2000 to 2004, with 73 percent of the sample remaining wary about privacy on the Internet in 2004 (up from 65 percent four years earlier). Texas respondents who already used offline government services demonstrated significant interest in using the same services online, and they were more accepting of voting and online tax filing than those surveyed in the Hart-Teeter study. Whereas only 30 percent of those surveyed by Hart-Teeter reacted favorably to the concept of online voting, nearly 47 percent of participants in the Texas survey were willing to vote online as of 2000, although this figure dropped to 37 percent in 2004, perhaps a reflection of growing privacy concerns as well as worries regarding the US voting system flaws evident in the 2000 presidential election. In addition, a greater percentage of Texans were willing to use the Internet for tax filing, and a significant percentage was willing to register online to vote.

However, the surveys indicated that few people had actually used any e-government services — only 29 percent in 2004, compared to Hart-Teeter's findings that about 70 percent of their sample had used e-government information.[9] Most commonly, the services assessed in the Texas study were paying utility bills, renewing drivers' licenses, renewing vehicle registration and filing a change of address form. Predictably, people who are more familiar with the Internet and spend more time with it also engage in more e-government transactions, and that in turn tracks with higher income levels, full time employment, and living in urban areas. In essence, the Texas surveys underscore the traditional biases in technological deployment (i.e., more broadband access in urban areas) and user skills and comfort ("Internet savvy" people will avail themselves of e-government more readily) as they influence use of and attitudes toward e-government services.

Respondents in the Texas 2000 and 2004 surveys themselves were somewhat skeptical about e-government: while most agreed that having government information available online would make government more available to all, they also acknowledged that the Internet itself is not sufficiently available to everyone to use it for e-government services. Agreeing with the findings of the Pew Foundation, about 56 percent of the 2004 respondents said they would prefer to see someone in person for a government service. There is a strong ethnic (minorities), age (older), and income (lower income) skew to this preference. In the 2004 survey, people also were concerned about providing credit card information to the state (64 percent), and even more (78 percent) were concerned about providing non-financial, personal information to the state online, with a clear majority, 70 percent, preferring that the state use an opt-in practice governing the use of and release of any personal information it collected.

In the Hart-Teeter survey, a smaller but still substantial proportion of survey participants reported concern over the security of their personal information in e-government, echoing results of the Texas surveys. Forty-six percent of Hart-Teeter respondents strongly agreed that the submission of personal information to government websites could enable government invasions of privacy, although a similar percentage also acknowledged that the release of such information could allow the government to provide better services (Hart-Teeter, p. 14). The Hart-Teeter survey did not distinguish between financial and non-financial personal information, a difference that often affects public attitudes on data disclosure. Also, it would be significant to discover current attitudes regarding opt-in choices, especially because the opt-out paradigm remains a standard.

With respect to how e-government services would be supported, respondents in the Texas study did not embrace fee-for-service schemes as enthusiastically as the participants in the Momentum study of 2000. The public demand in Texas varied according to the services offered — for instance, nearly 17 percent of participants were willing to pay up to ten dollars in convenience fees for online driver's license renewal, but only 9 percent reported willingness to pay this amount for the convenience of filing taxes online (Strover 2002). In the 2004 study, willingness to pay increased slightly, with about 31 percent of the sample reporting they would be willing to pay up to $3 for various government services. Regardless, the percentages of those willing to pay convenience fees in the Texas study are considerably lower than the overall figure reported in the Momentum survey, where 71 percent of individuals surveyed responded favorably to the idea of fees. Also, the Texas study examined this issue in more depth, looking at the varying amounts people are willing to pay for different services, rather than the more general approach of asking if respondents would be hypothetically willing to pay convenience fees reflected in other studies. It is possible that the level of detail in the Texas survey led to more cautious responses on the part of the participants. When faced with a realistic situation of certain, named services potentially costing specific amounts, respondents may have considered the scenario more thoughtfully, rather than simply being asked to give a yes or no response, as in the Momentum study.

The studies' findings on trust levels are important, as the diffusion of e-government applications at least partially depends upon citizens' confidence in established government institutions. A nationwide survey on privacy and trust by the Ponemon Institute and Carnegie Mellon University (2003) correlates with the earlier studies' results, finding that "the general public holds a relatively low or negative impression of various federal government organizations" (2004, p. 2). As the Hart-Teeter and Texas analyses already observed, citizens value the privacy of their personal information, and over 83 percent of respondents in the Ponemon survey reported that their privacy was important to them. (The Privacy Trust Survey, which drew upon a sample of over 6,300 adults, notes that citizens have varying levels of trust for different government agencies, with the US Postal Service achieving the highest trust rating, and the Office of the Attorney General and the Department of Justice receiving the lowest ratings.) Furthermore, respondents reported considerable concern over loss of civil liberties, with 64 percent claiming that this issue had a notable impact on their privacy trust. Other major concerns included surveillance into personal life, and government monitoring of Internet activities (2004, p. 2). These results reflect significant levels of distrust of public institutions, and are generally consistent with the findings of earlier e-government studies, especially the ones focused on Texas.

The Texas and Momentum studies both reflected public rejection of using general government revenues to support e-government. The Texas survey asked respondents to evaluate four choices of potential e-government support, including use of state general funds, revenues from advertising on state websites, convenience fees from e-government service users, and income from the sale of data collected by e-government sites. In both 2000 and 2004, using general revenue or revenue from data sales were deemed unacceptable: in 2004 only 14 percent of the sample approved of using general revenue funds for support (and another 39 percent deemed it "somewhat acceptable"), and only 4 percent approved of the state selling transaction-generated data for support (another 34 percent considered it somewhat acceptable). About 18 percent approved of user ("convenience") fees (plus 55 percent in the somewhat acceptable category), and another 18 percent approved of web advertising to support e-government (45 percent said it is somewhat acceptable); the latter figures on ad support are a slight drop from 2000's approval of advertising on a state site when 80 percent indicated it was entirely or somewhat acceptable. These results resonate with those of the Momentum study, where only 22 percent of participants supported the idea of taxpayer-based e-government, while 71 percent supported the scheme of using user fees to offset e-government deployment costs.

Although these user studies have differing scopes and time periods, the respective results reflect similar themes. Americans are cautious about information security issues, and not confident in the ability or inclination of the government to protect their confidentiality. Fee-based services are generally viewed as more acceptable means of support for e-government deployment than the use of general state funds, and respondents express the most interest in routine services like driver's license renewal or tax filing, services that reflect time savings. Online voting is acceptable for a minority of respondents in the Texas and Hart-Teeter surveys, although the more recent Hart-Teeter survey reflects less support for this service, which is often considered a prime example of e-government potential. Again, one explanation for this apparent decrease in support for online voting could be the confusion surrounding voting in the 2000 US presidential election, which may have dampened citizens' enthusiasm for innovative means of voting. The Hart-Teeter survey reflects appreciation of the potentials of e-government but also concern over issues surrounding its deployment.

Finally, the Texas survey on businesses and e-government found that businesses are increasingly dependent on the Internet, and that dependence is more pronounced for business-to-business and business-to-government transactions than it is for business-to-consumer transactions (Strover and Straubhaar 2004). Businesses were much more aware of and regular users of e-government services than were individuals in the other Texas surveys. Businesses in all sectors depend on the Internet, and nearly all of these larger businesses have at least some of their employees using the Internet for procurement, research or customer service. The most appealing e-government services they cite include undertaking criminal background checks, filing paperwork with state agencies, obtaining continuing education, obtaining, registering and renewing professional licenses, and tracking state regulations. (Undertaking criminal background checks has moved up in importance since 9/11.) As was the case with the survey of individuals, businesses are very concerned about security and privacy with respect to e-government. A small percentage of businesses (14 percent) felt e-government services were sufficiently desirable that they would be willing to pay a sizable, annual subscription fee for them. Overall, this survey finds that the Internet is seamlessly integrated into business processes, and its findings illustrates that companies think of e-government services primarily in operational terms — how can they conform to regulations, deliver paperwork to regulators, and so forth. It is striking that little or nothing emerged from the survey regarding accountability that might be achieved through more openness to the public.

The anticipated benefits and concerns surrounding online government are discussed more broadly in the section below, which describes the arguments of e-government theorists. These survey results convey the slow growth of e-government and confirm an operational penchant to cast e-government as a means for more efficiently delivering and offering the same services and information that already exist. Why e-government configurations have developed in this way can be explained in part by referring to the pressures of organizational continuity: agencies do via the Internet what they already do best without it; thus, they play to their strengths. They can be explained as well by acknowledging a limited impetus for the types of reforms that would accommodate more interactivity. In adopting many of the business practices common to the Internet — indeed, most e-government sites are contracted and "built" by private consultants — e-government operations seek to minimize any "non-programmable" contact with their personnel since this represents a critical cost savings. Encouraging more personal contact would increase costs, not save them.

Conclusion

There are several motivating factors behind implementation of online government, including heightened demand from citizens, a need for improved efficiency in the shrinking public sector workforce, a business community increasingly intolerant of inefficient state bureaucracy, and policy makers who are more willing to adopt technological solutions in order to save money (Abramson and Means 2001, pp. 2–3). E-democracy is not usually cited as a demand feature by the operators. Some also credit "elected and appointed officials who wish to build a better public image, achieve superior service, increase taxpayer and voter confidence, and manage risk and compliance more effectively" (Abramson and Means 2001, p. 3). Despite these multiple drivers of e-government adoption, Abramson and Means argue that contemporary implementations of e-government generally lack adequate planning, training programs, and benchmarking studies — business strategies the authors suggest the state would do well to adopt from private sector models.

The fact that federal and state e-government efforts have bothered to sponsor or pay attention to some of the empirical studies cited above suggests that benchmarking is a valued practice, but the broader issue of why these expensive and lightly used e-government services exist at all cannot be dismissed. The findings cited above underscore the extremely pragmatic concerns of state agencies — how much one should pay, how to financially support the service, which services people are most interested in, and so forth. The Pew study and the Texas studies go somewhat further in assessing how people *want* to interact with government, and what the conditions of accessibility are, but fundamental issues of control and democracy are left as hints in findings on trust and fears of privacy violations.

McNeal, Tolbert, Mossberger, and Dotterweich (2003) disagree that citizen demand is a primary factor in e-government adoption, basing their conclusions upon comparisons of different states' e-government implementations and corresponding state demographic characteristics, such as Internet access and dominant political party. They argue that state professionalism and state professional networks are more important than economic resources or user demand, and suggest that desire for more citizen participation is not a key element in current e-government operations. Using multivariate regression analysis to measure relationships between several variables, including the number of state websites offering online services to citizens, the demand for online services, measured by the number of households with Internet access, state general revenue per capita, demographic characteristics such as race, and the activity levels of state legislators in professional organizations, the authors conclude that "the data suggest that participatory politics and constituent demand do not drive adaptation of digital government" (p. 62). Referring to partisan government as a "critical causal factor" in e-government adoption, they explain that Republican-led legislatures may be concerned with facilitating smaller, more efficient government operations, and be more open to the adoption of private business practices in government (p. 66). The authors suggest that e-government has been primarily framed as an issue of administrative efficiency, rather than as an issue of participatory politics. "Our finding that innovation is not associated with direct democracy or political participation indicates that participatory goals are not presently a dominant factor in state programs." (p. 66). Online government services are offered to provide greater administrative efficiency, not to promote more direct citizen involvement in political decision-making.

Whereas some may argue for participatory democracy as a primary factor in e-government implementation, our review and analysis finds that this is not currently the case. Greater citizen demand and involvement may be a key factor in e-government adoption, but this analysis of state e-government efforts finds that in terms of site content and user reactions, e-government design and performance to date reflect a top-down process chiefly influenced by government professionals and somewhat relevant to businesses but not especially relevant to individuals.

There appears to be a disconnection between the concerns of

e-government designers and operators and the people who are expected to use the services. As Doty and Erdelez (2002) point out, "there is a real danger that the fragmented model of information technology planning and implementation common in government will serve as the de facto base for e-government development" (p. 383). Theorizations of the user as citizen and user as consumer are in conflict, and much legitimate debate occurs over the place of both the public and the private sectors in e-government. Since the online government initiatives of the early 1990s, private investment and cooperative developments in the US have been viewed advantageously in creating federal and local e-government services, but empirical surveys show that citizen response is less than overwhelming. The involvement of the private sector and the state's emulation of business-like concerns for efficiencies and cost savings may have negative consequences for the democratic potential of online government. To the extent that electronic government creates portals and generates new data about citizen-users — data that can be analyzed, bought and sold — the role of the state and the various collaborative arrangements established to manage e-government should be scrutinized continuously in terms of privacy, security, and the ethical use of information. Most fundamentally, the agencies behind e-government efforts need to grapple with e-democracy potentials and realize that their explorations of near-term efficiencies achievable through adapting their normal operations to an Internet mode represent only a small part of what should be possible. An alternative vision will require leadership and a willingness to reexamine and conduct public debate on what governance systems should be like and how they should operate in the 21st century.

Notes

1. The NII called for the development of a seamless open data network to bolster education and the private economy, as well as improve governance through digital technologies (McIver and Elmagarmid, 4).
2. The current web page for FirstGov.gov states "FirstGov.gov will help you find and do business with government online, on the phone, by mail or in person. You may select customer gateways — citizens, businesses and nonprofits, federal employees and government-to-government — to

find exactly what you need. For example, from your computer, you can apply for student financial assistance, buy government publications, apply for social security and other benefits, get a passport application, and so much more." http://www.firstgov.gov/index.shtml, last accessed on 31 May, 2004.

3. Rosen notes the average Briton may be photographed by 300 separate security cameras a day, due to the broadly deployed CCTV system (2004).

4. The authors find associations for percentage of homes online (r = .42), per capita income (r = .35), percentage of population with a high school or higher education (r = .34) and voting participation in the 2000 election (r = .30).

5. Internet users were defined as persons who reported accessing the Internet in the past 30 days.

6. The list of businesses in this survey were taken from the Dun and Bradstreet Intensive File, proportionately including businesses in financial, legal, insurance, real estate, construction, and transportation sectors.

7. Both surveys were telephone based and conducted in February-March, 2004. Interviewers spoke with 300 information officers or CEOs in most cases at those businesses, and the response rate was 64 percent. About 1000 household respondents were randomly selected within Texas, and that sample included an oversample of 200 households from rural regions of the state.

8. The businesses employed over 100 people, were chosen randomly, and headquartered in Texas.

9. One distinction between the two surveys is that the Texas survey inquired specifically about services, while the Hart-Teeter survey included services and simple information seeking.

References

Abramson, J., Arterton, F. C., and Orren, G. R. (1988). *The Electronic Commonwealth: The Impact of New Media Technologies on Democratic Politics.* New York: Basic Books.

Abramson, M. and Means, G., (Eds.). (2001). *E-Government 2001.* PricewaterhouseCoopers Endowment for the Business of Government series. Lanham, MD: Rowman and Littlefield.

Aldrich, D., Bertot, J. C., and McClure, C. R. (2002). "E-Government: Initiatives, Developments, and issues". *Government Information Quarterly* 19: 349–355.

Barlow, J. P. (1996). *A declaration of the Independence of Cyberspace.* Electronic Frontier Foundation. Accessed on 5 April, 2004 at http://www.eff.org/ ~barlow/DeclarationFinal.html.

Bimber, B. (1998). "The Internet and political transformation: Populism, community, and accelerated pluralism". *Polity* 31 (1): 133–160.

Chabrow, E. (2003). "Congress urged not to put privacy ahead of data mining for potential terrorists". *InformationWeek*, 25 March.

Chadwick, A. and May, C. (2003). "Interactions between states and citizens in the age of the Internet: "E-government" in the United States, Britain, and the European Union". *Governance*, 16 (2): 271–300.

Cohen, S. and Eimicke, W. (2001). "The use of the Internet in government service delivery". In M. Abramson and G. Means (eds.), *E-Government 2001*, page no.? Lanham, MD: Rowman and Littlefield.

Dahl, R. A. (1985). *Controlling Nuclear Weapons: Democracy Versus Guardianship.* Syracuse, NY: Syracuse University.

Doty, P. and Erdelez, S. (2002). "Information micro-practices in Texas rural courts: Methods and issues for e-government". *Government Information Quarterly* 19" 369–387.

Dyson, E., Gilder, G., Keyworth, G., and Toffler, A. (1994). "Cyberspace and the American dream: A Magna Carta for the knowledge age (Release 1.2, August 22)". *The Information Society* 12 (3): 295–309.

Ferber, P., Foltz, F., and Pugliese, R. (2003). "The politics of state legislature websites: Making e-government more participatory". *Bulletin of Science, Technology, and Society* 23 (3): 157–167.

Halchin, L. E. (2002). "Electronic government in the age of terrorism". *Government Information Quarterly* 19: 243–254.

Hart-Teeter. (2003). "The new e-government equation: Ease, engagement, privacy, and protection". Prepared for the Council for Excellence in Government.

Horrigan, J. (2004). "How Americans get in touch with government". *Pew Internet and American Life Project*, available online: www.pewinternet.org/ (accessed on 20 May, 2004).

Jaegar, P. T. (2002). "Constitutional principles and e-government: An opinion about possible effects of federalism and the separation of powers on e-government policies". *Government Information Quarterly* 19: 357–368.

Kampen, J. K. and Snijkers, K. (2003). "E-democracy: A critical evaluation of the ultimate e-dream". *Social Science Computer Review* Winter, 21 (4): 491–496.

Lan, Z. and Falcone, S. (1997). "Factors influencing Internet use — a policy model for electronic government information provision". *Journal of Government Information* 24 (4): 251–257.

Lessig, L. (2000). *Code and Other Laws of Cyberspace*. New York: Basic Books.

Love, J. (1992). "The marketplace and electronic government information". *Government Publications Review* 19: 397–412.

Lyon, D. (2003). *Surveillance after September 11*. Cambridge, UK: Polity Press.

McIver, W. J. and Elmagarmid, A. K. (eds.). (2002). *Advances in Digital Government: Technology, Human Factors, and Policy*. Boston: Kluwer.

McNeal, R., Tolbert, C., Mossberger, K., and Dotterweich, L. (2003). "Innovating in digital government in the American states". *Social Science Quarterly* 84 (1): 52–70.

Michaels, D. (2003). "Critics say freedom of information shouldn't come with access fee". *Dallas Morning News*, 6 April, 2003.

Momentum Research Group of Cunningham Communication. (2000). *Benchmarking the eGovernment Revolution: Year 2000 Report on Citizen and Business Demand*. Reston, VA: NIC.

Moulder, E. (2002). "Inside e-government: Applications for staff. Special Data Issue no. 6". Washington, DC: International City/County Management Association.

Musso, J., Weare, C., and Hale, M. (2000). "Designing web technologies for local governance reform: Good management or good democracy?" *Political Communication* 17: 1–19.

Netchaeva, I. (2002). "E-Government and e-democracy: A comparison of opportunities in the North and South". *Gazette: The International Journal for Communication Studies* 64 (5): 467–477.

Ponemon Institute. (2004). "Privacy trust survey of the United States government: An executive summary". Presented by Ponemon Institute and the CIO Institute of Carnegie Mellon University. Accessed on 5 April, at http://www.cioi.web.cmu.edu/research/2003PrivacyTrust SurveyExecutiveSummary.pdf.

Ross, J. (2003). "Data searches slow computer: County computer is overloaded by firms accessing public data". *Corpus Christi Caller-Times*, B1, 17 July.

Rosen, J. (2004). *The Naked Crowd: Reclaiming Security and Freedom in an Anxious Age*. New York: Random House.

Strover, S. (2002). "Citizens' perspectives on E-government". In W. J. McIver and A. K. Elmagarmid (eds.), *Advances in Digital Government: Technology, Human Factors, and Policy*, pp. 243–257. Boston: Kluwer.

———, Straubhaar, J., Inagaki, N., Gustafson, K., and Boaventura, A. (2004). "E-Government services in Texas: Results of a Texas Survey". Telecommunications and Information Policy Institute, University of Texas. Available online: www.utexas.edu/research/tipi (accessed on 31 May, 2004).

——— and Straubhaar J. (2004). "E-government, TexasOnline and Business in Texas". Telecommunications and Information Policy Institute, University of Texas. Available online: www.utexas.edu/research/tipi (accessed on 31 May, 2004).

West, D. (2003). "State and federal e-government in the United States, 2003". Center for Public Policy, Brown University.

11

—⁓⁓—

Good Governance through E-governance? — Assessing China's E-government Strategy

Junhua Zhang

Good Governance and China

Despite the divergence of definitions and interpretations of "good governance" among international agencies and scholars, there is quasi-consensus on the core elements of this concept: transparency, accountability, the rule of law and democracy. It is not within the scope of this paper to consider the implementation of "good governance" in developed countries. Regardless of different understanding of the term "good governance," one thing is certain — the very notion of "good governance" has created global competition in effectiveness, efficiency and accountability between political elites regardless of their differing political systems.

From an international perspective, the introduction of the idea and practices of "good governance" has enabled people to depart from Cold War rhetoric and ideology and to abandon some absolute value judgements in terms of "either you have it or you don't." Without renouncing universal values, more and more people from developed countries, especially policy-makers have realized that there should be different, contextual approaches in dealing with countries which still have a relatively long way to go on the road to democracy and prosperity. One of the ways international organizations seek to assist this process is by promoting sound administration. This strategy of incrementalism has clearly enjoyed a greater degree of acceptance among the countries attempting to modernize than the "hard" approaches previously taken. It is indisputable that China is among those most committed to modernization.

A review of various "good governance" approaches currently practised reveals the inclusion of the outside concept into the national internal policymaking process has encouraged more and more fledgling democracies and non-democratic countries to enter a global competition in "good governance." A comparison of governance levels in these countries conducted by the World Bank, for example, has at least stimulated the political elites of the respective countries to rethink their performance and image from a national as well as an international perspective.

To some extent, China's endorsement of e-government is also a response to the internationalization of the issue of good governance. Yet the motivations behind bringing government online and networking both government and citizens are manifold. For this reason it makes no sense to discuss the incentives for establishing Chinese e-government from one single angle. Instead, the real motivation behind the introduction of e-government can and should be revealed by examining the modernization strategy as well as administrative reform policy pursued by China's political elite over the past two decades.

Modernization and China's E-government

Generally speaking, the history of 20th century in China was a history of the continual struggle to modernize. The last twenty five years since Deng Xiaoping's accession to power have proved the most significant period in this process. This paper will not discuss in detail the Chinese leadership's varying perceptions and interpretations of the term "modernization" at different times. However, special mention should be made of an important change of paradigm in terms of development strategy that took place in the 90s. This shift was directly influenced by Alvin Toffler's theory of the three waves, which was first introduced into China in the mid 80s. In his work *The Third Wave*, Toffler assumes that most Western nations have already undergone two phases of development: the agricultural revolution and industrialization. Now they are embarking on the third phase known as informatization. Unlike the modernization theorist Walt Whitman Rostow, who sticks to a step-by-step development for "latecomers" (1960), Toffler argues that it is quite possible for developing countries to avoid the mistakes made by the industrial nations during industrialization and to catch up with them by promoting informatization during their modernization. Obviously Toffler's idea that modernization can include a "leap-frog development strategy" was very encouraging for the Chinese leadership. So it is hardly surprising that soon after the publication of his theory, there was an outbreak of 'Toffler fever' amid huge enthusiasm for the new evolutionary theory. Since then the term "informatization" (*xinxihua*) has been added to the Chinese Communist Party's (CCP) program, running parallel to the "four modernizations."[1] Thereafter, especially as China witnessed the efforts made by the Clinton administration to promote the Internet industry in the mid 1990s, the Chinese political elite became firmly convinced that informatization is the only step necessary to achieve the goal of modernization. Modernization through informatization (*yong xinxihua daidong xiandaihua*) has become one of the key policies implemented since then. It is notable that during Jiang Zemin's administration information and communication technology (ICT) has become a favourite with the CCP and the central government. The priority given to promoting ICT has been clearly underscored in various documents emanating from the CCP as well as the government. It was repeatedly emphasized in the blueprint released at the 16th Party Convention (Zhang 2001; Qi 2003: Preface; Jiang 2001: 108).

It should be noted that China's preference for ICT is intended as a long-term strategy. The importance attached to the role of informatization still dominates today's development policy in China even at a time when the new economy has been called into question in Western societies. The massive promotion of ICT has led to a degree of progress in building a new telecommunication infrastructure, of which many other developing countries can only dream. By the end of July 2003, China's telephone penetration had reached 30.22 percent of the whole population (in comparison to 11 percent in 1986), fixed phone line penetration was 15.56 percent while that of mobile phones was 13.86 percent. Official reports show 41.73 million Internet users.

Given both its heritage in political thinking and the existing political and economic system, the government is only too aware of its own key role in the modernization process. The political elite believe the introduction of e-government can accelerate the process of informatization in two respects. Firstly, it requires all government organs to be computerized and networked, so that they will set a good example for private enterprises and companies. Needless to say, this only works where ties between government and business are quite strong and the market economy has yet to reach maturity.

The second respect is closely related to the perception that the government is a major consumer of computer industry products. The drive by all levels of government to equip themselves with ICT will give a great boost to the national production of hardware and software as well as e-commerce. The goal of China having its own hardware and software industry has been a key factor in Chinese informatization. The concept of e-government dovetails well with this approach.

The discussion above has focused mainly on factors and expectations at the technical and technological levels. But there is also an important political consideration providing strong motivation for the Chinese leadership to set up an e-government. Inferior and irrationally designed structures of government and the poor morals of civil servants and cadres are widely accepted as posing a serious danger to the CCP. As modernization proceeds, public administration at various levels has proved unequal to the task of keeping up as long as it clings to its old working style. The problems in public administration China is facing nowadays are not new. However, the economic reforms have created additionally a breeding ground for a hitherto unparalleled criminality: rampant corruption and money-laundering have been made worse by insufficient flows of information, the rapid expansion of government organs, the ineffective control of the state's revenue and emerging interest groups in various government departments and provinces who work against the policy of the central government. Indeed, the fruits of the reform policy, which has given China a measure of economic successes, have been nibbled away by the bureaucracy itself. This has awakened considerable unease among the Chinese leadership as the CCP is quite aware of that these developments could jeopardize its continued political monopoly.

From this reason the Chinese leadership has felt a very real need to enhance its surveillance mechanisms to guarantee at least a minimal level of functioning of government organs. E-government is the ideal instrument to help the leadership strengthen its position in this respect since networked government organs will provide superiors with a better insight into the work flow of state workers.

China's E-government — The State of the Art

China's informatization of government (*zhengfu xinxihua*) is already about 20 years old. Its development can be divided into four periods. At the end of 80s the central government decided to embark upon an "Office Automatization Project." This was really the initial step designed to computerize office work and to build an internal e-network. This project established a good basis for subsequent efforts to promote e-government. During the 90s all organs at national and provincial levels were computerized. By the end of 1991 more than 47 government organs at the deputy provincial governor level and above were linked through an intranet. According to official statements, the purpose of this was to guarantee absolute security and to promote efficiency and serve the convenience of those higher-ups.[2]

The second phase began in 1993. Under the patronage of Jiang Zemin the State Council launched a project named "Golden Card" aimed at introducing smart cards and installing a national automated teller machine (ATM) network and a point-of-sale (POS) computer network. Almost simultaneously two other Golden Projects, the so-called Golden Customs and Golden Bridge, were also launched. The Golden Customs project seeks to promote network-based administration, the operation of foreign trade and the flow of related information, and the building of a CA (Certification Authority) system for foreign trade, whereas the Golden Bridge aims to build a nationwide broadband network known as the "China Golden Bridge Net (China GBN)."[3]

Within ten years of the launch of the first golden project, several other giant projects — all designated "Golden" — sprung up. To date there are 13 such golden projects. Most are still in their initial stages (see Appendix 1). Aside from the three mentioned above, the Golden Tax, Golden Finance, Golden Audit and Golden Trade projects have been singled out for special favour by the central government. This is because they reflect the priority of Chinese policy-makers at the top level, namely giving economic development the highest priority. A latecomer, the "Golden Shield" project, though hardly having anything to do with the economy, has been the focus of attention of the political elite as its special function is to control the Internet and counter delinquency both in terms cyber-dissidents and other internet crimes.

It is important to note that the Internet was introduced relatively late to China. This combined with a laxness among cadres and civil servants about switching to computers and Internet technology. By 1998, there were only 561 websites with gov.cn domain names.

Inspired by the American "new economy", the government realized that it had to encourage government organs to use network resources. At the instigation of China Telecom in January 1999 more than 40 government units at ministerial level forwarded a proposal for constructing an e-government. Heralded officially as the "Government Online" project (*zhengfu shangwang*) it proclaimed the third stage of China's e-government development. In the schedule drawn up by the Government Online Project Service Centre (GOPSC) it was projected that in the first year 60 percent of government organs at the ministerial level would be equipped with their own websites. By the year 2000 the number of online government organs was expected to grow to 80%. In order to provide government employees with more incentives for adopting the e-government, subsidies were offered to those institutions ready to set up their own websites. This campaign has yielded some positive effects: one year later, the number of gov.cn domain names had increased to 2,479 sites, and 720 governmental departments had their own www websites. Today, according to the last CNNIC (China Internet Network Information Centre) annual report, the number of gov.cn domain names has increased to more than 13,000.[4]

Parallel to this development, and in part spurred on by enthusiasm for the previously discussed idea of leap-frogging, some local governments began to experiment with their own concept of e-government. Cities in the coastal regions with high grade ICT environments and a sound basic infrastructure conceived ambitious plans to modernize their government structures and provide citizens with digital services. Words like "digitalized city" (*shuzi cheng*) or "digitalized harbour" (*shuzigang*) have become fashionable terms. In contrast to most other cities in China, where plainly there are few resources available for creating a sophisticated e-government, cities like Beijing, Tianjin, Shanghai, Guangzhou and Shenzhen have made concrete plans to implement e-governments by a process of establishing special teams for professional design and realization. Taking advantage of its special status, Beijing put forward plans for a so-called "48261 Project"[5] and proclaimed that it would become the first city in China with a digitalized and sophisticated e-government by the year 2005.

At the same time, some other e-government models have also emerged. In the year 2000 the Administration Committee of the *Zhongguancun Hichtech Park* opened a one-stop shop for investors and new university graduates from abroad (www.zhongguancun.com.cn). It was commissioned by the district authorities for technical realization and operation by a private commercial company. This model provides a way of connecting government and private enterprises in complementary digital services — a rare example of the type of co-operation which China must further encourage.[6]

In 2000 a fourth phase of China's e-government was launched, involving a holistic and down-to-earth conceptualizing informatization project. Characteristic of the new phase of China's e-government is that the GOPSC declared that government organs were not merely facing the phase of "e-government" in terms of bringing themselves online, but would also have to enter a phase of "e-governance." For the GOPSC "e-governance" means that the Government Online Project should lead to interplay between computerized and digitalized networks and real government work and that there should be a fundamental change in thinking and behaviour among government workers produced by a sophisticated, not a superficial e-government. Currently, many local governments feel content with just creating a website for themselves like a business-card without realizing the real meaning of e-government. The GOPSC hopes that a new stage will start by emphasising the difference between e-government and "e-governance" although Western experts find this somewhat misleading and irritating. It is no accident that 2002 was proclaimed the year of e-governance by the GOPSC.

The problems China's e-government faced after the launch of

the Government Online Project did not centre entirely on trying to meet the GOPSC target. Within the Internet industry, conflicts between various telecommunication carriers and operators significantly hampered the government's initiative to merge three networks (computer network, telecommunication network and TV network), a move laid down in the 10th Five-Year-Plan (Zhang, 2003) and which is designed ultimately to lead to the networking of local governments at a national level. The superficial and arbitrary e-government designed by local governments or their departments has impeded the networking of different small-size e-governments as well. In addition, a lack of funding and human resources had led to ambitious projects remaining half-finished.

In view of these difficulties the State Council decided to speed up the pace of building e-government by enhancing the authority allocated to top-down management by the central government. Many State Council documents issued in 2000 and 2001 reveal that the government has created a top priority project to be completed in between three and five years. It foresees three networks and one data bank forming the basis of Chinese e-government.[7] The three networks are: firstly, an intranet for high-ranking government officials, which is intended to be more "individual-oriented"; secondly, an intranet for civil servants; and thirdly, a public information network open to all. The data bank, which is to be specially designed for government employees, has four subordinate data banks. These are devoted to demographic information, laws and regulations, territorial resources and macroeconomics. In addition to the thirteen ongoing Golden Projects, there several new ones: a national digital networked system for urban environmental protection, a digital networked system for the prevention and reduction of natural catastrophes, and a digital networked system for the stimulation and promotion of the economy in China's western regions.[8]

Apart from the plans mentioned above, another decisive step with far-reaching consequences for the further development of Chinese e-government is the Project Demonstrating a Practicable Model of E-Governance (*zhongguo dianzi zhenggu yinyong shifan gongcheng*). At the end of 2000, a special team consisting of experts from Ministry of Science and Technology, State Informatization Office, Ministry of Public Security and other ministries, was established to design China's own e-government model to be applied to all levels of local government. The project emphasises security, sophistication, standardization and integrity. In November 2001 the team held a hearing to select several local governments to take part.

Chen Xiaozhu, Director of State Council Informatization Promotion Office said that the key projects of the office is to promote e-government in administration operation resources management, macro economy management, customers, taxation, finance, IC cards, auditing, public security, social security, agriculture, water resources, and quality assurance. In accordance with massive efforts made by the central government in promoting a secure, standardized e-government network, the Chinese *E-commerce Standard Committee* (ESC)[9] issued in March 2003 the *Guide of E-Government* and *Six Notices of Trial of E-Government Standards.*

Despite of much rhetoric about e-government, no completion target date has been set to date. Chinese experts seem to be uncertain what difficulties they might encounter. Judging by China's current level of success in building a basis for e-government, the scheme may take 3-5 years to complete. Applying the model at local government level may need a further 10 years.

Mapping out China's E-government Strategy

E-government has become a global phenomenon. To judge whether an e-government has been established in accordance with the model of good governance, one should first examine the objectives formulated and the strategy pursued in the implementation of e-government. Mapping out exactly what an e-government strives to achieve is a process which brings into focus both the political culture and the institutional framework of the countries in question. Enthusiasts of e-government often overlook that there is a straight interplay between the e-government designer and the product designed. It is an indisputable fact that e-government will, in the long run, change the way of thinking and behaviour of both its creators and users. In the initial stages the active role of the designer should not be neglected. The e-government's future path is determined in the first instance by the designer. Moreover, different perceptions of governance inevitably shape the e-government strategy.

As suggested before, in China there is much evidence of the non-performance of government work in the last two decades. The Chinese saying "the superior issues policy, but the inferior has a counter-policy" (*shangyou zhengche, xiayou duiche*), shows how very often central government cannot wholly rely on subordinate organs to implement its policies. As a result, government administration costs have been very high and there are not enough resources to fund such a giant bureaucratic machine. The Chinese leadership is only too aware of the fact that it cannot always get the exact information it wishes. Unlike the first and second generations of Chinese leaders, the third and fourth are dependent on performance and bureaucratic professionalism rather than personal charisma. That is why the former State Council headed by Zhu Rongji, introduced several administrative reforms and enhanced the vertical control mechanism in his legislative period to try to make government work more effectively and efficiently. A recent project in Shenzhen experimenting with a Chinese model of separation of powers demonstrates there are also attempts to create a horizontal control mechanism within the government. The new administration's programme foresees the continuation of existing reforms and even greater administrative changes to come. There are numerous barriers to cutting the costs of bureaucracy and leaders would probably settle for even partial success in the years to come.

A review of developments over the past two decades clearly shows that the existing information policy has assisted corrupt civil servants in lining their own pockets and abusing power. Citizens are poorly informed about laws and regulations because of the restrictive information policy, which obviously hampers even a very limited public participation. Consequently there can be no e-government in real sense without redefining what citizens should and should not know.

Last but not the least, China's accession to the WTO has also put Chinese government, and above all, local governments under immense outside pressure. Many new rules have to be introduced and China urgently needs a government based on professionalism in order to compete with member countries.

Against this background it is understandable that China has a vision, albeit not a very grand one, of e-government. Unlike developed countries China does not seem to cherish any ambition to build one of the world's top e governments. Instead, authorities merely express the hope that it will meet the average world standards in three or five years, without defining exactly what these world standards are. In the *E-government White Paper* published in 2000, the GOPSC declared their objectives to be as follows (Service Centre 2000: 53; Wu and Qi 2001: 108):

- To provide citizens with basic information about the function and structure of government organs;
- To enable the public to get access to laws, regulations and the workflow of government departments;
- To improve services and raise work efficiency by providing citizens with electronic service counters etc operated by various government departments;
- To promote economic development by informing the public about local industry and other sectors;
- To receive online information and feedback from citizens in the form of Emails and letters of complaint.

Yet, since China is a country where there is a major gulf between reality and rhetoric, the true targets for China's e-government are a long way away from the stated aims — at least in the short term. An examination of Chinese government at national and local levels indicates that China's e-government presently has four priorities:

- To establish a surveillance mechanism as soon as possible. This mechanism should enable central government decision-makers to prevent or trace huge economic losses caused by organized tax dodgers etc. Characteristic of these attempts are the aforementioned Golden Projects and other major schemes devised by central government.
- To improve economic performance providing investors, especially ones from abroad, with information and services. Chinese government websites are clearly targeting business and investment. The majority of websites do not suggest that a commitment to providing citizens with information is the norm.
- To secure the physical separation of the intranet from other platforms or portals as well as the Internet. From the very beginning Chinese authorities have repeatedly emphasized the security aspects e-government. The standard practice of

physically separating intranet from other networks indicates that China's leadership is very concerned about the vulnerability of e-government.

- To secure sufficient funding for the aforementioned major projects at any cost. As with real practice, there is a clear hierarchy in the funding of e-government. Major e-government projects are funded by the state budget while local governments have to "feed" their government websites or portals by themselves.

An analysis of China's e-government strategy suggests China will develop a kind of e-government which cannot be compared to that of developed nations. The key features of Chinese efforts to set up e-government can be summarized as follows:

1. Top-down and overall-planning combined with a trial and error approach implemented first in developed regions.

    The legal framework and respective guidelines for developing a Chinese e-government were firstly developed by the *State Informatization Leading Group affiliated to the State Council.* Up to date, the e-government policy has been embodied by several documents such as "Special Projects of Informatization of National Economy and Society" (Guomin jinji he shehui xinxihua zhongdian zhuanxian guihua), 'Guidelines for constructing a Chinese e-government' (woguo dianzi zhenwu jianshe zhidao yijian) and the 'Internal Document No. 17 (Li 2002)'. The government has adopted a purely elitist approach for designing a Chinese e-government. The advisory committee is committed to providing the leading group with information about technical realization and experiences of Western countries. Apart from the "Golden Projects" launched and financed by the central government or various ministries experiments in the developed regions have been encouraged, so far the local governments will solve the financial problems by themselves.

2. A contradiction between the ambition of modernizing public administration in a leap-frog way and the limited knowledge of how to make a government work well.

    The third generation of leadership embodied by Jiang Zemin and Li Peng represents the image of technocrats. It is unavoidable that idea of e-government was largely reduced to technical and instrumental dimension. There are signs among the fourth generation of the Chinese leadership that more interest has been shown in social sciences and administrative culture. However, it is hard to say whether the idea of good governance in terms of administrative culture will be penetrated through the responsible government officials in charge of the realization of e-government.

As Golden Projects and other aforementioned plans illustrate, China is trying to reshape the existing structure of public administration, particularly the financial and taxation sectors. To echo Max Weber: China has for a long time lacked a bureaucracy which can think and act rationally. The central government wants e-government to function in part as the driving force for these key sectors to introduce a new type of work flow as well as working style. Yet it is still hard to foresee whether public administration can be swiftly reformed in the leap-frog way the government expects. China is a country of incredible contrasts: on the one hand the government endorses brand new tools of governance, yet on the other it has one of the most ineffective and inefficient government organs. In this respect no one can predict whether in the short term China's e-government will reflect the central government's expectations.

3. Lack of ideas for financing the establishment of e-government.

    As a result of the aforementioned the problem, many e-government portals at provincial level downwards do not have any long-term plan, so that there is no sign of sustainable development with respect to the funding and content enlargement.

Apart from what has been mentioned above, China's insistence on absolute physical separation of the intranet from the Internet means the costs of e-government will be much higher than countries tackling the security problem in other ways. Given the limited budget for setting up e-government, achieving the rapid networking and digitalizing of government at the provincial level and below will be extremely difficult. Some east coast urban regions do not seem to have any big financial problems in establishing their local e-government. But local authorities in the interior, in particular those at prefecture and district level where 50% of government budget still stems from illegal or semi-legal sources (mostly through charging enterprises or rural citizens excessive fees) will have great trouble in meeting even minimal e-government standards.[10] The massive blind investment in e-image building by many local governments as well as some ministries in previous years shows that there is lack of accountability towards Chinese taxpayers.

Progress and Problems of China's E-government

Despite of the problems mentioned above, the progress made in the past few years cannot be ignored. The partial realization of Golden Tax and Custom Projects has already yielded its fruits. According to official statistics, smuggled goods seized by custom officials were worth 1.474 and 2.122 billion RMB in 1997 and 1998 respectively. Following the introduction of computerized declaration procedures, the value of smuggled goods was reduced to 0.313 billion RMB in 1999. And there were almost no registered smuggled goods one year later (Qu 2002; Chen and Li 2002).

It is highly significant that the legal conditions for the introduction of a modest level of e-government are being improved. There are four new laws or regulations closely related to e-government. One is the procurement law, which came into force at the end of 2002. It provides government at all levels with a legal framework for procurement in an electronic form. The second one is "The Regulation on Publicizing Government Information" (Li 2002). From the political science perspective, this regulation will, if effectively implemented, have a far-reaching impact on Chinese society. As the insiders have already revealed, once issued, it will commit all government organs to publishing most of the information which until now has remained locked in office desks. The implementation of this will be painful for two reasons: firstly, the CCP has got used to setting the agenda and letting the public know what it allows. Secondly, many civil servants have profited greatly from their monopoly of information and lack of government transparency.[11] When the regulation comes into force, they will have to give up at least part of their power.

One problem connected with "Publicizing Government Information" regulation lies in its incompatibility with the existing censorship practised in journalism. Until now China has refused to issue a press law because it might curtail the privileges of CCP's propaganda department in disseminating information. It is unclear what will happen when the forthcoming regulation collides with existing censorship. It is unlikely that there will be an answer to this soon.

To sum up, overall the Chinese leadership plays a productive role in establishing e-government. In some regions citizens will enjoy the fruits of China's e-government. Yet, the political system and the backward political culture of civil servants pose a serious threat to the modernization of public administration. China's e-government is not always being built in a modern and rational way. It also remains to be seen whether the completion of the major e-government projects will have any impact on e-government itself. Nevertheless, e-government will ultimately become one of important instruments for reformers within the leadership, who are trying gradually to bring China closer to a modest form of good governance.

Evaluating China's E-government Websites

Since e-government has become a global phenomenon, more and more e-government analysts have come to the conclusion that there should be a worldwide recognized standard for measuring the quality and the grade sophistication of a certain e-government website or portal. A worldwide accepted standard of comparison of various e-governments will certainly boost the incentive of respective "stakeholders" to improve the quality of their work and furthermore to enable them to become innovative. From this reason a strong need to set a series of criteria with which one can tell at which level a certain e-government can be positioned is emerging. Up to now, worldwide surveys on development of e-government have been carried out mainly by three organizations. One, by the Internet consultancy *Accenture*, involved researchers attempting to conduct business with 22 governments via the internet, role-playing citizens and businesses in their own countries. The following service sectors were investigated during the survey: human services, justice and public safety, revenue, defence, education, administration, transportation, regulation and democracy, and postal. In all, 165 services potentially offered, or more exactly supposed by the *Accenture* to be offered, were studied. According to degrees of overall maturity of the respective e-government, as shown in Table 11.1, 22 countries were ranked in four degrees: "Innovative Leader," "Visionary Follower," "Steady Achievers," and "Platform."

Without going into details of criteria employed during the survey, the ranking of the countries evaluated in 2001 is as follows:

Table 11.1 Maturity of the Respective E-government 22 Countries

Innovative Leaders (Degree I)		Visionary Followers (Degree II)	
Canada		Norway	Netherlands
Singpapore		Australia	United Kingdom
USA		Finland	
Steady Achievers (Degree III)		Platform Builders (Degree IV)	
New Zealand	Ireland	Japan	South Africa
Hong Kong	Portugal	Brazil	Italy
France	Germany	Malaysia	Mexico
Spain	Belgium		

Source: Accenture (2002): Rhetoric vs Reality — Closing the Gap.

It deserves special note that the Informatization Leading Group of China's State Council commissioned *Accenture* to conduct a special assessment of China's e-government in July 2002. The result of this analysis was submitted as a report known as "The Present State of Chinese E-governance — Establishing a Platform of Future Development." According to *Accenture*, the overall maturity of China's e-government has just reached 23% and China is still in the stage of building a platform. However, China might yet take a leading position among the less developed countries due to the steady growth of its infrastructure and research into e-government.[12]

The other international survey, which includes an assessment of China, was issued by the *World Market Research Center* in June 2001 and is based on methods employed by M. West in *An Assessment of City Government Websites* (Wes, 2001). Six criteria are used for evaluating the quality of e-government, namely: online service, privacy and security, disability access, foreign language access, advertisements and user fees, and public outreach. According to these measures, China comes 12th among all the countries surveyed with regard to online service, while in the overall scores China turned out to be quite low, being placed 85th among the 196 nations.

The third research of e-government was undertaken in the year of 2002 and 2003 by the United Nation together with American Society for Public Administration. Based on the report, 173 member countries with web presence were analysed. The research team developed a set of e-government index, with which a ranking list was made. Table 11.2 mirrors the scores respective countries have achieved in terms of e-government readiness.

As to the evaluation of e-government within China, there have emerged four institutions involved in evaluating government websites. Each of them has introduced different methods and the results of their surveys demonstrate a wide spectrum of state of the art of online service provided (mostly) by local governments.

In the following part, it is intended to discuss briefly the surveys conducted by two of these organizations.

Table 11.2 E-Government Readiness Rankings (2003)

Ranking	Country	Scores measured by the e-government index
1	USA	0.92
2	Sweden	0.84
3	Australia	0.83
4	Denmark	0.82
5	Great Britain	0.81
6	Canada	0.80
7	Norway	0.778
8	Switzerland	0.76
9	Germany	0.76
10	Finland	0.76
12	Singapore	0.74
74	China	0.41

Source: UN (2003): *World Public Sector Report: E-Government at the Crossroads*, pp. 144–151.

The Fortune Age, an IT consulting company based in Guangzhou, conducted a survey on 196 government websites last year. Among these websites, 96 are those of ministerial and provincial level, 100 are those of inferior organs of Guangdong province. The company developed a system for measuring the degree and scale of e-governance which comprises 30 indicators. The indicators are divided into four categories: 1) basic government information and content of government information; 2) online service; 3) main function of online administration; 4) concrete plans and actions for application and promotion of e-governance. The result of the survey reveals that China is still far away from e-government in the strict sense. According to the Fortune Age, China's e-government has fulfilled merely 22.6 percent of the requirements which a well-designed e-government should meet. This assessment has been widely cited by experts on e-government in China.

Another evaluation of China's e-government was made by the editorial office of *China Computer World Research (CCW Research)* in 2002. By order of the Office of State Informatization Leading Group affiliated to the State Council, the staff of the editorial office took several months trying to find a systematic and sustainable standard of e-government websites by focusing on the websites as well portals of 36 cities which are mostly capitals of their respective provinces in China. Three categories were conceived as major criteria for the assessment: 1) content related service regarding aspects which range from transparency of government information to local information; 2) functional service in terms of online service in connection with transactions ranging from online consulting, inquiry, application and procurement, and online complaint mechanism as well as interaction between government and citizens; 3) quality of construction. The latter comprises client-oriented design of websites, actuality and comprehensiveness of information and other special features of a website in terms of security, hit rate and the like. In the view of the editorial staff the main feature of e-government should appear from scores yielded through assessment according to the first and the second categories. During the evaluation, five classes of scores were applied: Excellent (8 points and upwards), good (7.0–7.9 points), satisfactory (6.0–6.9 points), unsatisfactory (0.1–5.9 points) and nonexistent (0). The result of the assessment is shown in Table 11.3 as follows:

Table 11.3 Scores for the Performance of Chinese Local E-government

Beijing	7.8	Kunmin	5.2	Shanghai	7.7	Chongqin	5.1
Guangzhou	7.4	Fuzhou	5.1	Nanjing	6.7	Guiyang	4.9
Dalian	6.7	Changsha	4.9	Haerbin	6.7	Changcun	4.7
Hanzhou	6.6	Shijiazhuan	4.6	Shenzhen	6.5	Nanchang	4.3
Qingdao	6.5	Tianjin	4.0	Xiameng	6.4	Yinchuan	4.0
Haikou	5.9	Xinin	4.0	Uhehaote	5.9	Zhengzhou	4.0
Hefei	5.9	Shenyang	3.4	Urumuqi	5.8	Lanzhou	3.3
Jinan	5.8	Xi´an	2.4	Wuhan	5.6	Lasa	0.0
Ninbo	5.4	Nannin	0.0	Chendu	5.4	Taiyuan	0.0

Source: CCW-Report in: http://www.ccw.com.cn/news2/other/indusdata/ (accessed 20 July, 2004)

The proportions of diverse quality can be demonstrated in Figure 11.1.

In respect to the first category, Beijing gained the highest scores, first of all regarding online publication of laws and regulation. As to the second category, the websites of Beijing, Shanghai and Guangzhou are considered be exemplary. Among the existent websites, 61 percent do not offer any online application or filing, 55 percent lack online procurement and search machines; half failed to install interactive consulting services.

Figure 11.1 Quality of municipal e-governments

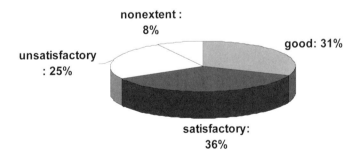

Source: CCW-Report in: http://www.ccw.com.cn/news2/other/indusdata/ (accessed 20 July 2004)

In assessing the surveys conducted by the four aforementioned organizations, two aspects deserve special mention. First, methodologically, it is difficult to legitimize any alleged well-balanced approaches applied by those who assess e-government. No e-government assessment is able to reflect the whole features of what an e-government really looks like, for it is difficult to see it through both "front office" and "back office" and the link between them in terms of workflow and institutional organization. Besides, the aforementioned organizations failed to realize that some criteria could be misleading in the sense that not all service provisions attributed as "online" or "digitalized" are really citizen-oriented. As Gartner, an Internet consulting company based in London, argues, better service levels can often be achieved without excessive reliance on web delivery.[13] Sweden, for example, has achieved higher tax collection rates and service levels by dramatically simplifying paper forms and preferring stronger back-office IT processes to an electronic front-end. This means taxes cannot be filed online yet, but the effort to file them is much lower than in countries where online filing and payments are possible. Many results of surveys also show that face-to-face or telephone interactions are still preferred for several services.

In addition, most organizations ignore the fact that there are different types of e-government websites or portals. Some countries are not keen on building a comprehensive portal or website like Singapore and the USA. China (www1.cei.gov.cn/govinfo/English/default1e.shtml) and Russia (www.gov.ru), for instance, have a very inconspicuous portal for websites of ministries and provincial governments. As well, some countries attach great importance to their government information website (in Germany: www.bundesregierung.de; in China: www.chinaorg.cn). In this case the question of whether these websites should also be regarded as part of e-government arises. The e-government websites in a real sense are mostly those created by municipal governments, especially in developing and less developed countries. In view of this fact, different approaches for assessing different types of e-government are called for.

For comparison on an international scope Accenture and the Word Market Research Centre have provided students of e-government with valuable perspectives. Yet, they mostly focus on

the e-governments of developed countries. In the surveys of
Accenture, China hasn't been regarded as a subject to be analysed.[14]
On the other hand, it is regrettable that the Chinese organizations
conducted their survey only at a national level. There is a resulting
lack of international comparison. As a result, it is difficult to non-
insiders to tell which stage China has factually achieved in the global
context.

Due to the difficulty of defining the criteria of *good*
e-government, it might be wise to introduce a more balanced
approach which contains three different types of analysis in assessing
China's e-government and other countries' e-government as well:
offline assessment, online assessment and outline assessment. While
online assessment refers to the examination of websites as the
aforementioned organizations do, offline assessment concerns two
aspects which reflect the ease of using e-government and its legal
environment in building e-government. Outline assessment
comprises surveys conducted among citizens and business circles for
the purpose of finding out their immediate relation to e-government.
Besides, many aspects of "back office" can only be revealed through
outline assessment, which appears to be not only time-consuming,
but also extremely difficult.[15] Due to the complexity of outline
assessment, in the following part only offline and online assessment
are to be discussed.

Offline Assessment (1)

Since 1999 China has developed a system of information indicators
known as the National Informatization Quota (NIQ)[16]. This system
covers various aspects of informatization: infrastructure, human
resources, education levels, etc. Thanks to its comprehensiveness this
system might be employed as the criteria of e-government readiness
mentioned above. According to the official report, the NIQ or the
overall level of China's informatization has reached a score of 38.46
in the year of 2000. Taking into account that 1999 and 1998 had
respectively scores of 30.14 and 25.89, there was apparently a leap in
China's informatization in the year of 2000.

Given that NIQ will influence the practicability and acceptability
of e-government in the respective regions, the following comparison
(see Table 11.4) reveals that despite of the increased efforts made by

the Zhejiang and Guizhou governments, these two provinces still lag very much behind Shanghai:

Table 11.4 Indicators of China's Informatization (2000)

Region	Develop-ment and use of resources	Constructure of informa-tion network	Application of informa-tion tech-nology	Information service and production	Human resources for infor-matization	Development environment of infor-matization	Increased scores in NIQ on national and regional level between 1999–2000	
							2000	1999
Total scores (at national level)	45.29	37.12	65.89	53.78	13.43	21.86	1.28	1.16
Shanghai	99.91	191.86	155.30	45.19	68.91	16.65	1.14	1.08
Zhejiang	72.43	59.03	86.53	33.49	9.86	34.68	1.39	1.15
Guizhou	2.16	157.84	40.38	5.62	4.45	21.01	1.48	1.20

Source: Centre of Assessment of National Informatization (2002), in: http://www.niec.org.cn/zt/xwtg31902.htm (accessed 23 April 2003). The criteria set by the Centre of Assessment of National Informatization are listed in the website: http://www.niec.org.cn/gjxxh/yjkt01.htm (accessed 23 April 2003).

Offline Assessment (2)

Another practicable offline assessment is examining the policy made by the respective governments in respect to promotion of e-government. Government documents and speeches made by political elites in relation to e-government are the main source. Based on analysis of government documents and speeches of state leaders, Table 11.5 provides a comparison by the author which reveals the difference between China, Germany and the UK in conceptualizing e-government and the realization of their plans.

Moving to online assessment, according to the core function of government and its respective website this kind of assessment consists of four parts: 1) G-C (government to citizens) service; 2) G-B (government to business) service; 3) administration/participation; and 4) technical realization. While the first three demonstrate the amount and quality of service which should be provided by a government normally in accordance with the concept of "good governance", the last criterion indicates the technical demand which a government website has to meet. In connection to these four categories three levels designated as "information," "com-munication", and "transaction" have been set for assessing the degree of maturity of e-government. The first level "information"

Table 11.5 China's E-government Environment in Comparison

Aspects which comprise e-government environment:	China internal *external*		Germany Internal external		UK internal external	
Political will on the side of leadership.	xxx	xxx	Xxx	xx	xxxx	xxxx
Analysis of e-readiness to face the issues.	xx	xxx	Xxx	xxx	xxxx	xxxx
Long-term vision, with strategic goals to relate e-government to development plans, to inform the public, get public support and facilitate monitoring and accountability.	xx	x	xxx	xx	xxx	xx
Identification of priorities to line up small, achievable components of the vision.	xx	none	xxx	xxxx	xxxx	xxxx
Regulatory and legal framework to assure sustainability of the effort.	x	x	xxxxx	xxxx	xxxxx	xxxx
Institutional structure in the centre and throughout the government at all levels to implement the vision	x	xxx	xxx			
Public involvement to respond to needs and fine-tune design of initiatives.	none	xx	xx			
Measures to reduce digital divide in employing e-government: training and education to achieve the needed level of skills among state servants and among the public at large.	xx	none	xxx	x	xxx	x

* Internal refers to the government initiative within governmental institutions, while external indicates presentation of e-government plan to the public.
Source: compiled by the author.

refers to "non-contact" relationship between e-government und the public. The second level "communication" indicates a "one-way" contact with the e-government on the side of the public. The third stage demonstrates the interactive relationship between the e-government and the public as well as interactive filing and payment (See Appendix 2).

Based on this methodological approach, five websites of different regions/countries were chosen for the purpose of comparative analysis: the websites of the Guizhou and Zhejiang provincial governments in China, the website of the municipal government of Shanghai, the website of the city of Taipei, and the website of the city of Los Angeles.[17] The result of the comparison is shown as follows:

Table 11.6 Comparison of Five Websites

Website of respective cities/regions	Service (G-C)	Service (G-B)	Administration/ Participation	Technical realization
Zhejiang	***	**	**	**
Guizhou	**	***	**	***
Shanghai	****	***	***	****
Taipei	*****	****	*****	****
Los Angeles	*****	*****	*****	****
nonexistent = 0% *		good<75% ****		
unsatisfactory<25% **		excellent >76% *****		
satisfactory <50% ***				

As to maturity of e-government, the following comparison indicates that the generally lower level of China's e-government and the uneven development within China as well.

Shanghai tive cities/regions	Service (G-C)	Service (G-B)	Administration/ Participation	Technical realization
Stage III: Transaction (active-active)	**	*	**	****
Stage II: Communication (passive–active)	****	***	***	
Stage I: Information (passive–passive)	*****	****	****	
nonexistent = 0% *		good<75% ****		
unsatisfactory<25% **		excellent >76% *****		
satisfactory <50% ***				

Guizhou tive cities/regions	Service (G-C)	Service (G-B)	Administration/ Participation	Technical realization
Stage III: Transaction (active-active)	*	**	**	***
Stage II: Communication (passive–active)	***	***	**	

Guizhou tive cities/regions	Service (G-C)	Service (G-B)	Administration/ Participation	Technical realization
Stage I: Information (passive–passive)	***	***	**	
nonexistent = 0%	*	good<75%	****	
unsatisfactory<25%	**	excellent >76%	*****	
satisfactory <50%	***			

Obviously, the Chinese government websites have mostly reached the first level in terms of service provision. The results above correspond with that of an analysis made by The Fortune Age. According to this report (2002), 87.8 percent of the 196 examined government websites are factually accessible. 7.6 percent of those websites that are working provide one or more download service. While 6.4 percent of them facilitate a modest degree of online submission of forms and the like, 2.3 percent of them make publication of the state in dealing with online requests. Although 18.6 percent of government websites grant users the opportunity to make online complaints, only 2.2 percent of them give answers to complainants[18]

Concluding Remarks

The analysis of the websites reveals that China's e-government is still in the infant stages. E-government touches only a tiny part of urban residents, to say nothing of the rural citizens which make up 63% of the whole population. Besides, there are big regional differences in the development of e-government between coastal cities and cities in the interior regions. While e-government in Beijing and Shanghai has achieved considerable progress and is in some respects even at the level of Western standards, many other regional governments lag behind. The backwardness of China's "front office" performance in certain regions goes mostly hand in hand with the crucial realities of government itself. One of problems lies in the structure of the government and power distribution between the party and government itself. The so-called separation between "sections" (*tiao*) and "department" (*kuai*), and accordingly dysfunctional communication has impeded greatly the connection of different government departments, be it virtual or visible. Another problem can be demonstrated in the educational level of government officials. Despite the fact that the educational level at the ministerial level has been significantly elevated during the last ten years thanks to the new recruitment policy of the central government, in some provincial governments there remains large number of government officials with relatively low educational levels. In the Province of Hainan for example, less than 30 percent of state workers are university graduates. In such cases, it is hard to realize the computerization of government work, let alone, e-government.

It is obvious that China's present priority lies mostly in establishment of an intranet in terms of networking government organs and monitoring government work digitally instead of using citizen-oriented front offices. In other words, China's e-government strategy reflects the state of an authoritarian system which is seeking a basis for legitimacy; so its present priority in building the e-government lies not in promoting participation and democracy, but rather in enhancing its own governmental functionality and professionalism. From the point of view of good governance, this moderate goal of e-government has its justification. On the other hand, it is notable that China's e-government might face a change of paradigm due to the power shift from Jiang Zemin to the fourth generation of leadership. The fact that Hu Jintao and his team are concerned not only about the technological aspect of public administration, but also about the aspect of administrative culture, indicates that Chinese government might adjust its strategy of e-government, which will differs from that represented by the Soviet-styled technocrats under Jiang Zemin's administration.

In the process of realizing the blueprint of e-government, there is apparently a change of approach in dealing with the resistance stemming from different interest groups. Instead of a decentralized approach in the realization of e-government, the central government claims to be the sole authority in designing the e-government model. As a result, at least at the ministerial level the political will of the leadership in connection with e-government seems to be able to be implemented in a more effective way. Yet e-government on the provincial and interior level will continue face tremendous resistance. The reason for these lies mostly in the lack of a clear vision of what e-government is, as well as the absence of a convincing explanation of how it should be realized. In addition, the problem of allocation of financial and human resources in realizing e-government at the provincial level remains unresolved.

The emergence of e-government indicates a new stage of competition regarding good governance. By 2001, among 190 members of the United Nations about 88 percent had already established government websites or portals. 55 countries have built e-government with a relatively satisfactory degree of interactivity. Yet more than 25 percent of existing e-governments are still in a very primitive stage. This reflects a low level of governance and lack of the government's responsibility towards the citizens. It is to be hoped that through implementing a set of worldwide acceptable evaluation criteria, more and more members of the United Nations will be encouraged to approach the concept of good governance. The fact that the Chinese government invited *Accenture* to assess its e-government shows that China is quite ready to join in this global competition in moving towards good governance. In this respect, a cautious optimism seems in order.

At the same time, one should bear in mind that the e-government is a phenomenon of a high degree of urbanization, especially with respect to e-participation. In the near term, due to fact that about 68 percent of Chinese population are still living in rural areas, it is not realistic for China to attain Western e levels. From this reasoning, e-government will have a limited reach in China in the next few years, even if its quality has been improved greatly.

Appendix 1. Summary List of the Golden Projects

Name of Project	Stake Holders	Vision of the project	Date of beginning of the project and date of (projected) completion
1 Golden Bridge (Jinqiao)	Ministry of Electronic Industry[19], Jitong Co. (operator as well as ISP)	China Golden Bridge Net (China GBN) Constructing a broadband telecommunication network	1993, by the end of 2004
2 Golden Customs (Jinguan)	Customs Control Administration/ MOFTEC	Realizing network-based administration, operation and information flow of foreign trade Building a CA system for the foreign trade,	1993. 2001 coming into operation
3 Golden (Jinka)	CardState Council	Installing automated teller machine (ATM) network and point-of-sale (POS) computer network. Issuing smartcards	1993, by the year 2003, issuing 200–300 million Smartcards
4 Golden Tax (Jinsui)	State Administration of Taxation	Computerizing and networking a tax return and invoice system	1994, unknown
5 Golden Shield (Jindun)	Ministry of Public Security	Police communication platform; Databanks; Setting up a digital Surveillance Centre for Public Security	1998, 5 years
6 Golden Health (Jinwei)	Ministry of Health	Establishing MIN (Medical Information Network) for the purpose of remote medical operation and data exchange; Introducing Golden Health Card	unknown
7 Golden Journey (Jinlü)	China National Travel Agency	Tri-network plus one databank: Intranet / Administrative Network / E-commerce and E-service Network / Public Information Databank at four levels: national, province, municipal and company.	2001, 5 years

Name of Project	Stake Holders	Vision of the project	Date of beginning of the project and date of (projected) completion
8 Golden Audit (Jinsheng)	Audit Court	To construct a mechanism for surveillance of treasury, banks, custom offices and revenue offices as well as preferential state-owned enterprises.	2002, 5 years
9 Golden Intelligence (Jinzhi)	Ministry of Education	Connection between CERNET and Internet 2; Establishing National School Network and University Campus Network;	1994, unknown
10 Golden Water (Jinshui)	Ministry of Water Resources	Building a flood forecasting and management network (Intranet and Internet); Becoming a back bone provider	2001, by the end of 2010
11 Golden Agriculture (Jinnong)	Ministry of Agriculture	Data bank. Overall system for agricultural production, information and technology	2003, 3 years
12 Golden Trade (Jinmao)	State Economic and Trade Commission/ Ministry of Information Industry	Setting framework of e-commerce; coordinating with projects of Golden Card / Customs / Audit; Establishing an ecommerce network for enterprises	1998. Within 3 years, helping 80% enterprises to be brought online.
13 Golden Finance (Jinchai)	Ministry of Finance	Government Financial Management Information System (GFMIS)	2002, by the end of 2008

Source: http://www.china.org.cn/chinese/zhuanti/283716.htm (accessed 12 April 2004)

Appendix 2: Criteria for Assessing E-government Websites

	Service (G-C)	Service (G-B)	Administration/Participation	Technical realization
Transaction Stage III (active-active)	1. download of forms and other documents 2. feedback mechanism of Stage II (1.4.5) 3. e-signature 4. e-payment 5. one-stop-shop service 6. response time to inquiries 7. length of time for procuring goods, service, info (from citizens' perspective) (less than 5 days) -	1. download of forms and other documents 2. online filing 3. feedback mechanism of Stage II (1.2.) 4. e-signature 5. e-payment 6. one-stop-shop service 7. response time to inquiries 8. length of time for procuring goods, service, info (from the business perspective)	1. feedback from the government organs; 2. e-signature between G-G; G-I; 3. report of online survey / voting 4. report of feedback to online complaints / suggestions or petitions 5. response time to inquiries (less than 3 days)	1. Accessibility of domain name (through search machines / easily remembered URL / links) 2. friendliness of browsers (Explorer / Netscape or others) 3. time to reach next page / link; 4. validity of links (more than 3: negative) 5. foreign language; 6. download of software for FDP and other audio-, video documents; 7. privacy: prohibit cookies / prohibit sharing personal information; 8. non-advertisements (more than 10: negative!) 9. masthead 10. notice and comment to masthead and response
Communication Stage II (passive – active)	1. Contact with the mayor (email) 2. Search machine 3. interactive city map 4. mail address or phone number or email for Stage I (except 1, 9) 5. feedback (notice and comment) 6. links to other websites / portals (more than 10) 7. Online filing: civil application / registration (civil certificates; personal identification, social security; vehicle registration), more than 10.	1. mail address or phone number or email for Stage I (except 8) 2. search machine 3. links to other websites / portals (more than 5) 4. feedback (notice and comment)	1. mail address or phone or email for Stage I (except 3) 2. discussion forum; 3. online survey 4. Suggestions or petitions; 5. permit applications for institutional use 6. privacy 7. links to other websites / portals 8. websites statistics report 9. non-censorship (negative)	

Inform-tion	Stage I (passive-passive)	Service (G-C)	Service (G-B)	Administration/Participation	Technical realization
		1. Info about the mayor / governor 2. info about district council (= P/A 1) 3. city events (cultural, sport, everyday life) 4. Tourist info (city map, sightseeing spots, hotels, restaurants, transportation) 5. General city info for residents (weather / gas, water and power / dwelling and streets / revenue / welfare system / hospital info / police) 6. Special info for residents: emergency info/ health / public safety. 7. info about civil application / registration (civil certificates; personal identification, social security; vehicle registration) 8. revenue info (taxation, customs, fee information) 9. up-to-dateness of information 10. education info (digital libraries and museums; education institutions; e-learning)	1. general business info (G-B); investment / market info; 2. procurement info (general info, bids; results of bids); 4. usiness statistics 5. ob ad. 6. ermits and licence (enterprises registration); 7. evenue info (taxation, customs, fee information); 8. aws and regulations; 9. nfo about e-learning for employees and employers	1. Government information (structure, staff, competence of various departments); 2. Info about parliament and parliamentarians (members of standing committee) 3. events calendar of municipal government 4. budget planning; 5. info about NGOs 6. social and political statistics; 7. City rules and laws; 8. Government announcement (special topics);	

		Service (G-C) 35 %	Service (G-B) 25 %	Administration/Participation 25 %	Technical realization 15%
Transaction	Stage III (active-active)	25%	30%	25%	100%
Communication	Stage II (passive-active)	35%	30%	35%	
Information	Stage I (passive-passive)	40%	40%	40%	

100 % = total score; 100% = score for respective fields;

Notes

1. The "four modernizations program" was put forward in 1974. It comprises the modernization of agriculture, industry, science and technology, and defence.

2. See http://standard.globalmfr.com/em/news.jsp?newsid=6548 (accessed on 2 February, 2004).

3. See http://www.china.org.cn/chinese/zhuanti/281319.htm (accessed on 28 August, 2004).

4. The 14th Survey Report (July, 2004), in http://www.cnnic.cn/en/index/0O/02/index.htm (accessed on 3 January, 2005).

5. Each number symbolizes the number of subprojects. For example, 4 stands for a city cable network, a LAN broadband network, a platform of public information, and a special network for administrative use. See http://www.china.org.cn/chinese/zhuanti/283242.htm (accessed on 23 March, 2004).

6. Admittedly, the *Zhongguancun Hichtech Park* was initiated by a software company aiming at making business rather than improving government work. Yet, as a by-product of its project, the district authorities had to partly change the structure of its service in order to attract more investment in their territory.

7. http://standard.globalmfr.com/em/news.jsp?newsid=6548 (accessed on 23 April, 2003).

8. http://www.e-gov.net.cn/news/news1/26.htm (accessed on 28 April, 2003).

9. ESC was co-founded by the Standardization Administration of China and the Information Office of the State Council in February 2002.

10. It is no accident that more than 90 percent of local authorities employ pirate copies of software while constructing their e-government. The author was informed about that during an interview with government officials conducted in Shenzhen and Haikou in July 2003.

11. It is said that the Chinese government still controls 80 percent of information which the society needs. See: Yuan Zhenhua (2001: 59).

12. Dianzi zhengwu: Zhongguo yu shijie de caju (E-governance: China' Distance to the Global Level), in *Jinji guanca bao*, 19 February, 2003, at http://www.echinagov.com/article/articleshow.asp?ID=1013 (accessed on 21 Feb 2003).

13. Gartner Advises European Governments: Too Much Focus on 'E', Will Not Deliver Better Services to the Public , in: http://www.gartner.com/5_about/press_releases/2001/pr20011126a.jsp (accessed on 24 December, 2002).

14. It should be mentioned that the Central Government was very

interested in the work by the Accenture. It specially asked the Accenture to make an overall assessment of the Chinese e-government in 2002. Unfortunately the result of the evaluation remains unknown.

15. It should be pointed out the "Balanced E-Government Index" set by a German research group 2002 (see Friedrich 2002, p. 149), might be considered as quite complete and incontestable. Yet, it mixes all three types of assessment together. As a result, it will be finally destined to fail due to the complexity of outline assessment.

16. A list of NIQ-criteria can be found in the website: http://www.cnii.com. cn/20021111/ca111600.htm (accessed on 21 July, 2003).

17. The investigated URLs of the local governments mentioned above are:
    1) www.sh.gov.cn
    2) www.gzgov.gov.cn
    3) www.zhejiang.gov.cn
    4) http://www.taipei.gov.tw/
    5) www.losangeles.feb.gov

18. http://www.ben.com.cn/WLZB/20030320/GB/WLZB%5E622%5E4%5E20R1002.htm (accessed on 20 March, 2003).

19. The Ministry of Electronic Industry was merged with Ministry of Post and Telecommunication in 1998 into the Ministry of Information Industry.

References

Accenture. (2002). "Rhetoric vs Reality — Closing the Gap". Available online: www.accenture.com.

Chen, W. H. and Li, L. (2002). "Dianzi zhengwu de fubai yufang zuoyong" (The Preventing Function of E-governance against Corruption). Available online: http://www.e-gov.net.cn/expert/chenwh/2.htm (accessed 30 July, 2003).

Friedrichs, S., Hart, T., and Schmidt, O. (eds.). (2002). *E-Government — Effizient verwalten — Demokratisch regieren* (E-Government — Effient Adminstration and Democratic Governing). Gütersloh: Verlag Bertelsmann Stiftung.

Jiang, Z. (2001). *Lun kexue jishu* (On Technonology). Beijing: Zhongyangwenxian chubanshe.

Li, G. (2002). "More effective demanding for the e-governance of the year of 2002". Available online: http://www.my.gov.cn/DZZW/yxxq.asp (accessed on 20 August, 2003).

Poluha, E. and Rosendahl, M. (2002). *Contesting 'Good' Governance: Cross-cultural Perspectives on Representation, Accountability and Public Space.* London: Routledge Curzon.

Qu, C. Y. (2002). "Xinxinhua jianshe, zhengfu yao xianxing" (Government Should Become Pioneer of Informatization). Available online: www.e-gov.net.cn/expert/chenwh/2.htm (accessed on 23 August, 2004).

Rostow, W. W. (1978). *The World Economy: History and Prospect.* Austin: University of Texas Press.

Service Centre of Government Online Project. (zhengfu shangwang gongchen fuwu zhongxin) (2000). "Zhengfu shangwang gongcheng baipishu" (White Paper of Government Online Project). Beijing.

Toffler, A. (1995). *Creating a New Civilization: The Politics of the Third Wave.* Atlanta: Turner Pub.

U.N. (2003). "World Public Sector Report: E-Government at the Crossroads". Available online: unpan1.un.org/intradoc/groups/public/documents/un/unpan012733.pdf (accessed on 12 March, 2004).

West, D. M. (2001). "Urban E-Government: An Assessment of City Government Websites". Available online: http://www.insidepolitics.org/egovt01city.html (accessed on 14 February, 2006).

Wu, A. and Qi, G. H. (ed.) (2001). *Zhengfu shangwang yu gongwuyuan shangwang* (Government Online and State Workers' Online). Beijing: Zhongguo shehui kexue chubanshe.

Yuan, Z. H. (2001). *Dianzi zhengwu* (E-government). Vol. I-IV. Beijing: Zhongguo zhigong chubanshe.

Zhang, J. H. (2003). "Network convergence and bureaucratic turf wars". In R. Hughes and G. Wacker (eds.), *China and the Internet: Politics of the Digital Forward,* pp. 83-99. London und NY: Routledge.

——— and Woesler, M. (eds.). (2003). *China's Digital Dream: The Impact of the Internet on Chinese Society.* Berlin and NY: Bochum University Press.

12

—៷៷—

The 2004 European Parliament Election, the Internet and Emergence of a European Public Sphere

Nicholas W. Jankowski

Renée van Os

Introduction

Elections for the European Parliament (EP), held 10–13 June 2004, marked the moment when ten new members to the European Union (EU) participated for the first time in the formation of this transnational governmental body. In many ways, hopes were high that engagement in the election would receive a substantial stimulus. Voter turnout to previous EP elections had been steadily declining and, for individual countries, frequently dipped under the psychologically significant 50-percentile mark. These and other conditions have led observers to remark on the "democratic deficit" at play in the EU, particularly with regard to the one elected governmental unit, the European Parliament. Various remedies have been suggested for this situation, one of which involves creation of a European public sphere. Such a transnational public sphere is difficult to actualize for a variety of reasons, and we explore the concept and these issues in this chapter.[1]

One new ingredient in this election, missing from previous EP elections, is the widespread availability of the Internet. Since the last EP election in 1999 the Internet has matured and become a relatively common component in elections. Empirical evidence is beginning to be compiled on this "interface" and we review the main themes and findings of this work. The focus of this chapter, similarly, is the role ascribed to the Internet, particularly World Wide Web applications, during the 2004 EP election campaign.

This chapter is part of a pan-European collaborative empirical investigation exploring use of the Web during the EP election and involving research teams in 11 countries. We sketch the contours of this investigation and provide illustrations from two of the Web spheres related to that election as played out in France and the Netherlands by political parties and candidates in these countries. We also present findings regarding Web site features found on a sample of the election-oriented sites in these two countries. Much work remains to be done in understanding the role of the Internet in elections and we conclude the chapter with a sketch of issues important for a longer-term research agenda.

Public Sphere in a Pan-European Context

Few concepts within the social sciences have been both cherished and contested as strongly as has the notion public sphere. Since introduction to English language scholars through translation of Habermas' (1989) work, *Structural Transformation of the Public Sphere*, concern with and debate about the concept has been continuous. The debate contributed to reconsideration of elements missing or insufficiently accentuated in the original formulation: gender and class bias have been acknowledged, multiple and counter spheres have been recognized, and commercial concerns of the media have been seen as detrimental to a flourishing public sphere (e.g., Calhoun 1992; Fraser 1992; Keane 1995). Scholarly attention has intensified since popularization of the Internet and early expectations suggested that this new technology might be the Holy Grail for solving social and political ills. Pioneering scholarship contributed to measuring the components of public sphere in Internet newsgroups (e.g., Schneider 1997) and subsequent assessments suggested multiple measures in Internet environments (Dahlberg 2001).

In this chapter we circumvent much of this work and take as our starting point the following basic description of the public sphere: "a mediated arena which facilitates the provision of information and civic engagement via open discussion and action on societal issues".

Application of this formulation to a pan-European context constitutes the thrust of this section.

One of the variations of this extended discourse is whether a transnational or global public sphere might exist or be developed (Fraser 2003; Calhoun 2002). One subdivision of this debate addresses the possibility of a European public sphere. A continuous stream of conferences, colloquia, research programs and scholarly articles has been devoted to exploring this last variant of the original concept.[2] Discussion of a European public sphere is particularly fuelled, on the one hand, by the increasing importance and success story of the European Union as an administrative and economic unit, and, on the other hand, by the disappointing and dismal failure of that same institution as a democratic body.

Scholars argue that, as public affairs, broadly interpreted, are more and more outgrowing the boundaries of the nation state, so the need for a new, supranational, European public sphere, becomes urgent. Kunelius and Sparks (2001), for example, advocate what they call a "radical reading" of Habermas' original formulation of public sphere in order to reopen the debate and viability of the concept at the pan-European level. Such a reading suggests that public affairs can no longer be confined to the parameters of the nation state, given that they are increasingly global in nature. In this regard, a European orientation is an extension of an already existing social reality. Secondly, the unity attributed to the public sphere in its classical formulation no longer corresponds to the reality of contemporary political diversity. Kunelius and Sparks suggest that the concept should be seen as a complex mosaic of overlapping and interconnected public spheres. Finally, they stress the process character of democracy where multiple public spheres may serve as potential sites for political discourse and engagement.

Some initial contributions to the discussion as to whether a European public sphere is theoretically possible focused on difficulties imposed by the diversity of languages across Europe, by the general lack of pan-European mass media,[3] and by the absence of a collective European identity. In the view of these scholars, a European public sphere is only able to emerge when Brussels becomes more of a political centre in which politically relevant decisions are taken that are at least partially independent from national governments (Koopmans et al. 2000, pp. 19–20; Schlesinger and Kevin 2000). Others, however, have argued against this stance, which seems to be based on an idealized picture of an almost homogenous national public sphere which is then transferred to the European level (e.g., Van de Steeg 2001; De Beus 2002; Risse 2003). Koopmans, Neidhardt, and Pfetsch (2000), for example, explain how some countries like Switzerland have managed to create a genuine national public sphere in spite the presence of three language groups in the country and no newspapers that can be considered national in character.

Following ideas of the first group of scholars, a distinction can be made between a European public sphere hovering above the spheres within the EU member states, as opposed to a "Europeanization" of national public spheres. This notion of Europeanized national public spheres, where European issues are addressed by national media, is considered the most possible and is, in fact, the version around which most empirical research has focused. This research considers the degree and nature of European-oriented content in national newspapers as indicators of the Europeanization of the national public spheres. The results of these studies differ: some (e.g., Semetko, De Vreese, and Peter 2000; Kevin 2001; De Vreese 2003) conclude that there is little European orientation evident in national newspapers; others (e.g., Koopmans and Pfetsch 2003) are less pessimistic and suggest that, for some pan-European issues, indicators exists for such orientation.

An assumption underlying most of these studies is that the media, usually national newspapers but occasionally television (e.g., Groothues 2004), serve as the main conduit for Europeanized national public spheres. In a sense, this assumption, however, is not surprising: since Habermas scholars have emphasized the importance of the media in contributing to the public sphere. The problem with this assumption is that a "voice" of the public is essentially missing in the content of most media. At best, such voice is conveyed through the journalistic style of interspersing quotations within highly structured "stories".

A substantial and disputable conceptual leap is made from measuring the presence of "Europe" in newspaper articles and drawing conclusions about a public sphere where open and equal exchange may take place. Information provision is distinct from communicative participation by members of a public. This second feature is either relegated to the political elite that may contribute an opinion column or in some other manner use the newspaper-supplied information in personal exchanges with others. In contrast, forms of talk radio and discussion programs on television where different standpoints and representatives of groups take part come closer to reflecting constituencies of the public than do the traditional newspapers usually noted as the vanguard of the public sphere (see, e.g., Coleman 2002). Similarly, the Internet provides opportunities for a diversity of actors to provide information on European issues, to facilitate open discussion on these issues, and to facilitate forms of civic engagement.

Citizen Interest in the European Parliament

The European Parliament enjoys a mixed status in the overall structure of the European Union. It is, in the first place, the only elected body within the EU and, in that regard, is accountable to citizens of the EU member states during elections held every five years. The EP has limited power and primarily collaborates on decisions with the Council of Ministers. Although elected, the EP suffers from a long-standing tainted reputation regarding legitimacy, often described as a democratic deficit. This deficit is reflected, in part, by the generally low and declining voter turnout at EP elections.

EP elections have been under continual criticism as having little significance to voters. Franklin (2001, p. 315), in a study of the factors causing decline in voter turnout, observes "Elections to the European Parliament have about as little salience in their own right as it is possible to imagine." The European Parliament has no impact on the orientation of the executive body of EU government, the European Commission, and cannot influence the composition of the other main body of EU government, the Council of Ministers, which is appointed by the governments of EU member states. These structural features, remarks Franklin (2001, p. 323), make "low turnout at European elections ... no surprise."

Low voter turnout at the 2004 EP election did, though, come as a disappointment to many observers. This feeling is reflected in newspapers headlines of stories published just after the election: "Apathy clouds EU voting," "Eurosceptics storm the Citadel."[4] Citizens in the new member states were the least involved in the 2004

Table 12.1 European Parliament Election Voter Turnout in Percentage

	1979	1984	1989	1994	1999	2004	Average
EU Members Pre 2004							
Austria					49.0	41.8	45.4
Belgium*	91.4	92.2	90.7	90.7	91.0	90.8	91.1
Denmark	47.8	52.4	47.4	52.9	50.5	47.9	49.8
Finland					31.4	41.1	36.3
France	60.7	56.7	48.8	52.7	46.8	43.1	51.5
Germany	65.7	56.8	62.3	60.0	45.2	43.0	55.5
UK	32.2	31.8	36.6	36.4	24.0	38.9	33.3
Greece*		77.2	80.1	80.4	75.3	62.8	75.2
Ireland	63.6	47.6	68.3	44.0	50.2	61.0	55.8
Italy*	84.9	83.4	81.4	74.8	70.8	73.1	78.1
Luxembourg*	88.9	87.0	96.2	85.8	87.3	90.0	89.2
Netherlands	58.1	50.6	47.5	35.6	30.0	39.1	48.5
Portugal			51.2	35.5	40.0	38.7	41.4
Spain			54.7	59.1	63.0	45.4	55.6
Sweden					38.8	37.2	38.0
New EU Member States 2004							
Cyprus						71.2	
Czech Rep.						27.9	
Estonia						26.9	
Hungary						38.5	
Latvia						41.2	
Lithuania						46.1	
Malta						82.4	
Poland						20.4	
Slovakia						28.4	
Slovenia						28.3	
EU average	65.9	63.6	63.8	59.0	61.0	48.2	

Source: Adapted from Franklin (2001); updated with election results published in *Financial Times*, 15 June 2004, p. 15.
* Countries with compulsory voting; disbanded in Italy, 1993.

election. As evident in Table 1, the overall average of voter turnout fell below the 50 percent level for the first time in the history of EP elections. Less than 30 percent of the eligible voters in five of the new member states cast ballots; only 20 percent of the voters in Poland went to the polls. In contrast, an average of 50 percent of the eligible voters in the other, older 15 member states, cast ballots. The lowest voter turnouts among these member states, just under 40 percent, were recorded in the Netherlands, Portugal, Sweden, and the UK. As a whole, citizens in the older EU member states participated more in this election than those in new member states.

Many factors contributed to this limited engagement. For one, EP election campaigns are generally not marked by intense campaigning, which is characteristic of many local and national elections. This is because, as mentioned above, the EP elections have no policy implications. As with previous EP elections, the 2004 event had no magnetic qualities with which to attract voters and the consequences were recorded at the polls. For another, EP elections are "second order" elections in that they are usually held during off years and tend to attract less attention by all political actors, especially parties, interest groups, candidates, and voters. Also, these elections primarily cover domestic issues and serve as a referendum for the presiding government (Kevin 2001).

These aspects cannot reduce the degree of discontent expressed during this election campaign, however. "Euro-skeptics" were elected in large numbers in many member states. A party in the UK that campaigned on a platform to withdraw from the EU quadrupled its seats in parliament, drawing some 2.5 million votes across that country. A new Dutch political initiative — based on a single issue, to fight corruption in Brussels — won two seats and collected almost 350,000 votes. Although relatively small numbers, given the 27 Dutch MEPs and the 4.7 million voters in total, this protest campaign was run on an economic shoestring, together with the candidate's integrity among voters. Similar expressions of discontent and protest voting occurred across EU member states, contributing to the earlier mentioned democratic deficit.

There is no certain solution to transforming this limited engagement of European citizens with EP elections. Often, institutional solutions are recommended such as increasing the powers of the parliament, instituting elections and other forms of accountability regarding the Commission, and promoting pan-European political parties. Ward (2001) rightly points out, however, that institutional reforms must be accompanied by strategies for engaging citizens in public discourse about and participation in European affairs. Such communication strategies should be initiated parallel to any institutional changes, Ward argues. In a similar vein, Warleigh (2003, p. 2) recommends "radical action" designed to empower European citizens in a manner emphasizing public deliberation, a framework termed *substantive* democracy by scholars such as Held (1988). This "radical reading" leads toward the same goal that Kunelius and Sparks (2001) recommend in their reinterpretation of the classical theory of public sphere: emphasis on public discourse in multiple settings and channels, designed to inform and guide political action. One possible venue for such a "reading" is the Internet, and some of the considerations for enjoining this information and communication technology in the political arena are discussed below.

The Internet and Election Campaigns

The Internet, it is often claimed, potentially provides space accessible to a wide variety of politically concerned — citizens, interest groups, social movements, parties, candidates, governments — to share information, discuss issues, and propose and engage in political action, on and offline. That claim having been stated, there remains considerable debate about the impact of such engagement. First generation "cyber-optimists" stress the opportunities for deliberation and direct decision-making among a broad spectrum of the public in an Internet environment (e.g., Rheingold 1993; Rash 1997). Later, "cyber-pessimists" warn that the Internet may widen the gap between the engaged and the apathetic (e.g., Margolis and Resnick 2000). These scholars claim that cyberspace increasingly reflects the political forces that dominate politics and social life in the real world, and that "political life on the Net is therefore mostly an extension of political life off the Net" (Margolis and Resnick 2000, pp. 2–3, 14).

Norris (2001, pp. 233–239) suggests that a balance should be found and proposes a middle-ground, what she calls the position of the "cyber-skeptic." This proposal is based on three observations:

First, political institutions are relatively conservative in their adaptation of digital technologies; second, the Internet is not particularly effective in mobilizing the disengaged, but better at reinforcing the already active; third, the "politics as usual" situation may be altered through upsetting the balance of resources generally in favor of established political institutions. This last observation, in particular, opens up possibility for substantial transformation of the political arena when "transnational advocacy networks and alternative social movements ... have adapted the resources of new technologies to communicate, organize, and mobilize global coalitions around issues" (Norris 2001, pp. 238–239).

With regard to this last point, Foot and Schneider (2002) see potential in new forms of political engagement in online arenas. Based on their study of the 2000 US elections, they argue that impact of the Internet can be found in changes at the structural level of the political system. They stress the importance of independent political Web sites developed by national and state advocacy groups, civic organizations and mainstream and alternative press. Complementing this perspective, they view the Web sites of political parties as components within a larger overall political arena. In their research, they concentrate upon the online structure of politically oriented Web sites, and the political action this online structure facilitates: information gathering and persuasion, political education, political talk, voter mobilization, candidate promotion and campaign participation. A similar perspective is argued by Benoit and Benoit (2000) and D'Alessio (1997), who mention advances in the sophistication of Web sites of minor parties across time. Norris (2003) also sees the existence of Web sites of minor and fringe parties as an asset to democracy, enabling citizens to learn more about the range of the electoral choices than was previously possible.

Ward, Gibson and Lusoli (2003) summarize the main areas where political transformation have been anticipated and argue that each of these areas is, in fact, a double-edged sword. At the end of their review, they conclude that, although a revolutionary transformation of politics is not to be expected, "our early research indicates that the Internet will make a modest positive contribution to participation and mobilization" (Ward, Gibson, and Lusoli 2003, p. 667). In all likelihood, as others (e.g., Bimber 1998) have suggested, the Internet may play a role in conjunction with other societal trends in contributing to a transformation of politics.

Some studies indicate that the Internet is primarily a playing field for traditionally strong parties and citizens already active in the "real" world of politics. In the United States, major parties usually have more sophisticated Web sites than minor parties (Dulio, Goff, and Thurber 1999; Klotz 1997; Puopolo 2001). Moreover, major parties usually have a more significant Web presence, resulting in more hyperlink connections than enjoyed by minor parties (Gibson and Ward 1998). This inequality can be partially explained by differences in financial resources (Klotz 1997).

Although the balance is changing, empirical studies on the possible consequences of the Internet for the public sphere have been mainly conducted within the political environment of the United States. Europe differs in substantial historical, political-cultural, and institutional respects. One difference is that many European countries have a tradition of highly structured party organizations, which might account for differences in development of party Web sites (Norris 2000, p. 279). However, in a comparative study, Gibson, Margolis, Resnick and Ward (2003) observe that Web sites in the UK and the US are largely similar. In both countries, political parties do not seem to fully exploit the possibilities offered on the Internet during political campaigns. They conclude that Web campaigning is settling into a conventional form in the US and the UK: "cyberspace is clearly not jolting traditional political actors into radically different styles of message delivery, nor is it leading to a more egalitarian world of political communication" (Gibson et al. 2003, pp. 66–67).

In contrast, in another comparative study of party Web sites in Europe and the US, Norris (2003, p. 43) finds that European sites contain more bottom-up elements than their American counterparts. She suggests the idea of a new, postmodern era of political campaigning, in which "the development of party Web sites will generate egalitarian patterns of party competition and more opportunities for citizen participation in party politics".

These ideas and empirical studies constitute the backdrop for our exploratory investigation of the 2004 EP election. The following question guides the work:

In what manner do political actors involved in the election campaign for the 2004 European Parliament incorporate the Web as an arena for contributing to a public sphere through dissemination of political information and facilitation of civic engagement via discussion and action?

Study Design

This study is part of an international collaborative investigation concerned with the role of the Internet during election campaigns.[5] Building on the experience and methodological procedures and tools developed by WebArchivist (http://www.webarchivist.org/), empirical projects were established around national elections in seven Asian countries, the United States, and the 2004 European Parliament election as played out in 11 EU Member States: Czech Republic, Finland, France, Hungary, Ireland, Italy, Luxembourg, the Netherlands, Portugal, Slovenia and the UK. The study focused on the Web spheres[6] that emerged in these countries during the campaign.

Sites were identified for inclusion in the Web sphere of a particular country through guidelines developed by WebArchivist, which involved consulting search engines, politically-oriented portals and other depositories of potential Web site addresses. All sites produced by political actors that seemed potentially relevant to the 2004 election were identified in an Internet-based tool for this purpose, including the actor categories business, candidate, citizen, party, press, and NGO. Sites were identified during a three-week period beginning eight weeks prior to the election.

Samples were drawn from those sites identified five weeks prior to the election in each country. A sample of 100 sites was randomly drawn per sphere, stratified across site producer types such that additional weight was given as follows: 30 percent candidates, 15 percent of sample to include parties, 10 percent government sites, 10 percent NGOs, 10 percent labor unions, and the remainder of the sample was distributed across other producer types. The sites in this sample were coded for the presence of 32 features, including items such as: candidate endorsements, comparison of candidate platforms, speeches, images, audio and video files, contact information, recruitment, voter registration, online newsletters, discussion forums, distribution of election materials offline, and promotion of campaign via e-paraphernalia (e.g., banners, screensavers). Coding was completed before the election.

Dutch and French 2004 EP Electoral Web Spheres

In this section, we describe some of the characteristics special to the Dutch and French 2004 EP electoral Web spheres, and a panorama of the sites identified. Subsequently, in the next section, we compare features found on candidate and party sites in these two countries. Table 12.2 provides an overview of the number of producer types of sites found in France and the Netherlands. In both countries 318 Web sites were identified in their respective 2004 EP electoral Web spheres as having the potential to provide electoral content.

In France, elections are organized at the regional level, in contrast to the Netherlands, where EP elections are held nationally. For elections of the President, National Assembly and Senate, the country is divided into 31 electoral districts; for the 2004 EP election these districts were collapsed to eight. As a result, the French political system is much more fragmented than in most other EU Member States, such as the Netherlands (Guyomarch and Machin 2001).

Table 12.2 Producer Types of Web Spheres in France and the Netherlands

Producer type	France	Netherlands
Business	8	13
Candidate	30	74
Citizen	27	14
NGO	50	35
Party	75	48
Press	30	29
Labor Union	18	30
Educational	2	4
Government	44	37
Political Professional	19	19
Portal	5	13
Religious	1	0
Total	318	318

First, major differences are present in the number of party Web sites — for France 75, for the Netherlands 48. Both in France and in the Netherlands most of the major political parties established Web sites devoted especially to the 2004 EP election. Large French political parties such as the *Union pour un Mouvement Populaire* (UMP, http://www.u-m-p.org/index.php) and *Union pour une Démocratie Française* (UDF, http://www.udf.org/index.html) are, in fact, associations of smaller political parties at the same side of the political spectrum, which partially explains the relatively large number of party Web sites in the 2004 French EP electoral Web sphere. Also, some parties established Web sites for each of the eight regions, such as the French Socialist Party, the third largest political party in the National Assembly (*Parti Socialiste*, www.parti-socialiste. fr). Some French parties were regionally oriented and, as a consequence, participated in only a few of the eight districts. Similarly, some NGOs and social movement organizations limit their activities to the regional level in France.

In general, the political system in the Netherlands is much more concentrated, having some ten political parties with delegations at the national, regional and European levels. As a result, in the Netherlands, all sites examined in the context of the 2004 EP election were intended for voters around the country. Furthermore, there are few minor or fringe parties or political movements that manifest themselves in the Dutch political arena with the intent of influencing public and political opinion, in contrast to the larger number of political actors in France with that objective. Some relatively small French political parties have seats in the European Parliament, whereas only large Dutch political parties were represented in the previous European Parliament.

Expressions of Euro-skepticism could be found in both the Dutch and the French 2004 EP election. In the French electoral Web sphere, a relatively large number of politically-oriented social movement organizations provided EP electoral content as well as content on the EU. These social movement organizations might best be described as political organizations participating in political debate on (European) political issues. Some also organized and facilitated political debates between candidates and citizens. One example is "Cercles Liberaux" (http://www.cerclesliberaux.com/), an organization divided into regional groups that "constitute a place

Figure 12.1 Web Site of 'Les Cercles Libéraux' (Consulted: 8 June 2004)

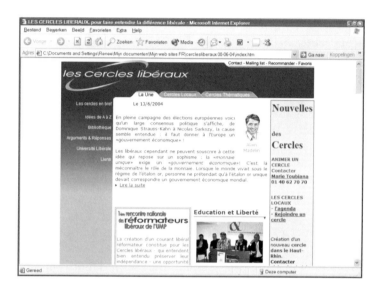

for free and independent reflection in the center of society; see Figure 12.1.

Some of these organizations consider themselves political parties, although they do not always run candidates in elections; others prefer the status of a political movement. They are usually opposed to further European integration, and are proponents of the more conservative stance known as promotion of a "Europe of Nations". About 30 social movement organizations were identified in the French EP electoral Web sphere. Expressions of Euro-skepticism were also manifested in the Dutch 2004 EP election, where four new political parties took part in addition to the more established parties. One of these new initiatives won two of the 27 seats in the new European Parliament, *Europa Transparant* (http://www.europatransparant.nl/), primarily on the basis of a single-issue campaign which criticized EU bureaucracy and corruptness; see Figure 12.2.

In both countries many candidates maintained their own campaign-oriented Web sites, although this was more prominent in the Netherlands than in France. Relatively more candidates had Web

Figure 12.2 Web Site of Dutch Party 'Europa Transparant' (Consulted: 7 June 2004)

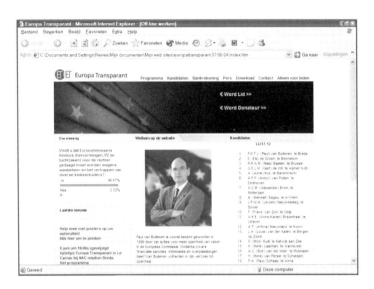

sites in the Netherlands (74) than in France (30). In France, some candidates placed an announcement on their Web sites, stating that they had chosen not to use the Web site during the electoral campaign. As previously mentioned, the elections in France were held at the regional level. As a result, regional branches of larger political parties produced their own campaign Web sites, placing the regional party leader in a central position, meaning that there were eight party candidates instead of a single candidate for each political party. This situation may have contributed to less need for individual candidate Web sites within these parties. There were, in fact, already regional Web sites focusing on regional candidates, sometimes with an endorsement from the national party leader, but always with links to the national Web site. Some candidates, those with personal Web sites, made reference to these regional Web sites, with an announcement that up-to-date election information could be found there, and not on the personal candidate Web sites. In other words, these regional Web sites constituted a central position in the French 2004 EP electoral Web sphere.

In the following section, we would compare features found on 2004 EP election candidate and party sites in France and the Netherlands. The comparison of these features is organized along two aspects of a public sphere noted in the exploratory research question: provision of information and opportunities for civic engagement through discussion and action.

Information Provision

Table 12.3 shows a selection of eight Web site features related to the provision of information on the EP election: explicit information on the election (ELECT), endorsement of candidates in the election (ENDOR), presentation of issue-related information (ISSUE), a calendar of election-related events (CALENDAR), comparison of candidates (COMPARE), information on the EP election campaign (INFOC), information on the voting process (INFOV), and presentation of audio-visual materials on the sites (AV). This data is shown for the sample of candidates and parties in France and the Netherlands. Because of the small number of cases involved and because all candidates in France are included, while only a sample of those in the Netherlands is included, the raw scores are shown in the cells along with ratios in parentheses and no statistical tests have been computed.

As would be expected, most sites in both countries, for both candidates and parties, presented election-related information, although the figures were lower for French sites. For issue-related information, however, both the French candidate and party sites presented less information than the Dutch sites. Few of the sites in either country placed endorsements of candidates on the sites – with the exception of about a quarter of the Dutch candidates that contained self-endorsements. Similarly, almost none of the sites compared candidates, with the exception of five French candidate sites.

The sites differed considerably with regard to presentation of calendars of election-related events. A majority of candidates in both France and the Netherlands provided this information, while much smaller fractions of the party sites in both countries maintained calendars of election-related events. Information focusing on the EP campaign and on voting procedures (e.g., registering to vote, voting

Table 12.3 Information-Related Features, French & Dutch Web Sites of EP Candidates & Parties

SITES	CASES	ELECT	ISSUE	ENDOR	COMPARE	CALENDAR	INFOC	INFOV	AV
	N	N (ratio)	N (ratio)	N (ratio)	N (ratio)	N (ratio)	N (ratio)	N (ratio)	N (ratio)
France									
Candidate	25	16 (.64)	15 (.6)	1 (.04)	5 (.16)	16 (.64)	5 (.16)	.24	8 (.32)
Party	14	8 (.57)	10 (.71)	0	0	5 (.36)	0	0	4 (.29)
Netherlands									
Candidate	30	30 (1)	25 (.83)	8 (.27)	0	22 (.73)	2 (.07)	2 (.07)	3 (.1)
Party	15	15 (1)	15 (1)	1 (.07)	0	12 (.8)	0	3 (.2)	5 (.33)

Note: It is not appropriate to compare percentages given the small N for candidates and parties; statistical texts are similarly inappropriate inasmuch as all French candidates are included in the data.

Abbreviations

CASES:	number of cases for site producer type
ELECT:	election-related information present on site
ENDOR:	endorsements of candidates present
ISSUE:	issue-related information present
CALENDAR:	a calendar of election-related events present
COMPARE:	comparison of candidates present
INFOC:	information on the electoral campaign
INFOV:	information on voting or voter registration present
AV:	audio-visual material present on site

regulations) was only found on a small minority of the sites in both countries, although French candidates seemed to do more in this regard than did Dutch EP candidates. Finally, audio-visual information (e.g., audio files of speeches, film clips) was found on about a third of the sites in each country for parties and candidates, albeit slightly less for Dutch candidates.

Part of the explanation as to why French candidates made limited use of their sites with regard to information provision has to do with national restrictions on campaigning just prior to the election. Some candidates placed announcements on their sites, indicating that they had decided not to circumvent this governmental restriction regarding campaigning. Those candidates seeking re-election primarily used their Web sites as a means to announce actions undertaken while serving as Members of Parliament (MEPs).

Dutch candidates produced somewhat more frequently personal Web sites for electoral purposes, although the completeness and sophistication of those Web sites varied considerably. Many did not have up-to-date electoral content, but only basic features such as biographies of candidates, pictures and presentation of positions on issues. Other candidates maintained two Web sites, one for campaigning purposes (prepared with a template provided by the party), and one general Web site, which would include material not related to the election and more personal in tone. Dutch MEPs and candidates also used their Web sites as a means to provide a measure of accountability, although this was done somewhat less frequently than in the case of French candidates. Furthermore, it was evident that some Dutch parties supported the establishment of candidate Web sites, possibly accounting for the relatively large number of candidate Web sites in the Netherlands that employed a basic structure in which candidates could easily construct personal Web sites. The Web site of a candidate for the Dutch Socialist Party (PvdA), for example, is similar to that of the general party Web site; see Figure 12.3.

Civic Engagement

Table 12.4 shows nine features related to aspects of the component of public sphere termed civic engagement: contact information for party or candidate (CONTACT), feature enabling a visitor to the site

Figure 12.3 Dutch Socialist Party Candidate Web Site (Consulted: 7 June 2004)

to join the party (JOIN), possibility to receive a newsletter or similar information from the party or candidate (GETMAIL), feature allowing site visitors to donate money to the election campaign, a discussion forum on the site that allows for contributions from site visitors (FORUM), feature enabling offline distribution of materials such as speeches and posters (OFFDIST), feature allowing site visitors to send materials to others (SENDLKS), possibility for site visitors to download e-paraphernalia (e.g., banners, posters, screen savers) and the possibility for site visitors to volunteer to party or candidate election activities (VOLUN). As with the previous table, the small number of cases involved and inclusion of all candidates in France in the sample precludes use of statistical tests; raw scores are shown in the cells along with ratios in parentheses.

The large majority of all sites in both France and the Netherlands provided contact information for candidates, parties and others involved with the Web sites. Only the party sites in both countries, however, generally provided information on joining those organizations; a small number of the candidate sites had such a

Table 12.4 Engagement-Related Features, French & Dutch Web Sites, EP Candidates & Parties

SITES	CASES	CONTAC	JOIN	GETMAIL	DONATE	FORUM	OFFDIST	SENDLKS	EPARA	VOLUN
		N (ratio)	N (ratio)	N (ratio)	N (ratio)	N (ratio)	N (ratio)	N (ratio)	N (ratio)	N (ratio)
France										
Candidate	25	24 (.96)	4 (.16)	8 (.32)	2 (.08)	5 (.2)	6 (.24)	1 (.04)	2 (.08)	1 (.04)
Party	14	13 (.93)	9 (.64)	10 (.71)	5 (.36)	5 (.36)	5 (.36)	1 (.07)	3 (.21)	1 (.07)
Netherlands										
Candidate	30	24 (.8)	9 (.3)	15 (.5)	1 (.03)	8 (.27)	5 (.17)	5 (.17)	4 (.13)	1 (.03)
Party	15	13 (.87)	13 (.87)	6 (.4)	10 (.67)	9 (.6)	9 (.53)	4 (.27)	1 (.07)	8 (.53)

Note: It is not appropriate to compare percentages given the small N for candidates and parties; statistical texts are similarly inappropriate inasmuch as all French candidates are included in the data.

Abbreviations

CASES: number of cases for site producer type
CONTAC: information provided for contacting party or candidate
JOIN: information and feature for joining party or organization
GETMAIL: possibility to receive newsletter or other information on election
DONATE: feature allowing visitor to donate money to election campaign
FORUM: possibility to contribute to a discussion forum hosted by the site
OFFDIST: possibility to distribute off-line of election-related materials
SENDLINKS: possible for visitor to send information on site to someone else
EPARA: e-paraphernalia available on the site such as banners, posters, screen-savers.
VOLUNTEER: possible to volunteer for election-related activities on the site

feature. Nearly three-quarters of the French party sites had features making newsletters and similar periodic news sources available; a little more than a third of the Dutch party sites contained this feature. Larger numbers of Dutch candidates, however, did include this feature: about half in comparison to about a third of the French candidates. Two-thirds of the Dutch party sites, compared to a third of the French party sites, had features allowing visitors to donate money to the campaign. Essentially no sites of Dutch and French candidates included this possibility.

Perhaps one of the most central features included in the list of variables related to civic engagement is the presence of a discussion forum. In the French party sites about a third had this feature, compared to some two-thirds of the Dutch party sites. About a fifth of the French candidate sites provided this discursive feature; Dutch candidate sites had slightly more discussion opportunities — a quarter of the sites. The possibility to distribute materials from the sites offline was present in all of the sites, with both French and Dutch parties offering more of such opportunities; half of all Dutch party sites contained this feature. Sending materials from the site to someone else was largely absent from all the sites, with the exception of Dutch party sites, where about a quarter provided this feature. Similarly, e-paraphernalia was an infrequent feature on the sites. Finally, only the Dutch party sites, about half, allowed site visitors to volunteer for election-related activities.

Many of these engagement features seemed, in summary, to be utilized only to a limited degree by both French and Dutch parties and candidates. Some of these features — donating money, becoming members, and volunteering — seemed to be centrally organized. Party Web sites, particular those of the more established political parties, both in France and the Netherlands, generally contained more engagement features than did candidate Web sites in both countries. Web sites of newly established political parties were, in general, less sophisticated than Web sites of the more established parties and, as a consequence, had fewer features facilitating civic engagement. About three-quarters of the established political parties had produced Web sites devoted specifically to the EP election; these electoral Web sites were less complex than the main party sites, primarily providing basic information in the context of this election.

Overall, the sophistication of the candidate and party Web sites varied considerably in France and the Netherlands during the 2004 EP election. Candidates seemed to use their Web sites mainly for provision of basic information on themselves and their positions on issues, whereas parties more often included engagement features. In comparison to the Netherlands, fewer French candidates had Web sites, but nevertheless within each of the eight districts there were sophisticated party Web sites with detailed information on regional candidates. Most political actors in both the Dutch and French 2004 EP electoral Web spheres offered at least basic electoral information on candidates, issue positions and on the European Union and the European Parliament.

Conclusion

In this chapter we have argued for an interpretation of public sphere that places emphasis on both information provision and civic engagement, the latter term encompassing discourse and action. This approach to public sphere is related to one of the more radical initiatives intended to reduce the distance and deficit many Europeans experience with regard to the EU, the European Parliament in particular. Discussions of the concept European public sphere and the variant Europeanized national public spheres convey the importance of some form of public engagement, but the discussions and related studies tend to focus on the role of traditional media in the construction of such public spheres. In this manner they miss what we consider the heart of the concept, civic engagement through discourse and action. Some alternative media, as well as the Internet, provide opportunity for such engagement.

The 2004 European Parliament election provided opportunity to investigate the extent to which the Internet played a role in the campaign, in our case focusing on features of information provision and civic engagement. As part of a larger project concerned with Internet and elections, also involving studies in Asia and the United States, 11 teams of researchers across Europe examined sites identified in the Web spheres of the respective countries for features related to provision of information about the election and to support of various forms of civic engagement in the context of the EP election.

The data presented in this chapter on the features present on party and candidate sites in France and the Netherlands related to this election represents a small slice of the political actors involved in this election, but does reflect two of the actors generally prominent. Based on the sites examined, these actors placed primary emphasis on information provision, with limited opportunities for civic engagement. A skeptical reading of this emphasis suggests that the parties and candidates entertained a very limited purpose for the Web, other than provision of an electronic version of campaign materials prepared primarily for other modes of distribution. This reading suggests that the Web played, at best, a minimal role in the overall political campaign strategy for parties and candidates in the 2004 EP election.

Somewhat less skeptical, we expect differences to emerge on the facilitation of information provision and civic engagement through discourse and action in further analysis between countries and other actors employing the Web in this election. We also expect that some site political actors envision this EP election as one small moment in a longer-term more encompassing "permanent campaign". It may be, in fact, too early to expect much Web activity during European elections, and certainly in those countries for which Internet penetration and use is relatively low (e.g., eastern and southern European countries).

These are early times for the empirical study of the role of the Internet in the political process. Much further work is required before we can adequately delineate the nature and extent of that role. Certainly, longitudinal study is required that follows up on this examination of Web site features provided on the Web sites of political actors during elections, and this exploratory investigation may serve as the launch for such an extended examination. Further, future study of political Web sites should extend beyond identifying site features and include substantive analysis of the content, particularly analysis of online discussions. The nature of such discussion is at the heart of the concept public sphere and merits close examination. Through such analysis it may be possible to determine the manner in which European issues are discussed and contribute to a pan-European public sphere. Such study must, however, be supplemented by research that explores the intentions of site producers, along with and experiences of those that make use of the sites for gaining information and engaging in politics. Research, in other words, is needed that explores the central components of the communicative process — site producers, site content, and site users — across time. Such a longitudinal, all-encompassing design may provide the empirical findings necessary to make an informed assessment of the emerging role of the Internet in construction of a European public sphere.

Notes

1. This chapter builds on publications the authors have prepared for other venues (Jankowski, Foot, Kluver, and Schneider, forthcoming 2005; Van Os, 2005).
2. Not all observers agree with this account: Kleinstuber (2001), for example, claims the scholarly debate around public sphere in Germany is essentially dead. Counter evidence includes: a conference "The European Public Sphere" at the Berlin European Academy in November 2003, a 5th Framework research programme on the public sphere in Europe, a Euricom colloquium on the topic in Tampere in 2000, and similar panels in Helsinki in 2003 and Florence in 2004. The journal *Javnost/The Public* devoted a theme issue to the concept European public sphere in 2001; see entries in the list of references for details.
3. The *Financial Times* has, in contrast, been successful across Europe because it is targeted toward a specialized niche market of readers.
4. "Apathy clouds EU voting," Aljazeeras.net, 13 June 2004, available online: http://english.aljazeera.net/NR/exers/BF48424E-BFAB-4637-440526970394.htm; "Eurosceptics storm the Citadel," BBC News, 14 June 2004, available online: http://news.bbc.co.uyk/go/pr/fr/-/1/hi/world/europe/3806503.stm.
5. Further information on the Internet & Elections project can be found at http://oase.uci.kun.nl/~jankow/elections/ and http://www.ntu.edu.sg/home/trkluver/asefhome.html.
6. Web sphere is defined as a "hyperlinked set of dynamically defined digital resources that span multiple Web sites and are deemed relevant, or related, to a central theme of object" (Schneider and Foot 2004, p. 118).

References

Benoit, W. L. and Benoit, P. J. (2000). "The virtual campaign: Presidential primary websites in campaign 2000". *American Communication Journal* 3 (3): 1–22.

Bimber, B. (1998). "The Internet and political transformation: populism, community, and accelerated pluralism". *Polity* 31 (1): 133–160.

Coleman, S. (2002). "BBC Radio Ulster's talkback phone-in: Public feedback in a divided public space". In N. Jankowski (ed.), *Community Media in the Information Age: Perspectives and Prospects*, pp. 107–122. Cresswell, NJ: Hampton Press.

Calhoun, C. (ed.). (1992). *Habermas and the Public Sphere*. Cambridge, MA: MIT Press.

——. (2002). "Information technology and the international public sphere". Paper presented at the International Sociological Association, Brisbane, 11 July. Available online: http://www.ssrc.org/programs/calhoun/publications/infotechandpublicsphere.pdf.

D'Alessio, D. (1997). "Adoption of the World Wide Web by American political candidates, 1996-1998". *Journal of Broadcasting & Electronic Media* 44 (4): 556-568.

Dahlberg, L. (2001). "Computer-mediated communication and the public sphere: A critical analysis". *Journal of Computer-Mediated Communication* 7 (1). Available online: http://www.ascusc.org/jcmc/vol7/issue1/dahlberg.html.

De Beus, J. (2002). "A European public sphere". Paper presented at the American Political Science Association conference, 29 Aug.–1 Sept. Available online: http://apsaproceedings.cup.org/Site/papers/015/015014DeBeusJos0.pdf.

Dulio, D. A., Goff, D. L., and Thurber, J. A. (1999). "Untangled web: Internet use during the 1998 election". *PS: Political science and politics* 32 (1): 53–59.

Klotz, R. (1997). "Positive spin: Senate campaigning on the Web". *PS: Political science and politics* 30 (3): 482–486.

Foot, K. A. and Schneider, S. M. (2002). "Online action in campaign 2000: An exploratory analysis of the U.S. political Web sphere". *Journal of Broadcasting & Electronic Media* 46 (2): 222–244.

Foot, K. A., Schneider, S. M., Dougherty, M., Xenos, M., and Larsen, E. (2003). "Analyzing linking practices: Candidate Web sites in the 2002 US electoral Web sphere". *Journal of Computer-Mediated Communication* 8 (4): 1–15.

Franklin, M. N. (2001). "How structural factors cause turnout variations at European Parliament elections". *European Union Politics* 2 (3): 309–328.

Fraser, N. (1992). "Rethinking the public sphere: A contribution to the critique of actually existing democracy". In C. Calhoun (ed.), *Habermas and the Public Sphere*, pp. 109–142. Cambridge, MA: MIT Press, 1991.

———. (2003). "Transnationalizing the public sphere". Paper presented at conference "Identities, affiliations, and allegiances", Yale University, Department of Political Science, 3-4 October. Available online: http://www.yale.edu/polisci/info/conferences/fraser1.doc.

Gibson, R. K. and Ward, S. J. (1998). "U.K. political parties and the Internet: 'Politics as usual' in the new media?" *The Harvard International Journal of Press/Politics* 3 (3): 14–38.

Gibson, R. K., Lusoli, W., and Ward, S. (2002). *Online campaigning in the UK: The public respond?* Paper presented at APSA 2002 Conference, Boston, September. Available online: www.ipop.org.uk/.

Gibson, R. K., Margolis, M., Resnick, D., and Ward, S. J. (2003). "Election campaigning on the WWW in the USA and UK. A comparative analysis". *Party Politics* 9 (1): 47–75.

Groothues, F. (2004). "Television news and the European public sphere: A preliminary investigation". Centre for European Political Communications, Working Paper. Available online: http://ics.leeds.ac.uk/eurpolcom/exhibits/paper_6.pdf.

Guyomarch, A. and Machin, H. (2001). "Political developments in their historical institutional context". In A. Guyomarch, H. Machin, P. A. Hall, and J. Hayward (eds.), *Developments in French Politics 2*, pp. 1–22. Houndmills Hampshire: Palgrave.

Habermas, J. (1989). *The Structural Transformation of the Public Sphere*. Cambridge: Polity Press.

Held, D. (1997). *Models of Democracy*. Cambridge: Polity.

Jankowski, N. W. and Selm, M. van (2000). "The promise and the practice of public debate". In K. L. Hacker and J. van Dijk (eds.), *Digital Democracy: Issues of Theory and Practice*, pp. 149-165. London: Sage.

Jankowski, N. W., Foot, K., Kluver, R., and Schneider, S. (f2005). "The Web and the 2004 EP election: Comparing political actor Web sites in 11 EU Member States". *Information Polity* info??

Keane, J. (1995). "Structural transformations of the public sphere". *The communication review* 1 (1): 1–22.

Kevin, D. (2001). "Coverage of the European Parliament elections of 1999: National spheres and European debates". *Javnost/The Public* 8 (1): 21–38.

Klotz, R. (1997). "Positive Spin: Senate campaigning on the Web". *PS: Political science and politics* 30 (3): 482–486.

Koopmans, R. and Pfetsch, B. (2003). "Towards a Europeanised public sphere? Comparing political actors and the media in Germany". ARENA Working Paper. Available online: http://www.arena.uio.no/publications/wp_03_23.pdf.

Koopmans, R., Neidhardt, F., and Pfetsch, B. (2000). "Conditions for the constitution of a European public sphere". Paper presented at Euroconference "Democracy Beyond the Nation-State", 5–7 October, Athens. Available online: http://www.wz-berlin.de/zkd/poem/pdf/koopmans_european_public_sphere.pdf.

Kunelius, R. and Sparks, C. (2000). "Problems with a European public sphere: An introduction". *Javnost/The Public* 7 (1): 5-20.

Margolis, M. and Resnick, D. (2000). *Politics as Usual: The Cyberspace Revolution.* London: Sage.

Norris, P. (2000). *A Virtuous circle: Political communications in post industrial societies.* Cambridge: Cambridge University Press.

———. (2001). *Digital divide? Civic engagement, information poverty and the Internet Worldwide.* Cambridge: Cambridge University Press.

———. (2003). "Preaching to the converted: Pluralism, participation and party web sites". *Party Politics,* 9 (1): 21–45.

Puopolo, S. T. (2001). "The Web and U.S. senatorial campaigns 2000". *American Behavioral Scientist* 44 (12): 2030–2047

Rash, W. (1997). *Politics on the Nets: Wiring the Political Process.* New York: W. H.

Rheingold, H. (1993). *The Virtual Community: Homesteading on the Electronic Frontier.* New York: Harper.

Risse, T. (2003). "An emerging European public sphere? Theoretical clarifications and empirical indicators". Paper presented at European Union Studies Association, Nashville TN, 27–30 March. Available online: http://www.fu-berlin.de/atasp/texte/030322_europe_public.pdf.

Schlesinger, P. and Kevin, D. (2000). "Can the European Union become a sphere of publics?" In E. O. Eriksen and J. E. Fossum (eds.), *Democracy in the European Union: Integration through Deliberation.* London: Routledge.

Schneider, S. (1997). "Expanding the public sphere through computer-mediated communication: Political discussion about abortion in a Usenet Newsgroup". PhD dissertation, MIT. Available online: http://www.sunyit.edu/~steve/.

——— and Foot, K. (2004). "The web as an object of study". *New Media & Society* 6 (1): 94–102.

Semetko, H. A., De Vreese, C. H., anf Peter, J. (2000). "Europeanised politics — Europeanised media? European integration and political communication". *Western Politics* 23 (4): 121-142.

Tsagarouisanou, R. (1999). "Electronic democracy: Rhetoric and reality". *Communications: The European Journal of Communication Research* 24 (2): 189–208.

Steeg, M. van (2001). "Aspects of a transnational European public sphere".

Paper prepared for Burgerschaft, Offentlichkeit und Demokratie in Europa, 6–7 July. Available online: http://www.uni-leipzig.de/~roose/ak/tagung/vandesteeg.pdf.

Van Os, R. (2005). "Framing Europe online: Political parties' qualifications of Europe in the context of the 2004 EP election in France". *Information Polity* 10 (3/4): 205–218.

Vreese, C. H. de. (2003). *Framing Europe: Television news and European integration.* PhD Dissertation, University of Amsterdam. Amsterdam: Askant.

Ward, D. (2000). "The democratic deficit and European Union communication policy. An evaluation of the Commission's approach to broadcasting". *Javnost/The Public* 7 (1): 75–94.

Ward, S., Gibson, R., and Lusoli, W. (2003). "Online participation and mobilisation in Britain: Hype, hope and reality". *Parliamentary Affairs* 56: 652–668.

Warleigh, A. (2003). *Democracy in the European Union.* London: Sage.

13

—ᴠ—

Shifting Approaches to Governing E-commerce: From Promoting New Technology to Controlling Uses

Stephen D. McDowell

Introduction

The focus in e-commerce discussions in international telecommunications regulation, trade, and investment negotiations in the 1990s was initially placed upon reducing or eliminating taxation, providing secure payment mechanisms, and building a digital infrastructure. Some countries saw the Global Information Infrastructure goals, national information infrastructure planning, and e-commerce applications on the World Wide Web as vehicles to stimulate the next wave of economic development, and to gain competitive advantage for leading national sectors. Expansion of international agreements to support trade in services (market access, non-discrimination, transparency), as well to promote transnational investment (dispute resolution, constrained role of government, privatization) supported this direction. Coordination of technology standards for various activities upon which e-commerce depended was also seen as a way to build a connected digital infrastructure, and to provide a path to a technology-enhanced future. Sales tax moratoria on online sales were declared in the United Sates as a way to allow the new technology and services to flourish. The first part of the paper reviews policy documents and debates in the second part of the 1990s to survey approaches to the governance of e-commerce in its first half decade.

New issues have emerged since the early 2000s in overall cyberspace governance, as well as a more grounded sense of e-commerce strengths and limitations. Ruby Roy Dholakia (2004, p. 115) calls this a "post-euphoric phase" that is typified by more examination of actual consumer and producer behavior in electronic markets (see for example, Josang, Ismail, and Boyd 2007; Ho, Kauffman, and Liang 2006; Lee, Lee, and Park 2007). The focus on uses has also been reflected in policy debates, including the emergence of numerous questions about controlling a wide range of uses. These include efforts to control children's access to pornography, to protect privacy and prevent identity theft and fraudulent payments, to limit spamming, to limit hacking, to eliminate copying and sharing of audio and visual materials, to understand the use of cookies to track consumer activities, and to limit viruses spread by e-mail. The early images of e-commerce should be re-examined since more recent research has not borne out initial impressions of activities and practices. The focus on controlling user behavior brings to the fore cultural issues about users and communications practices. Hence, it sets the context for e-commerce activities, and in ways more fundamental than enhancing security to enable continued expansion of e-commerce. This discussion will attempt to show the governance of e-commerce needs to be recognized as multifaceted and complex, and as posing both national and international challenges at the technology, policy, and cultural levels.

The paper examines shifts in policy research and debates about the governance of e-commerce over the past decade, focusing on the United States and multilateral forums. It proposes that we have seen a shift toward the emphasis of control of uses of economic transactions and other services in cyberspace, and away from concerns about promoting new technology and facilitating electronic services and transactions. The first part of the paper uses a review of policy documents and debates in the second part of the 1990s to provide an overview of approaches to governance of e-commerce in its first half decade. The second part of the paper outlines the emerging issues, many of which emphasize efforts to control consumer and user behavior. The paper concludes by raising a number of issues for research on the governance of e-commerce.

E-commerce: Initial Conceptualizations and Modes of Governance

E-commerce was presented in laudatory terms in the 1990s. New technologies would allow the "disintermediation" of transactions between buyers and sellers (Shapiro 1999), allow those in different geographic spaces to engage in commercial exchanges, and provide for many new business models and activities. While the press focused upon a variety of possibilities, business and policy researchers attempted to conceptualize and understand these new processes, as well as to examine them carefully.

Defining Electronic Commerce

Rolf Wigand (1997) noted that the term electronic commerce was at that time being used without distinguishing between electronic business, electronic markets, or electronic commerce. Wigand proposed that "[b]roadly speaking, electronic commerce includes any form of economic activity conducted via electronic connections. The bandwidth of `electronic commerce' spans from electronic markets to electronic hierarchies and also incorporates electronically supported entrepreneurial networks and cooperative arrangements (electronic networks). The market coordination mechanism is their common characteristic" (Wigand 1997, p. 2). More specifically, "[e]lectronic commerce denotes the seamless application of information and communication technology from its point of origin to its endpoint along the entire value chain of business processes conducted electronically and designed to enable the accomplishment of a business goal. These processes may be partial or complete and may encompass business-to-business as well as business-to-consumer and consumer-to-business transactions" (p. 5). A number of effects of the use of information technology, proposed by Wigand drawing from Malone et al. (1987), "may lead to the reduction of transaction and coordination costs" (p. 3). The communication effect meant that more information cold be communicated during the same amount of time, reducing transactions costs. The electronic integration effect meant that a "tight electronic linkage between buyer and seller is enabled." The electronic brokerage effect referred to an "electronic market where buyers and seller come together to compare offerings." The electronic strategic networking effect refers to that ways in which information technology "enables the design and deliberate strategic deployment of linkages and networks among cooperating firms intended to achieve joint, strategic goals gain competitive advantage" (Wigand 1997, p. 3).

In addressing issues of governing electronic commerce, Linda Garcia (1997) used a definition of electronic commerce focusing on "networks, economic process, and outcomes rather than specific activities (such as marketing) or actors (such as consumers or suppliers) or organizational forms (such as markets or firms)." Garcia states that "[v]iewed conceptually and as a whole, electronic commerce can be defined as the use of information and communication technologies to network economic activities and processes, in order to reduce information-related transaction costs or gain a strategic information advantage" (Garcia 1997, p. 18).

However, these thoughtful analyses are not representative of the expansive hopes, promises, and investment that were placed in online enterprises by entrepreneurs and members of the public in the late 1990s. This excitement led to high priced of initial public offerings of stocks with little or no revenue, and unconventional business plans. The efforts of governments to promote economic growth also contributed to this sense of a new sector, where the regular rules did not apply.

Government as Promoter in the United States

The Clinton-Gore Administration undertook the National Information Infrastructure Initiative almost immediately after coming into office in 1993. This began a national consultation process addressing issues such as economic development, universal access to new media services, investment, and the introduction of competition (Information Infrastructure Task Force 1993; Drake 1995). Investment in, access to, and use of high capacity electronic communications networks and services were increasingly portrayed as a new infrastructure essential to economic growth.

A United States Congress Office of Technology Assessment (OTA) report of 1994 noted how communication technologies may be used to restructure roles in economic transactions, and to reduce transaction costs. These might be the costs of searching for information, exchanging goods and services, or monitoring sales. (OTA 1994, p. 32). "As transaction costs begin to constitute a greater proportion of the total costs of production and exchange, a firm's economic performance, as well as a nation's competitiveness, will increasingly rest on its ability to efficiently process and distribute business-related information" (OTA 1994, p. 32.). Furthermore,

> Today, communication and information technology can be used to conquer time and space. With advanced networking technologies and the growing number of business applications they support, buyers and sellers — regardless of their geographic locations — can interact online in a virtual, electronic space. Under such circumstances, the network will, in effect, become the marketplace. Linking buyers and sellers directly, the need for information — as well as for costly intermediaries to transport, process and interpret it — will be significantly reduced. (OTA 1994, p. 32)

This report drew upon some of the leading research of that time in identifying these possibilities. The need for electronic enterprise capabilities was placed in the context of national productivity and competitiveness, and specifically alongside the National Information Infrastructure Initiative. In the OTA report, the savings in transactions costs for inputs into production and in relations with suppliers, and in the organization of production within the firm, were emphasized, rather than efforts to reach consumer markets. Although retail markets were mentioned, topics such as supply chains, software, technology and organizational innovation, technology standards, flexible workplace conditions, and regulatory needs were stressed.

The Telecommunications Act of 1996 (United States 1996b) was directed toward the existing telecommunications industry, with an eye to promoting investment in new technologies and services by introducing competition in the local telecommunications network, or promoting telecommunications facilities-based competition within different communication industry sectors or across different technical platforms (i.e., the telephone network, the cable network, and wireless services). Given the active lobbying by many groups from different industry sectors, the Act was formed more out of political compromise among existing industry actors than from a clear vision of the future of digital communication or of applications such as electronic commerce (Aufderheide 1999). Sales tax moratoria on online sales were declared in the United Sates as a way to allow the new technology and services to flourish.

For many analysts, finding ways to ensure open access to a variety of communication services, and enabling all users and providers to have connectivity with a wide range of suppliers and purchasers of goods and services on the network, were the core challenges for communication policies that were of importance for electronic commerce in this early phase. Linda Garcia argued that the goals of specific businesses in electronic commerce — to reduce transaction costs in their relationships with their customers — were different than the overall public policy goals which were to ensure widespread an diverse connectivity. "Unlike entertainment, the goal of electronic commerce is not to enhance diversity and to reduce consumer costs. Rather, electronic commerce aims to lower transaction costs, and thus to reduce diversity (or at least complexity). To achieve lower transaction costs, network integration — and not competition — will be key. If, in fact, competition were to give rise to closed systems and proprietary standards, it would most likely increased business transaction costs" (Garcia 1997, p. 28).

International Efforts to Promote E-commerce

In international discussions and debates on telecommunications regulation, trade, and investment negotiations in the 1990s, the initial focus in e-commerce discussions was placed upon efforts such as reducing or eliminating taxation and import and export duties on e-commerce transactions, providing secure payment mechanisms and enforceable contracts provisions, and building digital infrastructure to support a variety of applications including electronic commerce (Muir and Oppenheim 2002). Many international organizations concerned with economic development or trade and commercial issues have prepared policy research programs addressing e-commerce issues (OECD 2001b).

More directly connected with Internet technologies were the discussions and deliberations that grew out of the NII and the Global Information Infrastructure (OECD 1997) discussions, beginning with the "Framework for Global Electronic Commerce" (United States 1996a).

The OECD undertook a number of efforts to define e-commerce beginning in the late 1990s, as well as to harmonize ways to measure e-commerce among its members. A conference of economic ministers was held in Ottawa in October 1998 (OECD 1998). A conference on the measurement of electronic commerce was held in Singapore in December 1999. An "OECD Action Plan for Electronic Commerce" emphasized four major areas of emphasis. These are: firstly, enhancing information infrastructure, including "improving access to telecommunications and Internet services at the price, reliability, and speed levels needed for e-commerce"; secondly, "building trust for users and consumers of electronic commerce"; thirdly, "establishing ground rules for the digital marketplace"; and fourthly, maximizing benefits of electronic commerce (Tigre and O'Connor 2002). These categories were specified in more detail:

A. *Building Trust for User and Consumers*
1. Protection of privacy and personal data
2. Secure infrastructures and technologies, authentication and certification
3. Consumer protection
4. Other trust-related issues

B. *Establishing Ground Rules for the Digital Marketplace*
1. Commercial law
2. Taxation
3. Financial issues, electronic payment and movement of goods
4. Trade facilitation and market access
5. Intellectual property

C. *Enhancing the Information Infrastructure for Electronic Commerce*
1. Access to and use of the information infrastructure
2. Internet governance/ domain name system
3. Standards

D. *Maximizing the Benefits*
1. Economic and social impacts
2. Small and medium-sized enterprises
3. Skills development
4. Ensuring global participation (OECD, 2001b, p. 10).

Consumer protection in e-commerce was also addressed in the *OECD Guidelines for Consumer Protection in Electronic Commerce* (1999b). The goals of the *Guidelines* were "to help ensure that online consumers are no less protected when shopping online than when buying from their local store or ordering from a catalogue," and to "reflect existing legal protections available to consumers in more traditional forms of commerce by setting out core characteristics of effective consumer protection for online b2c transactions" (Donohu 2003). The emphases included in the *Guidelines* are:

1. Transparent and effective protection
2. Fair business, advertising and marketing practices
3. Online Disclosures
4. Transparent process for the confirmation of the transactions
5. Secure payment mechanisms and information on the level of security
6. Dispute Resolution and Redress
7. Privacy Protection
8. Education and Awareness (Donohue 2003).

The OECD also published advice for non-members countries on best practices for achieving e-commerce "readiness" (OECD 2000; Tigre and O'Connor 2002). An OECD Report of 2000 dealt with contributing to e-commerce readiness, by which is meant "preparing the technical, commercial, and social infrastructure necessary to support e-commerce" (OECD 2000, p. 77). It proposed that the stage of readiness would be followed by increasing intensity of e-commerce, and greater impact as these technologies and services diffused. Readiness issues included infrastructure, access technologies, pricing, and human resources. The main policy areas to be faced in e-commerce concerned enabling uses, diffusion processes, and shaping the business environment (OECD 2000, pp. 77–96).

This agenda combined a number of significant policy changes to support the building of telecommunications infrastructure and providing a competitive environment and stable regulatory environment in the context of privatization efforts (versus "excessively generous exclusivity agreements"). Among other issues that OECD experience in e-commerce highlighted were ensuring an "e-commerce conducive business environment," consumer protection, the protection of privacy, ensuring the security of transactions, and the authentication of electronic signatures. While the OECD members differed on privacy policy and also on the treatment of sales or consumption taxation on e-commerce transactions, it was noted that "[d]eveloping countries probably stand to gain in the near-term by adhering to a tax moratorium on e-commerce transactions, given the initially small revenues implications and the positive incentive effect on e-commerce diffusion (Tigre and O'Connor 2002, p. 8). Further, the "benefits of Internet for increasing productivity and competitiveness are associated with business-to-business (B2B) rather than business-to-consumer (B2C) (Tigre and O'Connor 2002, p. 10).

Some countries saw the Global Information Infrastructure goals, national information infrastructure planning, and e-commerce applications on the World Wide Web as vehicles to stimulate the next wave of economic development, and to gain competitive advantage for leading national sectors. This view was reinforced by the emphasis placed upon the availability of information and communications technologies deployed in the infrastructures necessary to support e-commerce. For instance, an OECD presentation in 2001 emphasized internet access prices, internet subscription levels, the number of internet hosts per 100 inhabitants, the number of secure internet servers per 100 inhabitants in a country, the level of broadband subscriptions by households, and the level of household ownership of computers (OECD 2001a),

Expansion of international agreements to support trade in services (through market access, non-discrimination, transparency), as well to promote transnational investment (dispute resolution, constrained role of government, privatization) supported this direction. Many of the agreements to liberalize trade and investment in the communication and ICT sectors were developed by the General Agreement on Tariffs and Trade (GATT), beginning with the trade in services negotiations that were undertaken alongside the trade talks in the Uruguay round of negotiations. At the conclusion of this round of talks, a new organization, the World Trade Organization, was formed as the successor to the GATT. Another agreement, the General Agreement on Trade in Services was pursued after the conclusion of the Uruguay Round. The World

Bank also published an extensive paper on e-commerce governance issues (Intven et al. 2003).

Coordination of technology standards for various activities upon which e-commerce depended was also seen as a way to build a connected digital infrastructure, as well as providing a path to a technology-enhanced future. The International Telecommunication Union (ITU) is the main multilateral body dealing with telecommunications issues, and especially telecommunications network technology standards. As of 2004 there were 189 member states and over 700 private sector members of the ITU. Numerous working groups address technology standards in order to allow various technologies and networks from across the world to interconnect with each other. The ITU has therefore been involved in coordinating many of the discussions among governments and industry players for the many layers and kinds of technology that interconnection to provide web-based services necessary for e-commerce (ITU 2004; Kahin and Abatte 1995). A number of internet use and governance issues were addressed in the meetings of the World Summit on the Information Society in Geneva in 2003 and Tunis in 2005. (ITU 2003, 2005). The main focus of these meetings was expanding access and applications of relevance for developing countries, as well as issues and modes of internet governance.

Tracking E-commerce in the United States

More recent research on electronic commerce has emphasized different characteristics and processes of e-commerce processes. Most striking has been a move to highlight retail sales applications and to address user behaviors that reduce the profitability of content and service providers. A methods discussion paper (Mesenbourg 2001) from the U.S. Bureau of the Census states "[i]t is useful to think of the digital economy as having three primary components — supporting infrastructures, electronic business processes (how business is conducted), and electronic commerce transactions (selling of goods and services online) (Mesenbourg, p. 2). While e-business is "any process that a business organization conducts over computer-mediated networks," electronic commerce is "the value of goods and services sold over computer-mediated networks" (p. 4). The issue of defining and measuring e-commerce transactions has become important for governments and international organizations across the world.

In the United States e-commerce data collection efforts by the Department of Commerce began in fall 1999 by asking firms if they were selling online and the volume of e-commerce sales (Mesenbourg 2001, p. 7). E-commerce questions were also added to surveys of firms in various economic sectors, including data collection of specific types of good s and services that were being sold online.

Despite the popular excitement about online sales directly to consumers, surveys in the United States found that the volume of e-commerce selling was higher as a proportion of total sales in merchant wholesale trade and manufacturing wholesale trade sectors (or business to business transactions) than in retail trade and selected service sectors (or business to consumer transactions). Electronic data interchange systems among businesses had been in place prior to the extensive expansion of the World Wide Web in the mid-1990s, and this was offered as a possible explanation of the differences. Studies also found that in each sector e-commerce activities were concentrated among a small number of industry groups (Mesenbourg 2001).

A more detailed analysis of the figures from 2002 in the United States indicated that "Business-to-Business activity, which depends critically on Electronic Data Interchange (EDI) dominated e-commerce." It represented 93 percent of e-commerce in 2002, and accounted for 19.6 percent of manufacturing shipments. 11.7 percent of merchant wholesale trader sales, 1.4 percent of retail trade sales, and 0.9 percent of selected service revenues (U.S. Dept of Commerce 2004a, p. 1). The "e-shipments" in the manufacturing sector were concentrated in five industry groups: transportation equipment, computer and electronic products, chemicals, food products, and beverage and tobacco. What is notable about the selected service revenues is that of the 41,463,000 million dollars of revenues in this sector in 2002, only 26.2 percent (or 11,059,000 million dollars) were information services. E-commerce as a portion of the industry group sales in information industries, at 1.2 percent of total sales, was only slightly higher than the e-commerce portion of selected service industries overall (0.8 percent) (U.S. Dept of Commerce 2004a, Table 4). The role of e-commerce revenues in information services categories remain small, including publishing industries (5,362,000 million, or 2.1 percent of overall revenues), broadcasting and telecommunications (2,549,000 million of 0.5 percent of overall revenues), and online information services (1,823,000 million dollars or 5.7 percent of overall revenues in this industry) (U.S. Dept of Commerce, 2004a, Table 4).

Tracking of e-commerce retail sales from 4th quarter 1999 to the fourth quarter of 2003 revealed a slow but steady increase as a proportion of retail trade sales. In 4th quarter 1999, 5,393,000 million dollars of e-commerce sales were reported, or 0.7 percent of total retail sales. This rose over fours years to $17,226,000 million dollars in 4th quarter 2003, or 1.9 percent of total retail sales for the quarter (U.S. Dept of Commerce, 2004b, p. 2). By 2005, e-commerce accounted for 26.7% (1,266,000,000 million) of total shipments in the United States. Merchant wholesale e-commerce made up 18.3% (945,000,000) of total sales in this sector). Retail e-commerce sales increased, but were only 2.5% (93,000,000 million) of the retail sector (U.S. Census Bureau 2007a). Business-to-business e-commerce accounted for 92.1% of all e-commerce in 2005, down from 92.2% in 2004, while business-to-consumer e-commerce (including retail and selected services) went from 7.8% to 7.9% of total recorded e-commerce from 2004 to 2005 (U.S. Census Bureau 2007a). Preliminary adjusted estimates for the first quarter of 2007 were $31,500,000 million for retail and selected service e-commerce sales, which would represent a growth of 18% over the first quarter of 2006. The 2007estimate accounted for 3.2% of total retail sales for the quarter, up from the portion in 2005 (U.S. Census Bureau 2007b).

Moving toward Governance as Control

New issues also emerged in early 2000s in overall cyberspace governance, as well as a more grounded sense of e-commerce strengths and limitations. As mentioned, this has been called a "post-euphoric phase" (Dholakia 2004, p. 115) in which business and policy research moved somewhat beyond the possibilities and potentials of the new technology to examining actual patterns of uses. Although the tracking of e-commerce has shown that business-to-business transactions make up over 90% of the volume, public debate on e-commerce governance has increasingly emphasized the illegal and improper uses of the internet and web-based services in retail and consumer transactions.

This focus on behavior and uses has also been reflected in policy debates, including the emergence of numerous questions about controlling a wide range of uses. These include efforts to control children's access to pornography (Thornburgh and Lin 2002; Zittrain 2003). National and international cooperative efforts have been undertaken to prevent identity theft and fraudulent payments (OECD 2003). National legislatures have also tried to limit spamming and hacking, and the spreading of computer viruses. Legislation has been passed to eliminate copying and sharing of audio and visual materials, and the World Intellectual Property Organization has launched efforts to protect trademark owners from "cybersquatting" by those attempting to register web names using existing trademarks (WIPO 2004).

The OECD has also launched a series of efforts to coordinate electronic commerce promotion among its members. Among the issues and initiatives addressed are the "culture of security," privacy online, network security, cross-border fraud, broadband access, the importance of electronic commerce for development, and measuring the information economy (OECD 2004). A 2005 report outlines national efforts to promote "a culture of security for information systems and networks in OECD countries" (OECD 2005), while a follow-up compares that "development of policies for the protection of critical information infrastructures" in Canada, Korea, the United Kingdom, and the United States (OECD 2007).

The International Telecommunication Union has also increased emphasis on network security, establishing a "Cybersecurity Gateway" web portal page to link to security activities in different ITU sectors (ITU 2007). A paper prepared in 2007 to follow up on the WSIS 2005 action line of building confidence and security in the use of ICTs provides, "a generic national framework for critical infrastructure protection" (Suter 2007).

Consumer advocates have argued that consumers need more protection in cross-border disputes concerning internet sales. Consumers International (2002a) noted, prior to an OECD conference on e-commerce, that alternative dispute settlement procedures would be more effective than national courts in facilitating appropriate solutions. Other efforts that have been identified as important to consumers are privacy protection, including the use of cookies to track consumer activities. Consumers International (2001) also found significant problems in the performance of online shopping sites. A study was also completed on the credibility of online information available to users (Consumers International, 2002b). It concluded that, "many sites are failing to provide adequate details in these areas, leaving consumers potentially at risk from inaccurate, incomplete or even deliberately misleading information." The study called upon consumers to "check the site's background," on business to "adopt best practice and provide more transparent information in order to build consumer confidence," and on governments to ensure, "that all existing laws in the offline world are applied equally online and ensuring that existing standards are enforced." However, less progress has been made in implanting some of these consumer protection measures than in developing strategies to limit certain types of behavior on the web.

The International Chamber of Commerce (ICC) has also published a series of studies to serve as resources for business and governments to enhance online security, including a guide to "information security assurance for executives (ICC 2003a), and a guide to "securing your business" (ICC 2004a) for smaller and entrepreneurial companies. It also prepared a compendium on "ICT and e-business policy and practice" for the first World Summit on the Information Society in Geneva in 2003 (ICC 2003b). The ICC position, as outlines in its policy statement on spam and unsolicited commercial electronic messages (ICC, 2004b), attempted to distinguish between spam and legitimate commercial messages, and sough educational and technical solutions alongside self-regulation by industry groups and government enforcement of existing legislation rather than developing new regulations.

In the United States, the focus on network security as been enhanced in the responses to the attacks of 11 September, 2001. The *National Strategy to Secure Cyberspace* was finalized in February 2003. A Cyber Security R&D Center web portal managed by the U.S. Department of Homeland Security and SRI International outlines a number of network security initiatives. These include Secure Protocols for Routing Infrastructure (SPRI), and the International Identity Theft Technology Council (ITTC). In discussion papers,

Aaron Emigh (2005) examines online identity theft, while a 2006 paper identifies the "crimeware landscape," including malware, phishing, and identifying theft software (Emigh 2006). The National Infrastructure Advisory Council, whose members are appointed by President from the public and private sectors, has prepared reports on "cyber vulnerabilities" (NIAC 2004a), on hardening the internet (NIAC 2004b), and on the convergence of physical and cyber technologies and related security management challenges (NIAC 2007).

Along with increased concern about privacy, identity theft, fraud, spamming and phishing and network security, the United Stated has previously introduced a succession of laws to limit children's access to indecent and sexual material online, beginning with the Computer Decency Amendment that was part of the Telecommunications Act of 1996, followed by the Child Online Protection Act in 1998. Both of these have been found unconstitutional, while the requirement that public libraries install filtering software in order to be eligible to receive federal subsidies for telecommunications costs has been upheld.

Compared to the features that were touted in discussions a decade ago, such as openness and multiple uses on the Internet, and the ability to "conquer time and space," the master metaphors for thinking about the web has shifted some way toward control of uses and enhancing network security.

Conclusion

Several questions arise from this brief review of the different directions and priorities in e-commerce research, and suggest that some of the commonplace claims need to be reconsidered. E-commerce has assumed a role as an agenda for national development in some documents, even though its overall role may be relatively difficult to determine. Similarly, closed networks still retain importance for electronic data interchange, compared to more open internet applications. Rather than focusing only upon the ability of web-based technologies to cross space and time, economic transactions within existing geographic markets can also be supported by e-commerce applications. While public perceptions focus upon retail sales, manufacturing and wholesale sector electronic data interchange are actually more significant by many orders of magnitude. While protection of intellectual property rights may be important for some sectors (such as publishing or media products and services), these represent a small portion of e-commerce sales. Although opportunities arising from using new technologies have been emphasized, the applications to which organizations put e-commerce tools are more important in determining its significance. Finally, consumer protection has assumed a less important role in policy debates than the support for efforts to build consumer trust in e-commerce applications. These issues are discussed in more detail below.

The emphasis on e-commerce has been used by a number of countries and international organizations to promote specific economic policies or economic reforms, rather than just the introduction and use of new technology. E-commerce has become more than an agenda for using new media, but also part of an agenda for national development. E-commerce "readiness" reports or scorecards, as with similar reports for e-government, have been used to push deregulation in telecommunications and information technology sectors, more efficiency in the provision of public sector goods and services, and more accountability in government agencies. E-commerce seems to follow in a long line of issues dealing with development and information and communication technologies. These include concerns over transborder data flow in the 1970s and 1980s, the efforts to promote investment in telecommunications in the 1980s to bridge "the missing link," the promotion of trade in services including telecommunications services in the 1980s and 1990s, and the idea of "knowledge societies" as a path to development in the 1990s. Each of these concepts became successively the focus of discussions, debates and policy research, and each combined fairly similar issues in different conceptual frameworks. What is perhaps most striking about the e-commerce agenda is that it is most clearly a path of development through economic growth, rather than through addressing human development needs. It is also a path of economic growth that requires extensive investment in communications and information and communication technology infrastructure, and continued and real time provision of reliable telecommunications and ICT services. As such, it is a very skills-intensive and technology-intensive path to development, and a path to development that stresses fuller integration in transnational supply chains.

The high priority on the Internet and broadband access to internet services may also need to be re-considered carefully in the context of e-commerce research. Certainly, technologies that span distance and allow for real time processing of transactions are important, but for high volumes of e-commerce in business-to-business users it may be useful to set up private or more secure network services. As stated above, a common view of e-commerce is that it was made possible by the world wide web technologies that were deployed in the mid-1990s, but this does not account for the private electronic networks used in firms in activities such as travel, finance, and manufacturing applications prior to the diffusion of the web or even after web diffusion. Clayton et al. (2003) note that in a British study, internet connections were often used alongside electronic data interchange. In 2000 they found, "established, closed, trading networks still account for much electronic trading; sales over these are almost times as great as sales via internet" (Clayton et al. 2003, p. 2). This also does not account for the extensive use of telephone service centers for marketing and for purchasing. If electronic mediation of commercial transactions is the core definition, then e-commerce policy research should also focus upon electronic networks other than the world wide web, and their use in conjunction with web technologies.

The core change that was highlighted in early conceptualizations, again as noted above, were the ability of web-based e-commerce applications to cross distance with little cost, and to be available at times convenient for the user rather than just business hours during the day. However, because a technology serves to cross space and time, does not mean that these modalities of usage will be the most important. It is also useful to not how e-commerce activities have strengthened existing local relations. For instance, Adelaar, Bouwman, and Steinfield examine how "click and mortar" companies, existing firms that have augmented existing marketing by integrating online activities, use e-commerce to "strengthen relations with existing customers in geographic markets where firms are already active" (Adelaar, Bouwman, and Steinfield 2004, p. 167). While these firms are also able to retain contact with firms that have moved away, and bring new customers on board with their exiting markets, "[c]ontrary to the usual expectations for e-commerce, click and mortar e-commerce are to a lesser extent used to penetrate new, more distant geographical markets, nationally and internationally (Ibid., p. 167). The importance of integrating electronic commerce and on-site retailing has been emphasized by numerous companies in the United States, which also face slowing rates of growth in e-commerce activities (Richtel and Tedeschi 2007).

The public perception of the importance or retail trade e-commerce activities, or the potential for growth in these area, has perhaps fueled the speculation in stocks of e-commerce companies like Amazon.com, online service providers (travel, hotels, consumer electronics), and internet access providers (AOL, MSN) and internet portals and search engines (Google, Yahoo). However, less visible but more important applications in terms of the proportionate volume of sales, have been e-commerce applications in manufacturing and wholesale trade. Similarly, many accounts of e-commerce focusing upon retailing claim that it originated in the mid-1990s, such as a 1999 OECD report that states, "Though only three years old, it has the potential to radically alter economic activities and the social environment" (OECD 1999, p. 9). While this may be true for business to consumer electronic sales, electronic networks for business to business transactions were in place prior to the public adoption of World Wide Web technologies in the mid-1990s. This disjuncture between perception and practice has important implications for governance and issues where efforts at governance of e-commerce have been directed. While the potential for retail sales has been much touted, the increased productivity and competitiveness of firms that make use of electronic data interchange technologies to join and participate in integrated supply chains may be more important for overall economic policy. This perhaps can be seen in the migration of jobs in business process operations, where effective telecommunications and data networks allow these operations to be integrated within and among firms across the globe.

While protection of intellectual property rights and the efforts to limit peer-to-peer sharing have attracted much media attention, they are relatively less important as economic activities than non-retail activities, and represent only a portion of the selected service revenues. This suggests that although media content creation and distribution activities are certainly important as part of cultural expression and cultural policy questions, the claims of their economic importance in e-commerce activities need to be considered carefully, as do claims that stronger digital rights management will enhance e-commerce. Additionally, as Lawrence Lessig has argued in *Free Culture* (2004), the efforts to introduce stronger intellectual property laws in the digital environment may reduce the exchange of ideas that contribute both to a vibrant political life as well as open research, investigation, invention and innovation. Tarleton Gillespie also argues that the Digital Millennium Copyright Act in the United States "anticipates a technological and commercial infrastructure for regulating not only copying but every facet of the purchase and use of cultural goods (Gillespie 2004, p. 239).

The mismatch also presents us with a problem for theory and research. The initial emphasis in the e-commerce research was on the potential of new information and communication technologies to lower transaction costs, and thus enable transactions across space and time to take place in new ways. Although the researchers cited here were careful to use the term "enable," in public debates over business and policy, it almost seems that "enabling change" became translated to a sense that e-commerce "will inevitably change" transactions and consumption patterns. Beyond enabling, there are many other important factors and contingencies that may contribute to actual systems and practices being implemented and used. The large volume of transactions and coordination in manufacturing processes, even before the fragmentation of production in the last decades, has been a challenge in this sector since its inception. James Beniger (1986) refers to this ongoing challenge in *The Control Revolution,* and notes the uses of the telegraph, data handling and processing (on paper), and mass media advertising in the 19th century to address the successive challenges posed by the growth of a national economy in the United States, and coordination of supply chains, manufacturing, distribution, and consumption. The use in business purposes is a core element of the definition of e-commerce, and the specific nature of these purposes and the uses that arise may be more important than technology change in determining the shape of e-commerce practices. Vladimir Zwass (2003, p. 7) notes, "[i]t needs to be stressed time and time again, that opportunities, including those that are technologically based, do not translate into realities without the necessary organizational processes, such as entrepreneurship and intrapreneurship, organizational learning, adoption, diffusion, and infusion of innovators, the culture of individual and group creativity, and executive support for change. There is no technological imperative. However, transformational technologies do change the force field and cannot be ignored." To restate, the uses and applications of electronic commerce by organizations and consumers should have theoretic priority over the focus on infrastructure expansion (broadband services, secure servers, ISP subscriptions) and over the possible uses and implications of new devices and software.

Protection of consumers' rights on online transactions has taken a backseat to the protection of intellectual property rights or the protection of credit information. Privacy protection has been an important concern for members of the public in considering computer communications over several decades, as evidenced by debates in the 1970s, and conflicts over transborder data flow in the 1980s (Baumer et al. 2004; Strauss and Rogerson 2002). The areas in which consumer rights are actively protected, such as in consumer credit information, are areas in which there is also a significant business interest at stake. For instance, elimination of credit card fraud is an issue of high importance for credit card companies in that while a consumer may be protected from losses due to fraud, the credit card company may be responsible for the losses rising from fraudulent uses. Similarly, identity theft poses a problem for consumers, but it also poses a problems for banks and other financial and credit institutions. Building the trust of consumers in online transactions, as well as protecting the assets of individual account holders and subscribers, thus becomes core values for providers of e-commerce goods, services, or transaction facilities. In these cases, the interests of consumers and the providers of e-commerce services may be more in line, but it is the active interest of the business sector that has led to significant change or efforts to introduce more effective legislation or regulation.

E-commerce possibilities and risks as represented in the late 1990s can be seen as political and social constructs, rather than merely technical potentials and allowances. Similarly, the claims about the responses aiming to enhance security to provide solid basis for e-commerce should also be closely examined. Civil society advocates at the World Summit on the Information Society were wary of the perceived efforts to expand state control in internet governance. As noted above, efforts to protect intellectual property in online behavior may protect a small value sector of the economy while contributing terms and conditions for general online behavior. Similarly, social, cultural, and political concerns about specific types of content and behavior, and the security of transactions and network integrity may lead to mechanisms to control uses and behavior in general. For instance, Minyan Wang (2007) argues that disjointed national efforts to introduce secure digital signatures to enhance security may actually limit e-commerce transactions.

These debates over uses and actual business activities bring to the fore cultural issues about users and communications practices, but also set the context for e-commerce activities. These policy questions are potentially more difficult to resolve than debates over infrastructure policies or trade practices. These questions and debates go directly to the core of domestic practices and law. The governance of e-commerce, especially with the move toward the examination of uses, needs to be recognized as multifaceted and complex. Governance strategies must address both national and international challenges in technology, policy, and economic and cultural practices and uses.

References

Adelaar, T., Bouwman, H., and Steinfield, C. (2004). "Enhancing customer value through click-and-mortar e-commerce: implications for geographical market reach and customer type". *Telematics and Informatics* 21 (2): 167–182.

Ang, P. H. (2005). *Ordering Chaos: Regulating the Internet*. Thomson Learning Asia.

Aufderheide, P. (1999). *Communications Policy and the Public Interest: The Telecommunications Act of 1996*. New York: Guilford Press.

Baumer, D. L., Earp J. B., and Poindexter, J. C. (2004). "Internet privacy law: A comparison between the United States and the European Union". *Computers and Security* 23 (5): 400–412.

Beniger, J. R. (1986). *The Control Revolution: Technological and Economic Origins of the Information Society*. Cambridge, MA: Harvard University Press.

Clayton, T. (2002). *Towards a Measurement Framework for International e-Commerce Benchmarking.* Available online: http://www.statistics.gov. uk/about/methodology_by_theme/benchmarking/default.asp.

———, Criscuolo, C., Goodridge, P., and Waldron, K. (2003). *Enterprise e-commerce: Measurement and impact.* Paper for UNCTAD workshop on Measuring Electronic Commerce, Geneva, September.

Consumers International. (2001). *Should I buy? Shopping online 2001: An international comparative study of electronic commerce.* Available online: http://www.consumersinternational.org/.

———. (2002a). *Credibility on the web: An international study of the credibility of consumer information on the internet.* Available online: http://www. consumersinternational.org/.

———. (2002b). *Consumer Redress in E-commerce in Need of Attention.* Press Release.

Dholakia, R. R. (2004). "Electronic Markets in the post-euphoric phase: Relationships, values, and behaviors". *Telematics and Informatics* 21: 115–121.

Donohue, M. (2003). *Consumer Protection Across Borders: OECD Work to Build Consumer Trust in the Digital Economy.* Presentation for OECD/UN/ World Bank Global Forum: Integrating ICT in Development Programmes. 5 March.

Drake, W. J. (ed.) (1995). *The New Information Infrastructure: Strategies for U.S. Policy.* New York: Twentieth Century Fund.

Emigh, A. (2005). *Online Identity Theft: Phishing Technology, Chokepoints and Countermeasures.* Available online: http://www.cyber.st.dhs.gov/ittc. html.

———. (2006). *The Crimeware Landscape: Malware, Phishing, Identity Theft and Beyond.* A Joint Report of the U.S. Department of Homeland Security — SRI International Theft Technology Council, the Anti-Phishing Working Group, and Ironkey, Inc.

Garcia, D. L. (1997). "Networked Commerce: Public Policy Issues in a Deregulated Communication Environment". *The Information Society* 13 (1): 17–31.

Gillespie, T. (2004). "Copyright and Commerce: The DMCA, Trusted Systems, and the Stabilization of Distribution". *The Information Society* 20 (4): 239–254.

Ho, S. C., Kauffman, R. J., and Liang, T. P. (2006). "A growth theory perspective on B2C e-commerce growth in Europe: An exploratory study". Electronic Commerce Research and Applications *(update??)*.

International Chamber of Commerce (2003a). *Information security assurance for executives: An international business companion to the 2002 OECD Guidelines for the security of networks and information systems: Towards a culture of security.* November. Available online: www.iccwbo.org.

—— *(2003b)*. ICC compendium on ICT and E-business: policy and practice. *December. Available online: www.iccwbo.org.*

—— *(2004a)*. Securing your business: An companion for small and entrepreneurial companies to the 2002 OECD Guidelines ... *July. Available online: www.iccwbo.org.*

—— (2004b). *ICC policy statement on "spam" and unsolicited commercial electronic messages.* 2 December. Available online: www.iccwbo.org.

Information Infrastructure Task Force (IITF). (1993). Global Information Infrastructure: Agenda for Action. *Washington, DC: U.S. Government Printing Office.*

International Telecommunication Union. (2004). *ITU and its Activities Related to Internet-Protocol (IP) Networks.* Geneva: ITU

——. (2007). "Cybersecurity Gateway". Available online: www.itu.int/cybersecurity/index.html.

Intven, H., Pfohl, R., Slusarchuck, C., and Sookman, B. (2003). "Legal and Regulatory Aspects of E-Commerce and the Internet". *The World Bank Legal Review: Law and Justice for Development* 1: 3–159.

Josang, A., Tsmail, R., and Boyd, C. (2007). "A survey of trust and reputation systems for online service provision". *Decision Support Systems* 43 (2): 618–644.

Kahin, B. and Abbate, J. (eds.) (1995). *Standards for Information Infrastructure.* Cambridge, MA: MIT Press.

Lee, S., Lee, S., and Park Y. (2007). "A prediction model for success of services in e-commerce using decision tree: E-customer's attitude towards online service". *Expert Systems with Applications* 33 (3): 572–581.

Lessig, L. (2004). *Free Culture: How Big Media Uses Technology and the Law to Lock down Culture and Control Creativity.* New York: Penguin

Malone, T., Yates, J., and Benjamin, R. (1987). "Electronic markets and electronic hierarchies". *Communications of the ACM* Volume 6: 485–497.

Mesenbourg, T. (2001). *Measuring Electronic Business.* Washington: U.S. Department of Commerce.

Muir, A. and Oppenheim, C. (2002). "National Information Policy developments worldwide III: E-commerce". *Journal of Information Science* 28: 357–373.

National Infrastructure Advisory Council (2007). *Convergence of Physical and Cyber Technologies and Related Security Management Challenges.* Available online: http://www.dhs.gov/xlibrary/assets/niac/niac_physicalcyber report-011607.pdf.

National Infrastructure Advisory Council (2004a). *Hardening the Internet.* Available online: http://www.dhs.gov/xlibrary/assets/niac/NIAC_ HardeningInternetPaper_Jan05.pdf.

National Infrastructure Advisory Council (2004b). *Prioritizing Cyber*

Vulnerabilities. Available online: http://www.dhs.gov/xlibrary/assets/niac/NIAC_CyberVulnerabilitiesPaper_Feb05.pdf.

Office of Technology Assessment, Congress of the United States. (1994). *Electronic Enterprises: Looking to the Future.* OTA-TCT-600. Washington, DC: U.S. Government Printing Office.

Organization for Economic Cooperation and Development. (1998). *OECD Action Plan for Electronic Commerce.* Prepared for OECD Ministerial Conference "A Borderless World: Realizing the Potential of Global Electronic Commerce", Ottawa, 7–9 October. Paris: OECD.

———. (1999a). *The Economic and Social Impact of Electronic Commerce: Preliminary Findings and Research Agenda.* Paris: OECD.

———. (1999b). *Guidelines for Consumer Protection in Electronic Commerce.* Paris: OECD.

———. (2000). *OECD Information Technology Outlook: ICTs, E-Commerce and the Information Economy.* Paris: OECD.

———. (2001a). *Business to Consumer Electronic Commerce: An Update on the Statistics.* Paris: OECD.

———. (2001b). *International and Regional Bodies: Activities and Initiatives in Electronic Commerce.* Paper for OECD Emerging Market Economy Forum on Electronic Commerce, Dubai, UAE, 16–17 January.

———. (2003). *OECD Guidelines for Protecting Consumers from Fraudulent and Deceptive Commercial Practices Across Borders.* Paris: OECD.

———. (2004). *Electronic Commerce.* Availableonline: http://www.oecd.org.

———. (2005). *The Promotion of a Culture of Security for Information Systems and Networks in OECD Countries.* Paris: OECD.

———. (2007). *The Development of Policies for the Protection of Critical Information Infrastructures: A Comparative Analysis in Four OECD Countries: Canada, Korea, the United Kingdom and the United States.* Paris: OECD.

Organization for Economic Cooperation and Development, Committee for Information, Computers, and Communications Policy. (1997). *Global Information Infrastructure — Global Information Society (GII-GIS) Policy Requirements.* Paris: OECD.

Richtel, M. and Tedeschi, B. (2007). "As Some Grow Weary of Web, Online Sales Lose Momentum". *New York Times* 17 June: 1, 16.

Shapiro, A. L. (1999). *The Control Revolution: How the Internet is Putting Individuals in Charge and Changing the World We Know.* New York: Public Affairs.

Strauss, J. and Rogerson, K. (2002). "Policies for online privacy in the United States and the European Union". *Telematics and Informatics* 19: 173–192.

Suter, M. (2007). *A Generic National Framework for Critical Information Infrasrtructure Protection.* Meeting Background Paper. Second

Facilitation Meeting for WSIS Action Lin C5: Building confidence and security in the use of ICTs.

Thornburgh, D. and Lin, H. (2002). *Youth, Pornography and the Internet.* Washington, DC: National Academies Press.

Tigre, P. B. and O'Connor, D. (2002). *Policies and Institutions for E-Commerce Readiness: What Can Developing Countries Learn for OECD Experience?* OECD Development Centre, Technical Papers No. 189. Paris: OECD.

United States (1996a). *A Framework for Global Electronic Commerce*, Draft 9, 11 December.

——. (1996b). *Telecommunication Act of 1996* (Public Law 104-104).

——. (2003). *National Strategy to Secure Cyberspace.* Available online: http://www.dhs.gov/xlibrary/assets/National_Cyberspace_Strategy.pdf.

United States, Department of Commerce. (2004a). *E-stats.* 15 April.

——. (2004b). "Retail e-commerce sales in fourth quarter 2003 were 17.2 billion, up 25.1 percent from fourth quarter 2002, Census Bureau reports". *U.S. Department of Commerce News.* 23 February.

——. (2007a). *E-stats.* 25 May.

——. (2007b). *Quarterly Retail E-commerce Sales, First Quarter 2007.* U.S. Census Bureau News. 16 May.

United States Congress, Office of Technology Assessment. (1992). *Finding a Balance: Computer Software, Intellectual Property, and the Challenge of Technological Change.* OTA-TCT-527. Washington, DC: U.S. Government Printing Office, May.

Wang, M. (2007). "Do the regulations on electronic signatures facilitate international electronic commerce? A critical review". *Computer Law & Security Report* 23 (1): 32–41.

Wigand, R. T. (1997). "Electronic Commerce: Definition, Theory, and Context". *The Information Society* 13 (1): 1-16.

World Intellectual Property Organization (2004). WIPO Continues Efforts to Stamp Out Cybersquatting. *Press Release, 17 January.*

Zittrain, J. (2003). "Internet Points of Control". *Boston College Law Review* 48 (1): 1–36.

Zwass, V. (2003). "Electronic Commerce and Organizational Innovation: Aspects and Opportunities". *International Journal of Electronic Commerce* 7 (3): 7–37.

14

The Development of E-commerce in Online News Media: Toward a Core Partnership Strategy[1]

Alice Y. L. Lee

Clement Y. K. So

Introduction

In the post-industrial society, online news sites play three major roles, providing a better information center (the information marketplace), a more interactive opinion forum (the opinion marketplace) and a more convenient digital shopping mall (the trading marketplace). This article examines only the trading marketplaces of online news sites. The Internet has provided a brand new platform for online news media to do e-business. In the late 1990s, a rosy picture was painted for the online news media, and it was predicted that they would be transformed from "advertisement deliverers" to "electronic traders" that would do a wide variety of e-business (Gipson 1999; Lee and So 2001; Noack 1999). The online news media were considered suitable for all kinds of innovative e-commerce projects, and it was thought that the online news media business would run very differently from that of its off-line counterparts.

After several years of practice, does the e-commerce performance of the online news media match the original optimistic conceptualization of the "digital trading marketplace?" Or does their e-commerce strategy reflect the philosophy of "e-business is business" and follow some business scholars' appeal for "going back to the basics?" (Fung 2001; Porter 2001). A longitudinal study was conducted in the first three years of the new millennium to examine the development of e-commerce in the online news media. The purpose was to evaluate the performance of the digital trading marketplace and analyze its development pattern. This study tries to assess a strategic model of e-commerce for the online news media and also provides guiding principles in e-commerce for online news practitioners.

In the mid-2000s, the Internet application has entered the Web 2.0 stage which puts great emphasis on interactivity and sharing. Web 2.0 enables users to engage in the production of Web content and the Web has changed from a "reading Web" to a "read/write Web." The participatory online media environment is not only changing the way in which people use the Web but also providing new opportunities for doing e-business (Kwok 2007; Yeung 2007). This article will also assess the implications of Web 2.0 for e-commerce in online news media.

Digital Trading Marketplace: Theoretical Background

Online news media organize and deliver their content in a flexible way that is very different from the traditional news media, and uses a medium format that is known as "open media code" (Lee and So 2001). This new format enables an online news site to operate like a digital marketplace, where people can get together, shop around and seek services. The unique characteristic of online news media, such as interactivity, connectivity and immediacy, turn news sites into desirable marketplaces. Unlike their offline counterparts that can generate revenue only through circulation and advertisements, online news media are capable of making money by becoming multi-dimensional electronic traders in B2B, B2C, and C2C businesses.

In the late 1990s, most of the news sites were free of charge. They did not follow the general practice of the traditional news industry of selling news content for revenue. Although many of them tried their best to generate income by recruiting online advertisements and sponsors, what they were eager to do at that time was to make money through the development of their "digital trading marketplaces." Internet technology cuts across all the boundaries of geographical region, gender, class, race, age, and business sector. The online media, housed on the Internet, can attract global consumers.

Theoretically speaking, therefore, the online news media are ideal trading marketplaces.

Moreover, encouraged by the white-hot new economy in the late 1990s, many news media enthusiastically devoted themselves to online business ventures, building up digital shopping malls and promoting trading of various kinds. For example, the *Los Angeles Times Online* set up a mall with 14 departments, including electronics, health and sports, computers, fashion, and flowers. In Hong Kong, the *Hong Kong Economic Times* developed six affiliated websites to join the e-commerce bandwagon (*Hong Kong Economic Times* staff, personal communication, 13 July, 2000). There is a view that news companies would lag behind if they were not prepared to take advantage of this "eventual spending spree" (Noack 1999, p. 20).

Contrary to the optimistic conceptualization of the digital trading marketplace, business scholars raised doubts about the myth of the Internet and called for the cautious development of e-commerce on the Net. It is warned that the Internet itself "will be neutralized as a source of advantage" when all companies come to embrace Internet technology (Porter 2001, p. 64). In other words, although the new medium format enabled online news media to serve as an ideal trading marketplace, their advantage would be diminish when every company could establish its own website and do e-business.

It is proposed that "e-business is just business" and that the real competitive edge comes from the traditional strengths of the news organization (Fung 2001; Porter 2001). Porter criticized the notion that the Internet changes everything and renders all the old rules obsolete. He proposed to "see the Internet for what it is: an enabling technology — a powerful set of tools that can be used in almost any industry and as part of almost any strategy" (Porter 2001, p. 64). Success would go to those companies that used the Internet as a complement to traditional ways of competition, rather than to those that set their Internet initiative apart from their established operations. Porter argued for a return to fundamentals. He deeply believed that the old rules would regain their currency and strategies that integrated the Internet and traditional competitive advantages would win out in many industries. It is important, he suggested, for companies to establish distinctive strategic positioning — by doing things differently from their competitors and relying on their own traditional strengths. Fung (2001, p. 118) echoed the view that "the same old economics of business remain very applicable in the cyberworld." Moreover, there is a need for an integrated approach to using the Internet, and media companies should not regard their websites as separate business entities. Following this line of analysis, the development of e-commerce on online news sites should go back to the basics of the news industry and follow the traditional principles of competition instead of launching aggressive online business projects in all directions.

By mid-2000, the bursting of the new economic bubble made many online publishers rethink their Web development plan and their methods of conducting e-commerce. The dot-com crisis led online publishers to realize that doing e-commerce was not as easy as they had previously thought. However, online publishers were still optimistic about the future of e-commerce, and refused to give up. They came up with various plans to sell goods and trade on the Web. A study of e-commerce in electronic newspapers in 2000 concluded that online newspapers were adopting a "network partnership model" as a survival strategy (So and Lee 2004). Building e-commerce partnerships can reduce costs and enhance the competitive edge of an online news site.

In addition to the partnership model, online publishers also took up a "content model" — asking the online news users to pay — as part of their e-commerce package (Scasny 2001). As about one-third of newspaper Internet operations still lost money heavily, online news media need to develop more aggressive e-business strategies (Gipson 2002). From the practitioners' point of view, the advertising-support model for online media was still regarded as the main driver of the industry. However, they began to believe that paid content would play a supplementary and complementary role (Outing 2003). Consulting firms also predicted that in the first decade of the 21st century, online media business would shift from free distribution to paid Internet subscriptions (*Reuters* 2001a). The argument is very straightforward: readers have to pay for their print newspapers, so it is also reasonable to ask them to pay for online content as well. Many online publishers believe that it is time to declare that the free content model has failed and the "authoritative content model" should step in (Friedman 2003). Yet, online the resistance of news readers to paying for content remains extremely high (CyberAtlas staff 2003; Sullivan 2002; Sun 2001). Readers still view the Internet as a source of free information (Bughin, Hasker, Segel, and Zeisser 2001). In 2002, a survey conducted by the Pew Internet and American Life project found that some of America's favorite websites had begun to charge fees as a result of the dot-com shakeup, but few people were willing to pay. The debate over adopting the "authoritative content model" as part of the e-commerce package has therefore drags on.

To examine how the online news media perform their e-commerce in the new millennium, it is necessary to conduct a tracking study. This study is guided by the following working hypotheses: (1) due to the bursting of the new economy and the downsizing of many online media, e-commerce on news sites are drawing back instead of making progress. (2) Online news media have failed to perform the role of multi-dimensional electronic traders and have shifted to a "return to core fundamentals" strategy. (3) Online news media still adopts the partnership model as a survival strategy.

Research Method

In this study 26 news sites from five regions were selected for analysis. These sites are representative of online news media in their region.[2] Among these five regions, the United States must be included due to its leading position in e-commerce. The United Kingdom was an obvious choice in Europe to represent an English-speaking country there. While the US and UK represent the West, Mainland China, Hong Kong and Taiwan represent the East. The three Eastern regions have cultural similarities but also major political and social differences. For example, although Hong Kong is now part of China, it distinguishes itself as a Special Administrative Region with a totally different political system and tradition, and it also had an early and aggressive start toward e-commerce.

An evaluation framework, based on the concept of the "open media code" (Lee and So 2002), was developed to evaluate the e-commerce performance of the news sites. The open media code is characterized by a weak classification between information contents and interactive information transmission. The evaluation framework consists of two parts: (1) the organization of content and (2) the mode of transmission, each constituting 50% of the scores in the evaluation (see Table 1). The first part (organization of content), was measured in terms of openness (a low hierarchical arrangement of e-commerce information), contextualization and networking (where e-commerce information is linked to the other part of the site), diversity (the diversity of the e-commerce items), and clarity (the clear organization of the e-commerce information). Each of the above four components has a share of 12.5% of the total score. The second part (the mode of transmission), was measured by means of interactivity, connectivity, search function, multimedia capability (e.g., 3D product display), immediacy (e.g., instant transaction) and customization. Each of these six components should be allocated 8.3% of the total evaluation score. However, customization is applicable only to the information marketplace and the opinion marketplace, not the trading marketplace. Thus, it does not contribute to the score in evaluating e-commerce activities here, deflating slightly the total score. A content analysis coding sheet was constructed accordingly to measure the e-commerce performance of the news sites.

The score of the e-commerce performance of individual sampled news sites was calculated each year according to the evaluation framework outlined in Table 14.1. The scores of news sites in the same region were added up and then divided by the total number of the sampled news sites in that region to produce an average score. The average score (see Table 14.2) represents the e-commerce

Table 14.1 Evaluation Framework for Individual News Sites

Classification of Content (50%)	– Openness (12.5%)
	– Contextualization and Networking (12.5%)
	– Content Diversity (12.5%)
	– Clarity (12.5%)
Mode of Transmission (50%)	– Interactivity (8.3%)
	– Connectivity (8.3%)
	– Searching (8.3%)
	– Multimedia Capability (8.3%)
	– Immediacy (8.3%)
	– Customization (8.3%)

* Full mark of coding sheet of each marketplace = 100%

performance of the online news media in a region for a particular year.

This study is a longitudinal research that focuses on the period from 2001 to 2003. One constructed week was selected as a sample date in each year for the content analysis. However, the constructed weeks were not designed in a traditional manner, due to the fact that the website content is not always available. The week of a particular year was chosen within a time span of several weeks, and there were two-day intervals between neighboring dates. This arrangement can greatly facilitate data collection and can minimize the overflow of content from one day to the next. The chosen dates in 2001 were June 11 (Monday), 14, 17, 20, 23, 26, and 29. In 2002, the dates were June 23 (Sunday), 26, 29, July 2, 5, 8, and 11. In 2003, the dates were July 11 (Friday), 14, 17, 20, 23, 26, and 29.

Personal interviews with six senior news managers and directors from Hong Kong media sites (three newspapers and three broadcast organizations) were conducted in 2004 to supplement and cross-check with the data from the content analysis. With promised anonymity, they were asked to comment on the growth of commerce, the business models for news websites as well as the trend in finding partnership.

Findings

The Growing E-commerce of the Online News Media

The first hypothesis of this study is not supported by the data. Despite the bursting of the new economy bubble in the mid-2000 and the financial crisis of the dot-com companies, e-commerce in online news media continued to grow and improve from 2001 to 2003. Although some of the earlier e-commerce items folded, new items kept emerging. A TV news director we interviewed believes that technology is still a pushing force. Tables 2 and 3 compare the e-commerce marketplace performance in the five regions from 2001 to 2003. In all five regions, the e-commerce performance of the online news media improved by 24.2% in terms of the score. It should be noted that the "growth" of e-commerce here is not measured in dollar terms. Instead, it is indicated by the growth in e-commerce items and the overall performance measured by the score

Table 14.2 Comparison of E-commerce Marketplace Performance in Five Regions (2001–2003)

	Year	Ranking				
		1	2	3	4	5
Openness	2001	US (5.1)	UK (4.3)	HK (2.31)	Taiwan (1.56)	China (0.78)
	2002	HK (6.3)	US (5.9)	Taiwan (4.69)	UK (3.91)	China (3.13)
	2003	US (7.4)	HK (6.3)	Taiwan (5.47)	China (3.91) — UK (3.91)	
Contextualization	2001	US (7.1)	UK (6.0)	Taiwan (5.47)	HK (3.94)	China (3.13)
and Networking	2002	US (7.4)	Taiwan (7.0) UK (7.0)	—	HK (6.77)	China (5.47)
	2003	US (7.0)	HK (6.8)	UK (5.47)	Taiwan (3.91)	China (3.13)
Diversity	2001	UK (8.4)	US (8.3)	Taiwan (4.41)	HK (4.32)	China (3.27)
	2002	US (10.5)	UK (9.4)	Taiwan (8.57)	HK (5.12)	China (4.69)
	2003	UK (10.0)	US (9.7)	Taiwan (8.79)	China (6.45)	HK (5.53)
Clarity	2001	US (7.4)	UK (7.0)	Taiwan (3.91)	China (2.34)	HK (1.56)
	2002	HK (7.3)	US (7.0)	Taiwan (6.25)	UK (4.69)	China (3.13)
	2003	US (8.6)	HK (7.3)	China (5.47) Taiwan (5.47)	—	UK (4.69)
Organization of	2001	US (27.9)	UK (25.8)	Taiwan (15.35)	HK (12.13)	China (9.52)
Content	2002	US (30.8)	Taiwan (26.5)	HK (25.43)	UK (25.01)	China (16.42)
	2003	US (32.7)	HK (25.8)	UK (24.03)	Taiwan (23.64)	China (18.96)
Interactivity	2001	UK (6.0)	US (5.1)	China (4.0)	Taiwan (3.9)	HK (2.9)
	2002	UK (5.7)	US (5.2)	Taiwan (4.9)	HK (4.7)	China (3.4)
	2003	US (6.1)	UK (6.0)	Taiwan (4.9)	HK (4.3)	China (3.1)
Connectivity	2001	UK (4.4)	US (3.8)	Taiwan (3.6)	China (2.5)	HK (2.3)
	2002	Taiwan (4.6)	HK (4.0)	UK (3.9) US (3.9)	—	China (3.2)
	2003	UK (3.9) US (3.9)	—	HK (3.8)	Taiwan (3.2)	China (2.8)
Searching	2001	US (5.6)	UK (3.1)	China (3.0)	Taiwan (2.3)	HK (2.1)
	2002	US (5.6)	Taiwan (5.2)	UK (4.7)	China (4.4)	HK (4.2)
	2003	UK (5.7)	US (5.6)	HK (4.7)	China (3.4) Taiwan (3.4)	—
Multimedia	2001	US (2.3) HK (2.3)	—	Taiwan (1.8)	UK (1.6)	China (1.0)
Capability	2002	UK (3.6)	US (3.5)	Taiwan (3.5)	HK (2.9)	China (2.1)
	2003	Taiwan (3.6)— UK (3.6)		HK (3.5)	US (3.4)	China (1.6)
Immediacy	2001	UK (8.3)	HK (6.7)	Taiwan (6.2)	US (5.2)	China (3.9)
	2002	Taiwan (8.3)— UK (8.3)		HK (6.9)	China (6.2) US (6.2)	—
	2003	Taiwan (8.3)— UK (8.3)		US (7.3)	HK (5.9)	China (4.2)

	Year	Ranking				
		1	2	3	4	5
Customization*	2001	—	—	—	—	—
	2002	—	—	—	—	—
	2003	—	—	—	—	—
Mode of	2001	UK (23.3)	US (22.0)	Taiwan (17.9)	HK (16.3)	China (14.4)
Transmission	2002	Taiwan (26.5)	UK (26.2)	US (24.4)	HK (22.7)	China (19.3)
	2003	UK (27.5)	US (26.2)	Taiwan (23.5)	HK (22.3)	China (15.0)
Marketplace Total	2001	US (49.9)	UK (49.1)	Taiwan (33.2)	HK (28.5)	China (24.0)
	2002	US (55.2)	Taiwan (53.1)	UK (51.2)	HK (48.1)	China (35.7)
	2003	US (58.9)	UK (51.6)	HK (48.1)	Taiwan (47.1)	China (33.9)

* No customization in the E-commerce marketplace.

in this study (e.g. the sites' interactivity, multimedia function, etc.). For example, in 2001, 265 product items and 98 service items were provided on our sampled sites, while in 2003 a total of 348 products items and 213 service items were available, representing prominent increase in the amount.

After 2000, the online media faced great financial difficulties. Many news sites were "burning money" and their business models did not generate enough money to meet their expenditure. However, online publishers remained optimistic about the business future of online media and were determined to hang on. Moreover, as the overall e-commerce market had been growing in the previous few years, this gave online publishers much confidence and hope. Surveys that were conducted in Hong Kong and the United States unanimously reported that consumers were getting used to shopping online (*Hong Kong Economic Journal* 2002; *Ming Pao Daily News* 2002). The 2002 *State New Economy Index Report* pointed out that in the United States, e-business was becoming a more important part of the economic base and the new economy was definitely here to stay (Atkinson, 2002). US online sales hit $50 billion in 2003 (BBCi 2004a). The e-commerce trade body, IMRG, reported that some 20 million British consumers planned to do their shopping via the Internet in 2004 (BBCi 2004b). The encouraging development in the overall e-commerce market certainly had a positive effect on the e-commerce performance of the online news media. Yet, one of our interviewees opined that the news websites should possess a clear business focus. With strong and unique functions the websites can serve a targeted audience better. Another interviewee said that e-commerce still offers opportunities and website managers have to be smarter in their approaches.

From Tables 14.2 and 14.3, we can see that the improvement of the digital trading marketplaces of news sites in various regions was prominent in both the organization of content and the mode of transmission, and even the diversity of e-commerce items had increased. The growth occurred not only in B2C online retailing but also in B2B retailing. The B2B examples include Times Online's news international syndication, USAToday.com's franchise center, and UDN's corporate news cutting service. In terms of B2C, the online retailing programs showed a high turnover rate, but on the whole they were on the rise. The findings show that the e-commerce programs were organized in an increasingly open and less hierarchical way, indicating that readers were no longer guided by the sites' strong e-commerce agenda (e.g., a concentrated virtual mall) and were shopping around on the site on their own. However,

Table 14.3 Changes of E-commerce Marketplace Performance in Five Regions (2001–2003)

	Hong Kong 2001–03 change (%)	Mainland China 2001–03 change (%)	Taiwan 2001–03 change (%)	United Kingdom 2001–03 change (%)	United States 2001–03 change (%)
Openness	170.6	401.3	250.6	**-9.1**	46.1
Contextualization and Networking	71.8	0.0	−28.5	−9.3	−1.5
Diversity	28.0	97.2	99.3	18.6	16.5
Clarity	367.3	133.8	39.9	**-33.3**	15.8
Organization of Content	113.0	99.1	54.0	−6.7	17.1
Interactivity	46.9	**−22.3**	26.7	0.0	20.6
Connectivity	64.8	10.8	**−10.8**	−10.5	2.1
Searching	124.5	10.9	44.6	83.6	0.0
Multimedia Capability	56.9	50.0	99.5	132.7	44.6
Immediacy	**−11.8**	7.8	33.2	0.0	39.9
Mode of Transmission	36.6	3.7	31.1	18.1	19.2
Overall Marketplace	69.2	41.6	41.7	5.1	18.0

the results indicate that the e-commerce sections were increasingly linked with the information sections of the sites. For examples, book columns were connected with online bookstores, and travel pages were linked to the travel agencies and online ticketing services. This kind of networking facilitates online retailing and services, but it also further blurs the line between advertisements, trading and information.

The digital trading marketplaces in the five regions also made improvements in their mode of delivery. Over the years, the news sites have improved the delivery of their products in many ways, particularly in their multimedia presentation, and search and connectivity facilities. Recent studies indicate that a 3D display of products is much more attractive than a 2D display (Jung 2004). More value-added rich content and more user-friendly website features can attract more online shoppers (Blake, Neuendorf, and Valdiserri 2004), and so news sites are working hard to update their tools. However, the multimedia presentation of products is still unsatisfactory. The results show that scores were low in the mode of transmission (see Table 14.2). Many products were still shown in photos and simple graphics, with just a few sites using interactive devices such as interactive calculators. However, over the years many sites have developed more sophisticated search functions.

Table 14.2 shows that among the five regions, the US ranked number one in doing e-commerce on their online news sites. The UK followed in second place while Hong Kong and Taiwan occupied the third and fourth position. Mainland China came last. The digital trading marketplaces in the US and UK were performing much better than their Asian counterparts. They led with very high scores in both their organization of content and their mode of transmission. In 2003, whereas the digital trading marketplaces in the US hit the score of 58.9, those in Mainland China stood only at 33.9. The performance of e-commerce in the US and UK sites was quite steady in the three-year period, but the development of e-commerce in the Asian sites fluctuated somewhat.

Redirecting the E-commerce Strategy: A Return to Core Fundamentals

Hypothesis 2 was supported by the data. Up to 2003, the online news media were no longer expecting to perform the role of multi-dimensional electronic traders, and they tried to redirect their e-commerce strategy. In the late 1990s, many news media were interested in turning themselves into portals because portals could attract a large Web audience, implying more advertising and business opportunities. Take hkcyber.com, a new online newspaper in Hong Kong as an example. This newspaper tried to build a cyber city named Skyworld. In the Skyworld there were many mini-webs that were loaded with a wide variety of information, chat-rooms and large number of virtual retailing shops (including jewelry and gold, books, clothes, and computer games) and service centers (such as e-banking, stocks and shares, and fortune telling).

A study on e-commerce in 2000 indicated that many online news media were heading in a similar direction by planning to set up e-business empires (So and Lee 2004). The portal dreams carried on into the early 2000s. Our data reflect that e-malls continued to be a strong e-commerce component in the first two years of the new millennium, but the scenario began to change in 2002 and the landscape of online media e-commerce looked completely different by 2003 (see Table 14.4). The tide of virtual e-mall subsided and became the smallest in proportion.

This study divides the e-commerce items of the news sites into three categories:

(A) In-house products and services:
These refer to the news media content-related e-business and their own company's in-house products and services. They include the e-paper's entry level subscription, their premium video, their special section premium (such as a horse racing page and adult columns), their archive, their stock market-related premium service, their wireless subscription, downloads for mobile phones, in-house souvenirs (e.g., BBC tapes, *New York Times* books, CNN clothing, ABC Network's Disney toys, The *Sun's* Page 3 girl posters), and in-house services (e.g., the CNN tour, Disney ticketing).

(B) Connected outside products and services:
These refer to the e-commerce programs in which the news sites play the role of middleman, linking up buyers with

sellers and service seekers with service providers. These products and services are not offered by the news media themselves: the news media merely provide a bridging service. These include travel, ticketing, real estate, jobs, cars and partnership mini-site products. The "commission" service is also included in this category. If an online reader clicks the link that is provided on the news site and makes a purchase in the linked online shop, then the news site will be paid by that online shop.

(C) Outside e-malls:

Many news media set up e-malls on their sites. This is a special corner for e-shopping, and the products offered in the mall are all outside products. There are two kinds of e-malls. One is a visual department-store e-mall, in which various products are displayed, prices are listed and instant transactions can be conducted on the news site. Another kind is an e-mall which functions like a classified advertisement section of a newspaper. Online shoppers click the brand name or the name of the shop, and then they go directly to that virtual shop to purchase items. The transaction is not carried out on the news site and the e-malls are basically retailing businesses that have nothing to do with the news.

The traditional news media generate revenue mainly from subscriptions/circulation and advertisements. In other words, the basic strengths of the news companies are their unique news products and their special role as middlemen. This study finds that the e-commerce strategy of the online news media is returning to these fundamental marketing principles. Table 14.4 shows that among all e-commerce categories, in-house products and services were increasing and ranked number one in 2003. The online news media began to sell their own content for revenue. They also emphasized providing connected outside products and services. The e-mall type of retailing business dropped dramatically over the three-year period. Outside e-malls on news websites do not work partly because they are not unique in their services and also due to the fact that consumers have security concerns when they want to buy expensive goods online. If the media sell their own products online,

Table 14.4 Partnership E-commerce vs. Non-partnership E-commerce (2001–2003)

E-Commerce Category	2001			2002			2003		
	Partner-ship	Non-Partnership	Total	Partner-ship	Non-Partnership	Total	Partner-ship	Non-Partnership	Total
In-house Products and Services	15 (4.2%) (A1)	68 (19.3%) (A2)	83 (23.5%) (A)	23 (4.1%) (A1)	135 (23.8%) (A2)	158 (27.9%) (A)	33 (6.0%) (A1)	171 (31.0%) (A2)	204 (37.0%) (A)
Connected Outside Products and Services	56 (15.9%) (B1)	13 (3.7%) (B2)	69 (19.5%) (B)	129 (22.8%) (B1)	21 (3.7%) (B2)	150 (26.5%) (B)	151 (27.4%) (B1)	41 (7.4%) (B2)	192 (34.8%) (B)
Outside E-mall	12 (3.4%) (C2)	189 (53.5%) (C)	201 (56.9%) (C1)	1 (0.2%) (C2)	258 (45.5%) (C)	259 (45.7%) (C1)	5 (0.9%) (C2)	151 (27.4%) (C)	156 (28.3%) (C1)
Total	83 (23.5%)	270 (76.5%)	353 (100.0%)	153 (27.0%)	414 (73.0%)	567 (100.1%)	189 (34.2%)	363 (65.8%)	552 (100.1%)

Note:

A1: In-house Products and Services (Partnership)

A2: In-house Products and Services (Non-partnership)

B1: Connected Outside Products and Services (Partnership)

B2: Connected Outside Products and Services (Non-partnership)

C1: Outside E-mall (Partnership)

C2: Outside E-mall (Non-partnership)

security is not a problem, and the media audience is already a customer base for in-house or connected outside products and services.

In the development of e-commerce in online news media, one outstanding phenomenon was the trend of registration and content subscriptions. The online news media began to require visitors to register, to amass data to help boost their advertising (Brown 2003). Online publishers argue that their sites need at least registration, so that they can obtain information on its users and can then offer targeted advertising (Gates 2002). Major electronic newspapers like nytimes.com and washingtonpost.com have been carrying out this policy for a long time. In this study, it was found that, in 2001 only 3.9% of our sampled sites required entry-level registration and 53.8% asked for voluntary or required registration in specific information sections. However, in 2003, 11.5 % of the sites sampled required entry-level registration, and 76.9% needed registration in specific information sections.

One step further on, the online news media have started to charge for their content. The *Wall Street Journal* was the first major US newspaper to make a subscription charge for access to its website, and started charging early on. After entering the new millennium, more online publishers thought that charging for online content might not be as bad a strategy as was often depicted, and they began to follow suit (Palser 2001). In our sample, the *Los Angeles Times* became the first major general news site to adopt a subscription model (Gates 2002). The Online Publishers Association conducted a survey in 2003 and found that 10% of online users were paying for some type of content (Krasilovsky 2003). This study substantiated this popular trend of selling content. Our findings show that content subscriptions rose from 32 items to 91 items, a jump of 184%. By 2003, among our sample sites, the i-cable.com, Atnext.com and scmp.com from Hong Kong and *The Times Online* from the UK required entry-level subscriptions. Out of the 26 sites sampled, 12 charged for archive stories and eight sites, including cnn.com, nytimes.com and chinatimes.com, required a video premium. News sites also charged for special sections like the horse-racing page, adult columns, the stock market and financial pages. As mobile technology became more popular, wireless subscription also became popular. Out of the 26 sites, 16 offered different kinds of wireless subscription services, which were particularly popular in the US.

Apart from selling content, the news media have also set up in-house stores on their sites to promote the products and services of their mother organizations and sister companies. Out of the 26 sites sampled, 11 had in-house stores. Examples include the ABC store, the CNN Turner store, Pearl Travel of *Ming Pao Daily News*, and the BBC Shop. Online publishers are increasingly seeing their sites as a complement to the business of their corporations, and are trying to integrate their online e-commerce with their offline business.

Acting as advertisement deliverers, the traditional news media play the role of middlemen by linking up consumers and advertisers. This study finds that online news media are also moving back to the middleman role, increasingly initiating e-commerce projects that aim to connect online readers with service providers. These kinds of e-commerce projects include career centers, real estate cars, and so on. Table 14.4 clearly demonstrates the rise of the e-commerce category of "connected outside products and services" and the decline of "outside e-malls." By 2002, many news sites were prepared to shrink the size of their virtual malls. In Hong Kong, the hycyber. com chopped its Skyworld plan, and in the US, latimes.com cut out its whole marketplace section. Meanwhile, the commission type of e-commerce program emerged in 2002. The service type of e-commerce programs, such as job recruitment, car sales, property sales and ticketing, also grew steadily. By 2003, the share of service-type e-commerce items reached 38%.

Online publishers now recognize that as Internet technology has become more popular, many companies have set up their own sites and have developed their online retailing applications. The advantage of the news site as a digital trading marketplace has been neutralized, as Porter (2001) suggested that it would be. The news media have no advantage in conducting general online retailing business and auctions. They therefore have to offer products and services that are unique and competitive. Turning back to the traditional news media-marketing strategy of selling news content and providing bridging services has become a rational choice. A radio news executive we interviewed agrees that the news media have to go back to the basics like selling news bulletins to outside companies such as bus and train companies, portal websites, mobile phone users and people requiring special financial information services.

It is interesting to note that the news sites in Mainland China put forward very few content subscription packages. This may be due to the fact that most of the news stories from Mainland China sites come from the same standardized official channels. Their news products are not unique, and have low economic value.

The Partnership Model as a Survival Imperative

Hypothesis 3 is also supported by the data. The online news media continued to adopt the partnership model as a survival need for their e-commerce projects. Table 14.4 shows that over the three years, partnership e-commerce programs have continued to grow. In terms of their share of e-commerce items, partnership items increased from 23.5% in 2001 to 27% in 2002, and further increased to 34.2% in 2003. In other words, one-third of the e-commerce programs were conducted in some type of partnership. A previous study in Hong Kong indicated that many electronic newspapers adopted a "network partnership model" to facilitate the establishment of flexible networking for the enhancement of competitive edge (So and Lee 2004). The present study further confirms this strategy. Although online news media are increasingly integrating with the business of their own news group, and are strengthening their internal partnership ties, they are also eager to establish outside partnerships. For example, in Mainland China, news sites are particularly interested in setting up e-commerce mini-sites with outside companies to sell specified products such as sports products, World Cup products, gifts, computer games, clothing, flowers, CDs, and books. Partnership items shared 85.5% of their e-commerce programs in 2003. These partnership mini-sites are basically operated by outside partners, and all the transactions are also handled by outside partners. The news media actually do not run these virtual shops. What they do is to guide online readers to these partnership shops, playing a bridging role instead of selling directly.

In other regions, the online news media were also active in finding e-commerce partners. In Hong Kong, atnext.com has lined up with YesAsia, an e-mall, to provide various mechanized products. Atnext.com gains commission if readers click through the link and make a purchase. Scmp.com links its site with various hotel partners for hotel booking services. The cts.com.tw in Taiwan has teamed up with toy manufacturers to sell toys. In the UK, news sites work with betting companies and banks to offer betting and mortgage services. In the US, it is very common for news sites to team up with sites such as cars.com, careerbuilder.com, apartment.com and movecenter.com to provide a wide range of online services and goods for their readers. Many sites also work with telecommunication companies to provide various kinds of wireless news download services.

Building partnerships is important for many news media because they can engage in e-commerce for a lower investment and using less manpower. Their own sites cannot attract as many online shoppers as many product and service providers, and so cooperation is beneficial for both parties. An interviewee from a newspaper organization pointed out that in Hong Kong, Wisenews is a company that focuses on collecting daily news contents from many newspapers in Hong Kong and the Greater China region and selling them to various clients. This company represents a successful model as it forges a partnership among direct competitors. It has its own unique niche.

Web 2.0 and the News Sites

Beginning from the mid-2000s, the world has entered the Web 2.0 age. The media environment has a new landscape. Facing the challenge of Web 2.0, the online news media are responding with a number of innovations. The new practices are mainly in their news section (information marketplace) and forum section (opinion marketplace). Many online news sites have integrated citizen journalism into their news gathering process. Some sites even provide corners for posting citizen journalistic reports. For example, the *Apple Daily* in Hong Kong invites readers to submit stories. ABC News launches an hour-long show based on user-generated video called "i-Caught" and put the clips on its news site. BBC has a collection of reader photos. Nytimes.com also encourages readers to send in photos and it showcases the best online. CNN.com and nypost.com offer videos sent in by readers. Moreover, almost all the news sites have added in the "blog" sections to enhance the participation of online readers. However, few changes are observed in the e-commerce section (trading marketplace) of the online news media.

Web2.0 has created ample e-business opportunities. YouTube, MySpace and other video sites are popular and making good profit. This study revisited all the sampled news sites in 2007 but found the impact of Web 2.0 on the e-commerce practice of the news sites is very limited. The overall e-commerce pattern has not changed much since 2003.

Yet, it is worth noting that e-commerce on news sites has no sign of drawing back. Like the e-commerce development in the first three years, the trading marketplaces are still active and growing steadily. A few new features have been added. For examples, in the US sites, printable coupons are available for e-shoppers. Another new feature is the launch of the shopping channels on a few sites. Products are promoted in the video shows and expert advice is offered. The CCTV.com e-shopping channel is operated round the clock. The ttv.com.tw e-shop invites guests to promote products in its TV Live program. While some new formats have emerged in the e-commerce sections, there are few Web 2.0 characteristics. The one with Web 2.0 feature is the consumer blogs on ETtoday which is not our sampled site. Online readers and celebrities share their shopping experience in their blogs in this site. Apparently, the online readers are more enthusiastic in sharing news and opinions on the news sites instead of engaging in e-shopping activities.

Hypothesis 2 of this study is still supported in 2007. Overall speaking, there is no sign that the online news media play the role of multi-dimensional electronic traders. Most online media sites focus on selling their unique media products and playing their traditional role as middleman of product promotion. The trend of registration and content subscriptions continues. Many online news sites keep on charging for their content. The only exception is the case of CNN. Starting from July 1, 2007 CNN.com stops charging for Pipeline live video service (US$25 per year) as bandwidth costs drop. However, other sites such as abc.go.com still charges for some videos and nytimes.com has charged US$50 a year for accessing certain columnists since 2005. The *Times* said it has 724,000 TimesSelect subscribers (Associated Press, 2007). Like the e-commerce pattern in 2003, many news sites, particularly those in HK, UK and USA, put emphasis on selling in-house products and services. They also play the middleman role of conducting e-commerce projects which connect online readers with service providers. In Mainland China and Taiwan, we can see that the outside e-malls of some news sites such as cctv.com and ttv.com.tw are more active than before. More efforts have been put into the e-mall project. For example, they develop shopping channels on the site to promote products. Across all the 26 sites, this kind of effort is limited to a small number of sites and it has not yet had great impact on the strategic development of e-commerce as a whole. This moderately revived confidence in e-mall may be due to the rising economy in Mainland China and Taiwan. People there begin to get used to online shopping as credit system improves.

In the Web 2.0 age, online news media still put emphasis on the partnership model of e-commerce. They continue to cooperate with estate companies, car companies, travel agencies and job recruitment agencies to provide e-commerce service. For e-malls, the TTV e-shop is actually part of the oBuy Allied Commercial City and the udn. com's shopping mall is also a partnership project with Monday.com.

Conclusions

Toward a Core Partnership Strategy

This study has evaluated the e-commerce performance of 26 news sites around the world in the first three years of the new millennium. Although their performance did not match the overly optimistic expectation of the early days, e-commerce has been gradually making progress. Over these three years, the digital trading marketplaces of the sites have kept changing their look, closing down old programs and bringing forth new initiatives.

Although the characteristics of the online news media have propelled them into being electronic traders rather than advertisement deliverers, their advantage in this field advantage did not last long. As all companies start to embrace the Internet, the online trading platforms of the news media then become ordinary marketplaces. However, news sites are still good locations for trading, because of their capability to attract large groups of online visitors. This study finds that, after experiencing ups and downs, online publishers have not given up their e-commerce dreams, but are redirecting their e-commerce strategy. They have shifted their thinking away from e-business-to-business and from e-strategy-to-strategy, as some business scholars suggested they should. They are returning to the basic business strategy of the traditional news media, selling their unique content products and making service charges by playing the role of middlemen. In addition, they have teamed up with e-commerce partners to reduce cost and risk.

The digital trading marketplace of the online news media has evolved with emphasis on different product categories in different years. In 2001, heavy emphasis was put on the direct sale of retail products in e-malls as category C accounted for the largest part of this type of business (56.9%, see Table 4). In 2002, content sales (Category A) and connected outside services (Category B) began to grow in both size and share. Although outside e-malls still grew in size, their share actually shrank to 45.7%. By 2003, Categories A and B outgrew Category C, which registered decreases in both size and share (28.3%). The trend of a growing number of partnerships is also noticeable. The combined approach of returning to the core fundamentals and building partnerships has become the strategic principle that has been adopted by many news sites. The characteristics of the core-partnership model of e-commerce include: (1) requirements for site registration and subscription; (2) individual content package for sale; (3) promoting and selling in-house products and services; (4) handling more connected outside products and services; (5) developing more service-type e-commerce items; and (6) building more internal and external partnership programs.

While some were still optimistic about the future of e-commerce, many of our interviewees recognized the limitations of doing e-commerce on news websites, and they adopted a more pragmatic approach. They came to realize that going back to the media basics is the way forward. To a certain extent, e-commerce has to be related to your own line of business, or certain synergy can be established between a news website and its sister enterprises or outside companies. Forming partnership with others is thus the key to a successful business.

A content online report once stated that "The Internet is evolving ... and there are unquestionably some significant changes.... The current evolution will see more sustainable business models emerging and greater numbers of roadblocks erected" (eMarketer 2002, p. 6). The number of Internet users has now reached critical mass in many countries. The growing global Internet population and the wider use of broadband will certainly benefit the development of e-commerce as more people will go online to shop. Although online practitioners claim that advertising remains the overwhelming source of income for supporting digital content, e-commerce will continue to play a significant complementary role in generating revenue for news sites. E-commerce strategy will, of course, continue to change, as it accommodates the new technological and economic environment of the 21st century. A revisit of the sampled news sites in 2007 shows that the core partnership strategy has not changed much in the past few years. With Web2.0, e-commerce on news sites may have some new initiatives. However, regardless of what the changes will be, the online news media's e-commerce strategy will probably orbit around the traditional strengths of the news industry.

Notes

1. The authors gratefully acknowledge funding support for this study by Competitive Earmarked Research Grants (HKBU2022/ 00H, CUHK4320/01H) from the Research Grants Council of Hong Kong.
2. Hong Kong sites: atnext.com, hkcyber.com, i-cable.com (broadcast), mingpao.com, singtao.com, scmp.com. Mainland China sites: cctv (broadcast), eastday.com (broadcast), people.com, 7cworld (2001 &2002) / SZNews (2003) [name change].
   Taiwan sites: chinatimes.com, cts.com.tw (broadcast), udnnews.com, ttv.com.tw (broadcast). UK sites: bbci (broadcast), sky.com (broadcast), The Sun Online, timesonline. US sites: abc.go.com (broadcast), cnn. com (broadcast), latimes.com, msnbc.com (broadcast), nypost.com, nytimes.com, usatoday.com, washingtonpost.com.

References

Associated Press. (2007). "CNN.com to stop charging for Pipeline live video service as bandwidth costs drop". Accessed on 25 May, 2007: http:// technology.scmp.com/techinternet/ZZZYD3VQV1F.html.

Atkinson, R. D. (2002). *The 2002 State New Economy Index: Benchmarking Economic Transformation in the States*. Washington, DC: Progressive Policy Institute.

BBCi. (2004a). "US online sales hit $50bn in 2003". Accessed on 25 February, 2004: http://newsvote.bbc.co.uk/mpapps/pagetools/print/news.bbc.co.uk/2/hi/business/3515287.stm.

BBCi. (2004b). "20m UK shoppers going online". Accessed on 31 March, 2004: http://newsvote.bbc.co.uk/mpapps/pagetools/print/news.bbc.co.uk/2/hi/business/3557519.stm.

Blake, B. F., Neuendorf, K., and Valdiserri, C. (2004). "Appealing to those most likely to shop new websites". Paper presented at the 54th Annual Conference of the International Communication Association, 31 May, 2004, New Orleans, USA.

Brown, D. (2003). "Searching for online gold". *American Journalism Review* 25 (5): 54–59.

Bughin, J. R., Hasker, S. J., Segel, E. S. H., and Zeisser, M. P. (2001). "What went wrong for online media?" *The McKinsey Quarterly* Number 4 Web exclusive. Accessed on 27 March, 2002: http://www.mckinseyquarterly.com/article_page.asp?tk=5....:17&ar+1121&L2=17&L3=6.

CyberAtlas staff. (2003). "Users still resistant to paid content". *CyberAtlas.* Accessed on 15 April, 2003: http://cyberatlas.internet.com/markets/retailing/print/0,6061_2189551,00.html.

eMarketer. (2002). *The Online Content Report: Executive Summary.* New York: eMarketer.

Friedman, D. (2003). "From free to fee in 10 easy steps". *Online Journalism Review.* Accessed on 23 February, 2004: http://www.ojr.org/ojr/business/106808483.php.

Fung, S. (2001). "Dotcoms in Crisis: Way forward for Online Journalism". Unpublished thesis. Green College, University of Oxford.

Gates, D. (2002). "News-sites hustle for profitability". *Online Journalism. Review.* Accessed on 26 July, 2002: http://www.ojr.org/ojr/future/p1026348638.php.

Gipson, M. (1999). "Commerce: The online solution?" *Presstime,* February: 35–41.

Gipson, M. (2002). "Playing the online game to win". *Presstime,* July/August: 26–31.

Hong Kong Economic Journal. (2002). "Consumers are getting used to shop online". *Hong Kong Economic Journal,* 8 November, p. 5.

Jung, Y. (2004). "Perceived costs and virtual experience: The added value of rich content in B2C E-commerce". Paper presented at the 54th Annual Conference of the International Communication Association, 31 May, New Orleans, USA.

Krasilovsky, P. (2003). "Newspapers want to charge for content, but will readers pay?" *Online Journalism Review.* Accessed on 4 September, 2003: http://www.ojr.org/ojr/business/1062025099.php.

Kwok, C. K. (2007). "New opportunities for sale in Web 2.0 age". *Hong Kong Economic Journal Monthly* no. 360: pp. 110–112.

Lee, A. Y. L. and So, C. Y. K. (2001). "Electronic newspaper as digital marketplaces". *World Futures* 57: 495–522.

Lee, A. Y. L. and So, C. Y. K. (2002). "Dissolving boundaries: The electronic newspaper as an agent of redefining social practices". In J. M. Chan and B. T. McIntyre (eds.), *In Search of Boundaries: Communication, Nation-states and Cultural Identities*, pp. 72–94. Westport, CT: Ablex.

Ming Pao Daily News. (2002). "Online retailing is showing hope". *Ming Pao Daily News*, 7 March, p. F2.

Noack, D. (1999). "Ebay: Users of newspaper Web sites open their cyberwallets". *Editor & Publisher* 10 July: 18–21.

Outing, S. (2003). "Top Online media execs see bright future". Accessed on 20 February, 2003: http://www.editorandpublisher.com/editorand publisher/fetures_columns/articledisplay.jsp.

Palser, B. (2001). "Pay-per-click". *American Journalism Review* p. 82.

Porter, M. E. (2001). "Strategy and the Internet". *Harvard Business Review* 79 (3): 62–78.

Reuters. (2001a). "Net access to boost media spending". Accessed on 7 June, 2001: http://news.cnet.com/news/0-1005-202-6209956.html.

Scasny, R. (2001). "Online news users have to pay: Change the product, give it more value and paid access will work". *Online Journalism Review*. Accessed on 5 December, 2001: http://ojr.usc.edu/content/print. cfm?print=663.

So, C. Y. K. and Lee, A. Y. L. (2004). "Doing e-commerce in electronic newspapers: Toward a network partnership model". In P. S. N. Lee, L. Leung, and C. Y. K. So (eds.), *Impact and Issues in New Media: Toward Intelligent Societies*, pp. 35-60. Cresskill, NJ: Hampton Press.

Sullivan, C. (2002). "Pay sites struggle, but the niche may get richer". *Editor & Publisher* 4 February: 19–20.

Sun (2001). "Web sites that lay off staff in the past year". Accessed on 28 February, 2002: http://www.the-sun.com.hk/channels/news/ 20010223/20010223025810_0001_2.html.

Yeung, W. L. (2007). "Web2.0 is changing the e-business world". *Information Technology Weekly* p. IT6.

15

—ₘ—

The Role of the Internet in Cultural Identity

George A. Barnett

Convergence Theory and Cultural Identity

Communication may be defined as a process of sharing information in which two or more participants reach mutual understanding. Mutual understanding may be achieved by the successive sharing of additional information (feedback). Usually several cycles of information exchange are required to change the initial differences that prevent understanding. The convergence model of communication posits reduced within-group variance to be the primary result of the communication process and a requirement for collective action and the achievement of social goals (Rogers and Kincaid 1981; Kincaid et al. 1983). Convergence theory may be applied to those communication situations in which the participants are social systems, such as ethnic groups or nation-states, each of which possesses a unique culture. Thus, cultural convergence theory suggests that the variance between groups or national cultures would become smaller over time as a result of international communication (Barnett and Kincaid 1983).

This chapter suggests that due to the increased communication among the peoples of the world via the Internet that the differences among national cultures will diminish, resulting in the formation of a single global culture. One outcome of this process of cultural convergence is that separate cultural identities will also disappear, replaced by a single transnational identity, albeit with considerable variation.

Convergence Theory and Communication Networks

Convergence Theory envisions the flow of information through a communication network shared by those who participate in the process. This information has profound effects on the members of the network, which are indicated by changes in the belief systems of the members and the structure of their network (the communicative relations among the participants). Local regions of greater communication density share more information and thus will be characterized by movements toward decreasing variance or difference of opinion at a greater rate than regions of less density.

The process of divergence, or movement toward increased within-group variance, occurs in closed social systems where there are no (or limited) information flows among its members. In network terms, they are disconnected or isolated. In this situation, over time members of such a system would be expected to become less similar to one another, and the system as a whole would reach a state of greater entropy or disorder. However when communication is unrestricted, the process leads toward reduced within-group variance among its members. The communication network is completely interconnected or dense. In this case, differences between its members are reduced through the iterative process of information exchange. The social system moves toward an equilibrium state where it remains as long as internal information flows are constant.

The laws of thermodynamics predict that all participants (individuals, groups or nation-states) in a closed system (the world system or global community) will converge over time on the average collective pattern of thought if communication is allowed to continue indefinitely over time. Thus, the convergence model of communication predicts that all participants in the world system will converge over time on the average collective pattern of thought if communication is allowed to continue unrestricted. Unlimited and unrestricted communication between cultures would eventually lead to a reduction in the differences between cultures and toward greater similarity of beliefs and values (homogenization) with the equilibrium value tending toward the average of the collective as expressed in its messages. Cultural convergence can only be delayed or reversed by the introduction of new information and/or the formation of boundaries that restrict the flow of information. Relatively bounded, isolated groups would experience greater convergence toward their own local system rather than the average of the larger global system, even though the net convergence of the entire system would continue to increase (Barnett and Kincaid 1983; Kincaid et. al. 1983).

Past discussions of cultural convergence theory have not take into account differences in the strength of ties among the participants in social networks. Typically, the strength of the links has been operationalized as the number of messages exchanged or the frequency of communication. This issue was not addressed at the time convergence theory developed because network theory was restricted to dichotomous measures (link-no link). Today, there are more sophisticated methods that allow for the consideration of the measured strength of a link (Richards and Barnett 1993).

Also, not addressed by the theory was the difference in the directionality, where one participant initiates the interaction a greater proportion amount of time. What are the differential impacts of encoding and decoding information? This issue was not addressed because communication was defined as a sharing of information between equals rather than considering the differences in power among the participants.

Thus, two additional propositions may be added to Convergence Theory. First, the stronger the link between individuals (or higher-level systems), the greater their reciprocal influence. Thus, the faster they will converge on a common set of beliefs. Second, the greater the proportion of messages initiated by an individual (or larger system), the more similar the final equilibrium set of beliefs will be to that initial state of beliefs. Alternatively, the smaller the proportion of messages initiated, the greater those beliefs will change to reach the final equilibrium state. These propositions may be generalized from the dyadic case to social networks composed of many individuals, nation-states. Thus, the equilibrium culture will be most similar to the nation encoding the greatest proportion of the system's messages.

This chapter describes one communication network, the

Internet, which links the members of the international community. Through the examination of the strength of the connections among the nations of the world system, it will be possible to predict its impact on their individual national cultures and to gain insights into the process leading to the formation of a global or universal culture. It begins by explicating the structural model of intercultural communication, which may be operationalized using the tools of network analysis. The chapter next describes the results of network analyzes of the international Internet. Based upon these findings, it draws inferences from cultural convergence theory to make a series of prognoses about what the short-term and long-term impact of the Internet on global culture.

A Structural Model of Intercultural Communication

Intercultural communication is the exchange of "cultural" information between two groups of people with significantly different cultures. While this definition is clearly circular, it can be clarified by specifying the meaning of its critical concepts. In other words, intercultural communication focuses on the exchange of information among two or more social systems embedded in a common context or environment that result in the reduction of uncertainty about the future behavior of the other system through an increase in understanding of the other social group.

In the past, scholars have limited its study to the individual level. However, intercultural communication occurs on many levels (Smith 1999), such as via mediated communication including the Internet. International organizations working through out the globe also link disconnected cultures facilitating understanding of the similarities and differences among groups. Intercultural communication is thus the exchange of information between well-defined groups with significantly different cultures.

To help understand the impact of the Internet on cultural identity one may adopt a structural model of communication (Barnett and Lee 2002). It is displayed in Figure 1. It represents the process of intercultural communication. It shows a sociogram of a communication network composed of two interacting groups each with its own culture. Individuals or other information sources (the media and other organizations) are represented as circles and the

Figure 15.1 The Structural Model of Communication

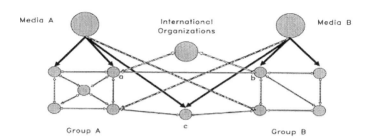

communication flows as lines. Arrows indicated the direction of information flows. This system is composed of two groups *A* and *B* with porous boundaries. Generally, communication *within* the groups is relatively dense compared to communication *between* the groups, which is sparse (Yum 1988).

Spanning the cultural boundary is a link between individual *a*, who is member of Group *A*, and *b*, a member of Group *B*. In network analysis terms, *a* and *b* are referred to as group members with *a bridge link* that connects the individual to a member of the other group. These links tend to be weaker, less frequent and deal with a narrower range of topics, than intragroup links (Granovetter 1973; Yum 1988). These individuals may be sojourners (Gudykunst and Kim 1997), individuals who travel to the other country for tourism, educational (Barnett and Wu 1995; Chen and Barnett 2000), business (Salisbury and Barnett 1999; Barnett, Salisbury, Kim, and Langhorne 1999), military (Kim 1998) or diplomatic (Kim and Barnett 2000) reasons. These interactions have been facilitated by innovations in telecommunications (the Internet) and transportation. *A* and *b* may also be immigrants, individuals moving relatively permanently to the other country but residing in a location composed primarily of members of their native group (Smith 1999). Through *a* and *b* information that reduces the uncertainty about the other group is communicated to the group of which they are a member. In other words, *a* and *b* serve as gatekeepers about information that facilitates the understanding of the other group.

C is a member of neither group. He/she is a *liaison* connecting both groups. As such, *c* is not bound by his/her membership to one particular culture. Generally, *c* is a product of a multicultural marriage, and generally, bilingual (Barnett 1996). Because he/she has the capacity to function in more than one culture effectively, he/she serves as a facilitator for contacts between nations. *C* is what Park (1928) calls a "marginal man" and Adler (1982) labels as a "multicultural man." Intercultural persons, develop a "third culture" perspective (Ellingsworth 1977; Gudykunst, Wiseman and Hammer 1977), which enables them to accurately interpret and evaluate intercultural encounters. Through *c* information about cultures *A* and *B* are passed on to the members of the other nation.

Intercultural communication concerns the linkages between Groups *A* and *B* that involve individuals *a*, *b* and *c*. These links also include the mass media and telecommunications, including the Internet (Korzenny, Ting-Toomey, and Schiff 1992; Ware and Dupagne 1994) because information that facilitates the understanding of Groups *A* and *B* is communicated via the mass media, either print (Kim and Barnett 1996) or electronic (Varis 1984). In this model, it is represented as *Media A*, the media expressing the culture of Group *A* and *Media B*, expressing Group *B's* culture. Typically, they are articulated in the unique language of each group. For example, American media is primarily in English. There may be only a few infrequent paths from *Media A* to Group *B* or *Media B* to Group *A*. This is the case with non-English language media into the United States, although Western media is widely distributed through out the world (Nordenstreng and Varis 1974). *Media A* is more strongly connected to individual *b*. The strength of *Media B's* connections to person *a* is also stronger. *C* receives both media sources. Barnett, Olivieria and Johnson (1989) report that bilinguals (*a*, *b*, and *c*) use the mass media in both of their languages that may emanate from more than one different group (*A* and *B*).

Also connecting the groups are international organizations that are not part of either group, but rather, part of global society transcending any single culture (Boli and Thomas 1997; Meyer, Boli, Thomas, and Ramirez 1997). These may be such organizations as the United Nations or the World Bank whose members are the nations of the world (IGOs), non-governmental issue-based organizations such as Amnesty International and Greenpeace (INGOs) (Boli and Thomas 1997; Jacobson 1979) or transnational corporations (Monge and Falk 1999; Walters 1995). These organizations bring people from different nations together in common forums.

Historically, these linkages among different cultural groups have increased, resulting in globalization — the process of strengthening the worldwide social relations which link distant localities in such a way that local events are shaped by circumstances at other places in the world (Giddens 1990). That is, events occurring at one place reduce the uncertainty of the future behavior of groups at other locations. The increase in transborder communication (*A* and *B* now have more and stronger ties) has led to the rapid global diffusion of values, ideas, opinions and technologies, i.e., the underlying components of culture. Transborder communication has opened cultural boundaries and begun the process of cultural convergence. It has created a global community with an increasingly homogenous culture, particularly regarding political, economic, educational and scientific activities although in the area of religion this process has been much slower (Beyer 1994; Robertson 1992).

Giddens (1990) argues that globalization is an inherent part of modernization. One consequence of modernization is the increase in time-space distanciation that renders physical distance less of a barrier to intergroup communication. This is due in part to innovations in telecommunications and transportation. Globalization stretches the boundaries of social interaction such that the connections among different social contexts or nations become networked across the globe. Thus, the communication between the two groups presented in Figure 1, may be generalized to all the nations of the world. The mass media and other communication technologies, especially the Internet, compress time and space becoming a catalyst for globalization (Giddens 1990; Robertson 1990). As a result, McLuhan's notion of the global village is becoming a reality.

Various forms of the Structural Model, also known as the Network Model, have been used to investigate intercultural (Yum 1984, 1988; Weimann 1989; Smith 1999), intergroup communication (Kim 1986) and international communication (Barnett 1999, 2001). Barnett and Lee (2002) recently reviewed this research in depth.

In a recent review of the role of nationality in the process of globalization Crofts Wiley (2004 p. 90) has argued that the contextualist approach assumes that the nation, "... is a porous, perhaps precarious, organization of economic, demographic, and cultural flows that must constantly be redefined and reinforced in the midst of a fluid geography." It is "a complex assemblage of flows, materials, bodies, and symbols." This complex of flows may be examined through the structural analysis of social and communication networks as described in this chapter.

The Network Structure of the International Internet

The Internet is one channel that directly connects people of different cultural and national groups from across the globe with one another. Information flows via the Internet may facilitate the convergence of national cultures leading to a universal set of beliefs including a change from national to global identity.

There has been little research that has examined international Internet flows. Ingwersen (1998) examined the international web links among Scandinavia, U.K., France and Japan and found Norway to be prominent on the web. Almind and Ingwersen (1997) found that Denmark's position on the web to be weaker than Norway and Sweden.

Halavais (2000) examined the role of geographic borders in cyberspace with a sample of 4,000 web sites. He analyzed their external hyperlinks, determining the total percentage of links from the sites to various countries and found that web sites were most likely to link to another site in the same country. When they did link across national borders, most often it was to hosts in the United States. In a study of the structure of global web commerce, Brunn and Dodge (2001) analyzed the inter-domain hyperlinks among 174 geographic TLDs (top-level domains, such as *.ca* for Canada). They treated web sites' incoming and outgoing links separately and developed a domain-by-domain matrix of inter-hyperlinks upon which they conducted descriptive statistics and cross-tabulation analysis by country and region.

Barnett, Chon and Rosen (2001) used data published by the Organization for Economic Cooperation and Development (OECD, 1998) to examine international hyperlink traffic among OECD countries. They found that, the United States was the most central country, the nucleus of Internet traffic. The next most central nations were the United Kingdom, Canada, Germany and Australia.

Most peripheral in the OECD were Iceland and Turkey. The Internet network of the OCED nations formed a single group. Also, the structure of the Internet was significantly related to the structure of the international telecommunications, air traffic, trade, science and student flow networks at earlier points in time, as well language and asynchrony, but not cost or physical distance. In combination, only telecommunications, air traffic, science citations, asynchrony and either trade or student flows were significant, accounting for over 62 percent of the structure of the Internet.

Ciolek (2001) examined the direction and volume of hyperlinks among ten East Asian countries. He found that Japan had the greatest volume of hyperlinks. However, most (92 percent) were directed to other Japanese web sites. Singapore imported 27 percent of its links, and China 25 percent. Indonesia attracts 30 percent of all pages with international links from the other nine countries.

There are other recent studies on international hyperlink networks that focus on a specific type of international linkage. Thelwall and Smith (2002) examined academic hyperlink connectivity among thirteen Asia-Pacific countries. They found that Australia and Japan have the most internationally visible academic Webs in the Asia-Pacific region in terms of total number of incoming and outgoing hyperlinks. Park (2002) analyzed the structure of hyperlink connectivity between South Korea and Taiwan. He found that the hyperlink network was very sparsely connected in terms of the number of South Korean web pages hyperlinking to Taiwan's pages.

Bharat, Chang, Henzinger, and Ruhl (2001) examined the structure of the WWW using Google and found that there was a much higher number of intra-national links than ties to other countries. Typically, only one percent of all links were to websites in another country. Further, when the links among the most central countries were removed, geographical, linguistic and political factors impacted the structure of the web.

Barnett and Park (2003) examined the structure of the international hyperlink network (n = 47) using Alta Vista and the Internet infrastructure (n = 63). The analysis of the hyperlink network revealed a dense completely interconnected system with a single group centered about the United States. Over 15 million web pages connected directly to the U.S. (not including .com or .net), more than three times any other nation. Next most central were Australia, the United Kingdom, China, Japan, Canada, and Germany. China emerged as a central node in international Internet flows. Most peripheral in the network were Uruguay, Luxemburg, U.A.E., Thailand, Slovakia and Romania. A multidimensional scaling resulted in two dimensions. Dimension 1 differentiated Latin America from East Asia, and Dimension 2, U.A.E. from Luxemburg. These results are consistent with Barnett, et al. (2001) who found that the Internet formed a dense completely interconnected network with a single group centered about the United States. Also, they found no clustering of nations. It is represented in Figure 2.

The infrastructure (bandwidth) network is fairly sparse. For the 47 countries that compose the hyperlink network, only 18.5 percent of the possible direct links were present. Again, the United States was the most central country, followed by the United Kingdom, Germany, Hong Kong, Singapore, Japan, France and Italy. Most peripheral in this network were Iceland, Lithuania, Morocco, Croatia and Guatemala. The cluster analysis resulted in three major groupings, 1) the English speaking countries (U.S., U.K., Canada, Australia, New Zealand) with Northern Europe and East Asia, 2) Latin America, and 3) Franco-German Europe. A multidimensional scaling resulted in two dimensions. The first dimension differentiated the Baltic Republics from North Africa Morocco and Algeria, and the second South America from Eastern Europe. It is presented in Figure 3.

Townsend's (2001, p. 1701) examination of the Internet bandwidth resulted in a similar conclusion,

> ... every region and nearly every country has a direct Internet connection to the United States, direct connections between other countries are less common. Furthermore, direct connections between different major regions such as Asia and Europe are practically nonexistent.... This structure dictates that the U.S. Internet infrastructure functions as a massive switching station for traffic that originates and terminates in foreign countries.

Barnett and Sung (2002) examined the relationship between the national culture, as operationalized by Hofstede (1990), and the structure of the Internet. They found that national culture is strongly related to a country's position in the Internet network. How central

Figure 15.2 International Internet Hyperlink Network

Thickness of the line indicates the number of hyperlinks between two countries. 50,000 links is the minimum for the presence of a link. The direction of the hyperlink is indicated by an arrowhead. The luminance of the country indicates its centrality in the network.

Figure 15.3 International Internet Infrastructure

Thickness of the line indicates the bandwidth capacity between two countries. 13Mbps is the minimum for the presence of a link. Color indicates membership in a cluster. Shades of a color indicate membership in a sub-cluster.

a country is in the network is significantly related to a nation's degree of individualism. In societies high in individualism, people look after their own interests, and value their independence. Societies low in individualism support group values and beliefs and seek collective interests (Hofstede, 1980). Using the results of the multidimensional scaling to represent the overall structure of the networks, they found that first dimension of the Internet was significantly related to individualism, the second to masculinity, and the third to power distance. Societies in high power distance are more autocratic. Low power distance societies value equality, with a preference toward democratic processes (Hofstede, 1980).

These results suggest that while there are some structural barriers in the infrastructure of the Internet that could restrict communication among nations. However, the actual pattern of information flows suggests one completely interconnected system. Thus, the potential for the convergence among the cultures of individual nation-states into a homogenous universal system of beliefs exists. The results also show that the U.S. encodes significantly more messages on the net than any other nation, putting it at the center of these flows. This suggests that if the status quo were to continue that universal culture is in the process of forming about the culture of the United States.

Implications of the Structural Model for National Identity: Current Trends

Barnett and Park (2003) and Barnett, et al. (2001) indicate that the nations of the world are components in a completely interconnected hyperlink network, unrestricted by cost or physical distance, although other (Halavais 2000; Ciolek 2001; Bharat et al. 2001) find that most hyperlinks are directed to other sites within the same country. Also, there are other barriers that restrict the flow of information among nations including, language and political policies implemented in the form of firewalls and other forms of network surveillance that prevent the access to websites containing particular content perceived as dangerous to individual societies.

Also, the infrastructure (bandwidth) may limit the flow of information among countries. It is sparse, creating barriers to the direct contact among nations. For example, there are no direct connections between any Islamic countries. All flows among these nations must be routed by way of the U.S., Japan, U.K., France, Germany, Hong Kong or Singapore. The later two provide links only between Indonesia and Malaysia. This suggests the capability of the core nations to monitor or restrict the flows within the Islamic world.

Focusing on the countries that are most central in the network finds that Internet flows revolve around the U.S. and the other English-speaking nations — UK, Canada, Australia, India, as well as Japan, Germany and France. This suggests that global identity will converge about Anglo-American or at a minimum, a liberal Western culture.

This position can be further supported by the examination of linguistic data. According to Global Reach (2003), 35.6 percent of the online population speaks English. Other European languages account for an additional 34.9 percent of the users, with 8.0 percent Spanish, 7.0 percent German, 3.7 percent French, and 3.3 percent Italian. Asian languages account for only 29.4 percent with Chinese, 12.2 percent, Japanese, 9.5 percent, and Korean, 4.0 percent. Arabic accounts for only 1.2 percent of the total number of users.

Further, Barnett and Sung (2002) found that Hofstede's dimension of individualism was significantly related to centrality in the network. Countries high in individualism include the U.S., U.K., Canada and Australia. This suggests that over time due to these nations' positions in the flow of Internet information that global culture will become more individualistic. People will identify less with their national or ethnic group; provide less support for these groups' values and beliefs and the interests of the collective. They will take on the culture that places great emphasis on the individual. Individual identity will become less closely tied to a nationality and more highly connected to a universal global civilization.

Based on his research on international telecommunication, Barnett (2001, p. 1650) discusses the implications of these patterns for the long-term development of a universal culture,

> Over the last two decades, the frequency of interaction among the nations of the world has increased steadily. While there is regionalization due to physical and cultural (linguistic) barriers, today, the world consists of a single integrated network of nations centered about North America and Western Europe. One potential consequence

of globalization is the cultural homogenization or the convergence of the indigenous cultures of the world into a universal culture.

While cultural convergence is the likely long-term outcome of international communication of which the Internet is only one channel, the globalization-localization dialectic suggests that globalization involves the linking of locals to the wider world while localization incorporates trends of globalization. As a result, in the near future local cultures could be developing hybrid characteristics (Pieterse 1995; Lemish 1998). Over time, with unlimited and unrestricted information exchange among people from different cultural groups, the potential consequence of the Internet is cultural homogenization, that is, the convergence of the indigenous cultures of the world into a universal culture. However, in the short-term international communication will more likely first lead to the development of a number of regional civilizations composed of nations who are culturally similar. The reason for this is that international communication includes a number of different channels where barriers of access, physical distance, cost and language have a greater impact than they do on the Internet. Additionally, different groups may interpret media content differently due to their unique histories. Further, while certain content areas such as music and sports have seemed to globalize other topics, especially religion, remain idiosyncratic. As a result, Barnett (2001, 2002) found that the current structure of the world's telecommunication system is organized along the lines of regional groupings of nations, generally with related cultures, similar to those suggested by Galtung (1993) and Huntington (1996).

The process of cultural globalization can be considered as homogenization and hybridization. Along with absorption of global patterns, culturally localized or hybridized adaptation plays a strong role. Global forms interplay with local, national, and regional patterns, producing a new pattern best characterized as hybrid (Bhahba 1994). Straubhaar (2002) argues that hybridization is the dominant pattern of cultural interaction over time. He asserts that multi-country markets are formed on a geocultural or cultural-linguistic basis. Thus, in the near future, while individual identity will transcend the local ethnic or national it may stop far short of global convergence that has been suggested for the long-term. It is likely that we may see individuals developing pan-Islamic, European, Latin American or North American identities.

Implications for National Identity: The Future

The notion that cultural convergence will lead to the evolution of a universal set of beliefs heavily based upon the culture of the United States and other liberal western nations that places great emphasis on individual identity assumes that the current structure of the Internet will remain relatively stable in the foreseeable future. However, Hargittai (1999) has shown that a nation's time of the adoption of the Internet is an important determinant of its position in the international Internet network, and Barabási (2002) has demonstrated that the Internet evolves as new nodes (web-pages) link to existing sites. Those nodes (web-pages) with the most connections at one point in time generally remain most central at later points in time. Comparing the results from Barnett and Park (2003) with the more limited description of the structure of the Internet from Barnett, et al. (2001), one finds that the same nations that composed the core in 1998 are still the most central nodes five years later. This suggests that the Internet's growth tends to reinforce the influence of those countries that are central in the network on the formation of global culture.

The research reviewed here suggests that the cultural identity as represented by the converged global culture will be dominated by the United States. Currently, it is the most central country in the international flow of information, controlling the world's channels of communication, including the Internet. This may be a result, in part, of its level of economic and technological development. It may also, be due to its geography. It abuts Latin America, and it has a presence on both the Atlantic and Pacific Oceans, facilitating its function as a gateway between Asia and Europe. Its centrality may also be because Americans speak English, the international language of science, education and business. Or, it may simply be due to U.S. demographics. American society is composed of people from all the world's cultures. Today, although the majority of Americans are of European ancestry, 10 percent come from Latin America, 12 percent have African ancestry, and 3 percent are from Asia (U.S. Bureau of the Census 1996). It is estimated that by 2050, the majority of the

American population will be other than European, with nearly 10 percent from Asia, 25 percent from Latin America, and 25 percent with African ancestry. The U.S., the source for the plurality of Internet messages, is a product of cultural convergence. Its culture will be changing in the future due to changes in demographics and the dynamic patterns of international information flows resulting from the process of globalization.

The structure of the Internet is dynamic, changing as non-Western countries increasingly come online. Since 2000, the number of Internet hosts in China has annually grown by 48.7 percent and by 55.4 percent in India (Internet Software Consortium 2003). For the United States, the number of host increased by only 2.3 percent, and 10.6 percent, for the U.K. Thus, if we assume that these rates of growth continue over time, both China and India will have an increasing impact on the converged universal culture in the future, and the western nations will have a proportionately less effect on the global system. Further, if we consider how the growth of Internet use in China will change the pattern of language use on the net, then the converged culture of the world system will have increasing Chinese elements, suggesting that global civilization will be some combination of Chinese and Anglo-American culture. In some sense it will be similar to Hong Kong or Singapore.

It should be pointed out that the Internet is still not available everywhere on the planet, especially in Africa, and parts of Asia and Latin America. Further, even in the United States, it is primarily an urban medium. In rural areas of peripheral nations, the Internet like all forms of telecommunication is non-existent.

My current research (Barnett and Jun 2004) examines the antecedent factors that influence the structure of the Internet. The initial results indicate that many factors are significantly related to the structure of the Internet. Generally, these are indicators of the domestic telecommunication and media infrastructure. International Internet flows are not related to the physical distance between nations or a country's level of political freedom. Among developmental indicators, GDP, international trade and media variables are significantly related to a nation's position in the network. Literacy and urbanization are not. As for cultural indicators, only individualism is significant. When examined in combination, only international trade and a nation's number of

Internet hosts are significant predictors of the structure of international Internet flows, accounting for between 63 and 86% of variance in a nation's position depending on the measure. Culture (individualism) is a significant predictor of only one measure of structure, the number of hyperlinks sent to other nations.

This research suggests what investments will produce greatest growth in Internet usage and output of messages to the net. Freund and Weinhold (2004) found that a growth in a nation's web hosts result in an increase in exports. Nations should encourage the establishment of web sites and thus increase their interdependency through international trade as well as encourage individual achievement if influence on universal culture is deemed a national priority. Countries that are putting the money into these activities will have the greatest long-term impact on global culture.

This chapter has argued that according to cultural convergence theory, the increased communication among the peoples of the world via the Internet will lead to the diminishment of differences among national cultures over time, eventually resulting in the formation of a single global culture. One outcome of this process is that unique national cultures will disappear, replaced by a single transnational identity. One caveat is that the Internet represents only one of many modes of communication between nations (Barnett and Lee 2002). Cultural information is still exchanged via interpersonal contacts, through international sojourners — tourism, military, business, student and migration, trade (artifactual communication), formal organizations (INGOs and transnational corporations), mail, other forms of telecommunications (telephone and facsimile), and the conventional mass media (print, film and electronic). Each medium may provide a set of different cultural images and its flows may be structured differently than the Internet. However, over the past decade, there is evidence for media convergence (Chon, Choi, Barnett, Danowski, and Joo, 2003), and past research indicates that these structures are congruent across these media (Barnett et al. 1999, 2001).

In summary, this chapter describes the Internet, which links the members of the international community. Through the examination of the strength of the connections among the nations of the world, it predicts the Internet's impact on individual cultural identity and the process leading to the formation of a global culture. It began by explicating the structural model of intercultural communication, which may be operationalized using network analysis. It next reviewed the results of network analyzes of the international Internet. Based upon these findings, it drew inferences from cultural convergence theory to make a series of prognoses about what the short-term and long-term impact of the Internet on global culture and national identity.

References

Adler, P. S. (1982). "Beyond cultural identity: Reflections on cultural and multicultural man". In L. Samovar and R. Porter (eds.), *Intercultural Communication: A Reader*, 3rd ed. Belmont, CA: Wadsworth.

Almind, T. C. and Ingwersen, P. (1997). "Informatic analyses on the world wide web: Methodological approaches to 'webometrics'". *Journal of Documentation* 53: 404–426.

Barabási, A. L. (2002). *Linked: The New Science of Networks.* Cambridge, MA: Perseus Publishing.

Barnett, G. A. (1996). "Multilingualism and transportation/tele-communication". In H. Goebl, P. H. Nelde, Z. Stary, and W. Wolck (eds.), *Handbook on contact linguistics: An international handbook of contemporary research*, Vol. 1, pp. 431–438. Berlin: Walter De Gruyter.

———. (1999). "The social structure of international telecommunications". In H. Sawhney and G.A. Barnett (eds.), *Progress in Communication Sciences: Advances in Telecommunications*, Vol. 15, pp. 151–186. Greenwich, CT: Ablex.

———. (2001). "A longitudinal analysis of the international telecommunications network: 1978–1996". *American Behavioral Scientist* 44: 1638–1655.

——— and Kincaid, D. L. (1983). "Cultural convergence: A mathematical theory". In W.B. Gudykunst (ed.), *Intercultural Communication Theory: Current Perspectives*, pp. 171–194. Beverly Hills, CA: Sage.

———, Olivieria, O. S., and Johnson, J. D. (1989). "Multilingual language use and television exposure and preferences: The case of Belize". *Communication Quarterly* 37: 248–261.

——— and Wu, Y. (1995). "The international student exchange network: 1970 and 1989". *Higher Education* 30: 353–368.

——— and Salisbury, J. G. T. (1996). "Communication and globalization: A longitudinal analysis of the international telecommunication network". *Journal of World System Research* 2 (16): 1–17.

———, Jacobson, T. L., Choi, Y., and Sun-Miller, S. L. (1996). "An examination of the international telecommunication network". *The Journal of International Communication* 3: 19–43.

——, Salisbury, J. G. T., Kim, C., and Langhorne, A. (1999). "Globalization and international communication networks: An examination of monetary, telecommunications, and trade networks". *The Journal of International Communication* 6 (2): 7–49.

——, Chon, B.S., and Rosen, D. (2001). "The structure of international Internet flows in cyberspace". *NETCOM* (Network and Communication Studies) 15 (1–2): 61–80.

—— and Lee, M. (2002). "Issues in intercultural communication". In W.B. Gudykunst and B. Mody (eds.), *Handbook of international and intercultural communication*, pp. 275–290. Thousand Oaks, CA: Sage.

—— and Park, H. W. (2003). "The structure of the international Internet". Paper presented at Association of Internet Research, Toronto.

—— and Sung, E. J. (2003). "Culture and the structure of international communication". Paper presented to the International Communication Association, San Diego.

—— and Jun, S. J. (2004). "An examination of the determinants of international Internet structure". Paper to be presented to the Association of Internet Research, Sussex, U.K.

Beyer, P. (1994). *Religion and Globalization*. London: Sage.

Bhahbam, H. (1994). *The Location of Culture*. New York: Routledge.

Bharat, K., Chang, B. W., Henzinger, M., and Ruhl, M. (2001). "Who links to whom: Mining linkage between web sites". *Proceedings 2001 IEEE International Conference on Data Mining (ICDM)*: 51–58.

Boli, J. and Thomas, G. M. (1997). "World culture in the world polity: A century of international non-governmental organization". *American Sociological Review* 62: 171–190.

Brunn, S. D. and Dodge, M. (2001). "Mapping the 'worlds' of the World Wide Web: (Re)Structuring global commerce through hyperlinks". *American Behavioral Scientist* 44: 1717–1739.

Chen, T. and Barnett, G. A. (2000). "Research on international student flows from a macro perspective: A network analysis of 1985, 1989 and 1995". *Higher Education* 39: 435–553.

Chon, B. S., Choi, J. H., Barnett, G. A., Danowski, J.A., and Joo, S. J. (2003). "A structural analysis of media convergence: Cross-industry mergers and acquisitions in the information industries". *Journal of Media Economics* 16 (3): 141–157.

Ciolek, T. M. (2001). "Networked information flows in Asia: The research uses of the Alta Vista search engine and 'weblinksurvey' software". Paper presented to Internet Political Economy Forum 2001: Internet and Development in Asia, The National University of Singapore.

Crofts Wiley, S. B. (2004). "Rethinking nationality in the context of globalization". *Communication Theory* 14 (1): 78–96.

Ellingsworth, H. (1977). "Conceptualizing intercultural communication". In B. Ruben (ed.), *Communication Yearbook I*, pp. 99–106. New Brunswick, NJ: Transaction.

Freund, C. L. and Weinhold, D. (2004). "The effect of the Internet on international trade". *Journal of International Economics* 62 (1): 171–189.

Giddens, A. (1990). *The Consequences of Modernity*. Stanford, CA: Stanford University Press.

Global Research. (2003). Global Internet statistics (by language). http://www.glreach.com/globstats/.

Granovetter, M. (1973). "The strength of weak ties". *American Journal of Sociology* 73: 1361–1380.

Galtung, J. (1993). "Geopolitical transformations and the 21st-century world economy". In K. Nordenstreng and H. Schiller (eds.), *Beyond National Sovereignty: International Communication in the 1990s*, pp. 28–58. Norwood, NJ: Ablex.

Gudykunst, W. B. and Kim. Y. Y. (1997). *Communicating with Strangers: An Approach to Intercultural Communication* (3rd ed.). New York: McGraw-Hill.

Gudykunst, W. B., Wiseman, R., and Hammer, M. (1977). "Determinants of a sojourner's attitudinal satisfaction". In B. Ruben (ed.), *Communication Yearbook*, pp. 415–426. New Brunswick, NJ: Transaction.

Halavais, A. (2000). "National borders on the world wide web". *New Media and Society* 2: 7–28.

Hargittai, E. (1999). "Weaving the Western web: Explaining the differences in Internet connectivity among OECD countries". *Telecommunications Policy* 23: 701–718.

Hofstede, G. (1991). *Cultures and Organizations: Software of the Mind*. London: McGraw-Hill.

Huntington, S. P. (1996). *The Clash of Civilizations: Remaking the World Order*. New York: Touchstone.

Ingwersen, P. (1998). "The calculation of web impact factors". *Journal of Documentation* 54: 236–243.

Internet Software Consortium (2003). "Distribution of top-level domain names". http://www.isc.org/ds/WWW-200201/dist-bynum.html.

Jacobson, H. K. (1979). *Networks and Interdependence: International Organizations and the Global Political System*. New York: Knopf.

Kim, C. (1998). "The changing structures of global arms trade 1987–1994: A network analysis on major conventional weapons trade". Paper presented to the International Communication Association, Jerusalem, Israel.

Kim, K. and Barnett, G. A. (2000). "The structure of the international telecommunications regime in transition: A network analysis of international organizations". *International Interactions* 26: 91–127.

Kim, K. and Barnett, G. A. (1996). "The determinants of international news flow". *Communication Research* 23: 323–352.

Kim, Y. Y. (1986). "Understanding the social content of intergroup communication: A personal network approach". In W. Gudykunst (ed.), *Intergroup Communication*, pp. 86–95. London: Edward Arnold.

Kincaid, D. L., Yum, J. O., Woelfel, J. and Barnett, G. A., (1983). "The cultural convergence of Korean immigrants in Hawaii: An empirical test of a mathematical theory". *Quality and Quantity* 18: 59-78.

Korzenny, F., Ting-Tommey, S., and Schiff, E. (1992). *Mass Media Effects across Cultures*. Newbury Park, CA: Sage.

Lemish, D. (1998). "Global culture in practice: A look at children and adolescents in Denmark, France and Israel". *European Journal of Communication* 13 (4): 539–556.

Meyer, J. W., Boli, J., Thomas, G. M., and Ramirez, F. O. (1997). "World society and the nation-state". *American Journal of Sociology* 103 (1): 144–181.

Monge, P. R. and Fulk, J. (1999). "Communication technology for global network organizations". In G. DeSanctis and J. Fulk (eds.), *Shaping Organizational Form: Communication, Connection, and Community*, pp. 71–100. Thousand Oaks, CA: Sage.

Nordenstreng, K. and Varis, T. (1974). *Television traffic — A one-way street? Reports and papers on mass communication* No. 70. Paris: UNESCO.

Park, H. W. (2002). "No diplomatic relationship between Korea and Taiwan on the web? Looking at an enemy's website". Paper presented at Tamkang University 2002 International Communication Convention, Taipei, R.O.C.

Park, R. E. (1928). "Human migration and the marginal man". *American Journal of Sociology* 33: 881–893.

Pieterse, J. N. (1995). "Globalization as hybridization". In M. Featherstone, S. Lash, and R. Robertson (eds.), *Global Modernities*, pp. 45–68. Newberry Park, CA: Sage.

Richards, W. D. Jr. and Barnett, G. A. (eds.). (1993). *Progress in Communication Sciences*, volume 12. Norwood, NJ: Ablex.

Robertson, R. (1990). "Mapping the global condition: Globalization as the central concept." *Theory, Culture & Society* 7: 15–30.

Rogers, E. M. and Kincaid, D. L. (1981). *Communication Networks: Toward a New Paradigm for Research*. New York: Free Press.

Salisbury, J. G. T. and Barnett, G. A. (1999). "A network analysis of international monetary flows". *Information Society* 15: 1–19.

Smith, L. R. (1999). "Intercultural network theory: A cross-paradigmatic approach to acculturation". *International Journal of Intercultural Relations* 23: 629–658.

Straubhaar, J. D. (2002). "(Re)asserting national media and national identity against the global, regional and local levels of world television". In J. M. Chan and B. T. McIntyre (eds.), *In Search of Boundaries: Communication, Nation-states, and Cultural Identities*, (page no.??). Westport, CT: Ablex.

Thelwall, M. and Smith, A. (2002). "A study of the interlinking between Asia-Pacific University Web sites". *Scientometrics* 55 (3): 363–376.

Townsend, A. M. (2001). "Network cities and the global structure of the Internet". *American Behavioral Scientist* 44: 1697–1716.

U.S. Bureau of the Census. *Population projections of the United States by age, sex, race, and Hispanic origin: 1995 to 2050.* Washington, DC: Government Printing Office.

Varis, T. (1984). "International flow of television programs". *Journal of Communication* 34 (1): 143–152.

Walters, M. (1995). *Globalization.* London and New York: Routledge.

Ware, W. and Dupsgne, M. (1994). "Effects of U.S. television programs on foreign audiences: A meta-analysis". *Journalism Quarterly* 71: 947–959.

Weimann, G. (1989). "Social networks and communication". In M. K. Asante and W. B. Gudykunst (eds.), *Handbook of International and Intercultural Communication*, pp. 186–203. Newbury Park, CA: Sage.

Yum, J. O. (1984). "Network analysis". In W. B Gudykunst and Y. Y. Kim (eds.), *Methods for Intercultural Communication Research*, pp. 95–116. Beverly Hills, CA: Sage.

———. (1988). "Network theory in intercultural communication". In Y.Y. Kim and W. B. Gudykunst (eds.), *Theories in Intercultural Communication*, pp. 239–258. Newbury Park, CA: Sage.

—⁂—

About the Editors

LEUNG, Louis is Associate Professor in the School of Journalism and Communication at The Chinese University of Hong Kong and was Assistant Professor at the University of Hawaii at Manoa. He currently serves as Director of Center for Communication Research conducting public opinion polls on issues related to media and society. He holds a PhD in Radio, Television & Film from the University of Texas at Austin. His research interests focus on the uses and impact of new communication technologies. He is co-editor of *Impact and Issues in New Media: Toward Intelligent Societies* (NJ: Hampton Press, 2004). Some of his recent publications have appeared in *Telecommunications Policy, Journal of Broadcasting & Electronic Media, Journalism and Mass Communication Quarterly, CyberPsychology & Society, Telematics and Informatics, New Media & Society, Asian Journal of Communication, and Gazette.*

FUNG, Anthony is an Associate professor in the School of Journalism and Communication at The Chinese University of Hong Kong. He received his PhD from the School of Journalism and Mass Communication at the University of Minnesota. His research interests included popular culture, youth and identity studies, cultural studies, political economy of communication and new media technologies. His research articles have been published in major international communication and cultural studies journals such as *Journal of Communication Inquiry, Gazette: A Journal for International Communication, Asian Journal of Communication, Cultural Studies, International Journal of Cultural Studies, Culture, Market and Consumption, New Media and Society,* and *Mass Communication &*

Society. He was editor and author of a few Chinese books on culture, policy and communication, including *Cultural Feeling: In the Voices of Their Own* (2000), *Cultural Feeling II: Passion, Sentiment, Obsession and Others* (2002), *Sensitive Music Areas* (2001), *The Special Administrative Region (SAR), Public Policy and Ethics* (2001) and *Hong Kong Popular Music Culture: A Cultural Studies Reader* (2004).

LEE, Paul S. N. is Professor and Dean of Faculty of Social Science and former Director of the School of Journalism and Communication at The Chinese University of Hong Kong. He received his PhD in Communication from the University of Michigan. His research interests include international communication, telecommunications policy, development communication and media criticism. He is author of *International Communication* (Taipei: Lai Ming Press, 1994, published in Chinese), editor of *Telecommunications and Development in China* (NJ: Hampton, 1997), co-editor of *TV Without Borders: Asia Speaks Out* (Singapore: AMIC, 1998 with Anura Goonasekera as co-editor) and *Impact and Issues in New Media* (NJ: Hampton, 2004 with Louis Leung and Clement So as co-editors). His publications also appeared in *Telecommunications Policy, Asian Journal of Communication, Journal of Communication, Gazette, Telematics & Infomatics* and *Media, Culture & Society*.

About the Contributors

BARNETT, George A. is Professor and Chair of the Department Communication at the University at Buffalo (SUNY). He received his B.A. and M.A. from the University of Illinois, in Sociology, and his PhD in Communication from Michigan State University (1976). Currently, he has been editor of *Progress in Communication Sciences* and has written extensively on organizational, mass, international and intercultural, and political communication, as well as the diffusion of innovations. His current research focuses on international information flows, in general, and telecommunications flows including the Internet, in specific, and their role in the process of social and economic development and globalization.

CHANG, Jay H. C. is an Assistant Professor in the Department of Communication Studies at the Hong Kong Baptist University. He received his Ph.D. from Syracuse University. His research interests include information processing, health communication, and campaign analysis and evaluation. His recent publications can be seen in *Journal of Broadcasting & Electronic Media,* and *Journal of Advertising & Pubic Relations.*

CHYI, Hsiang Iris is an Assistant Professor in the School of Journalism at The University of Texas at Austin. She was on the faculty at the University of Arizona (2004–2007) and the Chinese University of Hong Kong (2000–2004). She received her Ph.D. from the University of Texas at Austin, her M.A. from Stanford University, and her B.A. from National Taiwan University. Her research interests include the economics of new media, online journalism, communication technology, and news framing. She is interested in the relationship between online and traditional news media in multiple geographic markets. Her work has been published in journals such as: *Journalism & Mass Communication Quarterly, Journal of Media Economics, Newspaper Research Journal, International Journal of Media Management*, etc. Chyi has taught theoretical and skills courses such as Information Technology and Society, Multimedia Journalism, Directions in News Technology, Multidisciplinary Approaches to Information Technology, Media Economics, Multimedia Design and Development, and Communication Research Methods.

GUSTAFSON, Karen is a Doctoral candidate at the University of Texas at Austin. She received her Master's degree from the Radio-Television-Film department at the University of Texas in 1999, and is currently focusing on telecommunications and information technology policy. Her dissertation examines the policy discourse surrounding the deregulation and privatization of telecommunications in the United States, and the commercialization of the Internet. Her other interests include the social construction of technology and gender issues in online environments.

JANKOWSKI, Nicholas is a Visiting Fellow at Oxford Internet Institute, University of Oxford, and Associate Professor, Department of Communication, University of Nijmegen, The Netherlands. He has been involved in the investigation of electronic community media as related to political and social action since the mid-1970s. His publications include: *The People's Voice: Local Radio and Television in Europe* (Libbey, 1992); *The Contours of Multimedia* (Luton, 1996); *Community Media in the Information Age* (Hampton, 2001); and *A Handbook of Qualitative Methodologies for Mass Communication Research* (Routledge, 1991). He initiated and is editor of the Hampton Press book series *Communicative Initiatives & Democracy*. Currently he is co-organizing an international study of the role of the Internet during national elections; for details, see http://oase.uci.kun.nl/~jankow/elections/.

LEE, Alice Y. L. is Associate Professor at the Department of Journalism, Hong Kong Baptist University. Her research interests include media education, information literacy, online news media and knowledge society. She teaches courses in critical studies of the mass media, news media management, media education, television news reporting and broadcast journalism. She is the vice-chairperson of the Hong Kong Association of Media Education.

LYONS, Michael originally worked on the development of semiconductor devices for BT's optical fiber transmission systems before establishing a new research team to work on long-term strategic issues. For the past ten years, this team has studied the future impact of ICT on both the telecommunications industry and the wider society as well as developing computer-based simulation methods for strategic decision-making. Michael currently work includes the socio-economic impact of ambient intelligence and the application of complexity science to management. Both these research areas have major implications for the way businesses are structured and operated in the future.

McDOWELL, Stephen is John H.Phipps Professor of Communication and Chair in the Department of Communication at Florida State University in Tallahassee, Florida, where he has taught since 1996. His published work includes a book on India's communication policies, *Globalization, Liberalization and Policy Change: A Political Economy of India's Communications Sector* (and New York: St. Martin's; and Houndmills, U.K.: The Macmillan Press, 1997), as well as articles and book chapters dealing with international communications and communications policies in Canada, India, and the United States. McDowell has held fellowships with the Strategic Policy Planning Division of the Canadian federal Department of Communications in Ottawa (1987–1989), with the Shastri Indo-Canadian Institute in New Delhi (1989–1990), and a Congressional Fellowship supported by the American Political Science Association in Washington D.C. (1994–1995).

McMILLAN, Sally is Associate Professor in the School of Advertising and Public Relations at the University of Tennessee. She received her Ph.D. from the University of Oregon. Her research focuses on interactivity, definitions and history of new media, online research methods, health communication, and impacts of communication technology on individuals organizations and society and has been published in journals such as: *Health Communication, Journal of Advertising, Journal of Advertising Education, Journal of Advertising Research, Journal of Computer Mediated Communication, Journal of Interactive Advertising, Journal of Intercultural Communication Research, Journalism and Mass Communication Quarterly,* and *New Media and Society.*

NG, Vicky W. K. received her Master of Philosophy degree in Communication at the School of Journalism and Communication, The Chinese University of Hong Kong. Currently she works as a Client Service Manager (Customized Research) at A.C. Nielsen (China) Limited.

OS, Renée van is a PhD candidate at the Department of Communication, University of Nijmegen, The Netherlands. In her PhD project she is focusing on the potential of the Internet for enhancing the European democratic process, and its contribution to a European public sphere. At the moment, she is engaged in the Internet & Elections Project (http://oase.uci.kun.nl/~jankow/elections/), in which she is studying the nature of political action on and between election-oriented web sites during the European Parliament election campaign in the period May–June 2004 in The Netherlands and France. She received her Master's degree in Communication Science in September 2002, with a thesis entitled "Digital Democracy: A Case Study on the Role of Online Discussions within the Local Political Process" (e-mail: r.vanos@maw.kun.nl).

PATELIS, Korinna has been researching the socioeconomic structures of the Internet for the last 10 years. Her PhD was on The Political Economy of the Internet (Department of Media Communication — Goldsmiths College). She teaches at the Department of Media and Communications, University of Athens. Her research focuses on e-mediation, political economy and the Internet's taxonomy. Her publications include "E-mediation by America On-line," in R. Rogers (2000), *Preferred Placement: Web Epistemology and Knowledge Politics on the Web*, Maascrict: Van Eyck Academy for Design and Media, and "The Political Economy of Internet," in J. Curran (1999), *Media Organizations*, London: Arnold, and *Cyberspace as Capitalism*, Athens: Patakis Press (in Greek).

SO, Clement Y. K. is Director of the School of Journalism and Communication, The Chinese University of Hong Kong. His research interests include sociology and politics of news, Hong Kong press, citation analysis, and the development of communication as a discipline. He has co-authored *Global Media Spectacle: News War over Hong Kong*, co-edited *Impact and Issues in New Media: Toward Intelligence Societies, Television Program Appreciation Index: Hong Kong Experience*, and *Press and Politics in Hong Kong: Case Studies from 1967 to 1997*.

STROVER, Sharon is Philip G. Warner Regents Professor in the Radio-TV-Film Department at the University of Texas, teaches communications and telecommunications courses, directs the Telecommunications and Information Policy Institute, and chairs the Department of Radio-TV-Film Department. Some of her current research projects examine statewide networks and advanced broadband services, the digital divide, telecommunications infrastructure deployment and economic development in rural regions, and market structure and policy issues for international audio-visual industries. She currently works with various universities in Portugal in digital media education and research projects. Dr. Strover has worked with the U.S. Federal Communication Commission, The Appalachian Regional Commission, the Office of Technology Assessment, the Rural Policy Institute, the Ford Foundation, the European Union, the Texas Public Utility Commission, the Department of Information Resources and Department of Health and Human Services, the Tele-communications Infrastructure Fund Board, and the Aspen Institute, among other organizations. She is the former chair of the Mass Communication and the Communication law and Policy divisions for the International Communication Association. She received her doctoral degree from Stanford University and her undergraduate degree from the University of Wisconsin.

SUNDAR, S. Shyam is Associate professor and founding director of the Media Effects Research Laboratory (MERL) at Penn State University's College of Communications. He received his PhD from Stanford University. Dr. Sundar's research investigates psychological effects of technological elements unique to Web-based mass communication. His work has appeared in such leading journals as *Communication Research, Journal of Communication, Journalism & Mass Communication Quarterly, Journal of Advertising, Behaviour & Information Technology* and *Media Psychology*. He is a former head of the Communication Technology & Policy division of the Association for Education in Journalism & Mass Communication, and is currently chairing the organization's publications committee.

WILLNAT, Lars is Professor in the School of Journalism at Indiana University. Before joining IU in 2009, Professor Willnat taught at the George Washington University in Washington, DC and at the Chinese University of Hong Kong. His teaching and research interests include media effects on political attitudes, theoretical aspects of public opinion formation, and international communication. He has published book chapters and articles in journals such as Journalism & Mass Communication Quarterly, International Journal of Public Opinion Research, Political Communication, Journalism, and Gazette. Professor Willnat received his Ph.D. in Mass Communication from Indiana University in 1992.

ZHANG, Junhua obtained his BA in German literature and language in Shanghai. He then studied philosophy and political science at J. W. Goethe University in Germany and gained Ph.D. in philosophy. Since 1998 he has been teaching political science at the J. W. Goether University and later at the Free University Berlin. One of his research fields is comparative analysis of Internet policy in China. Up to date, several essays and articles about Chinese e-government and cyber war have been publicized in various journals and books. He co-edited with Martin Woesler *China's Digital Dream — Impact of the Internet on Chinese Society*.

Index

Accessibility, 215–228, 264
Accountability, 210–227, 235, 248, 276, 286, 312
Actuators, 55–60
Addiction, 13, 198
Administrative reform, 236
Adoption behaviors, 32
Advertisement deliverers, 323, 338, 342
Advertising
    clutter, 145–161
    repetition, 145–160
    vehicle, 148, 149, 158, 160
Agency, 126–131, 210–211
Ambient intelligence (AmI), 53–59, 76
Anonymization services, 72
Asia, 355–362
ATM, 239, 362
Attitudinal factors, 106
Audience as Source, 128
Audience fragmentation, 84
Authority, 16–20
Automating the mundane, 58, 60, 73
Average collective pattern, 348
Awareness, 217, 304

Back office, 254–255

Banner ad, 145, 147, 158
Beijing, 241, 253, 259
Blogs, 10, 27, 30, 341
Bureaucratization, 210
Business-to-business (B2B), 227, 299, 305–308, 342
Business-to-consumer (B2C), 308

Calming technology, 53, 59
Catalogues, 175, 178
Censorship, 169, 181, 249
China, 190, 193, 235–261, 333, 339–342
Civic engagement, 270, 273, 279, 284, 286, 289–291
Civil society, 316
Click-through, 147
Closed system, 348
CNNIC, 240
Cognitive factors, 32
Cognitive heuristics, 131, 141
Cold War, 235
Collaborative filtering systems, 127
Commercial exchanges, 299
Commercialization, 10–12, 15, 21
Common good, 73, 213
Common pool, 73
Communication

network, 348–350
patterns, 190
technology, 190–194, 299, 312
Communications practices, 298,
  317
Communicative participation, 272
Community communication, 191
Competitive advantage, 101, 105–
  107, 118, 119, 297, 300, 305
Computer games, 38–47, 201
Computer-based activities, 83
Connectivity, 324, 328, 355
Consumer protection, 303–305,
  310, 312
Consumer-to-business (C2B), 299
Content
  diversity, 328, 332
  model, 326–327
  aware, 56, 62, 68, 74
Context
  characteristics, 55–56
  clutter, 145–161
  aware applications, 62
  sensitive support, 68
Contextualist approach, 353
Contextualization, 328–332
Contingency-based interactivity,
  136
Control
  of information, 70, 72
  of services, 73
Controlling boundaries, 63–66
Convergence, 347–350, 353–354,
  358–364
Core-partnership model, 343
Credibility, 17, 133–134
Crimeware landscape, 311
Crystallization, 202
Cultural
  boundary, 351
  convergence, 347–350, 353,
    360–364

identity, 347–349
images, 363
life, 191
Culture of security, 309
Customization, 129–130, 138–142
Cyberculture, 189–202
Cyber
  optimists, 276
  pessimists, 276
  security, 310
  skeptic, 276
  space, 130, 276–278
Cyberspace governance, 298, 308
Cybersquatting, 309

DAGMAR
  defining-advertising-goals-for-
    measured-advertising-results,
    146
  the bandwagon effect, 129
Decrease (displace/substitute),
  38, 48, 84, 87, 97, 202
Democracy, 129, 210–215, 228–
  230, 235, 271, 276–277
Democratic
  deficit, 269, 273–275
  participation, 213
Demographic characteristics, 32,
  86, 229
Deng Xiaoping, 236
Deterritorization, 189
Digital
  divide, 165, 217, 222,
  me, 59–64
  shopping mall, 323
  trading marketplace, 323–325,
    338, 343
Digitalized
  city, 240
  harbour, 241
Dimensions of media use, 103
Disintermediation, 179–180, 299

Dis-intermediation narrative, 165–
 171
Displacement, 29, 46, 85–88, 94,
 103–119
Distal information, 132–135, 141
Divergence, 348
DNS, 175, 177
Domain name system, 303
Dot-com crisis, 326
Dysfunctional, 259

E
 -business, 306, 310
 -business-to-business, 342
 -Commerce, 36, 70–71, 238,
  297–317, 323–344
 -democracy, 210–211, 219,
  228–230
 -era, 215
 -generation, 11, 15
 -mediation, 175, 181
 -mediator, 174
 -malls, 334–338, 342
 -participation, 261
 -shipments, 307
 -shopping, 335, 341
 -TRUST, 71–72
Economic development, 172, 240,
 245, 297, 299, 302, 305
Economic transactions, 298, 301,
 311
Effectiveness of Internet
 advertising, 147
Election campaigns, 275–276, 279
Electronic
 brokerage effect, 299
 commerce, 299–316
 communication, 169, 209
 Data Interchange (EDI), 307,
  311–314
 government, 209, 230
 hierarchies, 299

markets, 298–299
 payment, 303
 signatures, 305
 strategic networking effect, 300
 traders, 323–324, 327, 334,
  341–342
Embedded intelligence, 55–57, 60
Entry level subscription, 334
Equilibrium culture, 349
Ethnographic study, 190
EU, 172–173, 269–290
Europeanization, 272
Exclusion, 103, 165–167
External environment, 32

Filtering devices, 175
Free distribution, 326
Functionality, 141, 260
Functions of leisure, 28–29

Gatekeeping, 127–129, 141
Germany, 354–359
Global
 civilization, 359, 362
 community, 348, 353
 culture, 347–350, 359–364
 identity, 354, 359
 Information Infrastructure,
  297, 302, 305
 participation, 303
 village, 353
Globalization localization
 dialectic, 360
Golden
 card, 239
 projects, 239, 242, 245–247
 shield, 240
Good governance, 235–236, 243,
 247, 256, 260–261
Government
 Online Project, 240–242
 Regulation, 71

Governmental functionality, 260
Guardian angel, 60–61

Habermas, 270–272
Hacking, 298, 309
Health
  communication, 15–16, 20
  -conscious individuals, 16
Heavy Internet users, 86
Hierarchy of effects model, 146
Home-centered leisure, 30
Home-work Interface, 62
Hong Kong, 102–109, 111–119,
  193–194, 202, 338–340
Hu Jintao, 260
Human-computer interaction
  (HCI), 126
Human-to-computer interactivity,
  15
Human-to-content interaction, 10,
  22
Human-to-human, 7–9, 15, 21–22
Hyperlink, 132, 354–358
Hyperplace, 200

ICT, 55, 57, 62–70, 76
Identity theft, 14, 61, 298, 309–
  311, 316
Identity verification, 60
Immediacy, 324, 328
Implications, 28, 30, 54, 70, 106,
  130–134, 137, 305, 314–316,
  358–361
Increase (supplement/
  complement), 16, 22, 38, 46,
  49, 84–88, 325, 338
Incrementalism, 235
Independent political Web sites,
  277
Individual cultural identity, 363
Individualism, 358–363
Individual-oriented, 242

Information,
  brokers, 175–178
  foraging theory, 132
  infrastructure, 297–305
  marketplace, 323, 328, 340
  provision, 216, 219, 272, 284,
    286, 290–291
  richness, 16–17, 23
  scent, 132, 141
  society, 57, 166–171, 180–181,
    306, 317
  society paradigm, 167–171, 181
  society policy, 167–170
  superhighway, 211
  -processing model (IPM), 146
Informatization, 237–255
Info-telecommunication
  infrastructure, 168
Inhouse stores, 338
Intellectual property, 168, 303,
  309, 312, 314–317
Intelligence, 53, 55–60, 63–64, 69,
  74–76, 373, 375
Intelligent spaces (I-Spaces), 53–
  59, 62, 70, 77
Interactive information
  transmission, 327
Intercultural communication, 350,
  352, 364, 374
Interdependency, 363
Intermedia competition, 101–103,
  106–108, 120
International
  community, 350, 363
  hyperlink networks, 355
  Internet, 350, 354, 356–357,
    361–364
  Internet flows, 354, 356, 362,
    363
  Telecommunication, 306, 309,
    359
  Telecommunication Union

(ITU), 306, 309
Internet
  Activities, 7, 10, 27, 32, 34, 36,
    38–42, 46, 48, 225
  Governance, 303, 306, 317
  Infrastructure, 171, 355, 357
  Penetration, 4, 172, 174, 291
  service providers, 175
  space, 191
Intertextuality, 175
Intra-national links, 355
Invisible technology, 53, 55
I-Office, 62, 66, 70

Jiang Zemin, 239, 246, 260
Job spill, 65
Journalism, 125, 249, 340, 369–
  376

Knowledge
  Networks, 86
  Societies, 312

Leisure
  Activities, 9, 27–36, 38, 41, 45–
    48
  Participation, 27–33, 36, 38–48
  · Satisfaction, 27–29, 31–35, 40–
    49
Liberalism, 213
Liberalist view, 191
Lifestyle, 27, 28, 59–60, 62, 71
Limited engagement, 275
Longitudinal study, 291, 323
Low-tech Elderly, 5, 6, 15, 21

Market
  Access, 297, 303, 305
  coordination mechanism, 299
McLuhan, 189
Media
  Convergence, 363

Economics, 101–102, 372
Environment, 101, 103, 324,
  340
Equation, 126
Landscape, 101
Media selection
  Behavior, 105
  preference, 109
Media-related activities, 29, 30, 34,
  38–42, 48–49
Media-related predictions, 83
Media-rich city, 102
Modality conditions, 138
Mode of transmission, 328, 332–
  333
Modernization, 196, 236–238,
  249, 353
Multimedia capability, 328, 332
Multimodality, 126, 138
Multi-tasking, 85, 87, 94
Multi-way reciprocal effects, 32

National identity, 358, 361, 364
Navigability, 126, 131–132, 134–
  135, 141
Navigational tools, 8, 171, 174
Negative responses, 13, 61
Net generation, 197
Network
  Integration, 302
  Model, 353
  partnership model, 326, 339
  Structure, 353
New media technology, 103
News cues, 133–134
Non-Internet users, 92, 105, 112–
  113, 222
Non-media-related leisure
  activities, 29, 41, 45

Obsession, 13, 370
Off switch, 57, 62, 76

Office
  Automatization Project, 239
Online
  Advertising, 13, 145, 147
  Arenas, 277
  Assessment, 255–256
  Network, 190, 309
  news usage, 86, 88, 92, 94, 95
  publishers, 119, 326, 331, 337–
    338, 342
  retailing applications, 338
  security, 310
  space, 191, 197, 199, 201–202
  transactions, 6, 14, 316
Open media code, 324, 327
Openness, 214, 227, 311, 328,
  330, 332
Opinion marketplace, 323, 328
Outline assessment, 255
Over-harvesting, 73

Paid Internet subscriptions, 326
PC communication devices, 190
Perceived
  Interactivity, 130
  Objectivity, 129
Performance-based online
  advertising model, 147
Permanent campaign, 291
Personality traits, 32
Personalization, 11, 14, 15, 23,
  129–131
Pervasive
  Communications, 55–57,
  Computing, 53–55, 72
Pervasiveness, 15, 23, 54
Platform for Privacy Protection
  (P3P), 71
Pluralism, 166, 168, 180, 215
Political
  Communication, 278, 371
  Discourse, 271

Economy, 165–166, 169, 171,
  172, 369, 373–374
Participation, 213–214, 217,
  229
Transformation, 277
Pornography, 298, 309
Portal sites, 127, 130, 175
POS, 239
Post-euphoric phase, 298
Post-industrial society, 323
Pricing mechanisms, 168
Privacy protection, 71, 218, 304,
  310, 316
Professional gatekeepers, 128
Professionalism, 229, 244, 260
Proximal cues, 132, 135
Psychographics, 4
Psychological space, 192
Public
  Discourse, 276
  information network, 242
  sphere, 181, 269–273, 276, 279,
    284, 286, 290–292, 374

Quasi-neoliberal, 169

Read/write Web, 324
Regulatory
  Agenda, 167–168
  Regime, 181
Relative constancy, 108
Repertoire, 31–32, 36, 38, 40–41,
  45, 47
Risk society, 69

Search engines, 175, 177–178,
  279, 314
Secure payment mechanisms, 297,
  302, 304
Self as Source, 128–129, 131, 142
Self-regulation, 71, 310
Self-selective nature, 83

Senior citizens, 4, 10, 15, 16, 19–21, 23
Singapore, 214, 221, 251, 254, 323, 355–356, 359, 362, 370
Size of repertoire, 32, 40–41
Social
  Context, 16, 18–19, 22, 23, 353
  Discourse, 165
  Interaction, 11, 13, 22–23, 35, 47, 85, 353
  Locators, 38
Socioeconomic status, 21, 32
Sourcing, 126–128, 130
Spamming, 298, 309, 311
Structural Model, 350–351, 358, 364
Substantive democracy, 276
Supplement effect, 88
Surveillance mechanisms, 239
Syndication, 332

Talk radio, 273
Taste and preference adaptor, 60, 61
Taxation, 243, 247, 262, 265, 297, 302–303, 305
Taxonomy, 174–175, 178–179, 181, 374
Technological
  Determinism, 191
  Developments, 30, 63, 361
  Grid, 166
  leisure, 27, 29, 32, 45–49
  Sources, 128
Technologically elite, 10
Technology standards, 197, 301, 306
Techno-phobia, 13
Telecommunications Act, 301, 311
Terrorism, 167, 170, 174–175, 178, 181

The democracy effect, 129
Time displacement
  Effect, 104, 105, 112
  Theory, 86
Trade facilitation, 303
Trade-off decision, 108, 116
Traditional
  leisure, 28–30, 38–40, 42, 45–47, 49
  mass media news, 83, 85, 87
  media use, 36, 88, 104, 110, 112
  news sources, 83–84, 88, 92, 94, 97
  newspapers, 126, 273
Tragedy of the commons, 73
Transborder communication, 353
Transnational identity, 348, 363
Transnational investment, 297, 305
Transparency, 72, 174, 217, 235, 248, 252, 297, 305
Two-way communication, 8

Ubiquitous computing, 55, 57
Ubiquitous sensors, 55–56
Universal
  Access, 166, 168, 300
  Culture, 350, 358–359, 360, 362–363
Urbanization, 261, 362
Usability, 135, 217

Virtual community, 198, 200–201
Virtual space, 30, 192, 197–201

Web 2.0, 324, 340–342
Web sphere, 270, 279–283, 290
Wireless subscription, 334, 337–338
Work-home interface, 63
WTO, 244

Young tech elite, 5, 6, 10, 14–15,
    21

Zero-order relationships, 46
Zero-sum time scenario, 94
Zhu Rongji, 244